THE REPUBLIC IN DANGER

The Republic in Danger

Drusus Libo and the Succession of Tiberius

ANDREW PETTINGER

OXFORD
UNIVERSITY PRESS

OXFORD
UNIVERSITY PRESS

Great Clarendon Street, Oxford, OX2 6DP
United Kingdom

Oxford University Press is a department of the University of Oxford.
It furthers the University's objective of excellence in research, scholarship,
and education by publishing worldwide. Oxford is a registered trade mark of
Oxford University Press in the UK and in certain other countries

© Andrew Pettinger 2012

The moral rights of the author have been asserted

First Edition published in 2012

Impression: 1

All rights reserved. No part of this publication may be reproduced, stored in
a retrieval system, or transmitted, in any form or by any means, without the
prior permission in writing of Oxford University Press, or as expressly permitted
by law, by licence or under terms agreed with the appropriate reprographics
rights organization. Enquiries concerning reproduction outside the scope of the
above should be sent to the Rights Department, Oxford University Press, at the
address above

You must not circulate this work in any other form
and you must impose this same condition on any acquirer

British Library Cataloguing in Publication Data
Data available

Library of Congress Cataloging in Publication Data
Data available

ISBN 978-0-19-960174-5

Printed in Great Britain
on acid-free paper by
MPG Books Group, Bodmin and King's Lynn

To Hayley, Sue, and Graham

Preface

In 2003, while reading modern works on treason trials in Rome, I came across the prosecution of M. Scribonius Drusus Libo, an aristocrat destroyed in AD 16 for seeking out the opinions of a necromancer. The case made little sense, and upon reading every relevant book and article I could find, it became clear that most scholars dismiss the episode as the trapping of a harmless fool by greedy prosecutors. A minority treat Drusus Libo more seriously, but these treatments are relatively short, indeed, the more recent discussions span a few pages only. Since the Government appeared to handle Drusus Libo with extreme caution, a more detailed investigation seemed to me worthwhile. This book, a revised version of a PhD thesis submitted to the University of Sydney in 2008, is the result of my investigation. Though much of the thesis was re-written, very little additional research was undertaken. Except where I was made aware of a new and important piece of research, relevant works published since 2008 have not been included.

The book is intended for scholars, but it is hoped that students and those with a general interest in the period will find the work accessible. To aid the reader, and allow for critical engagement with many of the conclusions, I have supplied, where possible, texts and translations vital to the argument. I consider this to be an important feature. Nonetheless, a reconstruction of the past is more than the sum of available evidence. The writing of history requires imagination; empathic in origin, creative in spirit: the glue by which fragments of knowledge are held together. The book includes many instances of comments and motives imagined, and where evidence for something is wholly lacking, such as what the conspirators of AD 16 hoped to achieve, an interpretation has been offered which is hypothetical in nature, but fits, nonetheless, with wider evidence, i.e., it is both possible and logical. Thus, the book serves also as a statement on method.

My work has benefitted from much criticism and learning received since the submission of the PhD. The corrections and opinions of my three examiners inspired much thought. In particular, discussion with Dr Yakobson led to a sharpening of my views on the nature of the Principate, while the anonymous readers of the Oxford University Press identified various mistakes and redundancies, and offered alternative interpretations on a number of points. The assistance of Atticus Cox with the translations of Dio and Plutarch, Peta Greenfield with checking the Latin texts, and Fiona Tweedie with reading and correcting the final draft, was invaluable, as were the patience and much appreciated abilities of the editing staff of the Oxford University Press. In addition, I must acknowledge the profound debt owed to my four mentors: my two supervisors Martin Stone, Peter Brennan, and also Kathryn Welch, and Keith McAllister. Without their support, belief and advice this book would not have existed. Indeed, I owe Martin individual thanks for countless hours spent talking about various aspects of the book and history in general. He went beyond the call of the supervisor, for which the author will remain forever thankful. Those listed above have each, in some way, improved this work; any remaining faults are of course my own.

Finally I thank my family. My parents, Sue and Graham, have been tremendously supportive, and deserve more than a book sincerely dedicated, while no form of praise could ever adequately recognise the indefatigable patience, fortitude, and love with which my wife Hayley has supported this long endeavour.

Contents

Introduction	1
1. An Urgent Summons and a Terrible Charge	5
The narrative	5
An emergency sitting of the senate	9
A terrible charge	17
2. The Treatment of an Enemy	29
Inability to obtain defence counsel	29
Drusus Libo *in custodia*	35
Damnatio memoriae and public offerings of thanks	37
3. The Adoption of Agrippa Postumus and the Friends of Gaius Caesar	47
The adoption of Agrippa	47
The wrong friends	53
4. Growing Pains	61
Agrippa and the *toga virilis*	61
Abdicatio and Agrippa	67
5. The Buck Stops Where?	75
The crisis	75
The sedition of Tiberius' rival L. Aemilius Paullus	93
6. Augustus' Final Arrangements	103
The *relegatio* of Agrippa	103
The *Lex Valeria Cornelia*	107
The elections of AD 7	114
7. The Exiles of the Younger Julia, D. Junius Silanus, and the poet Ovid	123
8. *Novus Principatus*: An Imperial Co-operative	135
9. The Hesitation of Tiberius	157
10. "Did You Hear About Agrippa?"	169
11. Germanicus: Successor to Tiberius or Augustus?	185

12. Alternative Government	195
An awkward alliance	195
A false dawn	207
Future directions	215
Appendix 1 A Prosopography of M. Scribonius Drusus Libo	219
Appendix 2 Family Trees	233
Appendix 3 Timeline	235
6 BC–AD 13	235
AD 14–AD 16	236
Bibliography	239
General Index	253
Index of Sources	258

Introduction

Modern scholars mostly treat the Principate established by Augustus as benign. Indeed, it is argued that Rome prospered on account of it. Romans supposedly agreed: senators, equestrians, plebeians, and Italians believed that under Augustus *res publica* was enhanced. Augustus himself called it the best state of affairs (*optimus status*). No serious opposition, they say, ever developed. The case of M. Scribonius Drusus Libo throws doubt on this view of things.

In September AD 16 M. Scribonius Drusus Libo committed suicide while the senate considered evidence that he was plotting to murder Tiberius, his heirs, the younger Drusus and Germanicus, and several important senators. Relying on Tacitus, scholars treat Drusus Libo as a harmless fool, caught in the net of hungry prosecutors. They argue that the case did not involve the politics of power. In this book I shall argue that it did, and that he was destroyed not by predatory prosecutors but by Tiberius' regime. The conspiracy of Clemens in AD 16 is crucial. While the senate was considering Drusus Libo's guilt, Rome was alive with news that Augustus' exiled grandson, Agrippa Postumus, reportedly executed when Augustus died, was actually marching on Rome. The resurrected Agrippa was in fact an ex-slave but there were reports of significant support from senators, equestrians, and members of the imperial household itself. The historical sources talk of civil war looming.[1] The present study places Drusus Libo among those secretly helping the slave Clemens. His family connections hold the key.

Drusus Libo's pedigree was impressive. He had a maternal connection with Pompey the Great, his father's family were key players during and after the civil wars, and through his great aunt Scribonia he was connected with Augustus' grandchildren, Gaius and Lucius

---

[1] Suet. *Tib.* 25.1 f.; Tac. *Ann.* 2.39.1 f.; Dio 57.16.3 ff.

Caesar, their sisters, the younger Julia and Agrippina, and with Agrippa's posthumous son. He was also attached, via adoption, to the Livii Drusi, the family to which Augustus' widow Livia and her lineage, Tiberius, Germanicus, and the younger Drusus, belonged.[2] These connections came with political clout, but with legitimacy they also brought trouble. Tiberius' rise to supreme power was at the expense of Augustus' grandsons, who were all dead by the time Augustus was laid to rest. Their supporters, however, remained unconvinced that life was possible under Tiberius. On hearing news that Agrippa had been put to death, a group of malcontents, unable to come to terms with Augustus' successor, approached Drusus Libo. My subject is the struggle between Tiberius and the supporters of Augustus' grandsons. It has serious implications for our understanding of the Principate.

The Principate was not benign: it was in fact brutal and destructive. This observation is not new. Ronald Syme used the words 'despotic and murderous', but Syme's view of the Principate no longer prevails.[3] Nor is my view exactly Syme's. For Syme, the Principate was a tragic affair, not because it was set up but because it was never seriously challenged. It was understood and accepted, he thinks, that Augustus had created a monarchy. But the Principate was in fact, as I shall show, a more fragile structure, depending, as many autocratic regimes do, not only on the consent of its members but on the goodwill and patience of those being governed. It was with good reason that the Principate was sold to the electorate, and the senate, as an emergency structure for the pacification of troubled provinces.[4] A power that was to be permanent was bestowed with time-limits.[5] Autocracy was dressed up as democracy in action. Despotic regimes that rule with a democratic mask are inevitably unstable, and require, of necessity, instruments for silencing enemies. The period covered in this book is crowded with instances of law and justice perverted. As

---

[2] See appendix for full discussion of Drusus Libo's connections.
[3] R. Syme, *The Roman Revolution* (1939), 439.
[4] Dio 53.13.1; 53.16.2-3; 54.4.1; 54.12.4-5; 55.6.1. R. Syme (1939) 313f., notes that Augustus justified the new system by utilizing the belief that Rome's provinces were in danger of collapse and ruin. Nevertheless, Syme does not link the success or failure of this justification to the Principate's stability.
[5] Dio 53.16.2-3. When, in AD 24, Tiberius received an extension of power without a time-limit, the Principate as a political system was transformed into something more like a monarchy, Dio 57.24.1.

with modern versions, the Principate attracted criticism and opposition. But as power was taken up into Tiberius' grasp, criticism and opposition hardened. Not all men acquiesced in the face of tyranny, nor did they simply lie low. The effect on the government was tangible: Tiberius' hold on supreme power was never guaranteed. This book is therefore a contribution to the study of the invention of the Principate at Rome.

1

An Urgent Summons and a Terrible Charge

THE NARRATIVE

Evidence of what happened to M. Scribonius Drusus Libo is frustratingly superficial. Only summaries and passing references survive. Tacitus provides the longest account, but the contemporary Velleius, the younger Seneca, Suetonius, and Dio also supply information.[1] An official record of Drusus Libo's posthumous conviction survives in the *Fasti Amiternini*:

Fer. ex s.c.q.e.d. nefaria consilia quae de salute Ti. Caes. liberorumque eius et aliorum principum civitatis deq(ue) r.p. inita ab M. Libone erant in senatu convicta sunt.

A holiday on account of the decree which (was passed) because the wicked plans commenced by M. Libo concerning the safety of Tiberius Caesar and his children and other men of consular rank and also concerning the State were defeated in the senate.[2]

The senate convened to investigate the allegations from 11 to 13 September AD 16, a period usually spent enjoying the Roman games (*Ludi Romani*).[3] The scenario was therefore unusual and foreboding. But suspicion of Drusus Libo had been developing for some time:

---

[1] Tac. *Ann.* 2.27–32; Vell. 2.130.3; Sen. *Ep. Mor.* 70.10; Suet. *Tib.* 25; and Dio 57.15.
[2] *CIL* 1² p 244; V. Ehrenberg and A. H. M. Jones (1955), 52.
[3] The *Ludi Romani* were held usually 4–19 Sept. In AD 20 the trial of Aemilia Lepida was interrupted by, probably, the *Ludi Romani*, Tac. *Ann.* 3.23.1. Cf. R. H. Martin and A. J. Woodman, *The Annals of Tacitus: Book Three* (1996), 217 f.

Firmius Catus senator, ex intima Libonis amicitia, iuvenem inprovidum et facilem inanibus ad Chaldaeorum promissa, magorum sacra, somniorum etiam interpretes impulit, dum proavum Pompeium, amitam Scriboniam quae quondam Augusti coniunx fuerat, consobrinos Caesares, plenam imaginibus domum ostentat, hortaturque ad luxum et aes alienum, socius libidinum et necessitatum, quo pluribus indiciis inligaret.

Firmius Catus, a senator and close friend of Libo, urged the short-sighted young man, given to empty things, to resort to the promises of astrologers, the rites of magicians, and also dream interpreters, reminding him of his great-grandfather Pompeius, his paternal aunt Scribonia, former wife of Augustus, his imperial cousins, his house crowded with ancestral images, and urging him to extravagance and debt: Firmius associated himself in these debaucheries and embarrassments in order to entangle Libo in more evidence.[4]

Catus, having collected witnesses, took his evidence to a certain Vescularius Flaccus, a friend of Tiberius'. Catus sought an audience with the princeps, but, having considered the evidence passed on by Flaccus, Tiberius declined. We are told that Tiberius then distinguished Drusus Libo with a praetorship and invited him to dinners.[5] Sometime later (Suetonius has two years) fresh and damning evidence emerged.[6] A necromancer named Junius had informed a prosecutor (*delator*), C. Fulcinius Trio, that Drusus Libo had paid him to invoke dead spirits. Suddenly chaos:

statim corripit reum, adit consules, cognitionem senatus poscit. Et vocantur patres, addito consultandum super re magna et atroci.

Immediately he [Trio] seized the accused, approached the consuls, and called for an investigation in the senate. And so the fathers were called, it being added that they were to deliberate upon a great and terrible matter.[7]

Drusus Libo, informed of the charge, sought out an advocate but, despite the support of noble women (*primores feminae*), was unsuccessful. The investigation began the next day, with the defendant carried to the doors of the senate in a litter accompanied by his brother, who was consul *ordinarius* for that year. Tiberius read out both the charge and the names of the *delatores*: Fulcinius Trio,

---

[4] Tac. *Ann.* 2.27.2 f.   [5] Ibid.   [6] Suet. *Tib.* 25.1 f.
[7] Tac. *Ann.* 2.28.3.

Firmius Catus, Fonteius Agrippa, and C. Vibius Serenus. Drusus Libo defended himself.[8]

The charges were designed to erode the defendant's credibility: Drusus Libo had allegedly consulted someone as to whether he would have enough money to cover the Appian road to Brundisium, followed by similar accusations. Then the bombshell:

Uni tamen libello manu Libonis nominibus Caesarum aut senatorum additas atrocis vel occultas notas accusator arguebat.

On one paper sinister or cryptic marks had been added to the names of Caesars or senators in Libo's hand, the accuser alleged.[9]

The evidence had an immediate effect. Drusus Libo denied the allegation, the prosecutor pressed, and so the defendant's slaves were sold to the State for interrogation. Thus the first day concluded. Before going home, Drusus Libo asked his relative P. Quirinius to deliver final pleas to Tiberius, but the desperate tactic was obstructed by the constitutional diligence of the princeps, who responded 'that he should ask the senate': *responsum est ut senatum rogaret.* Arriving home, Drusus Libo was confronted by troops in and around his house. Disturbed by the soldiers he relinquished hope and committed suicide. Seneca places Scribonia at the scene. It may be a literary convention, but Scribonia's presence does make sense. She certainly ranked among the *primores feminae* and, moreover, had supported other relatives in their moments of disgrace. Scribonia apparently encouraged her great nephew not to anticipate the executioner. The advice was ignored.

Death did not bring the investigation to a close. At some stage, probably when the verdict was read out, Tiberius swore an oath that he would not have supported death: *iuravitque Tiberius petiturum se vitam quamvis nocenti, nisi voluntariam mortem properavisset.* Many obviously considered death to be the appropriate punishment. Motions to remove Drusus Libo from public memory (*damnatio memoriae*) were then proposed. M. Aurelius Cotta Maximus Messalinus[10] proposed that Drusus Libo's image should not be carried in the funeral procession of any of his descendants, and Cn. Lentulus proposed that no Scribonius should bear the cognomen Drusus.[11]

---

[8] Ibid., 2.29.   [9] Ibid., 2.30.   [10] *PIR*² A 1488.
[11] Tac. *Ann.* 2.32.1.

Public acts of thanks were then performed. Offerings were made to Jupiter, Mars, and Concord, and 13 September was to be observed as a festival thereafter.[12] These last decrees were suggested by L. Pomponius Flaccus,[13] Asinius Gallus, M. Papius Mutilus,[14] and L. Apronius. Tacitus mentions another, but only L. P . . . remains. The initials could refer to at least four known senators during the period.[15] Drusus Libo's property was then divided among the *delatores*, and those *delatores* who were senators were awarded/received a praetorship, which probably means that Tiberius personally sponsored their candidacy.[16] Finally, a decree was passed expelling occult practitioners from Italy, two of whom, L. Pituanius and P. Marcius, were put to death.[17]

Most recent scholars, following Tacitus, dismiss Drusus Libo as relatively harmless: a stupid young man pursued by covetous prosecutors and left for dead by a hypocritical regime.[18] But certain items become incredible if the entire episode was orchestrated for the benefit of ravenous *delatores*: the fact of an emergency meeting of the senate (and during the *Ludi Romani*); the nature of the charge; Drusus Libo's inability to find an advocate; the continuation of the investigation after death; placing Drusus Libo into custody, rather

---

[12] Ibid.   [13] *PIR*¹ P 538.   [14] Ibid., P 92.
[15] R. J. A. Talbert, *The Senate of Imperial Rome* (1984), 246, lists L. Piso (cos. 1BC), L. Piso (cos. 15 BC), L. Plancus (cos. AD 13), or L. Voluseius Proculus (*suff.* 17?).
[16] There has been some debate over when these praetorships were taken up, see F. R. D Goodyear, *The Annals of Tacitus, Books 1–6*, Vol. 2 (1981), 280 f.
[17] Tac. *Ann*. 2.32.
[18] Drusus Libo is held to be an important conspirator by: L. Freytag, *Tiberius und Tacitus* (1870), 115 f; V. Duruy, *Historie des Romains*, IV (1879–85), 302; U. Silvagni, *L'Impero e le donne dei Cesari* (1909), 270; A. Lang, *Beitrage zur Geschichte des Kaisers Tiberius*, (diss. Jena., 1911), 26 ff; E. Ciaceri, 'L' Imperatore Tiberio e i processi di lesa maesta', *Processi politici e Relazioni internazionali* (1918), and *Tiberio Successore di Augusto*² (1944); F. B. Marsh, 'Tacitus and the Aristocratic Tradition', *CP*, 21: 4 (1926), 289–310 and *Reign of Tiberius* (1931), 58 ff; R. S. Rogers, *Criminal Trials and Criminal Legislation under Tiberius* (1935), 12–25; E. F. Leon, 'Notes on the Background and Character of Libo Drusus', *CJ*, 53: 2 (Nov. 1957) 77–80; B. Levick, *Tiberius the Politician* (1999), 149 f. Drusus Libo is considered to be not dangerous by: C. Merivale, *History of the Romans under the Empire*, V (1881–3), 219–21; J. C. Tarver, *Tiberius the Tyrant* (1902), 326 f; A. Von Domaszewski, *Geschichte der römischen Kaiser* I (1909), 277–8; A. Passerini, *Studi giuridici in memoria di P. Ciapessoni* (1947), 219 ff; F. H. Cramer, *Astrology in Roman Law and Politics* (1954), 254–5; R. Syme, *Tacitus*, II (1958), 400–1; D. C. A. Shotter, 'The Trial of M. Scribonius Libo Drusus', *Historia*, 21 (1972), 88–98; R. Seager, *Tiberius* (1972), 89–93; F. R. D. Goodyear (1981), 262 f; S. Rutledge, *Imperial Inquisitions: Prosecutors and Informants from Tiberius to Domitian* (2001), 158 f.

An Urgent Summons and a Terrible Charge

than encouraging voluntary exile; the implementation of *damnatio memoriae*; marking 13 September a holiday, and the invocation of Concord. Concord is particularly suggestive. Her presence implies that Drusus Libo's disgrace accompanied a profound rupture in Rome's socio-political fabric. There is, therefore, a major discrepancy between the facts of the case as they have come down to us, and the explanation provided by Tacitus. As Rogers and Levick supposed, and I shall argue, the conspiracy of the psuedo Agrippa Postumus (i.e. the slave Clemens) in AD 16 best explains the contradiction: Drusus Libo was supporting a plan to bring down the government.[19] The structure of the argument will fall roughly into two parts. First I shall argue that Tiberius and his government treated Drusus Libo seriously rather than as a harmless fool. I shall then propose a new historical interpretation for the years 6 BC–AD 16 to demonstrate that Tiberius' right was seriously contested, and that his opponents had been supporters of Augustus' grandsons. We shall start by considering the fact that Drusus Libo was forced to endure a senatorial investigation.

AN EMERGENCY SITTING OF THE SENATE

Only suspicion dogged Drusus Libo before the senate meeting, but real trouble emerged when the necromancer he consulted, a certain Junius, proved more ambitious than himself. Impressed by the situation, Junius sought out the most celebrated prosecutor of the day (*celebre ingenium*). L. Fulcinius Trio was decisive:

statim corripit reum, adit consules, cognitionem senatus poscit. Et vocantur patres, addito consultandum super re magna et atroci.

Immediately he [Trio] seized the accused, approached the consuls, and called for an investigation in the senate. And so the fathers were called, it being added that they were to deliberate upon a great and terrible matter.[20]

---

[19] R. S. Rogers (1935), 12–25; B. Levick (1999), 149 f. Both treatments are brief. Rogers offered merely a thought without evidence. Levick nevertheless rests her case upon a belief that Rogers' hypothesis was 'convincingly shown'. Levick's treatment, moreover, spans all of four pages, and thus produces more questions than answers.

[20] Tac. *Ann.* 2.28.3.

An extraordinary meeting of the senate (*senatus indictus*) to determine Drusus Libo's intention signals an emergency. During the late Republic the senate might respond to the possibility of revolution by asking the consul to 'see to it that the State should suffer no harm', the so-called *senatus consultum ultimum* (SCU).[21] But this was conceptually impossible in the early Principate, when the safety of the *res publica* was supposed to depend on a princeps.[22] Tiberius apparently uttered the formula once, when, in AD 24, the consul L. Visellius Varro prosecuted C. Silius Caecina Largus, but Tiberius' intention is suspect:

Precante reo brevem moram, dum accusator consulatu abiret, adversatus est Caesar: solitum quippe magistratibus diem privatis dicere: nec infringendum consulis ius, cuius vigiliis niteretur ne quod res publica detrimentum caperet. Proprium id Tiberio fuit scelera nuper reperta priscis verbis obtegere.

The defendant requested a brief delay so that the accuser could retire from the consulate, but Caesar opposed: 'It was by all means usual for magistrates to name a day for the trial of private citizens: nor should the right of the consul be infringed, by whose vigilance it depends that the State should suffer no harm.' It was characteristic for Tiberius to conceal his latest evil inventions with ancient words.[23]

Tiberius' opinion, irrefutable and cynical, had the effect of presenting Silius as a danger to the State.[24] To justify the consul's participation (who may have been driven by personal enmity), Tiberius evoked

---

[21] The principal treatments are: G. Plaumann, 'Das sogenannte senatus consultum ultimum', *Klio*, 13 (1913), 322–86; H. L. Last *CAH*[1] 9, 82 f; A. Lintott, *Violence in Republican Rome* (1968), 149–74, and *The Constitution of the Roman Republic* (1999), 89–93; T. N. Mitchell 'Cicero and the Senatus Consultum Ultimum', *Historia*, 20 (1971), 47–61; A. Drummond, *Law, Politics and Power: Sallust and the Execution of the Catilinarian Conspirators*, Historia Einzelschriften Heft, 93 (1995), 79–107.

[22] Cf. Th. Mommsen, *Staatsrecht* 3.2.1240 f.; H. Dessau, *Geschichte der römischen Kaiserzeit*, Vol. 1 (1924–30), 23.140; H. Volkmann, *Zur Rechtsprechung im Principat des Augustus: historische Beiträge* (1935), 33; J. Bleicken, *Senatsgericht und Kaisergericht—eine Studie zur Entwicklung des Prozeßrechtes im frühen Prinzipat* (1962), 40–3. For the view that the SCU did not inspire senatorial *cognitio* in the Principate, see W. Kunkel, *Über die Entstehung des Senatsgericht* (1969) = *Kleine Schriften* (1974), 267–323 and A. H. M. Jones, *The Criminal Courts of the Roman Republic and Principate* (1972), 93, who both argue that its contested status would have been enough to make its use as a precedent for senatorial *cognitio* fifty to sixty years later unlikely.

[23] Tac. *Ann.* 4.19.

[24] Tac. *Ann.* 4.17. For a general discussion of the charge against Silius, with bibliography, see A. A. Barrett, *Agrippina: Sex, Power and Politics in the Early Empire* (1996), 34 f. and S. H. Rutledge (2001), 142.

through the language of the SCU an atmosphere of emergency. The device was, moreover, used to convey another message. Velleius praised Tiberius for, among other things, restoring the senate's *maiestas*.[25] With less enthusiasm, Tacitus, Suetonius, and Dio have the senate playing a larger role under Tiberius than Augustus.[26] Their works contain, in fragmentary form, Tiberius' most important message to posterity, something like: 'I simply facilitate imperial administration, while the consuls with the senate run the show.' By invoking the SCU, Tiberius implied that his supreme position in no way affected the traditional *potestas* and *auctoritas* of the consuls: Tiberius' Principate was *in practice* a restored Republic! This improvised application of rhetorical colour does not explain why Drusus Libo was scrutinized in the senate rather than a court. The explanation lies instead with the senate's established right to hear evidence of conspiracy when due process was impracticable.

L. Fulcinius Trio did not waste time by seeking out the praetor presiding over the *quaestio maiestatis*, instead, as with all national emergencies, he went straight to the consuls. Ordinarily, Trio would have sought out the appropriate praetor and applied to prosecute Drusus Libo. The praetor would then have summoned Drusus Libo to appear before him to discuss the charge (*nominis delatio*). Satisfied that the evidence deserved trial, the praetor would then publish the charge and name Drusus Libo defendant (*reus*) before fixing a day for the trial to begin. In cases of *maiestas* the *reus* was given ten days in which to organize a defence or else enter into exile.[27] Trio hurried to the consuls because the evidence demanded their knowing and the senate's immediate response: the idea of seeking out the appropriate praetor, and thus giving Drusus Libo time to expedite his plans, would not have suggested itself. The praetor would instead be asked to consider the matter only once the senate had published its opinion (*praeiudicium*), at which point, had Drusus Libo not taken his own life, the *iudices* would have been hard pressed to produce anything but a verdict of guilty. In seeking out the consuls, Trio knew well that precedent justified his decision.

---

[25] Vell. 2.126.
[26] Tac. *Ann.* 4.7.2; Suet. *Tib.* 30.1, 31.1; Dio 57.6.2, 57.15.9.
[27] For procedure, see A. H. J. Greenidge, *The Legal Procedure of Cicero's Time* (1901), 459 f. On giving the accused ten days when the charge was *maiestas,* see Asc. *In Corn.* 59C.

On 18 October 63 BC M. Licinius Crassus, M. Marcellus, and Q. Caecilius Metellus provided to the consul, M. Tullius Cicero, evidence that suggested an impending insurrection by L. Sergius Catilina. Cicero summoned the senate the next day. Nothing came of this meeting but further suspicion that Catiline was up to no good, but when more damning evidence emerged two days later senators were again summoned, and this time the SCU was passed. For five weeks Cicero sought proof that a massacre was imminent, until finally a group was caught in the early hours of 3 December leaving Rome with sealed letters for Catiline. Cicero led those captured to the temple of Concord where senators were assembled. Having been examined by the senate, Catiline's associates were put under arrest and for two days their fate was uncertain while senators considered the options. On 5 December they were put to death. Whilst the decision to execute the prisoners was controversial, the senate's right to investigate the matter was not. This right was acknowledged even, or perhaps especially, during the early Principate.

In 26 BC, C. Cornelius Gallus, prefect of Egypt, was alleged to have extorted from provincials, put up images of himself in Egypt, inscribed a list of his achievements on the pyramids, and slandered Augustus in private.[28] Augustus reacted to the allegations by publicly withdrawing friendship (*renuntiatio amicitiae*) and inviting the senate to investigate the matter:

metu nobilitatis acriter indignatae, cui negotium spectandum dederat imperator...

in fear of the keenly disgusted nobility, to whom the emperor had given the affair to be looked into...[29]

The plundering of Egypt and thus the tempting of local inhabitants to revolt—which was not unheard of, especially for the Alexandrians—was for Augustus a matter worthy of senatorial scrutiny.[30] The

---

[28] Dio 53.23.5; Suet. *Aug.* 66.2; *De Gramm.* 5; Jerome *Chron.* 164H; Amm. Marc. 17.4.5; Servius *ad Georg.* 4.1, *ad Eclog.* 10.1; Ovid *Am.* 3.9.63; *Tr.* 2.446. There is no evidence of an inscription on a pyramid, but an inscription from Philae in Latin, Greek, and Hieroglyphic does celebrate his actions. The Latin can be found at *ILS* 8995.

[29] Amm. Marc. 17.4.5.

[30] The slander cited by Ovid had already been punished by *renuntiatio amicitiae*, contra Bauman (1967), 182–3. Daly, 'The Gallus Affair' *Latomus*, 164 (1979), 289–311 is probably correct to associate Suet. *De Gramm.* 16 with Augustus' decision to sever ties, not the formal indictments. Suetonius tells us that one of the gravest charges

productive capacity of Egypt was vital to the overall health of the economy, and hence the empire. Senators, on finding sufficient proof that Gallus was guilty, agreed that his actions were of national significance:

καὶ ἡ γερουσία ἅπασα ἁλῶναί τε αὐτὸν ἐν τοῖς δικαστηρίοις καὶ φυγεῖν τῆς οὐσίας στερηθέντα, καὶ ταύτην τε τῷ Αὐγούστῳ δοθῆναι καὶ ἑαυτοὺς βουθυτῆσαι ἐψηφίσατο.

The whole senate voted that he should be convicted in the courts and, having been deprived of his estate, exiled, and that his estate should be given to Augustus, and that they themselves should offer sacrifices.[31]

Gallus committed suicide before the decree took effect. The pressure on the *quaestio* to rubber-stamp the senate's *praeiudicium* was enormous: a verdict of not guilty was improbable and Gallus knew it. Four years later, in 22 BC, the *res publica* supposedly faced a more serious threat when the noble L. Terentius Varro Murena and a certain Fannius Caepio were put to death for planning revolution.[32] Though the sources do not explicitly give the senate a role before the trial took place, inference and logic would suggest that it had one.

No detailed account survives of the episode, but enough remains to construct a basic narrative: a plot was formed to bring down Augustus' government;[33] a certain Castricius gained knowledge of the conspiracy and informed Augustus.[34] Augustus called for his most trusted advisers, one of whom was Maecenas. Maecenas related the information to his wife, Terentia, who in turn told her brother L. Terentius Varro Murena.[35] The conspirators—aware that the game was up—fled Rome. At some point, probably early the next day, a decision was made to send troops after the pair.[36] Tiberius then

---

levelled at Gallus by Augustus was that he had living with him a certain Q. Caecilius Epirota, a freedman of Atticus who had been dismissed for having made innapropriate advances towards his daughter, Pomponia (she was also Agrippa's first wife).

[31] Dio 53.23.7. Gallus was equestrian. He could not therefore be charged under the *lex repetundis*. However, he could be, and probably was, charged under the *lex maiestatis*. It is possible, nevertheless, that the senate judged that Gallus should, despite the law, be convicted in the courts *de repetundis*.

[32] I have followed the chronology established by M. Swan, 'The Consular Fasti of 23 B.C., and the Conspiracy of Varro Murena', HSCP, 71 (1967), 235–47.

[33] Vell. 2.91.2; Macr. 1.11.21; Sen. *De Brev. Vit.* 4.5.

[34] Suet. *Aug.* 56.4.

[35] Suet. *Aug.* 66.3, who supplies Marcellus for Maecenas.

[36] To be inferred from Macr. 1.11.21.

took the matter to the praetor presiding over the *quaestio maiestatis* and named Caepio as defendant.[37] Caepio was condemned *in absentia*; Murena was then subjected to the same process. Caepio was finally caught in Naples.[38] Murena was caught with a peripatetic philosopher from Seleuceia named Athenaeus, who, we are told, supported popular politics.[39] Those caught were taken to Rome and put to death, except Athenaeus, who was found not guilty and released. Finally, thanks were voted as if it were a victory.[40]

The decision to send troops after the conspirators, accompanied no doubt by a public declaration that the pair were wanted for questioning and ought to be considered fugitives, would have come from the senate. Senators may even have suggested that the pair ought to be tried for *maiestas*. It would certainly explain the voting of *supplicationes* after the trial. It is inconceivable that Augustus was so clumsy as to take a matter of national importance straight to the praetor, when he had spent so much energy convincing the public, and especially senators, that his new *res publica* was built upon senatorial *auctoritas*, and especially impolitic to exclude the senate from something which belonged to it.[41] I believe that on hearing news that Caepio and Murena had fled Rome, Augustus immediately summoned senators for the purpose of producing a united response. Tiberius then approached the praetor to prosecute both men *in absentia*, arguing in court that their fleeing was in fact an attempt to enter into exile and should therefore be treated as confession.[42] Most in the jury agreed. The men were brought back to Rome for execution because they were not trusted in exile. The role of the senate was vital here, as it must also have been for the investigations into the acts of the elder Julia, Titus Labienus, anti-government pamphlets in AD 6, Agrippa Postumus in AD 7, and Falanius and Rubrius in AD 15.[43] The idea that the senate was the appropriate

---

[37] Suet. *Tib.* 8.1.
[38] Macr. 1.11.21.
[39] Strabo 14.5.4.
[40] Dio 54.3.3.
[41] *Res Gestae* 34.1 is the obvious example of this.
[42] Dio 54.3.3. The key is the construction ὡς καὶ φευξόμενοι. Dio has the sense 'as if ": i.e. they were convicted *as if they were actually going* into exile. Dio used 'as if' because an intention to go into exile was the interpretation of the prosecutor - they never actually reached a place of exile.
[43] For the elder Julia, see Dio 55.10.13 f; Suet. *Aug.* 65.2. For Titus Labienus, see Sen. *Cont.* 10. *praef.* 8; for anti-government pamphlets in AD 6, see Dio 55.27.3. For

An Urgent Summons and a Terrible Charge

space for the discussion of matters supposedly concerning the safety and health of the *res publica* compelled Tiberius to claim in AD 20 that:

Id solum Germanico super leges praestiterimus, quod in curia potius quam in foro, apud senatum quam apud iudices de morte eius anquiritur.

In this way only we will have placed Germanicus above the laws (*super leges*), that his death will be investigated in the curia rather than in the forum, before the senate rather than before the judges.[44]

The *Senatus Consultum de Pisone Patre* reveals that senators were not limited to discussing the circumstances of Germanicus' death:

Ti(berius) Caesar divi Aug(usti) f(ilius) Aug(ustus) pontifex maxumus, tribunicia potestate XXII, co(n)s(ul) III, designatus IIII ad senatum rettulit qualis causa Cn. Pisonis patris visa esset et an merito sibi mortem conscise videretur . . . et quid de Visellio Karo et de Sempronio Basso, comitibus Cn. Pisonis patris, iudicaret senatus . . .

Tiberius Caesar Augustus, son of the divine Augustus, pontifex maxumus, in the twenty-second year of his tribunician power, having been consul three times, consul designate for the fourth time, referred (the following) to the senate: how the case of Cn. Piso the father had seemed, and whether his suicide seemed justified . . . and what the senate judged concerning Visellius Karus and Sempronius Bassus, members of Cn. Piso the father's retinue . . .[45]

---

[44] Agrippa Postumus, see Suet. *Aug.* 65.4. The affairs of Falanius and Rubrius in AD 15 (Tac. *Ann.* 1.73) should not be dismissed as unimportant. Falanius was accused of having allowed an *infamis* to become a *cultor Augusti* in his house and to have sold a statue of Augustus by default of having sold his house. Rubrius was alleged to have used Augustus' name while committing perjury. Tiberius suggested to the consuls that both cases should be dismissed, but we should be cautious before writing them off as unimportant episodes. Augustus had been made a god less than a year before, and perceived violations against his *numen* had not, therefore, been appropriately defined. The senate was being asked to make a ruling that would affect tens of thousands of Romans. It is not unreasonable to assume that mass panic would have swept Rome had the senate voted to condemn in the *quaestio maiestatis*. Panic may have spread already. Any situation with the potential to cause an emergency was therefore dealt with by the senate. It is interesting, however, to note Tiberius' intervention. He wanted the senate to deal with the questions quickly. But the senate was in a tricky situation. To describe the acts as legal too quickly could appear impious, while to consider the matters too long could cause widespread anxiety: senators were probably relieved when Tiberius took the initiative.

[44] Tac. *Ann.* 3.12.7.
[45] *SCPP* 4–11. W. Eck, A. Caballos, and F. Fernández, *Das senatus consultum de Cn. Pisone Patre* (1996), 231 take *iudicare* at *SCPP* 11 to be technical, but M. Griffin, 'The Senate's Story', *JRS*, 87 (1997), 256 and J. S. Richardson 'The Senate, the Courts, and the SC de Cn. Pisone patre', *CQ*, 47 (1997), 516, show that the term maintains a

16   *The Republic in Danger*

Before Piso had even reached Rome, where accusations of murder awaited, the younger Drusus had been forced to remind a growing mob that men were innocent till proved guilty.[46] The plea to justice had little effect. While senators were in session a large group allegedly assailed the doors of the senate house:

Simul populi ante curiam voces audiebantur: non temperaturos manibus si patrum sententias evasisset. Effigiesque Pisonis traxerant in Gemonias ac divellebant, ni iussu principis protectae repositaeque forent.

At this same time voices of the people were heard in front of the *Curia*: they promised violence if he should evade the opinions of senators. They dragged statues of Piso to the Gemonian stairs and were breaking them up when, by order of the princeps, they were rescued and replaced.[47]

Popular unrest made operation of the regular court impossible. The *auctoritas* of the senate was needed to settle excited citizens and arrest the possibility of further violence. As with Augustus' decision regarding allegations against Gallus, Tiberius decided that politics demanded the senate's participation.[48]

Piso subsequently suffered *damnatio memoriae* because his suicide was found deficient in merit.[49] Judging the indictments against the *comites*, the senate decreed:

Visellio Karo et Sempronio Basso comitibus Cn. Pisonis patris et omnium malificiorum socis ac ministris, aqua et igne interdici oportere ab eo pr (aetore), qui lege{m} maiestatis quaereret, bonaq(ue) eorum ab pr(aetoribus), qui aerario praeesse<n>t, venire et in aerarium redigi placere.

That Visellius Karus and Sempronius Bassus, members of Cn. Piso the father's retinue, allies and assistants in all of his wicked crimes, ought to be interdicted from fire and water by the praetor who investigates (crimes) under the *lex maiestatis*, and that their property be sold by the praetors

---

standard meaning throughout the text which is far more general. Cicero uses *iudicare* and other legal terminology to describe the senate's debate on the arrested Catilinarian conspiracy, Cic. *In Cat. passim*.

[46] Tac. *Ann.* 3.8.2.
[47] Tac. *Ann.* 3.14.4–6.
[48] Tac. *Ann.* 3.10.3, see especially R. H. Martin and A. J. Woodman (1996), 132. See also Dio 53.21.5–6. Cf. W. Kierdorf, 'Die Einleitung des Piso-Prozesses', *Hermes*, 97 (1969), 246–51.
[49] SCPP 71: *Quas ob res arbitrari senatum non optulisse eum se de[b]itae poenae...* "That on account of these reasons the senate deemed that he did not subject himself to the punishment he deserved..."

responsible for the *aerarium*, and that the collected proceeds be placed in the *aerarium*.[50]

The senate passed its judgment on the guilt of the accused and prescribed the appropriate punishment, but the legal implementation of these decisions required the *quaestio*: as with its investigation into Gallus forty-five years earlier, the senate's judgment was preliminary not *de iure*.[51] As the above cases make clear, the senate had an important role within the Roman constitution that survived the transition from the late Republic to the governments of Augustus and Tiberius. It remained the space in which matters perceived to be national emergencies were discussed. Some cases, such as those of Falanius and Rubrius, were put to senators because the decision could have far-reaching legal effects, while others, such as allegations against Catiline's associates, and Caepio and Murena, required an immediate response to a perceived threat. The fact that Trio hurried to the consuls, who in turn summoned an emergency meeting of the senate, is therefore our first piece of evidence that Drusus Libo was thought to have posed a serious and immediate threat. It is now time to consider the charge.

A TERRIBLE CHARGE

Et vocantur patres, addito consultandum super re magna et atroci.

And so the fathers were called, it being added that they were to deliberate upon a great and terrible matter.[52]

The spectacle of senators hastily summoned 'to deliberate upon a great and terrible matter' led to a generally held impression that

---

[50] Ibid. 120–3.
[51] This is not to be confused with the senate's right to pass legal judgment in cases involving allegations under the heading *repetundae* and which satisfy the requirements of the *senatus consultum Calvisianum*. The text is published as Edict V in R. S. Sherk, *Rome and the Greek East to the Death of the Augustus* (1984), 130–2. J. S. Richardson (1997), 517, wonders whether the praetor took the decision of the senate as equivalent to the votes of the jury, but this cannot be right, since *tribuni aerarii* and *equites* who, along with senators, made up the *decuriae iudicum*, would still need to acquiesce in a court procedure.
[52] Tac. *Ann.* 2.28.

Drusus Libo was finished before even the submission of evidence. Friends and family displayed their pessimism by refusing appeals to both *amicitia* and *pietas*. In Tacitus' narrative, the consuls' decision to summon senators was in response to evidence that Drusus Libo had employed a necromancer to raise dead spirits. This was not a crime. The crime lay in the nature of his conversation with the necromancer.

Though details of the indictment are not extant, most scholars assume that *maiestas* was at least one of the charges. But while some hold that his occult interests were the basis of the *maiestas* charge, others believe that they were merely incidental, and that occult practices did not then constitute *prima facie maiestas*, even when the princeps was affected.[53] Rutledge, whose notable contribution is the latest, has put forward a third possibility: Drusus Libo was never indicted for *maiestas*, only occult practices in so far as they contravened the *lex Cornelia de sicariis et veneficis*.[54] A reconsideration of the relationship between Drusus Libo's alleged activity and Roman criminal law is therefore warranted.

In AD 11 Augustus responded to interest in his failing health by publishing his horoscope and forbidding the practice thereafter. No Roman was to employ a seer to discover one's own, or another's, time of death:

καὶ τοῖς μάντεσιν ἀπηγορεύθη μήτε κατὰ μόνας τινὶ μήτε περὶ θανάτου, μηδ' ἂν ἄλλοι συμπαρῶσίν οἱ, χρᾶν· καίτοι οὕτως οὐδὲν τῷ Αὐγούστῳ τῶν καθ' ἑαυτὸν ἔμελεν ὥστε ἐκ προγραφῆς πᾶσι τὴν τῶν ἀστέρων διάταξιν, ὑφ' ὧν ἐγεγέννητο, φανερῶσαι. οὐ μὴν ἀλλ' ἐκεῖνό τε ἀπεῖπε...

---

[53] Organizing scholars into camps is necessarily an over-simplification of the nuances which exist in each individual approach, but is nevertheless a fair representation of an obvious pattern. Occult practices equal *maiestas* in the case of Drusus Libo: J. C. Tarver (1902), 326; R. S. Rogers (1935), 16; R. Seager (1972), 89 f. and 'Review of R. A. Bauman Impietas in Principem', *JRS*, 66 (1976), 230–1; D. C. A. Shotter (1972), 92; P. Brunt (1980), 257, n. 10; D. Ogden, *Greek and Roman Necromancy* (2001), 156, and possibly F. R. D. Goodyear (1981), 268. That occult practice was a subsidiary/side issue: A. Lang (1911), 26–35; F. B. Marsh (1931), 58–60; B. Walker, *The Annals of Tacitus* (1952), 91–5; F. H. Cramer (1954), 254–5; R. Syme (1958), 399–401, and (1986), 256, 259; R. Macmullen, *Enemies of the Roman Order: Treason, Unrest and Alienation in the Empire* (1966), 130 f., 326, n. 4; P. Garnsey (1970), 110; R. A. Bauman (1974), 60–1.

[54] S. H. Rutledge (2001), 158–161. Rutledge is cautious, and acknowledges that *res novas moliri* could be evidence for a charge of treason; nevertheless, he seems to prefer *sicariis et veneficis*.

It was forbidden for seers to prophesy to anyone alone or on the topic of death, even if others were present. Even so, Augustus was so far from caring about such matters when he himself was concerned that he published by edict for all to know the arrangement of the stars under which he had been born. Nevertheless he forbade this practice.[55]

Augustus' response was limited. Astrology was not criminalized, only consultations between one person and a seer and questions about death, which must mean questions about both death (*mors*) and health (*salus*). Augustus' official horoscope (lacking a time of death)[56] was certainly published to overwhelm the widespread interest in his health, though a question *de salute principis* was not specifically made a crime. Augustus' personality was sufficiently protected by the general ban on questions *de salute alicuius* - a further prohibition would have been redundant. But did Augustus intend a breach of the ban to constitute a breach of the *lex maiestatis*?

Shortly after the investigation into Drusus Libo a *senatus consultum* outlawed all practice of astrology and magic in Rome.[57] Another—passed sometime later—determined that all Roman *mathematici*, *chaldaei*, and *harioli* should be interdicted from fire and water and have their property confiscated, whilst their foreign counterparts should be put to death.[58] We cannot be sure to what extent the decrees differed in penalty, since they seem to have been telescoped over time, but obviously the first was not considered sufficient. A description of the second survives in Ulpian:

Denique extat senatus consultum Pomponio et Rufo cons., factum, quo cavetur, ut mathematicis Chaldaeis ariolis et ceteris, qui simile inceptum fecerunt,

---

[55] Dio 56.25.5.

[56] Dio 76.11.1; see P. M. Swan, *The Augustan Succession: An Historical Commentary on Cassius Dio's Roman History, Books 55–56 (9 B.C.–A.D. 14)* (2004), 280.

[57] Tac. *Ann.* 2.32, Dio 57.15.8; cf. P. M. Swan (2004), 280. This certainly refers to AD 16.

[58] Ulpian, 'Proconsular Functions Book 4', in *Mosaicarum et Romanarum Legem Collatio* 15.2.1. The date is not secure. The decree states *Pomponio et Rufo cons . . .* The *suffecti* for AD 16 were C. Vibius Rufinus and C. Pomponius L.f. Graecinus. The *ordinarii* for AD 17 were L. Pomponius Flaccus and C. Caecilius Rufus. R. S. Rogers, 'The Date of the Banishment of the Astrologers', *CP*, 26 (1931), 203 f. argues for AD 16, he is followed by F. H. Cramer (1954), 238 f. They do not provide new evidence. F. R. D. Goodyear (1981), 284 f. takes Ulpian to mean AD 17. Though Tacitus and Dio date the decree to AD 16, I believe Goodyear is probably correct. A date of AD 16 would have produced *Pomponio et Rufino . . .* not *Pomponio et Rufo . . .* The second decree was probably published at the very beginning of AD 17.

aqua et igni interdicatur omniaque bona eorum publicentur, et si externarum gentium quis id fecerit, ut in eum animadvertatur...Saepissime denique interdictum est fere ab omnibus principibus ne quis omnino huiusmodi ineptiis se inmisceret, et varie puniti sunt ii qui id exercuerint, pro mensura scilicet consultationis. Nam qui de principis salute, capite puniti sunt vel qua alia poena graviore adfecti...

In short, a *senatus consultum* from the consulship of Pomponius and Rufus is extant in which it is laid down that astrologers, *Chaldaei*, seers and others who engage in similar practices are to be interdicted from fire and water and all of their property shall be confiscated, and if a foreigner has done this he should be punished with death... A prohibition has often been imposed by almost every emperor on those who meddle at all in such follies, and those who practice it have been variously punished, obviously according to the seriousness of the consultation. Those who have inquired into the safety of the princeps have been put to death or have had some rather serious punishment inflicted on them..."[59]

Tacitus, Suetonius, and Dio also give versions of the decree/s:

Facta et de mathematicis magisque Italia pellendis senatus consulta.

Decrees of the senate were also passed expelling *mathematici* and *magi* from Italy.[60]

Expulit et mathematicos sed deprecantibus ac se artem desituros promittentibus veniam dedit.

He also expelled the *mathematici* but pardoned those who came to him promising to give up their art.[61]

...τούς τε ἀστρολόγους καὶ τοὺς γόητας, εἴ τέ τινα ἕτερον καὶ ὁποιονοῦν τρόπον ἐμαντεύετό τις, τοὺς μὲν ξένους ἐθανάτωσε, τοὺς δὲ πολίτας, ὅσοι καὶ τότε ἔτι, μετὰ τὸ πρότερον δόγμα δι' οὗ ἀπηγόρευτο μηδὲν τοιοῦτον ἐν τῇ πόλει μεταχειρίζεσθαι, ἐσηγγέλθησαν τῇ τέχνῃ χρώμενοι, ὑπερώρισε· τοῖς γὰρ πειθαρχήσασιν αὐτῶν ἄδεια ἐδόθη.

As for the astrologers, magicians and anyone who practiced divination in any other way whatsoever, he put the foreigners to death and banished all the citizens who, even then, were accused of still practicing the art after the former decree by which it was forbidden to be involved in any such activity in the city; for to those amongst them who obeyed immunity was given.[62]

---

[59] Ulpian, *Mos. et. Rom.* 15.2.1.   [60] Tac. *Ann.* 2.32.   [61] Suet. *Tib.* 36.
[62] Dio 57.15.8–9.

An Urgent Summons and a Terrible Charge

As a general description we can add a statement by the jurist Paulus:

qui de salute principis vel summa rei publicae mathematicos hariolos haruspices vaticinatores consulit, cum eo qui responderit capite punitur.

One who consults *mathematici*, *harioli*, haruspices or soothsayers concerning the safety of the princeps or the wellbeing of the State, along with one who responds (i.e. the practitioner), is capitally punished.[63]

Expulsion of all citizen 'astrologers, chaldeans, seers and others who engage in similar practices' is a purge: Tiberius had criminalized the lot.[64] The ban was soon ignored, since astrologers can be found working in Rome four years later, but as a legal measure it marks a radical departure from Augustus' approach. Both Ulpian and Paulus make reference to *salus principis* but the words *fere omnes principes* in Ulpian need not encompass Augustus, and it is clear from Paulus' reference to *caput* that he is citing a much later interpretation, when interdiction had ceased to be the penalty for that crime.[65] Ulpian thus began his discussion with the decree of AD 17 because it was antecedent to consultations *de salute principis* being interpreted under the heading *maiestas*. Allegations against Aemilia Lepida four years later demonstrate the development.[66] Charges of adultery (*adulteria*), poisoning (*venena*), and asking seers about the house of Caesar (*quaesitum Chaldaeos in domum Caesaris*) were added to an indictment for false testimony (*falsum*). *Quaesitum Chaldaeos in domum Caesaris* was argued to have constituted *maiestas*.[67] Tiberius asked the senate not to consider the charge of *maiestas*, and later when the defendant's

---

[63] *P. S.* 5.21.3.

[64] A partial parallel is the emergency measures against the followers of Bacchus in the 180s BC, except that genuine followers were allowed to continue worship by registering with the appropriate magistrates. No such deal was made in AD 16 and 17. Cf. R. Macmullen (1966), 133, taking Dio and Suetonius to mean that those pardoned were allowed to continue practiing their art, so long as they avoided certain topics.

[65] Though *caput* had earlier covered death and *interdictio*, a differentiation appears in *P. S.* 5.29.1: *His antea in perpetuum aqua et igni interdicebatur: nunc vero humiliores bestiis obiciuntur vel vivi exuruntur, honestiores capite puniuntur.* 'Formely, they (who were convicted of treason) were permanently interdicted from fire and water: but now *humiliores* are thrown to the beasts or burnt alive, whilst *honestiores* are capitally punished.' Paulus is referring to legal penalties under the *lex maiestatis* during his own time. See also Callistratus, *Judicial Examinations* book 6 = *Dig.* 48.19.28.13.

[66] *PIR*² 1.71 no. 420.

[67] Tac. *Ann.* 3.22; Suet. *Tib.* 49.1.

slaves were handed over to the consuls he asked that the interrogation not include the issue concerning his family.[68] The incarceration and interrogation of slaves was administered according to the *lex Iulia de adulteriis*, which was not a capital offence.[69] When a capital offence was discovered, it came under the *lex Cornelia de sicariis et veneficis*: an intention to poison her ex-husband.[70] Since Aemilia did not plan to harm Tiberius or his family, the allegation of astrology was allowed to slide. At the very worst she had too liberally indulged in silly games fashionable with aristocrats.[71] The prosecutors saw things differently.[72] They understood that the *senatus consulta* of AD 16 and 17 had more significant legal effect than mere outlawry; any enquiry into any aspect of the imperial family was *prima facie maiestas*. The only known bridge between the *senatus consultum* of AD 11, the *senatus consulta* of AD 16 and 17, and the investigation of Aemilia Lepida is the case of Drusus Libo.[73]

Since C. Vibius Serenus was chosen to represent the prosecution in the peroration, he must at some stage have dealt with Fulcinius Trio's evidence.[74] Vibius began with a rhetorical device for character

[68] Tac. *Ann.* 3.22–23.
[69] For sale of slaves in cases of adultery, see *Dig.* 40.9.12.1. See P. Brunt, 'Evidence Given under Torture in the Principate', *ZSS*, 97 (1980), 256–65. Cf. R. A. Bauman (1974), 174.
[70] R. A. Bauman (1974), 174; R. H. Martin and A. J. Woodman (1996), 212.
[71] R. S. Rogers (1935), 51–56; R. H. Martin and A. J. Woodman (1996), 210 f.; cf. R. A. Bauman (1974), 175. S. H. Rutledge (2001), 91–2, 349, n.32, mistakenly believes that *maiestas* was not thrown out, but was, in fact, the charge that decided the nature of the penalty. This seems to be based on a belief that interdiction plus confiscation must equal *maiestas*, but this is not true. If it was thought that Lepida had intended to murder Quirinius with poison, then interdiction and confiscation would have been appropriate; see Marcian, *Institutes* book 14 = *Dig.* 48.8.3.5 and *P. S.* 5.23.1–2.
[72] R. S. Rogers (1935), 51–6; F. H. Cramer (1954), 256; R. Seager (1972), 130; S. H. Rutledge (2001), 91–2, cf. E. Ciaceri (1918), 254–5; R. A. Bauman (1974), 173 f.
[73] The decree of AD 11 probably extended the scope of the *lex Cornelia de sicariis et veneficis*, and possibly the *lex Cornelia de iniuria*. So U. Brasiello, *La Repressione Penale in Diritto Romano* (1937), 231 ff; E. Levy, *Gesammelte Schriften*, vol 2 (1963), 348, and R. A. Bauman (1974), 61, who argues for the *lex Cornelia de sicariis*. The Roman economy was dominated by inheritance. As such, young men and women eager to know the future health of a relative were probably the most common victims of Augustus' decree. Thus the penalty was probably not terrible.
[74] Tac. *Ann.* 2.30: *donec Vibius, quia nec ipsi inter se concederent et Libo sine patrono introisset, singillatim se crimina obiecturum professus*... "then Vibius, as they would not concede to one another, and Libo had entered without legal counsel, offered to state the charges against him singly..." At *Ann.* 4.29.4, Tacitus states: *Nam post damnatum Libonem missis* AD *Caesarem litteris exprobraverat suum tantum studium sine fructu fuisse*... "For after the condemnation of Libo, he [Vibius] sent to

assassination: Drusus Libo's addiction to occult practices evidenced an ambitious spirit.[75] Other tales were told and when the defendant had been sufficiently humiliated, Vibius submitted evidence that shocked Drusus Libo into denial and forced the sale of his slaves to the *actor publicus*. According to Tacitus:

Uni tamen libello manu Libonis nominibus Caesarum aut senatorum additas atrocis vel occultas notas accusator arguebat. Negante reo adgnoscentis servos per tormenta interrogari placuit...Ob quae posterum diem reus petivit domumque digressus extremas preces P. Quirinio propinquo suo ad principem mandavit.

On one paper sinister or cryptic marks had been added to the names of Caesars or senators in Libo's hand, the accuser alleged. When the defendant denied this it was resolved to interrogate under torture the slaves who recognized the handwriting...On account of this the defendant asked to adjourn till the next day, and having departed for home entrusted his final prayers to the emperor to his relative P. Quirinius.[76]

Drusus Libo did not kill himself until after Tiberius refused his plea, but the driving force was the senate's explosive reaction to this single *libellus*. He realized, on witnessing senators' expressions, that the situation was hopeless. A list of imperial and senatorial names is in itself suggestive, but it became impressive when the accompanying marks were described as *atrocis vel occultas*.[77] It is clear from the official commemoration of the trial that a majority in the senate agreed with the prosecutor's description:

Caesar a letter reproaching him that his energy was without reward..." R. H. Martin and A. J. Woodman, *Tacitus: Annals Book IV* (1989), 165, are probably correct to suggest that Vibius was complaining because he had not received a level of reward consistent with the other three accusers, pointing out that since Vibius was proconsul in Spain *c.* AD 22, he must already have held the praetorship, or in fact, may have been a praetor designate when the rewards were offered, cf. R. A. Bauman (1974), 60–1.

[75] Tac. *Ann.* 2.30.
[76] Ibid.
[77] F. R. D. Goodyear (1981), 276, takes *vel* to be distributive, which means that neither term describes the *notae* collectively. Some were obviously threatening whilst others appeared mysterious. This is at the expense of H. Furneaux (1896), 319: 'deadly or at least mysterious symbols.' Goodyear's approach better suits the mood, since the obviousness of some of the *notae* perfectly explains Drusus Libo's immediate denial. This is not to say, however, that the *libellus* was a forged plant. If Libo's enemies wanted to hang him on planted evidence, they would not have made some *notae* too obscure. Indeed, the message of the *libellus* as a whole would have been clear cut.

Fer. ex.s.c.q.e.d. nefaria consilia quae de salute Ti. Caes. liberorumque eius et aliorum principum civitatis deq(ue) r.p. inita ab M. Libone erant in senatu convicta sunt.

A holiday on account of the decree which (was passed) because the wicked plans commenced by M. Libo concerning the safety of Tiberius Caesar and his children and other men of consular rank and also concerning the State were defeated in the senate.[78]

The words *de salute Ti. Caes. Liberorumque eius et aliorum principum civitatis* so parallel the description of the *libellus—nominibus Caesarum aut senatorum*—that the decree clearly inspired Tacitus' report, though the poetical *atrox* is probably Tacitus' own touch. The *libellus* was also the clearest evidence of the *res magna et atrox* which had prompted the emergency investigation in the senate - it was supplied by the necromancer Junius. It is not hard to imagine how Junius came to possess the document: Drusus Libo wrote the list at home before taking it to Junius for consultation; Junius explained that he needed to hold on to it: 'the incantations will take a few days'; Drusus Libo left the document with Junius, who, as soon as the situation allowed, took it to one of the best prosecutors in Rome, L. Fulcinius Trio.

The *senatus consulta* that followed the investigation and the execution of the two *mathematici*, L. Pituanius and P. Marcius, reinforce the link between Junius' *libellus* and the *res magna et atrox*. Pituanius was flung from the Rock, whilst the consuls decapitated Marcius outside the Esquiline Gate at sound of trumpet.[79] Though they were probably tried first, the decision to execute was discretionary, much like the executions of Caepio and Murena.[80] Pituanius and Marcius were evidently guilty of acts more serious than a mere breach

---

[78] *CIL* I² p. 244. The phrase *de re publica* evidences the charge of *maiestas*, contra S. H. Rutledge (2001), 159.

[79] Tac. *Ann.* 2.32.

[80] A comparison with the *comites* of Piso is instructive. On that occasion the senate voted for interdiction, even though they were found to have been complicit in Piso's activities, *SCPP.* 120-1. R. Macmullen (1966), 133, suggests, rightly, that the nature of their death was a show of strength by Tiberius and his government. Still, it is strange that L. Pituanius and P. Marcius received different forms of the death penalty: one thrown from the Rock and the other decapitated by the consul at the Esquiline Gate. It is possible that one was a citizen and the other an alien. 'Thrown from the Rock' was a traditional form of the death penalty for citizens, whilst 'decapitation' signals the inapplicability of the *leges Porciae*. But that would not account for their citizen-like nomenclature.

of the Augustan edict of AD 11, which was not a capital offence. More probably they were judged to have participated in Drusus Libo's conspiracy by way of their talents.

The role of the occult in this episode weighed on the mind of Tiberius, and in doing so forged a bridge between the decree of AD 11 and those of AD 16 and 17. Debate in the senate during the drafting of the latter, however, shows that a total ban was not universally favoured:

καὶ σύμπαντες δ' ἂν οἱ πολῖται καὶ παρὰ γνώμην αὐτοῦ ἀφείθησαν, εἰ μὴ δήμαρχός τις ἐκώλυσεν. ἔνθα δὴ καὶ μάλιστα ἄν τις τὸ τῆς δημοκρατίας σχῆμα κατενόησεν, ὅτι ἡ βουλὴ τοῦ τε Δρούσου καὶ τοῦ Τιβερίου, συνέπαινος Γναίῳ Καλπουρνίῳ Πίσωνι γενομένη, κατεκράτησε, καὶ αὐτὴ ὑπὸ τοῦ δημάρχου ἡττήθη.

And all the citizens would have been acquitted contrary to his [Tiberius'] opinion, if a certain tribune had not obstructed. And here indeed one would particularly observe the form of democratic government, in so far as the senate, being in agreement with Cn. Calpurnius Piso, overruled Drusus and Tiberius, and was itself defeated by the tribune.[81]

Senators believed that a purge of occult practitioners (citizens) was unjustified, and were willing to oppose Tiberius publicly. Senators who had recently passed posthumous penalties upon the memory of Drusus Libo and, perhaps, ordered the execution of his accomplices were now agreed that Drusus and Tiberius were overstepping the mark. Interest in the occult affected every level of society. High levels of participation made Tiberius' policy unenforceable, and senators knew it. Opposition was perhaps also encouraged by a belief that the occult played only a subsidiary role in the Drusus Libo affair, as can be seen in the description of his intention in the sources.

Tacitus describes Drusus Libo's intentions with *moliri res novas;* Suetonius has *res novas clam moliebatur;* Dio has δόξαντά τι νεωτερίζειν; Velleius has *nova molientem* and *scelerata consilia;* Seneca has *maiora sperantis quam illo saeculo quisquam sperare poterat aut ipse ullo;* while the government itself used *nefaria consilia ... de r.p.*[82] An intention to cause revolution will have always resulted in *maiestas,* but a diminution of *maiestas* will not always have been

---

[81] Dio 57.15.9.
[82] Tac. *Ann.* 2.27.1; Suet. *Tib.* 25; Dio 57.15.4; Vell. 2.129, 130; Sen. *Ep.* 70.10; *CIL* I² p. 244.

caused by an intention to cause revolution; the sources unequivocally agree that senators believed Drusus Libo was aiming at revolution. The link to divination rested on the allegation, accepted as fact, that the defendant had given the list of names to a necromancer. It is here pertinent to refute the theory of Ogden that the dead spirits raised by Junius were meant to kill the people listed on the parchment.[83] Lucan, Heliodorus, and Dio are our best sources for the Roman conception of necromancy, and they show that dead spirits were not roused to kill but to prophesy.[84] Ogden has nevertheless drawn our attention to an important problem: how do we combine the parchment with the nature of Junius' expertise? The parchment on its own required a context. A context could only be supplied by a question. Vagueness would have been important, but it would need to be specific enough to gain an adequate answer. The question also had to be such that Tiberius could show indifference, whether real or feigned. Suspicion would not be aroused by something like 'will a certain venture be profitable?'[85], but perhaps by 'what does my future hold should anything unfortunate happen to the men on this list?' If this question were put to Junius in combination with a written list comprising members of the imperial family and other important men of State, it would account for both Junius' initial reaction and that of senators upon hearing the evidence.

Junius judged immediately that Drusus Libo was up to no good and wanted no part in it. Drusus Libo was deemed to have been plotting a coup in which the intended victims were represented on the list; the suspicion formed the basis of the indictment. The charge of having consulted magical practitioners, however, played only a subsidiary role. Its use as evidence was more important. Without obvious proof of Drusus Libo's plot, senators could only infer intent from Junius' evidence. The fact that he also breached the edict of AD 11 was probably an afterthought. As a result of this investigation the door was left open for such questions to be considered treasonable in the future, but that reaction (favoured by a minority) should not blind us to the true nature of the charge, which was intent to cause revolution

---

[83] D. Ogden (2001), 156; a similar idea was also put forward by R. Seager (1972), 92 f: 'In practical terms it was believed that Libo intended to liquidate all possible rivals by black magic and so attain the Principate himself.'
[84] Lucan *Phars.* 6.588–830; Heliod. 6.12–15; Dio 79.7.4.
[85] Apparently a popular question according to the *Tabula Aristobuli*, displayed in F. H. Cramer (1954), 24.

An Urgent Summons and a Terrible Charge

as interpreted under the *lex maiestatis*. Still, clarification of the charge does not make Drusus Libo an actual revolutionary. He is considered a dupe by most scholars, foolish enough to fall prey to more ferocious members of society, *delatores*. Such a view is certainly supported by at least two ancient writers. Seneca writes: *adulescentis tam stolidi quam nobilis,* 'a young man, more stupid than noble', while Tacitus has: *iuvenem inprovidum et facilem inanibus,* 'a short-sighted young man, given to empty things'.[86] Though a tradition which rationalized Drusus Libo's behaviour as that of a thoughtless young fool had taken hold within a generation, there is sufficient evidence to show that he was not underestimated by those who destroyed him. In the next chapter it will be argued that the treatment of Drusus Libo during and after the investigation was not consistent with the scorn shown to young fools who stumble into trouble, but rather the fear inspired by those who threaten revolution.

[86] Sen. *Epist.* 70.10; see also Tac. *Ann.* 2.27.

2

The Treatment of an Enemy

INABILITY TO OBTAIN DEFENCE COUNSEL

Advocacy maintained, from Republic to Principate, its moral force within the Roman social conscience. A belief that people should be defended regardless of the charge remained axiomatic.[1] Exceptions were rare and, usually, repudiated. Seneca denounced as impious Drusus Libo's abandonment:

Cum aeger a senatu in lectica relatus esset non sane frequentibus exsequis (omnes enim necessarii deseruerant impie iam non reum sed funus)...

When, sick, he [Libo] had been carried away from the senate in a litter, with few following, for by then everyone associated with him had *undutifully* deserted him, now that he was no longer a defendant but a corpse.[2]

Seneca's treatment is loaded with stoic conceit—Drusus Libo's lot should have held firm against fear. Tacitus, cynical rather than stoical, displays more sensitivity: 'every one refused, with different pretexts but the same fear (*formido*)'.[3] Dread accompanied the senatorial investigation, with *formido* carrying both shock and fear. Such fear would emerge again for the investigation into acts of sedition by Cn. Piso in AD 20.[4]

---

[1] Pliny *Ep.* VI 29; Cf. Tac. *Dial.* 7. J. A. Crook, *Legal Advocacy in the Roman World* (1995), esp. 119-45, and 172-97.
[2] Sen. *Ep. Mor.* 70.10.4-6; Seneca, furthermore, did not understand the refusal of Libo's family since he did not consider Libo to be dangerous.
[3] Tac. *Ann.* 2.29.
[4] The case of C. Junius Silanus in AD 23 is a different proposition, though it was also a case of *maiestas*. Silanus, governor of Asia in 22, was charged with *repetundae* for *saevitia* and *pecuniae captae* by the people of Asia, Tac. *Ann.* 3.66.1 f. Tac. *Ann.* 3.67.2, writes: *Et ne quis necessariorum iuvaret periclitantem maiestatis crimina subdebantur,*

Cn. Calpurnius Piso was charged with several alleged crimes: engaging in an unauthorized war with Parthia and Armenia while administering Syria;[5] inflicting capital punishment on provincials without trial;[6] the crucifixion of a Roman citizen;[7] patronizing soldiers under his command and allowing them to call themselves *Pisoniani*;[8] attempting (*conatus*) to produce (*excito*) civil war;[9] and murdering Germanicus by way of poison.[10] Most were interpreted under the *lex maiestatis*, but the *lex repetundarum*, the *lex Porcia*, or the *lex Julia de vi* might also have appeared.[11] Piso asked five eminent men to take up the challenge of defending him. Each of them declined. Three advocates were eventually found; their participation perhaps secured by Tiberius.[12] Germanicus' popularity, and the violent reaction of the plebs to his death, provided the five preferred

---

vinclum et necessitas silendi. 'And that not a friend might help him in his danger, charges of treason were added, a bond to guarantee silence.' That is, that Silanus could not procure advocates because the charges were too intimidating, R. H. Martin and A. J. Woodman (1996), 465; cf. D. C. A. Shotter 'The Trial of C. Junius Silanus', *CP*, 67: 2 (1972), 129, with a different interpretation. Charges of treason were registered by Mam. Aemilius Scaurus [*PIR* ² A-404; *RE* 1¹.583-4; S. Rutledge (2001), 186], Junius Otho (*PIR*¹ I-788) and Bruttedius Niger [*PIR*² B-158; *RE* 3.907; S. Rutledge (2001), 204]. The precedents cited by them were cases of *repetundae* during the Republic, see E. Badian, 'Mam. Scaurus Cites Precedent', in *Studies in Greek and Roman History* (1969), 106-10. Hence Silanus was prosecuted for the same crimes by two separate parties under two separate laws, Cic. *In Piso* 21.50 and Marc. *Inst.* 14 = *Dig.* 48.4.3 for acts of *repetundae* pursued under the *lex maiestatis*. During the trial Tiberius cited, in his mind, a parallel case: the recent (AD 13?) prosecution of L. Valerius Messala Volesus for *saevitia* and probably *seditio*, Sen. *De Ira* 2.5.5; Sen. *Contr.* 7.6.22. Messala Volesus, as proconsul of Asia, executed 300 people in one day, and was accused of parading round the corpses while saying, 'oh what a kingly act.'

[5] *SCPP* 37-8.
[6] Ibid., 50-2.
[7] Ibid.
[8] Ibid., 54-5.
[9] Ibid., 45-46.
[10] Tac. *Ann.* 3.12; Dio 57.18.10 = Zon. 11.2 and Xiph. 135.
[11] The charge of murder should have come under the *lex maiestatis*, since Germanicus held *imperium*, but Piso allegedly believed the *lex Cornelia sicariis et veneficis* was appropriate, Tac. *Ann.* 2.79.
[12] Tacitus *Ann.* 3.11 says only that three men, Piso's brother, L. Calpurnius Piso, M. Aemilius Lepidus (*cos.* AD 6), and Livineius Regulus (*suff.* AD 18) 'came to [Piso's] support'. Tiberius is lauded at *SCPP* 20-2 however for encouraging Piso's sons to defend their father: ...*filiosque eius arcessitos hortatus sit, ut patris sui causam defenderent, ita ut eum quoq(ue), qui ordinis senatori nondum esset, ob eam rem introduci in senatum vellet et copiam utriq(ue) dicendi pro patre et pro matre ipsorum et pro M. Pisone faceret,* 'when his [Piso's] sons had been summoned, he encouraged them to defend their father's case, going so far as to be willing for even the one who

candidates with a manifest reason for unease. The angry mob was evidently indifferent to philosophical dogma. It was interested however in 'justice', i.e., Piso's punishment.[13] There was no political advantage to be obtained by helping the perceived enemy of a Caesar. Indeed, supporting Piso might be dangerous. Eventually, however, men did help Piso, whereas Drusus Libo remained bereft: *Libo sine patrono introisset.*[14]

Piso's advocates were assured by reports that the government 'wanted' a fair trial. Such pronouncements were not made in the case of Drusus Libo. His only support (aside from being escorted into the senate by his brother Lucius and the intercession of P. Quirinius) came from a group of women whom Tacitus describes as being *primores feminae*: women from Rome's nobility. The cameo has attracted insufficient attention in modern scholarship:

Libo interim veste mutata cum primoribus feminis circumire domos, orare adfinis, vocem adversum pericula poscere, abnuentibus cunctis, cum diversa praetenderent, eadem formidine.

Libo, meanwhile, changed clothes and with women of consular rank went round from house to house, speaking to his in-laws and asking them to speak against [his] danger; every one refused, with different pretexts but the same fear.[15]

Scribonia, Drusus Libo's great-aunt, was probably among the *primores feminae*. Scribonia is said to have counselled her grand-nephew on his decision to commit suicide: 'What pleasure do you find in doing another's work?'[16] Scribonia may be referring to the executioner,

---

was not yet of of the senatorial order to be brought into the senate for this business and to grant each the opportunity of speaking on behalf of their father and mother and M. Piso'. Tiberius evidently wanted Piso to have defenders, and he may well have suggested that others might fill the void. Nothing is known of Livineius Regulus, while fraternal loyalty would explain the appearance of L. Piso the augur, but the presence of M. Lepidus, a member of Tiberius' inner circle, suggests a favour for the *princeps*.

[13] At the time of Piso's 'trial' a mob allegedly assailed the doors of the senate house: Tac. *Ann.* 3.14.4. Drusus had already been forced to make a public show of moderation by suggesting that justice be allowed to take its course, Tac. *Ann.* 3.8.2.

[14] Tac. *Ann.* 2.30.1.

[15] Tac. *Ann.* 2.29.1. Scribonia's identity can be inferred on account of her presence at Drusus Libo's house, as can Drusus Libo's wife, since her relatives (*adfines*) were the ones sought out, but we have no other evidence with which to identify other women.

[16] Sen. *Ep. Mor.* 70.10.

but she also means Tiberius. A commonly held belief that Tiberius wanted the defendant destroyed would partly explain his decision to swear an oath, *the very next day*, that he would have vetoed the use of capital punishment.[17] The efforts of the *primores feminae* were, not surprisingly, ineffectual. No one would speak on Drusus Libo's behalf when the government was suspected of engineering his destruction, especially since Tiberius was remaining silent—a situation radically different from that which developed in AD 20. This does not mean, however, that the *domus Caesaris* was united in agreement. The efforts of the *primores feminae*—a public protest by women of consular rank—were probably supported by Livia, now Julia Augusta. Advertised by the government as the embodiment of beneficence, Livia was treated as the de facto *Mater Patriae*; women from noble houses may have sought her consent.[18] The awkward behaviour of Drusus Libo's brother, L. Scribonius Libo, also deserves mention.

---

[17] It is also interesting to note that Drusus Libo was eventually prosecuted only once the *delator* L. Fulcinius Trio was involved; he was apparently a close friend of Sejanus, Dio 58.25.2. We do not know when Sejanus and Trio became friends, but when Trio prosecuted Drusus Libo his talents were already celebrated: *celebre inter accusatores ingenium*, Tac. Ann. 2.28.3. Since the *delator* was in Rome a public prosecutor, the two had probably already met. If that is the case, then the prosecution of Drusus Libo may well have been supported by important elements of the government. This further diminishes the possibility that senior figures, i.e., Tiberius, Germanicus' close friends, Drusus, Sejanus, etc., supported the efforts of the *primores feminae*.

[18] On Livia and the organization of women in the political arena during the early Principate, see N. Purcell, 'Livia and the Womanhood of Rome', *PCPhS*, 32 (1986), 78–105. Livia was credited with having saved the conspirator Cn. Cornelius L. f. Cinna Magnus (cos. AD 5) (Drusus Libo's maternal uncle) from having to stand trial, Dio 55.22.1; she supported the elder Julia on Rhodes, J. Linderski, 'Julia in Regium', *ZPE*, 72 (1988), 181–200, esp. 187; she provided financial assistance to the younger Julia on Trimerus, Tac. Ann. 4.71.4. Tacitus goes on to say: *quae florentis privignos cum per occultum subvertisset, misericordiam erga adflictos palam ostentabat*, 'who, having overcome the prosperity of her step-children by intrigue, publicly offered compassion to her victims'. Livia also secured a pardon for Piso's wife Plancina in AD 20, *SCPP* 115–20. The latter deserves further attention. The *SCPP* provides the best evidence for how the government constructed Livia's image: ... *Iuliae Aug(ustae), optume de r(e) p(ublica) meritae non partu tantum modo principis nostri, sed etiam multis magnisq(ue) erga cuiusq(ue) ordinis homines beneficis* ...'Julia Augusta, who was most deserving of the *res publica*, not only because she gave birth to our princeps but also because of her many and great kindnesses to men of every order'. Inherent in the description is a belief that Livia was the *Mater Patriae*, though the impression was strictly unofficial. See A. Barrett, *Livia* (2002), esp. 186–214, which includes many instances of Livia's benefaction and philanthropy. Livia was a mother not just to Tiberius but to society at large; a leading example to all women and a source of comfort to all men.

The Treatment of an Enemy 33

Willing to accompany his brother into the senate but unwilling to speak, L. Libo's behaviour was that of a man leading a lamb to slaughter.[19] Fraternal obligation should have freed L. Libo from the implied prohibition affecting others, unless he knew the facts. If L. Libo knew that his brother was guilty it would better explain his remaining silent. He could bring himself only to accompany his brother into the senate. Drusus Libo was alone after that. Thus two explanations for the desertion of Drusus Libo: a belief that he was involved in something serious and a belief that the government wanted him destroyed. A further point requires consideration.

A search for advocates took place before details of the charge were publicized.[20] *Adfines* therefore responded to a general atmosphere, not specific knowledge of the allegations.[21] The consuls called the emergency meeting of the senate to discuss the alleged designs of a young noble *in* a city alive with news that Agrippa Postumus, assumed dead, was marching towards Rome:

Vulgabatur interim per Italiam servatum munere deum Agrippam, credebatur Romae; iamque Ostiam invectum multitudo ingens, iam in urbe clandestini coetus celebrabant, cum Tiberium anceps cura distrahere, vine militum servum suum coerceret an inanem credulitatem tempore ipso vanescere sineret.

It was meanwhile rumoured throughout Italy that Agrippa had been saved by heaven, at Rome it was believed; already huge crowds greeted him at Ostia, already secret meetings were held in the city, while the attention of Tiberius was distracted with conflicting concerns: should he put down his own slave by military means or allow idle credulity to vanish over time.[22]

The government would not have used the phrase *Agrippa munere deum servatus*.[23] It is probably an authentic record of rebel

---

[19] Not explicit but implicit.

[20] The indictments were read to the senate by Tiberius on the first day of the investigation, Tac. *Ann.* 2.29.2.

[21] Though it cannot be discounted that some were actually complicit and thus knew too much.

[22] Tac. *Ann.* 2.40.1 and Dio 57.16.3 place the affair after the trial of Drusus Libo, at the end of AD 16. Since Suet. *Tib.* 25 treats this period thematically, his ordering of events is not applicable. If the affair was brought to a close at the end of AD 16, Clemens and his band of followers must have been traversing Italy while Drusus Libo was being prosecuted. They would have needed at least six months to march through northern Italy to Gaul and then back down the west coast of Italy to Rome, all the while recruiting men.

[23] Cf. J. Bellemore, 'The Death of Agrippa Postumus and escape of Clemens', *Eranos*, 98 (2000), 93–114.

propaganda.[24] Claiming divine support is a common instrument of persuasion and speaks directly to the true believer, an important element in any mass movement bent on causing revolution. It also attempts to persuade those who, being often bored, down on their luck, or fatalistic, are attracted to new movements offering change. The sources agree that the message had an effect:

Eodem anno mancipii unius audacia, ni mature subventum foret, discordiis armisque civilibus rem publicam perculisset.

In the same year the audacity of a single slave, but for prompt measures, would have struck down the *res publica* with discord and civil war.[25]

Dio writes:

... καὶ ἐς τὴν Γαλατίαν ἐλθὼν πολλοὺς μὲν ἐνταῦθα πολλοὺς δὲ καὶ ἐν τῇ Ἰταλίᾳ ὕστερον προσεποιήσατο, καὶ τέλος καὶ ἐπὶ τὴν Ῥώμην ὥρμησεν ὡς καὶ τὴν παππῴαν μοναρχίαν ἀποληψόμενος. Ταραττομένων τε οὖν ἐπὶ τούτῳ τῶν ἐν τῷ ἄστει, καὶ συχνῶν αὐτῷ προστιθεμένων ...

And having gone to Gaul, he won many to his cause there and many later in Italy, and finally he set out for Rome as one intending to win back his grandfather's domain. And so with those in the city having been excited at this and with considerable numbers having joined themselves to him ...[26]

Suetonius states

Nam et servus Agrippae Clemens nomine non contemnendam manum in ultionem domini compararet ...

For a slave of Agrippa, Clemens by name, had organised a not contemptible force to avenge his master ...[27]

The force that assembled between Ostia and Rome cannot have been in the hundreds, but instead numbered in the thousands. For contemporaries to use the language of civil war, Clemens must have marched with a large group of men and enjoyed the support of many more throughout Italy and Rome. A few hundred would have been easily defeated by the 4,500 praetorians and 1,500 urban cohorts alone.[28] This provides an appropriate context in which to explain the

---

[24] A source like Servilius Nonianus might have included things he had heard being said in Rome, or, the idea may have survived in anonymous political pamphlets. The latter were particularly common in Rome.
[25] Tac. *Ann.* 2.39.1.   [26] Dio 57.16.3.   [27] Suet. *Tib.* 25.1.
[28] W. Nippel, *Public Order in Ancient Rome* (1995), 90 f.

behaviour of Drusus Libo's relatives and friends.[29] Concerning the Clemens affair, Tacitus states:

Et quamquam multi e domo principis equitesque ac senatores sustentasse opibus, iuvisse consiliis dicerentur, haud quaesitum.

Though many from the imperial house, equestrians and senators were said to have supported [Clemens] with money and assisted with their advice, there was no public inquiry.[30]

The imperfect passive of *dico* indicates a contemporary idea, not a Tacitean construction. In AD 16 people were saying that important individuals were supporting Agrippa. Such an opinion would surely have affected the atmosphere surrounding Drusus Libo's pending investigation for acts that concerned the safety of the government; an effect enhanced by the perceived cold silence of Tiberius. Unfortunately for Drusus Libo, few are ever willing to go down with a sinking ship.

DRUSUS LIBO *IN CUSTODIA*

Once a decision was made to sell Drusus Libo's slaves to the treasury, an adjournment was allowed and the defendant proceeded home, where he was met by soldiers in and around his house:

Cingebatur interim milite domus, strepebant etiam in vestibulo ut audiri, ut aspici possent.

Meanwhile the house was being surrounded by soldiers, and they were even making a noise in the entrance so that they could be heard and seen.[31]

Custodia prevented voluntary exile. Provided a defendant did not present a threat to the *res publica*, it was in the interests of the

---

[29] The scene is reminiscent of the behaviour of Catiline's friends as he entered the senate on 8 Nov. 63 BC. Cicero (*In Cat*.1.16) apparently said to Catiline: 'A short time ago you entered the senate. Who from that crowd, from all your many friends and intimates greeted you? If no one else has received such treatment within the memory of man, are you waiting for condemnation to be voiced aloud, although you have been convicted by the hostile verdict of their silence? What of the fact that at your arrival the seats near you emptied, that the moment you sat down all the ex-consuls whom you had repeatedly marked out for death left the seats around you bare and empty . . . ?'
[30] Tac. *Ann*. 2.40.3.   [31] Tac. *Ann*. 2.31.1.

government and the prosecution that the defendant be allowed to quit Italy. The State would secure a conviction and the prosecution their compensation. But if the defendant was suspected of planning violence *contra rem publicam*, voluntary exile was untenable. *Dignitas* might sometimes demand that suspects be placed in the somewhat paradoxical 'free custody' (*libera custodia*), but either way, serious malcontents were usually held against their will.[32]

On 4 December 63 BC the senate decided that P. Cornelius Lentulus Sura, M. Cornelius Cethegus, L. Statilius, and M. Caeparius had attempted to conspire with the Allobroges against Rome, and decreed that they ought to be kept in *libera custodia*.[33] Cicero further alleged that they were acting in concert with Catiline, who, it was established, had gathered an army in northern Italy for the purpose of commanding violence (*vis*) against the State. Cato, in Sallust's version of his speech before the senate, put the motion that the nefarious plans of the wicked citizens placed the *res publica* in the greatest danger, and since they had planned *caedes, incendia* and other *crudelia facinora* against the State, they should be put to death, to which Sallust adds that a *senatus consultum* was passed 'in terms of Cato's resolution'.[34] It should be noted that these men were not 'enemies of the Roman People' (*hostes populi Romani*) but 'wicked citizens' (*scelesti cives*), in contradistinction to Catiline and Manlius, who were in arms against the State. The arrested conspirators were nevertheless executed.[35]

---

[32] Only four explicit examples of *libera custodia* are recorded before the case of Drusus Libo: the custody of Dassius Altinius in 213 BC, Livy 24.45.8; the Bacchanalian priests in 186 BC, Livy 39.19; King Perses of Macedonia in 168 BC, Vell.1.11; and the arrested leaders of the Catilinarian conspiracy in 63 BC, Sall. *Bell. Cat.* 47. P. Garnsey (1970), 148 n. 3 includes the imprisonment of Jugurtha after his defeat by Marius, but Plut. *Mar.* 12 suggests actual incarceration, not *libera custodia*, and Livy *Per.* 67 actually uses *in carcere*.

[33] Sall. *Bell. Cat.* 47: ... *itaque Lentulus P. Lentulo Spintheri, qui tum aedilis erat, Cethegus Q. Cornificio, Statilius C. Caesari, Gabinius M. Crasso, Caeparius nam is paulo ante ex fuga retractus erat Cn. Terentio senatori traduntur.* 'Lentulus was therefore handed over to P. Lentulus Spinther, who was then aedile, Cathegus to Q. Cornificius, Statilius to C. Caesar, Gabinius to M. Crassus, Caeparius, who, having fled, was recently caught and brought back, was given to the senator Cn. Terentius.' Cic. *In Cat.* 3.14; Plut. *Cic.* 19.

[34] Sall. *Bell. Cat.* 53.

[35] Cicero's use of the term *hostes* in his fourth Catilinarian of 60 BC (e. g. *In Cat.* 4.15) was not original, but an apologetic attempt to legitimize his execution of the conspirators. This is clear from the reaction to the proposal to execute them by Caesar in 63 BC—evident by the phrasing of Cato's *sententia*.

Lentulus Sura allegedly sought the assistance of various gangs, with apparent success. The conspirators were thus in alliance with a large armed force, with whom, it was feared, they would organize riots. Keeping the conspirators away from their supporters was therefore crucial.[36] I believe that a similar fear inspired senators to order the urban, or praetorian, prefect to assemble soldiers in and round Drusus Libo's house. The conspiracy of Clemens, with the belief that he possessed noble allies in Rome, again holds the key. Tacitus writes of secret meetings taking place in Rome, while Dio writes of many 'in the city' joining Clemens' cause.[37] Conspiracies, by definition, take time to plan; secret meetings must have occurred before Drusus Libo was indicted. As such, the decision to use armed soldiers rather than entrust Drusus Libo to one of the senior magistrates is suggestive. The government suspected that Drusus Libo was part of a larger conspiracy which might involve still other highly placed *nobiles* and took adequate precaution. The presence of soldiers reinforced the belief that Tiberius supported the defendant's prosecution.[38]

DAMNATIO MEMORIAE AND PUBLIC OFFERINGS OF THANKS

Drusus Libo's death did not bring the investigation to an end.[39] This phenomenon would later occur only when the defendant was charged with sedition. During Tiberius' Principate, however, it was not a fixed rule in law.[40] This is best evidenced by the treatment of Drusus Libo:

---

[36] Indeed, Sallust writes that in response to the senate's decree, Lentulus Sura's freedmen and some associates communicated with the gang leaders to help free their patron. Cicero, informed of this, summoned the senate to discuss the future of the prisoners, Sall. *Bell. Cat.* 50.

[37] Tac. *Ann.* 2.40.1; Dio 57.16.4.

[38] As was the case with Piso, Tac. *Ann.* 3.14.4–5.

[39] E. Volaterra, *RSDI* (1933), 393–416, argues that suicide proved guilt, basing his opinion on *Dig.* 48.21.3 pr.; also M. Griffin (1997), 260–3. But Tacitus' own words imply that the prosecution had work still to do, i.e., Drusus Libo was not yet guilty. Having narrated the death of Drusus Libo, Tacitus writes at *Ann.* 2.31.3: *Accusatio tamen apud patres adseveratione eadem peracta* ...

[40] For the belief that post-mortem prosecution is to be identified with sedition, see comments allegedly made by Marcus Aurelius in the case of Avidius Cassius, *Cod. Just.* 9.8.6pr; Ulpian *Disp.* 8 = *Dig.* 48.4.11. R. S. Rogers, 'Treason in the Early Empire', *JRS*, 49 (1959), 90–4, is of the view that post-mortem prosecutions were always a guide

the State took no part of his confiscated estate.[41] The estate, nevertheless, was entirely broken up and shared by his accusers.[42] At this point, Tiberius swore an oath that he would have vetoed a penalty of death: the death penalty was obviously well supported. Finally, propositions to restrict the Scribonii's ability to memorialize Drusus Libo were decreed, public acts of thanks were offered to Jupiter, Mars, and Concord, and 13 September was declared a holiday.[43] I shall deal first with the decision to control the public memory of Drusus Libo.

The practice of *damnatio memoriae* occurred in the early and middle Republic, when the responsibility of sanctions resided in the familial *potestas* of the *pater familias*.[44] In the late Republic, however, the State encroached on this ancient privilege.[45] By the time of Drusus Libo's conviction, precedent existed to justify punitive measures against the family as a whole. The first of these measures indicates that he was considered by a majority of senators to have intended actual harm against the State.

M. Aurelius Cotta Maximus Messalinus (cos. AD 20) was close to the *domus Caesaris*.[46] He was with Ovid in AD 8 when news arrived of the poet's banishment and afterwards provided material and

---

to the severity of a charge. I believe he is wrong. Though the jurist Macer applies the procedure to cases of *maiestas* while commenting on the *senatus consultum Turpillianum* of AD 61 (*Dig.* 48.16.15.3), it should be remembered that he lived after Marcus Aurelius, so that his comments probably constitute a reassessment of the S. C. Turpillianum in light of Marcus Aurelius' innovation. For evidence that post-mortem prosecution in cases of sedition was not a fixed rule in law in the early Principate, see esp. the case against Cremutius Cordus in AD 25, *Con. ad Marc.* 22. Seneca tells us that 'the big issue in court was whether accused persons lost their legal right to die'. Obviously there was no extant ruling. Seneca then writes: *dum deliberatur, dum accusatores iterum adeunt, ille se absolverat*, 'while the matter was being debated, while the accusors were arguiing their case a second time, he gained his acquital [by suicide].' A second plea by the prosecution shows that a legal consensus was proving impossible to establish. The senate finally clarified the situation in law - presumably good enough for the praetor - by ruling in favour of the heirs, Tac. *Ann.* 4.30.

[41] Tac. *Ann.* 2.32.1. C. W. Chilton (1955), 70, claims that 'When Libo Drusus committed suicide in 16 his property was not confiscated but divided amongst his accusers'. Libo's family might not have agreed. Payment of the delatores out of Libo's estate surely represents the annulment of his testament.

[42] F. R. D Goodyear (1981), 280; cf. R. A. Bauman, (1974), 60 n. 46.

[43] Tac. *Ann.* 2.32.1 f.

[44] H. Flower, *Ancestor Masks and Aristocratic Power in Roman Culture* (1996); J. Bodel, 'Punishing Piso', *AJP*, 120 (1999), 43–57.

[45] Cf. H. Flower (1996), 104.

[46] On his nomenclature and various questions surrounding his identity, see R. Syme (1986), 235 f.

psychological support to the 'exile'.[47] Friendship with Augustus none the less remained intact. Ovid believed (as late as AD 11) that Cotta Messalinus could successfully intercede with the princeps.[48] Until at least AD 32 he remained close to Tiberius.[49] His proposal concerning Drusus Libo is thus politically significant: that the image of Drusus Libo should not be carried in the funeral procession of any of his descendants.[50] Cotta Messalinus probably anticipated Tiberius' approval - a prominent noble allied to the government would not knowingly exasperate the princeps. The history of this particular punishment shows that Cotta Messalinus held Drusus Libo to be an enemy of the Roman people (*hostes populi Romani*).

C. Julius Caesar, in 69 BC, displayed Marius' *imago* at the funeral of his aunt Julia. Plutarch writes that among the spectators: 'there were some who shouted that this was the revival of honours which *by laws and decrees* had been properly put to rest'.[51] Flower and Bodel have nevertheless taken the view that no sovereign body had ruled against such action, since Caesar had come to no harm.[52] But aside from the fact that Plutarch mentions explicitly 'laws and decrees', that Caesar was not arraigned for his audacity is evidence only that the senate was unwilling to supply a judgment (*praeiudicium*).[53] It would probably have been difficult to find a jury to convict him. Sulla, having declared Marius a *hostis*, seems to have sought prohibitions against his memory from both the senate and *comitia*.[54] The treatment of Brutus and Cassius is also relevant. Tacitus writes that at the funeral of Junia in AD 22 the *imagines* of Brutus and Cassius were the more conspicuous by their absence.[55] The *lex Pedia* of 43 BC allowed for men to be

---

[47] *Tristia* 5.9; *Ex. Pont.* 1.9.25–30; 2.8. The last may imply financial assistance.
[48] Ovid *Ex. Pont.* 1.9.24–30.
[49] Tac. *Ann.* 6.5.
[50] Ibid., 2.32.1.
[51] Plut. *Caes.* 5, 6.
[52] H. Flower (1996), 58, n. 128, though at 103, n. 68 she states that Sulla had banned Marius' *imago*, and offers no further comment on what this meant; J. Bodel (1999), 47–8: 'On what authority the portrait of Marius was banned from funeral processions in the time of Sulla we do not know, but it must have been a private affair, for when Caesar reintroduced the *imago* at the funeral of his aunt Julia in 69 B.C., he contravened no law and suffered no penalty.'
[53] Plut. *Caes.* 6.
[54] Owing to the impotence of the *concilium plebis* under Sulla, it seems doubtful to me that 'law' could refer to a plebiscite. In 88 Sulla required the senate to outlaw Marius, App. *BC.* 1.60; Val. Max. 3.8.5. Plut. *Sulla* 10.
[55] Tac. *Ann.* 3.76; also Pliny *Epist.* 1.17.3.

convicted *in absentia* for either *vis* or *maiestas*, denying the convict Roman citizenship.[56] It probably provided for the treatment of their *imagines* also. Augustus is said to have favoured L.Sestius, who: 'had always been an enthusiastic follower of Brutus, had fought with him in all his wars, and even at this time kept his memory alive, preserved images of him, and delivered eulogies of him'.[57] Piety towards the shade of Brutus does not preclude sanctions. The *lex Pedia* may have prohibited only public display, or Octavian may simply have been exhibiting an extreme tolerance, in the same way that he 'tolerated' the history of Cremutius Cordus, who wrote that Cassius was the 'last Roman'.[58] Certainly not every opportunity to prosecute dissent was taken. A degree of *moderatio* and *clementia* by Augustus was necessary after the violent display of power during the thirties BC and the reconciliatory government which followed. With these cases - the rebellions of Marius, Brutus, and Cassius - Cotta Messalinus compared the conspiracy of Drusus Libo. That he believed Tiberius would agree with the comparison is more important than whether or not his belief was correct. The second instance of *damnatio memoriae* against Drusus Libo evidences a more complex situation.

The second opinion: 'that no Scribonii should take the cognomen Drusus' was that of Cn. Cornelius Lentulus the Augur (cos. 14 BC). Owing to his age (in his late sixties or early seventies in AD 16), Lentulus was probably closer to Tiberius than was the much younger Cotta Messalinus. Tacitus describes him as a 'very close friend' (*intimus amicus*).[59] When mutiny among the Pannonian legions was reported in Rome in September AD 14, Lentulus was asked to accompany the younger Drusus.[60] Singled out by the troops for having the most influence over the young prince, he was assaulted—with rocks—accordingly (despite the presence of L. Aelius Sejanus).[61] As with Cotta Messalinus, Lentulus should be viewed as having anticipated Tiberius' approval with regard to the proposal. Prohibiting a family the use of a *nomen* always concerned the *praenomen*; the case of Drusus Libo is the only instance attested in which a *cognomen* is involved.[62] That the

---

[56] Vell. 2.69.5.   [57] Dio 53.32.4, dated 23 BC.   [58] Tac. *Ann.* 4.34.
[59] Tac. *Ann.* 4.29.1; also Dio 57.24.8.   [60] Tac. *Ann.* 1.27.
[61] Ibid.; for Sejanus, *Ann.* 1.24.
[62] It must be pointed out that instances of this phenomenon are rare, as noticed by the editors of *L'année épigraphique* (1995) 54 adn: '*Mais ce phénomène est rare et de telles interdictions n'ont jamais eu un caractère systématique.*' The first recorded instance is the case of M. Manlius Capitolinus (cos. 392 BC), in which the family

cognomen was 'Drusus' signals a motivating force more complex than justice; it signals aristocratic politics.

The name Q. Caecilius Drusus Libo survives only on a single inscription found in the middle of the twentieth century:

> M SCRIBONIVS STORAX
> Q CAECILI DRVSI LIBONIS
> PAEDAGOGVS
> TVLLIA CLEOPATRA CONIVGI SVO FEC

M. Scribonius Storax, governor of Q. Caecilius Drusus Libo, put this up for his wife, Tullia Cleopatra.[63]

Comprehending the boy's nomenclature has proved difficult, but the answer lies within the text.[64] It is logical to suppose that the *paedagogus* was a freedman and that his former master was a certain M. Scribonius. We know of only one M. Scribonius. Now, if the *paedagogus* was a freedman of the boy's natural father, then the boy would have been born M. Scribonius Drusus Libo. Adoption by a Q. Caecilius would therefore produce Q. Caecilius Scribonianus: it is not a great leap to Q. Caecilius Drusus Libo. Moreover, since adoption occurred while the boy was still young, a 'favourite teacher' might reasonably have remained on duty.

The existence of Q. Caecilius Drusus Libo shows that Lentulus' proposal was enforced, and that the Scribonii responded accordingly. Prohibiting the *cognomen* 'Drusus' indicates a political context. Lentulus wished to deny a noble family use of a name associated

---

council ruled that no Manlius was ever to assume the name 'Marcus', Livy 6.20.14; Cic. *Phil.* 1.32 (with emendations by Shackleton Bailey) and Quint. 3.7.20. The next regards a decision by the Claudii to stop using the *praenomen* 'Lucius' because it had become sullied by its association with murder and robbery, Suet. *Tib.* 1. The final instance is a *senatus consultum* of 30 BC prohibiting the Antonii from using the *praenomen* 'Marcus', Dio 51.19.3; Plut. *Cic.* 49. The Antonii responded with Iullus Antonius, a *praenomen* claimed through Antony's mother, Iulia; a clever irony.

[63] *AE* (1964), 82.

[64] J. Scheid, 'Scribonia Caesaris et les Julio-Claudians. Problèmes de vocabulaire de parente', *MEFR*, 87 (1975), 349–75. Scheid makes him the natural son of a Scribonia, assumed to be the sister of M. Scribonius Drusus Libo. She thus married a Caecilius, but that fails to explain the *cognomen* Drusus in the boy's nomenclature; E. J. Weinrib, 'The Family Connections of M. Livius Drusus Libo', *HSCP*, 72 (1968), 247–78. R. Syme (1986), 260, proposed that the boy was born a Caecilius and was adopted by a Scribonius.

with supreme power. Drusus Libo, by implication, must have stressed this aspect of his personality. To Lentulus at least, Drusus Libo had been attempting to establish himself as a viable substitute or alternative to the reigning Claudian dynasty. I have argued in Appendix 1 that the *cognomen* was not appropriated but inherited from his uncle on the condition that he take his uncle's name (*condicio nominis ferendi*). The difference is important. *Condicio nominis ferendi* provided the heir with the testator's collection of *imagines*. On entering Drusus Libo's *atrium*, one would have been confronted by the images of Claudians, Scribonians, and Pompeians. Lentulus—and I think Tiberius—perceived in the Scribonii an ambition in direct conflict with the Claudian monopoly (perhaps then another item to explain the behaviour of L. Libo). But the child's adoption shows that consolidation of Claudian 'assets' was less important than arresting an immediate Scribonian threat.

Only one Q. Caecilius of sufficient significance is attested for this period, Q.Caecilius Metellus Creticus Silanus (cos. AD 7), and epigraphic evidence connects him to the Scribonii.[65] Tacitus believed that he was perhaps too close to Germanicus, inferred in part from

[65] *ILS* 9433: *Q. CAECILIUS CAECILIAE CRASSI L. HILARUS MEDIC CAECILIA DUARUM SCRIBONIARUM L. ELEUTHERIS EX PARTEM DIMIDIAE SIBI E SUI* 'Q. Caecilius Hilarus, *libertus* of Caecilia (wife of) Crassus, physician; Caecilia Eleutheris, *liberta* of two Scribonian women, part (of his tomb) for themselves and for their own (i.e. family).' Caecilia Crassi = Caecilia Metella, daughter of Q. Caecilius Metellus Creticus (cos. 69). Her husband was M. Crassus, eldest son of the triumvir M. Licinius Crassus (cos. 70). R. Syme (1986) stemma XVIII, has shown that Caecilia Metella was a great aunt to Q. Caecilius Metellus Creticus Silanus. Caecilia Eleutheris poses a problem. Why she is not Scribonia Eleutheris is unclear. The answer must lie with rules governing informal manumission: *manumissio inter amicos* and *manumissio iusta ac legitima*. Pliny *Epist*. 7.16 is apposite. See S. Treggiari, *Freedmen During the Late Roman Republic*, Oxford (1969), 20–36. Legal curiosities aside, the freedwoman stands as testimony to a connection between the Caecilii and Scribonii Libones during the late Republic. Q. Caecilius Drusus Libo evidences the continuation of close ties. On this inscription, see H. Dessau, *ILS*, III (1916), addenda 9433: *Quomodo liberta earum Caecilia appellari potuerit incertum*; H. Gummerus, *Der Arztestand im romishen Reiche*, I, Societas Scientiarum Fennica, Commentationes Humanarum Litterarum, III, 6 (1932), 47, no. 163; H. Bloch, 'The Funerary Inscription of the Physician of Caecilia Crassi in the Fogg Art Museum', *HSCP*, 86 (1982), 141–50; R. Syme (1986), 260, 275. Syme was cautious about the *duae Scriboniae*: 'Not necessarily Scribonia Caesaris and a daughter of old Libo, as suggested by H. Bloch.' There is, however, no evidence connecting the Scribonii Curiones with the Caecilii, and the existence of Q. Caecilius Drusus Libo surely limits our search to within the walls of the *domus Scribonii Libonis*. Scribonia Caesaris and her niece are the most obvious candidates within that house.

Tiberius' decision to replace him as governor of Syria with Cn.Piso in AD 17, but mostly from the fact that a daughter was for a time betrothed to Germanicus' eldest son, Nero.[66] His parentage is unknown, but his eventual rank implies close affinity with the Junii Silani, who profited under Augustus and Tiberius.[67] Intimately connected with Tiberius' dynastic plans, Creticus Silanus stood near the centre of the aristocracy.[68] A formal ceremony cannot have occurred until Creticus Silanus returned to Rome from Syria, i.e., towards the end of AD 17. A reconstruction is helpful. Immediately following the *senatus consultum de M. Libone* (?) the *cognomen* Drusus was probably dropped from the young boy's nomenclature. The situation persisted until Creticus Silanus had returned from Syria and a formal adoption then altered the boy's agnatic status. No longer a Scribonius, the boy could again use the cognomen Drusus; a privilege that adoption did not preclude. But would the adoption have been organized without the regime's approval? Based on what we know of Creticus Silanus, the answer must be no.

The adoption probably had both political and financial dimensions. Drusus Libo's entire property was confiscated, leaving his young son nothing to inherit. One year after the affair, when cooler heads prevailed (instigated perhaps by Germanicus' return), it may have been thought decent to ensure that an innocent child of excellent family did not suffer, financially or politically, on account of his father's behaviour.[69] If the reconstruction is correct, it would suggest that Lentulus' aim was particular; establishing a Claudian monopoly of the *cognomen* Drusus was not his intention. Lentulus planned instead to check immediately a destructive ambition perceived within the Scribonii. Once the threat had dissolved the child was allowed to move on, carrying his heritage with him.

Following declarations of *damnatio memoriae* the senate decreed votive offerings to Jupiter, Mars, and Concord, the last of which is

---

[66] Tac. *Ann.* 2.43.   [67] R. Syme (1986), 98.

[68] For the possible connections between Drusus Libo and the Caecilii, see Appendix 2.

[69] Indeed, the adoption may simply have been one of convenience, with little actual involvement in the child's life by Creticus Silanus. It is interesting to note that the child kept a Scribonian *paedagogus* and that the inscription bearing his name was found in the Scribonian *columbarium*. Either way, the government's position *vis-à-vis* the boy may have informed the more generous approach to Cn. Piso's children in AD 20, to whom the senate decreed their father's property, *SCPP* 93–100.

pregnant with the image of a fractured society.[70] Concord had always functioned as discord appeased; perhaps used most famously by L. Opimius after suppressing the Gracchans and later Cicero in the Catilinarian affair. She signalled the end of schism and the restoration of unity. Her presence in the affair of Drusus Libo is therefore suggestive. If Drusus Libo acted alone, then votive offerings to Concord were unnecessary. Indeed, Concord's appearance requires more than a few accomplices; L. Pituanius and P. Marcius would not by themselves merit her attention. Concord expresses instead a more profound suspicion: Drusus Libo shared the hopes of many. We must again return to the contemporary belief that many from the imperial house, equestrians, and senators were helping the pseudo-Agrippa.[71]

That the goddess was not honoured after the Clemens affair is due perhaps only to the absence of a senatorial inquiry, but that does not preclude the possibility of the Clemens affair inspiring her summons *vis-à-vis* Drusus Libo. If Drusus Libo was suspected of attending 'secret meetings in the city' (*clandestini coetus in urbe*), then Concord would have been quite appropriate. Moreover, an explicit statement linking the two items would not have been required. Suspicion could be left to inference. Indeed, I do not propose that Drusus Libo was alleged to have participated in the Clemens affair, but that he was treated as if he had.

As I have so far shown, Drusus Libo was considered dangerous. He was charged with planning sedition under the *lex maiestatis* and treated appropriately. The case against him seemed, on the face of it, weak, but there was none the less strong suspicion, perhaps knowledge even, that he was guilty. The government certainly perceived destructive ambition and, despite Tiberius' show of reticence, desired the defendant's downfall. Indeed, Lentulus' proposal exhibits political realism. The affair cannot be explained as an attempt by *delatores* to bag a 'big fish'. But it is impossible to explain this conclusion if our interpretation is limited to facts about the case; an irony which has

---

[70] Tac. *Ann.* 2.32: *Supplicationum dies Pomponii Flacci sententia constituti, dona Iovi, Marti, Concordiae, utque iduum Septembrium dies, quo se Libo interfecerat, dies festus haberetur, L. P*** et Gallus Asinius et Papius Mutilus et L. Apronius decrevere*, 'Days of public thanks were constituted on the advice of Pomponius Flaccus, offerings were given to Jupiter, Mars, and Concord, and 13 Sept., on which day Libo had committed suicide, was made a public holiday on the motion of L. P[...], Gallus Asinius, Papius Mutilus and L. Apronius.'

[71] Tac. *Ann.* 2.40.

hitherto caused dismissive analyses by most modern scholars. I have so far argued that the Clemens affair provides the solution. Clemens' conspiracy, active in Rome during the affair of Drusus Libo, provides positive explanations: an emergency sitting of the senate; unattained advocacy; praetorians in and round the defendant's house; *damnatio memoriae*; the execution of Drusus Libo's accomplices; Concord's appearance; and the marking of a holiday. There was, of course, no direct evidence linking Drusus Libo with Clemens, but that is no bar. Suspected, or indeed known, collusion would affect senators just as much. Still, a satisfactory theory must cohere with a broader historical model. Does the correlation make historical sense? Does it produce less contradiction or more? These questions cannot be solved by the approach taken so far, but require now an investigation of political activity on a larger scale. We have arrived at the question of connecting Drusus Libo with the supporters of the Pseudo-Agrippa. To answer it, we must consider the history of Agrippa Postumus and his supporters.

3

The Adoption of Agrippa Postumus and the Friends of Gaius Caesar

THE ADOPTION OF AGRIPPA

Marcus Agrippa Postumus was adopted by Augustus on 26 June AD 4. On this same day Augustus adopted Tiberius Claudius Nero as well. A *lex curiata* ratified the arrangements and equipped both with the filiation *Augusti f.* Similarities end here.[1] While Agrippa could yet impress with his new name, Tiberius was also given *tribunicia potestas* for a period of ten years and *imperium* for battle in Germany.[2] Tiberius, moreover, was adopted for the sake of the Republic (*rei publicae causa*). Tiberius was to be Augustus' successor.[3] There were caveats, however. Tiberius was made to adopt Germanicus,[4] who in turn married Augustus' granddaughter Agrippina.[5] The recall of Tiberius' ex-wife and Augustus' daughter from the island of Pandateria may also have been discussed at this time. In his study of Julia, daughter of Augustus, Linderski shows that Suetonius' statement about her recall is ambiguous:

---

[1] Vell. 2.104.1; Suet. *Aug.* 65.
[2] Vell. 2.103; Dio 55.13.1a = Zon. 10.36; Suet. *Tib.* 16.1.
[3] Vell. 2.104.1. R. Seager (1972), 31; J. H. Corbett, 'The Succession Policy of Augustus', *Latomus*, 33 (1974), 87–97, esp. 92 f.; B. Levick (1999), 49 f.; R. A. Bauman (1992), 104 believes that the official rider gave 'the dynastic arrangement a constitutional force that they had not had before'.
[4] Suet. *Tib.* 15.3; Dio 55.13.1a = Zon. 10.36.
[5] Suet. *Aug.* 64.1; R. Syme (1986), 94, n. 6. Following *PIR*² J 221, R. A. Birch, 'The Correspondence of Augustus: Some Notes on Suetonius, Tiberius 21.4–7', *CQ*, 31:.1 (1981), 155–61 and 'The Settlement of 26 June A.D. 4 and its Aftermath', *CQ*, 31:.2 (1981), 443–56, esp. 449, places the marriage of Germanicus and Agrippina in the spring of AD 5, though he argues that the arrangements belong in AD 4. But as R. Syme (1986), 94 n. 6, points out: 'there is no cause for delaying the marriage . . .'.

Post quinquennium demum ex insula in continentem lenioribusque paulo condicionibus transtulit eam.

'It was not until five years later that he moved her from the island to the mainland and treated her with less rigueur.'[6]

Though we can include 2 BC in the *quinquennium*, registering Julia's transfer to AD 3, the Latin also allows us to exclude 2 BC, which would place Julia's transfer to Rhegium in AD 4. The softening of Julia's conditions may well have been part of the negotiations leading up to 26 June.

Dio and Suetonius cite enthusiastic calls for her full restoration by the people in the year of her instalment at Rhegium.[7] Highly placed individuals probably were in support of, or encouraged even, the popular protest. Possibilities include the younger Julia, L. Aemilius Paullus (cos. AD 1), M. Aemilius Lepidus (cos. AD 6), and L. Scribonius Libo (cos. AD 16). Age probably excludes Libo, while Aemilius Lepidus' friendship with Tiberius makes advocacy of Julia unlikely. L. Aemilius Paullus, Lepidus' brother, is our best candidate. That he was chosen to share the consulship with Gaius Caesar evidences the necessary influence. That his wife was Julia's eldest daughter shows he had the motive. The manner of his eventual demise is the best evidence, however: he was condemned for treason.[8] I propose that L. Aemilius Paullus, either at the request of his wife or in collaboration with her, helped to incite a popular demonstration in support of his mother-in-law's full restoration. Dio gives Augustus' reaction: 'fire should sooner mix with water than she should be restored' but then adds 'yet later the people brought such pressure to bear that she was at least brought from the island to the mainland'.[9] If public pressure was maintained it would provide L. Aemilius Paullus with a legitimate opportunity to offer Augustus a suggestion, such as 'perhaps a partial compromise to placate the people while not damaging your position'. It would not be given in private, but in a forum like the *consilium principis* or the family council. As the younger Julia's husband, it would be difficult for him to pretend indifference, but the suggestion would not be enough to concern the princeps. Indeed, Augustus

---

[6] Suet. *Aug.* 65.3, J. Linderski (1988), 181–200; Dio 55.13.1 is similarly vague.
[7] Dio 55.13.1. = Xiph. 103, 19–28; Suet. *Aug.* 65.3.
[8] Suet. *Aug.* 19; *Scholia in Iuvenalem Vetustoria* 6.158.1-2 ed. by P. Wessner (1967).
[9] Suet. *Aug.* 65.3.

would have been well aware of Aemilius Paullus' personal situation. We can also postulate the inspiration behind the popular protest in support of the elder Julia: it was said that Tiberius was to become heir. Scholars have wanted to add another caveat: Agrippa's adoption.[10]

It is clear from the evidence that Tiberius was to succeed Augustus. Agrippa was only 15, Germanicus was 18, and the younger Drusus 17. In contrast, Tiberius was almost 46.[11] It is true that Gaius and Lucius were 14 when marked for succession, but at that time Augustus enjoyed relatively good health, or else the appearance of it. Since then almost a decade had passed and Augustus probably felt that too little time remained for appropriate training.[12] Tiberius had been consul twice and had been invested with *tribunicia potestas* for a period of five years shortly before his withdrawal to Rhodes; he was an experienced general and his mother was the indefatigable Livia. Augustus therefore adopted Tiberius because he was the most likely candidate.[13] Why then did Augustus adopt Agrippa?

Agrippa had not yet received the *toga virilis*.[14] His only superior qualification was genetic: Augustus' blood coursed through his veins.[15] With Gaius and Lucius dead, the younger Julia married to her cousin L. Aemilius Paullus, and Agrippina destined to marry Germanicus, Agrippa appeared to be in limbo. He was not old enough to enter public life, his mother was exiled, and his father was dead. It has therefore been argued that the adoption exhibits Augustus' sentimentality.[16] This may in part be true, but ignores an obvious objection: why did Tiberius not adopt Agrippa instead? It would have

---

[10] B. Levick, 'The Fall of Julia the Younger', *Latomus* (1976), 301–39; R. A. Birch (1981), 446 f.

[11] Tiberius was born 16 Nov. 42 BC; Germanicus was born in 15 BC; Drusus was born in 14 BC, and Agrippa in 12 BC.

[12] One of the reasons Tiberius gave for his desire to quit Rome in 6 BC was the ascendancy of Gaius and Lucius, Suet. *Tib.* 11.5.

[13] Vell. 2.104.1–2.

[14] That occurred in AD 5, Dio 55.24.4.

[15] J. H. Corbett (1974), *passim*, argues that blood connection was not considered better than adoptive relations, cf. Tacitus' reaction to the theory that Augustus had Agrippa put to death, Tac. *Ann.* 1.6: *ceterum in nullius umquam suorum necem duravit, neque mortem nepoti pro securitate privigni inlatam credibile erat.* 'But he never became so callous that he would destroy his own grandchildren, nor is it credible that his grandson died so that his step-son could feel secure.'

[16] A. E. Pappano, 'Agrippa Postumus', *CP*, 36 (1941), 30–45, esp. 32–3.

50   *The Republic in Danger*

provided a clearer picture. Augustus → Tiberius → Germanicus → Drusus → Agrippa: a line of succession ordered by age and experience. Yet Augustus took Agrippa on himself. A clue lies in the descriptions of Agrippa provided by the ancient sources.

It was once fashionable to believe that Agrippa was insane or a dim-witted brute.[17] Such descriptions misinterpret the language. Velleius uses *furor*, and describes him as possessing a deformed or perverse character: *mira pravitate animi atque ingenii in praecipitia*.[18] Dio cites a devotion to servile pursuits (δουλοπρεπής) and a propensity for violent anger (τῇ τε ὀργῇ προπετεῖ ἐχρῆτο), and Tacitus and Suetonius both use the term *ferox*.[19] Contemporaries were said to have described Agrippa as *trux*, while Suetonius echoes Dio's 'servile pursuits' with *ingenium sordidum*.[20] Some scholars perceived in *trux* and *furor* evidence of an unstable mind; Agrippa was subjected to the psychoanalytic approach.[21] But the method was based on a mistaken premiss. Ancient descriptions reveal moral not mental inadequacy: Agrippa was deemed deficient in moral character.[22] Dismissive analyses of Agrippa Postumus based on his mental ability can be, therefore, dismantled on the grounds of methodology alone.[23] Augustus' treatment of the future emperor Claudius during the same period is

---

[17] M.P. Charlesworth, 'Tiberius and the death of Augustus', *AJP*, 44 (1923), 145–57, esp. 149; F. B. Marsh (1931), 40; E. Hohl, 'Primum facinus novi Principatus', *Hermes*, 70 (1935), 350–5. Influenced no doubt by the meteoric rise of psychoanalytic theory at the time; J. Beranger, 'L'Hérédité du Principat note sur la Transmission du pouvoir Impérial aux Deux Premiers Sicles', *REL*, 17 (1939), 117 f = *Principatus* (1972), 137–152; R. Seager (1972), 37.

[18] Vell. 2.112.

[19] Dio 55.32.1–2.; Tac. *Ann*. 1.3; Suet. *Aug*. 65.1–2.

[20] Tac. *Ann*. 1.4; Suet. *Aug*. 65.1–2.

[21] E. Hohl (1935), 350–5.

[22] A. E. Pappano (1941), 37–8, argued that Agrippa was a bitter adolescent, angry at the unfairness of his upbringing. Pappano may be right, but it cannot be inferred from the sources. Any reason offered for his behaviour will be purely speculative. F. Norwood, 'The Riddle of Ovid's Relegatio', *CP*, 58: 3 (1963), 150–63, esp. 162 n. 18, nevertheless agrees with Pappano. R. A. Birch (1981), 443–56, interpreted the language as conveying political not psychological stupidity.

[23] R. Detweiler, 'Historical Perspectives on the Death of Agrippa Postumus', *CJ*, 65 (1970), 289–95, nevertheless refutes the psychoanalytic approach on rational grounds. He points out that Augustus would not have introduced into his dynastic plans anyone with a hint of clinical insanity.

The Adoption of Agrippa Postumus

instructive.[24] Suetonius believed he was in possession of a letter from Augustus to Livia on the subject of Claudius' character. Augustus wrote:

Nam si artius, ut ita dicam, holocleros, quid est quod dubitemus, quin per eosdem articulos et gradus producendus sit, per quos frater eius productus sit? Sin autem ἠλαττῶσθαι *sentimus eum et* βεβλάφθαι καὶ εἰς τὴν τοῦ σώματος καὶ εἰς τὴν τῆς ψυχῆς ἀρτιότητα, *praebenda materia deridendi et illum et nos non est hominibus* τὰ τοιαῦτα σκώπτειν καὶ μυκτηρίζειν εἰωθόσιν.

For if he is, so to say, complete, what reason have we for doubting that he ought to be advanced through the same grades and steps through which his brother [Germanicus] has been advanced. If however we feel that he is inferior and damaged in the fitness of his body and mind, material for making fun of him and us must not be offered to people accustomed to mocking and sneering at such things.[25]

This was written in AD 12, when Claudius was 21.[26] It is significant that Augustus began the letter with 'I have now discussed with Tiberius what we should do about your grandson Claudius . . . we agree that a decision ought to be taken once and for all.'[27] Augustus' position is unambiguous: Claudius would either have a career or he would not. Nothing was left to chance. If it was agreed that Claudius was a problem, he would be hidden from the public's view and treated like a child or invalid. It is therefore unlikely that Agrippa was identified as mentally deranged or defective, but Claudius may yet hold the key:

atque ex contubernio sordidissimorum hominum super veterem segnitiae notam ebrietatis quoque et aleae infamiam subiit, cum interim, quanquam hoc modo agenti, numquam aut officium hominum aut reverentia publice defuit.

And from his intimacy with the most sordid of men he was exposed to the infamy of drunkenness and gambling, in addition to his old characteristic of slowness. Nevertheless in the meantime, despite his conduct, he never lacked either attention from men or respect from the public.[28]

Though Agrippa was only 15, it is not inconceivable that he surrounded himself with, or was surrounded by, unsuitable people. His

---

[24] B. Severy, *Augustus and the Family at the Birth of the Roman Empire* (2003), 196, believes it is a useful comparison, but for Agrippa's *abdicatio*, not his adoption.
[25] Suet. *Claud.* 4.1–2.   [26] Dio 55.27.3.
[27] Suet. *Claud.* 4.1.   [28] Ibid., 5.

'truculence' was that of any teenager involved with the 'wrong' crowd and deemed to be 'uncontrollable'. He was not interested in activities that were associated with intelligence at Rome (oratory, legal studies, philosophy, poetry, and history), nor was he a model of discipline and restraint. *Ferox* implies 'wild' conduct, while *ingenium sordidum* encapsulates drinking, gambling, brawling, and low sports. He was considered idle and unfocused, typified by the story that he 'spent most of his time fishing'.[29] We can, therefore, use the treatment of Claudius to postulate reasons for Agrippa's adoption.

Agrippa was not adopted in order to be put out of the way. Augustus had decided instead that Agrippa was fit to play some part in the settlement.[30] He was unready for public advancement, but he would not be obscure. The political situation probably informed Augustus' decision.[31] Popular sympathy for the elder Julia would affect her only surviving son; Agrippa represented hope to those who had attached themselves, and thus their political future, to Gaius and Lucius.[32] As with their support for the restoration of Julia from exile, people were probably asking 'What about Agrippa?' L. Aemilius Paullus, the younger Julia's husband and Agrippa's brother-in-law, is again important.[33] His involvement in the recall of Julia from Pandateria was suggested above, but his connection to Gaius Caesar, with whom he was allowed to share the consulship, would be a more significant factor in his decision to cultivate a relationship with Agrippa.[34] Gaius died on 24 February AD 4, four months before Agrippa's adoption.[35] It is likely

---

[29] Dio 55.32.1–2.

[30] R. Detweiler (1970), 189, argues that Augustus was desperate to maintain a reserve of successors. But this does not explain why Agrippa was adopted by Augustus and not by Tiberius. It can hardly be maintained that Agrippa was considered superior to Germanicus.

[31] Cf. B. Severy (2003), 190: 'more private concerns may have led [Augustus] to accept paternal responsibility for this apparently unruly young man'.

[32] This is the argument of B. Levick, 'The Fall of Julia the Younger', *Latomus*, 35 (1976), 301–39, though it will become apparent that the present study differs considerably in its interpretation of the politics.

[33] R. A. Birch (1981), seems to argue that L. Aemilius Paullus, upset that he was overlooked in the settlement of 26 June AD 4, set about using Agrippa to drive his own political ambition; B. Levick (1999), 54, treats L. Aemilius Paullus and Agrippa as equals within an anti-Tiberian faction. Both approaches are unlikely—Agrippa was too young.

[34] It is reasonable to assume that Gaius was allowed to choose his colleague, or at best was allowed to offer his preference to Augustus.

[35] *ILS* 140; Dio 55.10.9; Vell. 2.102.3; Suet. *Aug.* 65.1.

that some who had invested heavily in Gaius began to show an interest in Agrippa. He was only a boy, but so was Gaius when designated consul in 6 BC.[36] Agrippa was in fact one year older. Interest in the young Agrippa might therefore have played a part in Augustus' decision to adopt. Free from *patria potestas* and due to wear the *toga virilis*, the prospect of a rich and uninhibited Agrippa entering the Roman political scene *sui iuris* would surely have alarmed Augustus and Tiberius, especially if surrounded by Gaius' old 'mates'. Agrippa's adoption was not forced on Augustus by vociferous supporters, but was an attempt to control a potentially uncomfortable situation.

Here is my proposed scenario: Augustus, Tiberius, and Livia were discussing Tiberius' adoption. Tiberius agreed to adopt his nephew Germanicus; Augustus then turned the discussion to Agrippa's future: 'Agrippa should already have taken the *toga virilis*. His future must be planned now'. Agrippa's behaviour was a concern, as was his choice of friends. They therefore agreed that Agrippa must be adopted before the *toga virilis* was taken. Tiberius would not accept the responsibility; Augustus said that he would adopt Agrippa himself, to keep a close eye on him and act as a personal instructor. Satisfied, Tiberius and Livia agreed. Finally, in order not to confuse the line of succession, and perhaps to explain further the decision to adopt two people at once, it was decided that to Tiberius' adoption would be added the phrase *rei publicae causa*.[37] Interest in Agrippa by Gaius Caesar's old friends made this conversation necessary.

THE WRONG FRIENDS

Most who invested in Gaius did so at the expense of friendship with Tiberius. In AD 1 Gaius, during an eastern tour, was faced with a

---

[36] Dio 55.9.2.
[37] Again a direct comparison can be made with Augustus' treatment of Claudius, Suet. *Claud.* 4: 'While you [Livia] are away, I shall certainly invite young Claudius to dine every day; rather than leave him to the exclusive company of Athenodorus and Sulpicius. If only he would show greater concentration and behave with less capriciousness in his choice of someone to imitate in his movements, deportment and gait.' For the alternative view see R. A. Birch (1981) 446: 'Tiberius . . . might well have preferred nothing at all to be done for Agrippa.'

Parthian coup that affected the political situation in Armenia.[38] Before reaching Syria, he stopped at Samos to meet with Tiberius.[39] Gaius probably asked Tiberius about his experience with Armenian politics, and Tiberius enquired about events in Rome.[40] Velleius writes: *convento prius Ti. Nerone, cui omnem honorem ut superiori habuit* 'he first met with Tiberius Nero, whom he treated with all honour as [his] superior.' Both observed appropriate decorum.[41] Suetonius provides a commentary:

Namque privignum Gaium Orienti praepositum, cum visendi gratia traiecisset Samum, alieniorem sibi sensit ex criminationibus M. Lolli comitis et rectoris eius.

For when he crossed to Samos to visit his stepson Gaius, who was overseer of the East, he found him somewhat estranged through the accusations of Marcus Lollius, a member of Gaius' staff and his instructor.[42]

The meeting ended and Gaius travelled to Syria, where he met with the Parthian king Phrataces on an island in the Euphrates. During the meeting Lollius was somehow undermined. Velleius was a military tribune on Gaius' staff and provides a firsthand account:

Quo tempore M. Lollii, quem veluti moderatorem iuventae filii sui Augustus esse voluerat, perfida et plena subdoli ac versuti animi consilia, per Parthum indicata Caesari, fama vulgavit. Cuius mors intra paucos dies fortuita an voluntaria fuerit ignoro.

It was at this time that there were revealed to Caesar, through the Parthian King, the treacherous designs, revealing a crafty mind given to stratagems, of Marcus Lollius, whom Augustus had wished to be the adviser of his still young son; and rumour spread. Concerning his death, which occurred within a few days, I do not know whether it was accidental or voluntary.[43]

'Caesar' must here refer to Gaius: Phrataces alleged that he had information that Lollius was up to no good. The elder Pliny provides some details:

---

[38] See F.E. Romer, 'Gaius Caesar's Military Diplomacy in the East', *TAPA*, 109 (1979), 199–214.
[39] Suet. *Tib.* 12.2; Vell. 2.101.1.
[40] Tiberius had earlier installed the pro-Roman Tigranes II on the throne, Joseph. *AJ* 15.105; Suet. *Tib.* 9.1; Dio 54.9.5–7, though Vell. 2.94.4 has Artavasdes.
[41] Vell. 2.101.1.
[42] Suet. *Tib.* 12.2.
[43] Vell. 2.102.1. F. E. Romer (1979), 210, n.33, takes the language to mean 'treasonable'. Though a whiff of *maiestas* hovers, it was not necessarily the case.

Hoc fuit quare M. Lollius infamatus regum muneribus in toto oriente interdicta amicitia a C. Caesare Augusti filio venenum biberet, ut neptis eius quadringentiens HS operta spectaretur ad lucernas.

It was for this that M. Lollius, having made himself infamous by taking gifts from kings throughout the orient and having his friendship renounced by Gaius Caesar, son of Augustus, drank poison, that his granddaughter should be shown in the lamplight wearing HS 400,000.[44]

The HS 400,000 was the value of jewels Lollius had received in the east, apparently one of the many payments which caused his disgrace.[45] But why pay Lollius? Presumably certain eastern rulers were hoping to influence his advice to Gaius. If his senior adviser was in the pay of Parthia's opponents, or even those who were nominally 'friends', it would have proved very awkward for Gaius, who was negotiating peace with the Parthian king. Gaius was either ignorant of Lollius' activities or pretended as much. Payments were either way deemed insidious once exposed. Given the nature of the negotiations, however, Phrataces probably used the incident to question the intentions of Rome. Gaius dealt swiftly with his *rector*, placing himself above suspicion while protecting others from contamination. But how was Phrataces informed? Evidence of collusion could have been noticeable, but Gaius' claim to ignorance would have been consequently untenable. It is possible that the information was leaked from within Gaius' entourage. Suetonius cites a revealing incident:

...familiari quondam convivio mentione eius orta exstiterit qui Gaio polliceretur, confestim se, si iuberet, Rhodum navigaturum caputque exsulis sic enim appellabatur—relaturum.

When mention was made of him [Tiberius] at a private dinner party, a man who was there assured Gaius that if he would say the word he would at once sail to Rhodes and bring back the head of 'the exile', as he was commonly called.[46]

Suetonius had information that the episode *was* the catalyst for Tiberius' request to return to Rome, a request supported by Livia. The story probably reached Tiberius through P. Sulpicius Quirinius. In his obituary of Quirinius Tacitus writes:

---

[44] Pliny *NH* 9.118.   [45] Ibid.   [46] Suet. *Tib.* 13.1–2.

...*datusque rector C. Caesari Armeniam obtinenti. Tiberium quoque Rhodi agentem coluerat: quod tunc patefecit in senatu, laudatis in se officiis et incusato M. Lollio, quem auctorem Gaio Caesari pravitatis et discordiarum arguebat.*

He was appointed adviser to Gaius Caesar in Armenia and also actively cultivated Tiberius who was at Rhodes: He [Tiberius] now disclosed all this in the Senate, praising the services of him [Quirinius] to himself while censuring Marcus Lollius, whom he accused of having been the author of Gaius Caesar's wrongdoing and disagreeable behaviour.[47]

Patefacio means that Quirinius' disclosures had been kept secret. Moreover, for *Rhodus* to make sense, the secret correspondence must belong to a period before Tiberius returned to Rome (which he did soon after Lollius died). Indeed, *datusque rector C. Caesari Armeniam obtinenti* does not exclude the possibility that Quirinius was already in the camp when made *rector*.[48] It is, therefore, likely that Quirinius informed Tiberius, through a messenger, about the hostile atmosphere within the camp. Tiberius blamed Lollius for everything. Suetonius continues:

Quo praecipue non iam metu sed discrimine coactus est tam suis quam matris inpensissimis precibus reditum expostulare impetravitque adiutus aliquantum etiam casu. Destinatum Augusto erat, nihil super ea re nisi ex voluntate maioris fili statuere; is forte tunc M. Lollio offensior facilis exorabilisque in vitricum fuit.

This especially brought home to him that his position was not now fearful but dangerous, and so he pleaded for his return with urgent prayers, in which his mother joined, and he obtained it, although partly owing to chance. It had been decided by Augustus that nothing should be determined in this matter that was not agreeable to his elder son; it happened that Gaius was now at odds with M. Lollius and so was open and placable towards his step-father.[49]

When Augustus' letter reached Gaius, Lollius was disgraced but still alive. Since we know that only a few days separated Lollius' disgrace from his death, Augustus' message must have reached Gaius immediately after Phrataces' allegations. Quirinius thus informed Tiberius

---

[47] Tac. *Ann.* 3.48.
[48] He had previously been governor of Galatia, during which time he had won the *insignia* of a triumph, Tac. *Ann.* 3.48. He was, therefore, the type of person Augustus would have wanted to accompany Gaius in the east.
[49] Suet. *Tib.* 13.2.

about the threat some months before Gaius and Phrataces met.[50] If Quirinius and Tiberius continued to correspond secretly in the intervening period, then we may have found our whistle-blower. Quirinius was evidently adept at concealing his correspondence, and must certainly have opposed Lollius (if only in secret). Moreover, the only known beneficiaries of Phrataces' revelations were Tiberius and Quirinius himself.[51] Quirinius' knowledge of Augustus' reply is irrelevant (though he may well have known about a response), for the benefits of destroying Lollius were self-evident.

It has been argued that the disgrace of Lollius and the rise of Quirinius signal the ascendancy of Tiberius, but that is too much.[52] Quirinius was probably the most experienced individual left, and since his correspondence with Tiberius was kept secret until after his death, the alliance went unnoticed. The nature of Tiberius' recall shows, moreover, that Gaius' unease with him persisted, despite the setting aside of animosity:

Permittente ergo Gaio revocatus est verum sub condicione ne quam partem curamve rei p. attingeret.

Therefore with Gaius' permission he was recalled, but on the condition that he take no part in public life or hold any responsibility.[53]

The combination of *pars* with *cura* seems redundant. But Suetonius had access to the imperial correspondence, and we know that letters between Augustus and Gaius survived to the time of Aulus Gellius.[54] We may instead have the exact phrase used by Gaius. Gaius was not being redundant, he was eliminating loopholes. Exclusion from every

---

[50] It would have taken a few days, perhaps almost a week for Quirinius' message to reach Tiberius. Tiberius' message would then have to travel over 1,400 km to Rome. Augustus' message would then travel well over 2,000 km to Gaius on the Euphrates. These represent the shortest distances between the points. The real distances travelled would have been much greater.

[51] Quirinius was made Gaius' *rector*, Tac. *Ann.* 3.48.

[52] D. C. A. Shotter, 'Cn. Cornelius Cinna Magnus and the adoption of Tiberius', *Latomus*, 33 (1974), 306–13, esp. 309 f.

[53] Suet. *Tib.* 13.2, also relevant is 15.1: *Romam reversus deducto in Forum filio Druso statim e Carinis ac Pompeiana domo Esquilias in hortos Maecenatianos transmigravit totumque se ad quietem contulit, privata modo officia obiens ac publicorum munerum expers.* 'On his return to Rome, after introducing his son to public life, he moved at once from the Carinae and the house of the Pompeys to the gardens of Maecenas on the Esquiline, where he led a very retired life, merely attending to his personal affairs and exercising no public functions.'

[54] Gell. 15.7.3.

'part' of public life and every 'responsibility' means attendance in the senate and all public positions, including those that did not require senatorial insignia. Obscurity in Rome rather than in Rhodes was alone conceded. This is not evidence of Tiberius' ascendancy. It is evidence of Gaius' clemency and power. It is also evidence that Gaius' clemency had limits: he was still suspicious (and perhaps fearful even) of Tiberius, along with other members of his entourage. Quirinius' promotion did not bring full cordiality between Gaius and Tiberius.

Suetonius believed that within Gaius' entourage Tiberius was referred to only as the *exul*. Such opinions must be widely held in order to be both institutionalized and publicly known. Revelations about the depth of hostility within his own circle forced Gaius to show clemency; the potential insinuation that he, like members of his staff, wanted Tiberius dead needed to be promptly dismissed. But deep-set feelings are put aside; they do not vanish. Having arrived in Rome with Gaius' corpse, Gaius' *paedagogus* and some *ministri* were executed:

Paedagogum ministrosque C. fili, per occasionem valitudinis mortisque eius superbe avareque in provincia grassatos, oneratis gravi pondere cervicibus praecipitavit in flumen.

He [Augustus] ordered that the *paedagogus* and aides of his son Gaius, since they had taken advantage of their master's illness and death to commit acts of arrogance and greed in his province, be thrown into the river with heavy weights about their necks.[55]

The reason for execution is suspect. Gaius died in the coastal city of Limyra while returning to Italy with his entourage; they probably cheated some local merchants. Velleius provides a more plausible explanation. It was believed that a wound suffered in battle severely affected Gaius' physical and mental abilities:

Nec defuit conversatio hominum vitia eius adsentatione alentium (etenim semper magnae fortunae comes adest adulatio), per quae eo ductus erat ut in ultimo ac remotissimo terrarum orbis angulo consenescere quam Romam regredi mallet.

Nor was there lacking the companionship of persons who encouraged his defects by flattery (for flattery always goes hand in hand with high position)

---

[55] Suet. *Aug.* 67.2.

as a result of which he wished to live in life long retirement in a remote and distant corner of the world rather than return to Rome.[56]

The 'remote and distant corner of the world' was apparently Syria.[57] The exact location is not known, but Antioch, one of the great cities of the Mediterranean world and the seat of provincial government, is the obvious choice.[58] It would not have escaped Gaius' notice that his father was highly thought of in the area, 'Agrippa' being one of the most common Italian names in Syria.[59] Evidently the government held Gaius' entourage responsible for his psychological condition, alleging that Gaius was led astray. This can also be inferred from the identity of Syria's next *legatus Augusti pro praetore* following Gaius' death: P. Sulpicius Quirinius.[60] Having dismantled Gaius' entourage in AD 4, Augustus and Tiberius probably sought to dampen any lingering influence the group held in the east by introducing one of Tiberius' most loyal supporters.[61] The execution of Gaius' *paedagogus* and aides thus signalled a new political order. The sudden ascendancy of Tiberius, for so long an object of ridicule and derision for the newly established smart-set, must have seemed to wipe away the very foundations of an aspiring political order. Young men on the up, confident that the future was theirs, were of a sudden left uncertain and feeling vulnerable. Many hitherto influential men in Rome would no doubt sympathize with king Archelaus of Cappadocia's experience:

Rex Archelaus quinquagesimum annum Cappadocia potiebatur, invisus Tiberio quod eum Rhodi agentem nullo officio coluisset. Nec id Archelaus per superbiam omiserat, sed ab intimis Augusti monitus, quia florente Gaio Caesare missoque ad res Orientis intuta Tiberii amicitia credebatur.

---

[56] Vell. 2.102.3; also Dio 55.10a.8.
[57] Dio 55.10a. 8.
[58] Jos. *AJ* 17.132; *CAH* 10^2 712 f.
[59] Jos. *AJ* 16.25 on Agrippa doing 'good works' in the east, and his general popularity; *CAH* 10^2 725.
[60] Jos. *AJ* 17.355; On the post, see Dio 53.13.5; A. H. J. Greenidge (1911), 434 f; J. W. Rich (1990), 144 f.
[61] The group had fostered anti-Tiberian feeling in the various cities in which they stayed. Suetonius (*Tib.* 13.1) tells us that during his Rhodian exile the people of Nemausus in southern France 'threw down his statues and busts.' Gaius' enmity may plausibly have enjoyed international recognition, though, as an Augustan veteran colony, Nemausus had some strong eastern connections (its coinage features the crocodile). Gaius, moreover, was a patron of the town: *CIL* XII 3155.

For fifty years King Archelaus had been in possession of Cappadocia; to Tiberius a hated man, because while he was at Rhodes Archelaus showed him none of the respect he deserved. The neglect was due not to arrogance, but to advice from the intimates of Augustus; for, as Gaius Caesar was then flourishing and had been sent to settle affairs in the East, the friendship of Tiberius was believed to be unsafe.[62]

When, in AD 4, Gaius' disenfranchised friends transferred their interest to the young but soon-to-be-of-age Agrippa, Augustus probably decided that an adoption was necessary. It is, therefore, significant that on receiving the *toga virilis* in AD 5, Agrippa 'obtained none of the same privileges as his brothers' and a year later suffered *abdicatio* and was sent to the town of Surrentum.

[62] Tac. *Ann.* 2.42.

4

Growing Pains

AGRIPPA AND THE *TOGA VIRILIS*

Scholars vest Dio's remark concerning Agrippa's lack of 'privileges' with importance:

κἂν τῷ αὐτῷ ἔτει τούτῳ ὅ τε Ἀγρίππας ἐς ἐφήβους, μηδενὸς τῶν αὐτῶν τοῖς ἀδελφοῖς τυχών, ἐσεγράφη·

In this very same year Agrippa was enrolled among the youths of military age but obtained none of the same things as his brothers.[1]

Dio's own treatment of the enrolment of Gaius and Lucius is lost. Our knowledge comes instead from his epitomator Zonaras:

Τῷ δ' ἐφεξῆς ἔτει δωδέκατον ὑπατεύων ὁ Αὔγουστος εἰς τοὺς ἐφήβους τὸν Γάϊον ἔταξε καὶ ἐς τὸ βουλευτήριον ἅμα εἰσήγαγε καὶ πρόκριτον ἀπέφηνε τῆς νεότητος ἴλαρχόν τε φυλῆς γενέσθαι ἐπέτρεψε... Καὶ μετ' ἐνιαυτὸν καὶ ὁ Λούκιος τὰς τιμὰς ὅσαι τῷ Γαΐῳ τῷ ἀδελφῷ αὐτοῦ ἐδέδοντο ἔλαβεν.

In the following year, while consul for the twelfth time, Augustus enrolled Gaius among the youths of military age, and at the same time introduced him to the senate, declared him First of the Youth, and allowed him to be cavalry-commander of a division... And after a year Lucius too received the honours which had been given to his brother Gaius."[2]

If Zonaras has followed Dio correctly, then these are the 'things' implied in Dio's treatment of Agrippa. Dio understood that Agrippa was not presented to the senate, declared First of the Youth (*Princeps*

---

[1] Dio 55.22.4.
[2] Dio 55.9.9–10 = Zon. 10.35. Also *Res Gestae* 14.1: 'The senate decreed that from the day in which they were led into the forum they should be included in public meetings.'

Iuventutis), or made the commander of a cavalry division (*sevir turmae*) upon receiving the toga of manhood (*toga virilis*).[3] We can add also privileges gained by Gaius the year before his taking the *toga virilis*:

καὶ μετὰ τοῦθ᾽ ἱερωσύνην μέν τινα αὐτῷ καὶ τὴν ἐς τὸ συνέδριον συμφοίτησιν τό τε συνθεᾶσθαι καὶ τὸ συνεστιᾶσθαι τῇ βουλῇ ἔδωκε·

And after that Augustus granted to Gaius a priesthood and attendance at senate meetings and the right to sit with the senators at shows and banquets.[4]

The comparing of Agrippa with his brothers is not necessarily Dio's own construction.[5] Agrippa's supporters would have 'wondered aloud' at the difference. They had marked him as an investment for the future and the lack of paraphernalia was a concern. This should be credited to the ascendancy of Tiberius.

In 6 BC Tiberius left Rome and retired to Rhodes. The move has been variously interpreted, both in antiquity and today, but a general theory has emerged which credits his decision to the political force of Gaius and Lucius Caesar. The linking of Tiberius' retirement with the popularity of Gaius and Lucius was conceived in antiquity.[6] But the interpretation is new: Tiberius retired because he opposed the decision to designate Gaius consul at age 14.[7] Dio implies that Gaius was elected by the *comitia centuriata* against the wishes of Augustus:

---

[3] For *Sevir Turmae*, see S. Demougin, *L'ordre équestre sous les Julio-Claudiens* (1988), 217–43.

[4] Dio 55.9.4. P. M. Swan (2004), 84, n. 79, makes an interesting point: 'Why do Dio and Augustus highlight Gaius' privilege of attending the senate when, according to Suetonius, Augustus: "permitted the children of senators, immediately they donned the *toga virilis*, to wear the broad stripe [on their tunics] and attend the senate" (*Aug.* 38.2)'. Swan suggests that Gaius may have been able to speak to a known formula: 'senators or those with the right to express their opinion in the senate', cited in the Cyrene Edict (V. Ehrenberg, and A. H. M. Jones (1955), 139 f.) If Swan is right, then Gaius was allowed to express political opinions at a very young age. It was probably the case, however, that Gaius was allowed to express an opinion because he was consul designate from 6 BC to 1 BC.

[5] Cf. J.W. Rich (1990), 227, with a general comment about his treatment of 6 BC: 'Dio's interpretation is unconvincing and may be partly his own construction'.

[6] Dio 55.9.5–8; Suet. *Tib.* 10.1–11.1, 5; Tac. *Ann.* 1.53.1, 6.51; Vell. 2.99.1–2.

[7] The general argument of B. Levick, 'Tiberius' retirement to Rhodes in 6 B.C.', *Latomus*, 31 (1972), 779–813; cf. F. B. Marsh (1931), 37f. and R. Seager (1972, rev. 2005), 23–9, who suggest that Tiberius simply determined that he had been superseded.

τά τε γὰρ ἄλλα καὶ ὕπατον τὸν Γάιον μηδὲ ἐς ἐφήβους πω τελοῦντα προεχειρίσαντο. ἠγανάκτησε, καὶ προσεπηύξατο μηδεμίαν τοιαύτην καιρῶν ἀνάγκην ὁποία ποτὲ αὐτὸν κατέλαβε γενέσθαι, ὥστε τινὰ νεώτερον εἰκοσιετοῦς ὑπατεῦσαι. ἐπειδή τε καὶ ὣς ἐνέκειντό οἱ, τότε ἔφη χρῆναί τινα τὴν ἀρχὴν ταύτην λαμβάνειν, ὅταν μήτε τι αὐτὸς ἁμαρτάνειν καὶ ταῖς τοῦ δήμου σπουδαῖς ἀνθίστασθαι δύνηται.

Among other things they [the people] elected Gaius consul while he had not yet even reached military age. He [Augustus] was irritated and prayed that no such necessity of circumstances should take place, as had once happened to himself, that someone younger than 20 should become consul. When the people continued to press him he said that a man should assume that office when he was capable of not making any mistake himself and resisting the impulses of the people.[8]

Tacitus writes:

necdum posita puerili praetexta principes iuventutis appellari, destinari consules specie recusantis flagrantissime cupiverat.

And though they [Gaius and Lucius] had not yet laid aside the *praetexta* of boyhood, he eagerly wished, though with the appearance of declining, that they be named *principes iuventutis* and be destined for consulships.[9]

Tacitus' analysis is unlikely.[10] The election of Gaius was not in Augustus' interest; it made ridiculous the proposition that the *res publica* was anything but a monarchy.[11] Furthermore, had Augustus really wanted a designated consulship for his son, he would surely have chosen the elections of 5 BC, when Gaius took the *toga virilis*.[12] It should also be noted that Augustus took Tiberius' decision to retire poorly. If Tacitus' interpretation is sound, Augustus would more likely have said 'good riddance!'[13] Instead, Augustus was probably annoyed with Tiberius for leaving him alone with Gaius and the

---

[8] Dio 55.9.2.
[9] Tac. *Ann.* 1.3.2.
[10] Cf. R. Syme (1939), 417, though Syme seems to take a different position in (1986) 83 f.
[11] R. Syme (1939), 417; R. Seager (1972), 29 f.
[12] Cf. J. W. Rich (1990), 227, who sees Dio being fooled; P. M. Swan (2004), 84, follows Dio's interpretation, at the expense of Tacitus.
[13] Tiberius received *tribunicia potestas* for five years at this time, Dio 55.9.4 f. Zonaras understood Dio to mean that Augustus hoped that it would 'bring Gaius and Lucius to their senses'. It seems to me more plausible that Augustus wished to make it obvious that he hoped Tiberius would succeed him.

young 'radicals'.[14] We can use Dio, Tacitus, and the *Res Gestae* to postulate Augustus' response to the people:

> I thank you for the support you have shown my house, but according to the custom of our ancestors such acts are only required when the Republic is in peril. I ask instead that my son be allowed to mature, and that he take the consulship in five years time.[15]

Augustus made the best of a bad situation. He was obviously not comfortable with a 14-year-old consul, but felt unable to defeat completely a popular movement in full swing. Tiberius retired in protest.[16] Gaius either interpreted Tiberius' position as a personal attack or his supporters offered him the interpretation: 'Tiberius is jealous and wants to destroy your career before it can begin'. Such suggestions can have devastating effects on a 14-year-old (especially if Tiberius was already an estranged step-father). The interpretation was perhaps in part correct. Gaius' designation threatened to cut short Tiberius' own special position, though Tiberius no doubt claimed to be simply unimpressed by the designation of a boy.[17] In AD 20 Tiberius presented his adoptive grandson, Nero, to the senate:

> *Neronem e liberis Germanici iam ingressum iuventam commendavit patribus, utque munere capessendi vigintiviratus solveretur et quinquennio maturius quam per leges quaesturam peteret, non sine inrisu audientium postulavit. Praetendebat sibi atque fratri decreta eadem petente Augusto.*

> He [Tiberius] commended Nero, the son of Germanicus who was now entering manhood, to the senate, and asked, not without laughter from the audience, that he be freed from having to take an office of the vigintivirate and that he be allowed to seek the quaestorship five years earlier than the law

---

[14] Cf. R. Seager (1972), 29 f., who argues that Augustus intended for Gaius to supersede Tiberius, thus making him superfluous. Seager maintains that Tiberius' proposed mission to Armenia was a convenience: 'with the princes' guardian thus kept occupied, the coast would be clear for the grooming of Gaius and Lucius'.

[15] RG 14; J. W. Rich (1990), 227, suggests that the people did not propose that Gaius be made consul at 14, but understood instead that an interim period would be required. This is possible, but perhaps diminishes too much the atmosphere which must have lingered over the *comitia* by insisting on a level of reason that may not have been present.

[16] Vell. 2.99.2 f.; Dio 55.9.5; B. Levick, (1999), 38 ff.; R. Syme, (1939), 47 f. and (1986), 83 f.

[17] He offered other reasons as well, such as tiredness and a wish to dedicate his remaining time to studies, Dio 55.9.6 f.; Vell. 2.99.2.

Growing Pains 65

allowed. His justification was that Augustus had requested the same decree for himself and his brother.[18]

Why did senators laugh? The process was not itself funny. Augustus' nephew Marcellus, Tiberius, his brother Drusus, Gaius, Lucius, Tiberius' nephew Germanicus, and his son Drusus had all received the dispensation.[19] It was a request the audience should have expected. Senators were instead amused by the irony of the situation; they were laughing at Tiberius, possible only if Tiberius was acting contrary to a previously held position. It is suggested here that the previously held position was opposition to accelerated public careers. But we must be careful to differentiate the treatment of Marcellus, Gaius, and Lucius from the treatment of Tiberius, the elder Drusus, Germanicus, and the younger Drusus. This is apparent by examining the age at which they reached certain positions.

	Quaestor	Ornamenta Praetoria	Consul
Marcellus		18	23*
Tiberius	18	23	28
Drusus I	20	23	29
Gaius			20
Lucius			20*
Germanicus	21	23	26
Drusus II	23	24	27

* Not taken

Augustus reformed the *cursus* so that the quaestorship could be reached at 25, the praetorship at 30, and the consulship at 33.[20] Twenty-six to 29 are relatively young ages for the consulship, but they are significantly older than 20–23. A *lex Plaetoria* and a subsequent praetorian edict had been devised, much earlier, to protect those under 25 who were *sui iuris* from their own economic ignorance by providing for restitution when the terms of a financial agreement were evidently misunderstood. On reaching 25 the law held that

---

[18] Tac. *Ann.* 3.29.
[19] Marcellus = Dio 53.28.3–4; Tiberius = Dio 53.28.3–4, Tac. *Ann.* 3.29; the elder Drusus = Dio 54.10.4, Tac. *Ann.* 3.29; Gaius and Lucius = Dio 55.9.2, 10, *RG.* 14; Germanicus = Suet. *Gaius* 1.1; the younger Drusus is a slightly different proposition. He did not take the quaestorship until he was 23 (Dio 56.25.4), but nevertheless took the consulship at 28 (Dio 56.28.1).
[20] Dio 52.20.1 f.; in actuality the ages were probably much older on average.

young men were responsible either way.[21] Thus, for Augustus, a man could be trusted with the people's finances when he could be trusted with his own. The designation of Marcellus, Gaius, and Lucius before even the age of 20 was therefore an outrageous innovation both politically and sociologically, whereas the designation of Tiberius, the elder Drusus, Germanicus, and the younger Drusus, though still exceptional, were nevertheless radically different propositions. I propose that Tiberius was satisfied with the standard used to accelerate his own career and the careers of his brother Drusus, Germanicus, and the younger Drusus, but not that of Gaius and Lucius. Tacitus highlights the boys' immaturity when designated:

Nam genitos Agrippa Gaium ac Lucium in familiam Caesarum induxerat, necdum posita puerili praetexta principes iuventutis appelari, destinari consules specie recusantis flagrantissime cupiverat.

For he had brought the children of Agrippa, Gaius and Lucius, into the house of the Caesars; and though they had not yet laid aside the *praetexta* of boyhood, he eagerly wished, though with the appearance of declining, that they be named *principes iuventutis* and be destined for consulships.[22]

Tacitus' language is pregnant with cynicism and irony. He confirms their immaturity by reference to a childlike image: *puerili praetexta*. More striking than: 'they were not yet men'. The style is Tacitus' own, but probably reflects the amused disbelief of a conservative commentator uncomfortable with the election of a 14-year-old. The designation of a boy was, after all, evidence that people did not take the business of government seriously, for voters could not have believed that Gaius would add value to debate in the senate. Indeed, it undermined the very concept of senatorial authority. Either way, Tiberius was among those startled by the development. But in 6 BC most failed to recognize the nuance of Tiberius' position: opposition to Gaius' accelerated career was interpreted as opposition to all accelerated careers. Evidently the subsequent careers of Germanicus and the younger Drusus did not dispel public opinion (even though Tiberius, as their father, must have acquiesced). When the time came to present Nero to the senate, Tiberius was forced, for the first time, formally to

---

[21] W. W. Buckland, *Textbook of Roman Law*, 3rd edn., ed. by P. Stein (1963), 169–73; J. Crook, *Law and Life of Rome* (1967), 116–18. The *lex Plaetoria* was passed sometime in the late third or early second century BC.
[22] Tac. *Ann.* 1.3.2; also Dio 55.9.2.

request a practice he was thought to have opposed—it was laughable. But the mockers were wrong, and Tiberius no doubt stood before them with a clear conscience.

Agrippa had grown up with his brothers in the limelight. Their election to the consulship and their entrance to manhood would have been discussed often. He may have remembered both episodes and probably anticipated similar treatment. The ascendancy of Tiberius meant that Agrippa would be left wanting and no doubt frustrated. Agrippa would probably have taken the quaestorship five years in advance of the legal age had he not suffered *abdicatio*, while the style in which he took the *toga virilis* is evidence only that the title *Princeps Iuventutis* and premature designations to the consulship were no longer considered appropriate (indeed, had they been appropriate, Germanicus and Drusus might also have expected them).[23] Agrippa, like Germanicus and the younger Drusus, was subject to a new political order that took the business of governing more seriously. He was not named *Princeps Iuventutis*; he was not made the commander of a horse division; he was not allowed to speak at senate meetings; and, as far as we know, he was not a *pontifex*. Analysing from effects to causes, Agrippa may have discovered discrimination. A consideration of his subjection to *abdicatio* the very next year suggests that he was probably right.

ABDICATIO AND AGRIPPA

The elder Pliny and Suetonius both mention *abdicatio* in relation to Agrippa Postumus. Pliny wrote:

---

[23] A. Degrassi, *Inscr. Ital.* (1931), 14.1, 183 quotes a fragment from the *Fasti Ostiensis*: *Agrippa Caesar*... Numerous attempts to provide a solution exist. None is convincing. Degrassi inserted *abdicatus est*..., a solution championed by B. Levick, 'Abdication and Agrippa Postumus', *Historia*, 21 (1972), 674–97, esp. 694, and (1999) 57. In the former Levick wrote: 'but there are difficulties. The least is that the Ostians after the event are speaking of Agrippa Caesar.' Having identified the problem, Levick provides no plausible explanation, but simply moves on. Others infer a local magistracy: L. Vidman, *Fasti Ostienses,* 2nd edn. (1982); R. Syme (1986), 113, n. 57. It may simply represent recognition of his birthday (though a priesthood cannot be ruled out).

68   *The Republic in Danger*

In divo quoque Augusto, quem universa mortalitas in hac censura nuncupet, si diligenter aestimentur cuncta, magna sortis humanae reperiantur volumina ... abdicatio Postumi Agrippae post adoptionem, desiderium post relegationem.

Also in the case of the divine Augustus, whom the whole of mankind enrols in the list of happy men, if all the facts could be carefully weighed, great revolutions of man's lot could be discovered ... making Agrippa Postumus an *abdicatus* after he had been adopted, and the yearning for him after his relegation.[24]

Suetonius wrote:

Tertium nepotem Agrippam simulque privignum Tiberium adoptavit in foro lege curiata; ex quibus Agrippam brevi ob ingenium sordidum ac ferox abdicavit seposuitque Surrentum.

He adopted in the forum via a *lex curiata* his third grandson Agrippa at the same time as his step-son Tiberius; after a brief period he made Agrippa an *abdicatus* because of his raw and wild nature, and he secluded him at Surrentum.[25]

Suetonius took his source/s to mean that *abdicatio* occurred first, followed by the transfer of Agrippa from Rome to Surrentum. He continues:

Agrippam nihilo tractabiliorem, immo in dies amentiorem, in insulam transportavit saepsitque insuper custodia militum.

As Agrippa did not become more manageable, but rather each day became more insane, he transported him to an island and, moreover, surrounded him with a military guard.[26]

Transporto corresponds with Pliny's *relegatio*, the nature of which will be considered later. The sequence is nevertheless *abdicatio* then *sepono* and finally *relegatio/transporto*: Agrippa suffered *abdicatio* and was then sent away/packed off to Surrentum, afterwhich he was relegated to an island.[27] Dio, though failing to mention Surrentum, provides a similar picture:

[24] *NH* 7.147–50.
[25] Suet. *Aug.* 65.1.
[26] Suet. *Aug.* 65.4.
[27] S. Jameson, 'Augustus and Agrippa Postumus', *Historia*, 24 (1975), 287–314, esp. 292, takes Pliny's *pudenda Agrippae ablegatio* in the same passage to refer also to Agrippa Postumus. But Pliny refers not to Agrippa Postumus but his father M. Vipsanius Agrippa. In 23 BC Vipsanius Agrippa was sent to Syria in the wake of

... αὐτῷ τε τῷ Αὐγούστῳ πολλάκις ὑπὲρ τῶν πατρῴων ἐπεκάλει. καὶ οὐ γὰρ ἐσωφρονίζετο, ἀπεκηρύχθη, καὶ ἥ τε οὐσία αὐτοῦ τῷ στρατιωτικῷ ταμιείῳ ἐδόθη, καὶ αὐτὸς ἐς Πλανασίαν τὴν πρὸς Κύρνῳ νῆσον ἐνεβλήθη.

... and he often accused Augustus himself regarding his inheritance, and since he was not of moderate mind he was made an *abdicatus* and his property was handed over to the military treasury, and he was himself exiled to Planasia, an island near Corsica."[28]

The nature of *abdicatio* is disputed. Though a legal force is implied, its sole appearance in the juristic literature is for the purpose of denying it such a quality:

Abdicatio quae Graeco more ad alienandos liberos usurpabatur et apokeryxis dicebatur Romanis legibus non comprobatur.

Abdicatio, which was used in Greek custom to alienate children and was called *apokeryxis*, is not approved by Roman law.[29]

Abdicatio was an alien concept which Roman lawyers rejected. It is therefore curious that Agrippa's exposure to *abdicatio* seems to have had legal consequences.[30] The solution to this paradox requires an examination of the term's perceived effects.

Some scholars propose that *abdicatio* was connected to *emancipatio*, in that it provided the same effect: the abdicated son ceased to live under the *potestas* of his father.[31] On that reading, Augustus saw fit to remove Agrippa from the line of succession and relinquish his

---

rumour that he and Augustus' nephew Marcellus had had a falling out, Dio 53.32.1. Suetonius (*Aug.* 66.3 and *Tib.* 10.1) writes, however, that Agrippa left of his own accord. Velleius 2.93.2 uses elements from both stories. Velleius writes that Augustus provided Agrippa with a special commission in the East to cover the fact that Agrippa had decided to leave Rome on account of his poor relationship with Marcellus. There is some dispute as to the accuracy of these reports, see R. Syme (1939), 342 f.; R. Seager (1972), 20 f.; J. W. Rich (1990), 167 f.

[28] Dio 55.32.2. Cary's Loeb translation uses 'not of sound mind' and is followed by P. M. Swan (2004), 209. But Dio refers not to insanity but to moderation and temperance.

[29] *Cod. Iust.* 8.46.6.

[30] Some dismiss *abdicatio* as purely fictional, so W. W. Buckland (1963), 132 n. 6, and R. Düll 'Iudicium domesticum, Abdicatio, und Apokeryxis', *ZSS*, 63 (1943), 75, n. 3. They may be right, but Augustus evidently used it with real effects. The case of Agrippa Postumus must, therefore, be considered separately.

[31] H. Volkmann, *Zur Rechtsprechung im Principat des Augustus* (1935), 109–10; A. Momigliano, 'Review of The Cambridge Ancient History Vol. X. The Augustan Empire 44 B.C.–A.D. 70', *JRS*, 34 (1944), 113; J. A. Crook, 'Oktavian und das Testament Cäsars by Walter Schmitthenner', *CR*, 4.2 (1954), 152–4; B. Levick, (1972), *passim*. For

potestas over him, making him *sui iuris*. This implies that whatever Agrippa had done, Augustus was satisfied that Agrippa could be controlled without *patria potestas*. It is therefore necessary to determine whether *abdicatio* was a technical term, which carried within it the idea of *emancipatio*.

For a term to have a technical meaning, its usage must be consistently applicable within given parameters; temporal variations in meaning make parameters important. It is fortunate that the term *abdicatio* is most prolific in a writer who lived during the Augustan period: the elder Seneca. Only a few samples are required:

Si quis me audit adoptari, iam putat abdicatum ... Laudat me pater, cum abdicet, laudo ego patrem, cum abdicer; haec una inter nos disputatio est: iste me dignum putat beato patre, ego me meo.

Those who hear I am to be adopted regard me as having already been 'abdicated'... My father praises me while 'abdicating' me, I praise my father while being 'abdicated'. This alone is in dispute between us: he believes that I deserve a wealthy father, I believe I deserve my own".[32]

Abdicatio here prepares the son for adoption, which will, in turn, dissolve *patria potestas*.[33] The son's emotional response is the key. If the son was *sui iuris*, he could not have been *forced* into an undesirable adoption? Evidently the son was not *sui iuris*. Seneca later writes

Quos abdicatione non potuit terrere, putat se castigaturum adoptione. Non ille tuum filium concupiscit: suos corrigit. Cum illos correctos putaverit, me satis minatum abdicabit.

Those whom he could not scare with 'abdication', he believes he can punish by adoption. But he does not covet your son: he wants to fix his own. When he believes they have been reformed, he will 'abdicate' me, the threat of me having been sufficient.[34]

---

the opposite view, see esp. M. Wurm, *Apokeryxis, Abdicatio und Exheredatio* (1972), esp. 22–64.

[32] Sen. *Cont.* 2.1.9.

[33] Furthermore, Seneca has produced a situation in which *abdicatio* is not punishment for a recalcitrant son but is, in fact, a reward. This would have seemed an extreme case. The clear majority of our examples depict *abdicatio* as a form of punishment, Sen. *Cont.* 2.1.15: *Quare abdicas? Numquid dies noctesque inpendo turpibus conviviis? Plurimum vivo in lupanari? Si nescis quae crimina obiciantur, ab amico disce*, 'Why do you abdicate me? Do I spend night and day at foul dinner parties? Do I spend most of my life in brothels? If you do not know the charges that are usually made, learn from your friend.'

[34] Sen. *Cont.* 2.1.28.

Growing Pains

In this *controversia*, a father adopts a man in order to punish his own sons, who are *abdicati*. *Abdicatio* is utilized as a short-term solution to behavioural problems, initiated and later to be revoked by the father. The sons are still subject to the power of their father; *abdicatio* has not made them *sui iuris*. Importantly the legal status of an *abdicatus* was a topic of dispute among rhetoricians. Seneca cites a question popular in declamatory schools:

an abdicatus non desinat filius esse; an is desinat qui non tantum abdicatus sed etiam ab alio adoptatus est?

Does an *abdicatus* cease to be a son? Does he cease [to be a son] who is not only an *abdicatus* but is even adopted by another.[35]

Seneca does not offer his opinion, nor are we offered the general view. The question is instead left hanging, with no clear answer in sight. If *abdicatio* were a form of *emancipatio* clarity should have prevailed. Indeed, the question would have been superfluous. The above examples make it difficult to maintain that where *abdicatio* is mentioned the results of *emancipatio* are meant. Quintilian provides evidence that *abdicatio* affected inheritance:

Quibus similia etiam in vera rerum quaestione tractantur. Nam quae in scholis abdicatorum, haec in foro exheredatorum a parentibus et bona apud centumviros repetentium ratio est.

Similar methods are also used with questions that occur in real life. For the question of *abdicatio*, which occurs in the schools, is related to those who are disinherited by their parents in the forum and those who reclaim their property in the centumviral court.[36]

And

Heredi scripto opponitur lex: 'abdicatus ne quid de bonis patris capiat.'

The heir by testament is opposed by the law: "an *abdicatus* shall not receive his father's property".[37]

---

[35] Ibid., 1.1.13. Adoption evidently inspired much philosophical discussion. Though adoption dissolved agnatic status, we know that an adopted man could not marry his former sister: legal constructs did not replace certain 'natural' laws even for the Romans.

[36] Quint. 7.4.11.

[37] Quint. 3.6.98, also 96: *Abdicatus ne quid de bonis patris capiat*, 'An *abdicatus* cannot take possession of his father's estate.'

Nam quae in scholis abdicatorum does not help with regard to Agrippa Postumus, but it nevertheless confirms that, in the early Principate, *abdicatio* was a fictional device. If, however, this fictional device provides specific results, it is, probably, that a son was treated *as* an *exheredatus*. This theory alone explains how an *abdicatus* was adopted against his will: he was still subject to *patria potestas*. Three aspects of Agrippa's situation are now evident: when Dio writes that Agrippa's 'property was given to the treasury', he means that Agrippa was disinherited; *sepono* evidences the maintenance of *patria potestas*; and Agrippa was punished.[38] Before considering the ramifications of this analysis, the details of his disinheritance deserve further comment.

It is likely that on 26 June AD 4 Augustus ceased to administer Agrippa's property as *tutor*, becoming instead its owner. Augustus' tutorship is likely but not definitely known. He was already the adoptive father of Gaius and Lucius when Agrippa was born, and M. Vipsanius Agrippa would surely have wanted his boys to grow up in the same house; it would have been hazardous to entrust the boy with anybody else.[39] As *tutor* Augustus would have provided Agrippa with pocket-money (*peculium*); he would have continued to provide assistance after 26 June AD 4, when Agrippa's property became his. Agrippa probably held the view that Augustus was too frugal before and after his adoption.[40] It is noteworthy, however, that Augustus donated Agrippa's money to the *aerarium militare*; it must have been a very large amount. Perhaps Agrippa accused Augustus of avarice when informed of his impending adoption. Either way, *abdicatio*, in the case of Agrippa Postumus, meant dishonour and the withdrawal of his property. At the same time Augustus ordered his adopted son to Surrentum: the boy was grounded without funds. Donating Agrippa's inheritance to the military treasury represents then a moral

---

[38] Dio 55.32.2. Dio must, of course, mean the part of Augustus' estate left to Agrippa in a testament, cf. *CAH* 10² 201. It is important to note, moreover, that had Agrippa been *sui iuris* he could have refused the adoption.

[39] Suet. *Aug.* 64.3 is important: *Nepotes et litteras et natare aliaque rudimenta per se plerumque docuit, ac nihil aeque elaboravit quam ut imitarentur chirographum suum...*, 'He [Augustus] himself, for the most part, taught his grandchildren how to read, swim and other basic skills, and he strived to make them copy his own handwriting.'

[40] B. Levick (1999), 59–60, places the accusation after Agrippa was 'abdicated'; thus, for Levick, once he had left the Julian gens. As has been shown above, however, this cannot be right; *abdicatio* did not equal *emancipatio* for Agrippa.

point. Augustus did not adopt Agrippa to acquire his wealth, nor was *peculium* withheld for private gain: he would not expose himself to slander from Agrippa or his friends.

The weight of evidence indicates that Agrippa did something deserving punishment. But it must be significant that Augustus chose *abdicatio* instead of *emancipatio*. The use of a Greek device with only fictional relevance in Rome reveals a delicate game. Agrippa was publicly reprimanded, impoverished, and rusticated. The source of the problem was evidently in Rome, and Agrippa was to stay well away from it. Augustus probably hoped that Agrippa's attitude would eventually improve (he was still a teenager), but retention of *patria potestas* signals caution.[41] Augustus perceived dangerous potential within Agrippa, a perception that, as I have argued above, encouraged his adoption. It would have been more reasonable to place Agrippa under Tiberius, beside Germanicus and the younger Drusus. By adopting Agrippa himself, Augustus admitted that his situation was different. Overdue for the *toga virilis* and unencumbered by *patria potestas*, Agrippa posed a problem; he could one day be used to symbolize an alternative line of power. It must be significant then that from the time of Agrippa's adoption to his becoming an *abdicatus*, Rome experienced social and political unrest. In order to test whether Agrippa's *abdicatio* could be related to wider political events, we must consider in detail the problems which affected Rome in both AD 5 and 6.

---

[41] This point is made by S. Jameson (1975), 292. See Sen. *Cont.* 2.1.28 and Quint. 7.4.27. Some have argued, however, that Agrippa must have been emancipated, because he is not named by Suetonius (*Aug.* 101), as a beneficiary, or as an *exheredatus*, in Augustus' will, see generally A. Momigliano (1944), 112–15; B. Levick (1970), *passim*; J. Linderski (1988), 188–200. It was made clear in Roman law that if a child, whether a *heres* or *exheredatus*, was passed over in a will, then the will was deemed to be void, *Inst.* 2.13. Since most hold that Suetonius has offered a complete account of Augustus' will in so far as it affected his descendants, they therefore argue that Agrippa must not have been named in the will, i.e. he was no longer *in potestate*. Since I have shown that *abdicatio* cannot mean *emancipatio*, I believe there is only one obvious answer. Agrippa was named in Augustus' will as an *exheredatus*, but the reference was ignored by Suetonius, who did not believe that the issue required notice, since exheredation was established not by Augustus' will but by the *senatus consultum* of AD 7, legalizing the incarceration of Agrippa on Planasia. It should be noted, however, that no one would surely contest a will, in public, in which the only victim was thought to be Agrippa Postumus. It may be that Augustus had put together a defective will knowing that no one would dare challenge. After all, Agrippa's *abdicatio* was hardly by the book!

5

The Buck Stops Where?

THE CRISIS

The year AD 5 witnessed the antecedents of a crisis that would burden the years immediately following:

...*per dies octo Tiberis impetu miseranda clades hominum domorumque fuit.*

...for eight horrible days men and homes were destroyed as the Tiber attacked.[1]

Τότε δ' οὖν ἐπί τε τοῦ Κορνηλίου καὶ ἐπὶ Οὐαλερίου Μεσσάλου ὑπάτων σεισμοί τε ἐξαίσιοι συνέβησαν, καὶ ὁ Τίβερις τήν τε γέφυραν κατέσυρε καὶ πλωτὴν τὴν πόλιν ἐπὶ ἑπτὰ ἡμέρας ἐποίησε, τοῦ τε ἡλίου τι ἐκλιπὲς ἐγένετο, καὶ λιμὸς συνηνέχθη.

And so at this time, in the consulship of Cornelius and Valerius Messalla, enormous earthquakes occurred and the Tiber washed away the bridge and made the city navigable for seven days; and there was also a partial eclipse of the sun, and a famine occurred.[2]

Low crop yields and the flood probably caused decreased supply.[3] In AD 64 a food shortage occurred when fire, sweeping through the city, destroyed grain stores.[4] Given that in AD 5 the city, which could just

---

[1] Cass. *Chron.* 604.
[2] Dio 55.22.3.
[3] G. Rickman, *The Corn Supply of Ancient Rome* (1980), 63; Cass. *Chron.* 604 links flood and famine, which is accepted by G. S. Aldrete, *Floods of the Tiber in Ancient Rome* (2007), 132. See also Dio 54.1.1–2, for a very similar combination of flood, plague, and famine.
[4] Suet. *Nero* 38.1; Tac. *Ann.* 15.39.3; Dio 62.16.5, see P. Garnsey, *Famine and Food Supply in the Graeco-Roman World* (1988), 224.

mean the Aventine, was navigable for a whole week, most stored grain was probably ruined, stores closest to the river spoiled first.[5] Ostia was no doubt similarly inundated, preventing immediate relief. As with most major floods, nearly all stored products (not just produce) were probably destroyed, increasing demand and exposing residents to very high short-term prices. Jerome had evidence that in AD 5 the price of grain inflated to HS 110 for one month's ration to a member of the *plebs frumentaria*, extraordinarily high when we consider that in the wake of the great fire of AD 64, the price was apparently HS 3.[6] But very high short-term prices would not have been the only problem. Water-borne disease, caused by the presence of faecal matter and general decay, often accompanies the flooding of major population centres, and would certainly have caused death in a pre-industrial city of Rome's size. In an unspecified period of Augustus' reign, Pliny connects disease in the city (*pestilentia urbis*) with famine in Italy (*fames Italiae*). Famine and disease are obvious partners, but the effect was no doubt devastating when combined with large-scale flooding.[7] Swan uses the solar eclipse to date these events to the beginning of the year, since an eclipse is recorded for 28 March AD 5.[8] But another eclipse occurred on 22 September.[9] There is no conclusive evidence for either date. A food shortage in the following year (AD 6) might suggest one long period of decreased supply from the end of AD 5 into AD 6.[10] Winter generally slowed import rates, which may explain why low supply persisted despite the receding

---

[5] G. S. Aldrete (2007), 129–41, who adds weakened buildings, injuries, and drownings. See also his excellent analysis of the extent of flooding on pp. 42–9.

[6] Jerome *Chron.* 170; Tac. *Ann.* 15.36.

[7] Pliny *NH* 7.149.

[8] P. M. Swan (2004), 155. Swan believed that the eclipse was either noticed in Rome or recorded in Roman Africa and communicated to Rome. It must be understood that the path of the eclipse began where the southern tip of Sudan intersects with the south-west point of Ethiopia, and stretched across the south of the Sahara to the southernmost tip of Morocco—a long way from Roman Africa.

[9] Recorded by NASA, and can be verified at http://sunearth.gsfc.nasa.gov/eclipse/ Secat/SE0001-0100.html. As with the eclipse of 28 March, this second eclipse could not be seen in Rome: it was a few hundred miles off the west coast of Indonesia. The most logical solution is to believe that eclipses were predicted. Indeed, this would seem to be supported by recent archaeological evidence in the shape of a time-measuring device that appears to have had a dial specifically associated with accurately predicting eclipses, J. Marchant, 'In Search of Lost Time', *Nature*, 444 (30 November 2006), 534–38.

[10] Dio 55.26.1.

flood. Piracy in Sardinia and rebellion in North Africa would not have helped.[11]

The seriousness of the above situation was exploited by the armies, who demanded better conditions at the end of AD 5. As with most other governments, the senate decided not to test the patience and loyalty of a discouraged military. Members of the praetorian guard were to therefore recieve 5,000 drachmas upon completion of sixteen years' service, while other soldiers were voted 3,000 drachmas upon completion of twenty years' service.[12] In AD 5 there were 28 legions, each containing on paper 5,500 men, and 9 cohorts of praetorians, each with 500 men.[13] That gives us 154,000 legionaries and 4,500 praetorians. A very large number had evidently survived their years of service and expected immediate payment. A soldier's severance package would consist of either cash or a plot of land, though land was more often provided as the government sought to minimize large money payments.[14] Nevertheless, Dio believed that the amount of money required in AD 5 was enough to threaten the *fiscus*:

Δι' οὖν ταῦτ' ἀπορῶν χρημάτων, γνώμην ἐς τὴν βουλὴν ἐσήνεγκε πόρον τινὰ διαρκῆ καὶ ἀείνων ἀποδειχθῆναι, ὅπως μηδενὸς ἔξωθεν μηδὲν λυπουμένου ἀφθόνως ἐκ τῶν τεταγμένων καὶ τὴν τροφὴν καὶ τὰ γέρα λαμβάνωσι.

And so lacking money for this, Augustus put a motion in the senate for a sufficient and permanent revenue source to be established to ensure that

---

[11] Vell. 2.116.2; Dio 55.28.1–4; Florus 2.31; Orosius 6.21.18. Dio writes that the Gaetulians 'ravaged the neighbouring territory' while an inscription (V. Ehrenberg, and A. H. M. Jones (1955), 63) testifies to war: *Marti Augusto sacrum auspiciis imp. Caesaris Aug. pontificis maximi patris patriae ductu Cossi Lentuli cos. Xxviri sacris faciundis procos. Provincia Africa bello Gaetulico liberata civitas Lepcitana.* 'Dedication to Mars Augustus by the city of Lepcis, for, under the auspices of Imperator Caesar Augustus, Pontifex Maximus, Pater Patriae, and the command of Cossus Lentulus, consul, XVvir Sacris Faciundis, pronconsul, the province of Africa was freed from the Gaetulian war.' Rome had other suppliers, but overall supply would necessarily have been diminished, or at least interrupted; cf. G. Rickman (1980), 66–71, argues that Africa provided considerably more grain than did Egypt. Thus, for Rickman, events in North Africa had a great effect upon supply in Rome.

[12] Dio 55.23.1–5. 5,000 drachmas equals HS 20,000, and 3,000 drachmas equals HS 12,000.

[13] See basic accounts in H. M. D. Parker, *The Roman Legions* (1971), 92; J. C. Mann, *Legionary Recruitment and Veteran Settlement During the Principate* (1983); W. Nippel (1995), 92 f.

[14] P. M. Brennan, 'A Rome Away from Rome: Veteran Colonists and Post-Augustan Roman Colonization', in J. P. Descoeudres (ed.), *Greek Colonists and Native Populations* (1990), 491–502.

soldiers should receive maintenance and rewards abundantly from fixed revenues, without injury to any other party.[15]

Augustus, sensitive to the issue of taxation and concerned about laying the burden on citizens and provincial taxpayers, delayed making a decision until the next year, AD 6, when a new treasury, the *aerarium militare*, was created. Dio explains the delay:

...ἐπειδὴ μηδεὶς πόρος ἀρέσκων τισὶν εὑρίσκετο, ἀλλὰ καὶ πάνυ πάντες ὅτι καὶ ἐζητεῖτο ἐβαρύνοντο...

Since no source [of revenue] acceptable to anyone was found, rather absolutely everyone was distressed that one was even being sought...[16]

These must have been a difficult few months for Augustus, who was confronted with threats by legionaries and praetorians if he did not improve their conditions of employment, while also facing universal opposition to any further taxation. Augustus states that he donated HS 170,000,000 to the new treasury, and Dio adds that foreign kings and cities also made contributions.[17] Revenue was nevertheless insufficient to meet expenditure, and so after much deliberation a 5 per cent tax on 'inheritance and legacies left by the dying to anyone except the closely related or poor' was initiated and earmarked for military severance pay.[18] The catalyst for this somewhat courageous decision is not hard to find. In the winter of AD 5/6 parts of Illyricum became restless; in late January or early February restlessness became outright rebellion across the entire region. Augustus had no option but to decide in favour of the troops.

Velleius describes some of the early incidents:

Oppressi cives Romani, trucidati negotiatores, magnus vexillariorum numerus ad internecionem ea in regione quae plurimum ab imperatore aberat caesus, occupata armis Macedonia, omnia et in omnibus locis igni ferroque vastata.

---

[15] Dio 55.24.9.
[16] Dio 55.25.1.
[17] RG 17; Dio 55.25.3. Dio tells us that private citizens were forbidden to make private donations. Wealthy citizens were happy to part with their money, but not through taxation. Augustus, for his part, would not countenance wealthy individuals being identified as patrons of the armed forces: tension between traditional Republican concepts and new political realities.
[18] Dio 55.25.5; 'closely related' probably means that heirs in the first degree and possibly even second degree were not taxed.

Roman citizens were overpowered, merchants were massacred, a very large number in the special detachment in the region which was the furthest distance from the commander, were killed, Macedonia was taken by arms and everywhere and everything was destroyed by fire and the sword.[19]

This is followed by Rome's response:

Quin etiam tantus huius belli metus fuit ut stabilem illum et formatum tantorum bellorum experientia Caesaris Augusti animum quateret atque terreret. Habiti itaque dilectus revocati undique et omnes veterani viri feminaeque ex censu libertinum coactae dare militem. Audita in senatu vox principis decimo die, ni caveretur, posse hostem in urbis Romae venire conspectum... Itaque ut praesidium militum[20] res publica ab Augusto ducem in bellum poposcit Tiberium.

For the war inspired such great fear that the spirit of Caesar Augustus, steady and firm from experience in so many wars, became shaken and terrified. Thus a levy was held, from every quarter veterans were recalled and men and women were compelled, according to the census, to give up some freedmen as soldiers. The voice of the princeps was heard in the senate to say that, unless precautions were taken, the enemy could come in sight of the city in ten days... and so the State demanded from Augustus the protection of the soldiers and Tiberius as leader in the war.[21]

According to Dio, and possibly an inscription found in Tuzla, the levy (*dilectus*) included freeborn citizens.[22] We can date Rome's response to the beginning of AD 6. Velleius states that he, as quaestor designate, was among those dispatched to the front lines.[23] Quaestorian elections usually occurred early in the year, which means that the levied forces did not leave Rome until spring at the earliest.[24] A *terminus post quem* is provided by Velleius, who seems to have reached camp shortly before summer.[25] The senate's decree should therefore be

---

[19] Vell. 2.110.6; Oros. 6.21.23 f.
[20] The word is debated, see A. J. Woodman, *The Tiberian Narrative* (1977), 161, for a brief discussion.
[21] Vell. 2.111.1–2. I have departed here from my usual practice of supplying the Loeb text and have used instead that of A. J. Woodman (1977).
[22] Dio 55.31.1–2; and V. Ehrenberg and A. H. M. Jones (1955), 168; cf. Suet. *Aug.* 25.2; Pliny *NH* 7.149.
[23] Vell. 2.111.3.
[24] A. J. Woodman (1977), 162; Pliny *Ep.* 4.15.6.
[25] Vell. 2.112.1. The point is disputed. A. J. Woodman (1977), 162–163, provides a good examination of the various positions, and shows that Velleius must have left early in the year.

dated somewhere between March and May. The response was possibly a *tumultus* declaration. The mobilization of veterans and a *dilectus* are certainly suggestive, but Dio supplies evidence of a decree suspending *inter alia* the activities of the courts.[26] Writing about an earlier period Asconius states:

Bello Italico ... crebraeque defectiones Italicorum nuntiarentur, nanctus iustitii occasionem senatus decrevit ne iudicia, dum tumultus Italicus esset, exercerentur.

In the Italian war ... news constantly arrived of rebellions among the Italians; on taking the opportunity to suspend public business the senate decreed that the courts should not remain in use for the duration of the Italic upheaval.[27]

It is nevertheless possible that the Illyrian rebellion and persistent famine caused successive emergency decrees with overlapping consequences. Under AD 6 Dio cites the following decisions:

(i) Foreigners (excepting doctors and teachers), gladiators, and unsold slaves were evacuated to 100 miles distance;[28]
(ii) Senators were permitted to 'travel wherever they wished', and the decisions reached by those who stayed were considered valid, i.e. even if there was not a *quorum*;[29]
(iii) Most members of Augustus' retinue and the retinues of other high officials were dismissed;[30]
(iv) The courts were put into recess;[31]

---

[26] Dio 55.26.1.
[27] Asc. 73–74C; A. Lintott (1968), 153–5. Augustus' own words are suggestive, since *tumultus* was originally declared when there was a sudden raid of Etruscans or Gauls, Vell. 2.111.1: 'The voice of the princeps was heard in the senate to say that, unless precautions were taken, the enemy could come in sight of the city in ten days.'
[28] Dio 55.26.1; Suet. *Aug.* 42.
[29] Dio 55.26.2. This represents a temporary suspension of the rules governing senators' movements outside Italy, Dio, 52.42.6 = 29 BC, see R. J. A. Talbert (1984), 139–40. It may be inferred that much of Italy was subject in AD 6 to a low food supply. Augustus himself suggests that there was something wrong with agricultural production, Suet. *Aug.* 42.3: *ut tandem annona convaluit, impetum se cepisse scribit frumentationes publicas in perpetuum abolendi, quod earum fiducia cultura agrorum cessaret*, 'He writes that when the grain supply improved, he was very much inclined to abolish the public supply of grain for good, because reliance on this had discouraged agriculture.'
[30] Dio 55.26.1.
[31] Ibid.

(v) Expensive celebrations were to be curtailed, particularly banquets on Augustus' birthday;[32]
(vi) Two ex-consuls were appointed to watch over the grain and wheat supply and produce a fixed ration amount for sale; and[33]
(vii) Those listed on the grain dole were provided with a double serve of the new ration amount.[34]

These are certainly from *senatus consulta*. Evacuation shows that food was scarce and that people were on edge. At least some decisions belong to late August or September, since the effect of Augustus' birthday (23 September) on food supply was anticipated. I propose that a *tumultus* declaration was passed between March and early May. Public business ceased until it became clear, perhaps by July, that Rome was in no immediate danger from an invasion. By then food supply had slowed dramatically, causing another emergency decree affecting, *inter alia*, celebrations for Augustus' birthday. Extreme measures tend to harm a population's general psychology. It could be that frustration and/or desperation fuelled deliberate acts of destruction. Dio states that fire destroyed parts of the city, but Ulpian provides more useful information: *pluribus uno die incendiis exortis*, 'many fires had broken out in one day.'[35] Lightning is a possibility, but arson is more likely.[36] Coming not long after severe floods, with food supply still low, destructive fires must have further tested the patience of urban residents. People were not only exposed to damaged property and disease but inflated prices for staple produce.

---

[32] Ibid., 26.3.

[33] Ibid., 26.2. This arrangement lasted only until AD 7, when, as Dio (55.31.4) writes, two ex-consuls, attended by lictors, were made grain curators. The policy of AD 6 must have been to protect the market from inflationary pressures, see P. M. Swan (2004), 180, cf. P. A. Brunt, 'Princeps and Equites', *JRS* 73, (1983), 42–75, argues that the ex-consuls were to acquire more grain not police private contractors; G. Rickman (1980), 64–6, also suggests that the problem was one of procurement, since private contractors were proving inefficient in times of hardship.

[34] Dio 55.26.3; Suet. *Aug.* 41.2.

[35] Dio 55.26.4–5; *Dig.* 1.15.1–3; Suet. *Aug.* 30.

[36] Ovid (*Trist.* 2.267–268) provides us with a contemporary opinion: 'What is more useful than fire? For whoever is planning to burn a house arms his criminal hands with fire.' The intention of P. Lentulus Sura and his co-conspirators in 63 BC to deliberately to light fires across Rome is apposite. It was evidently the best method for causing widespread panic, while diverting public attention from other activities, in their case the assassination of members of the government, Sall. *Bell. Cat.* 42.

The government's response evinces suspicion and anxiety: a massive fire-fighting force was mobilized.

Rome had hitherto relied on 600 slaves under the direction of the *vicomagistri* to fight fires.[37] In AD 6 this organization was abolished and replaced by a force of either 3,500 or 7,000 *liberti*, directed by an equestrian prefect (*praefectus vigilum*).[38] The nature of the task required officers to undertake policing duties in addition to the putting out/prevention of fires.[39] As a night patrol, the *vigiles* could not help but witness a variety of crimes: arson, looting, opportunistic violence, etc.[40] In time the *praefectus vigilum* could even pass sentence, but during our period criminals were probably handed over to the city prefect (*praefectus urbi*), who, unlike the *praefectus vigilum*, had use of a gaol.[41]

The relationship between fire and burglary was topical in Augustan Rome:

qui sive tectis iniectus est sive fortuitus, ruinae et incendia illa urbium excidia sunt; quippe non defendunt sua, sed in communi periculo ad praedandum ut hostes discurrunt appetuntque aliena, et in suis domini a validioribus

---

[37] Organized in 7 BC; Dio 55.8.6–7. For a general discussion on arrangements before then, see P. K. Baillie Reynolds, *The Vigiles of Imperial Rome* (1926).

[38] Dio 55.26.4–5; for 7,000 see P. K. Baillie Reynolds, (1926), 22; for 3,500 see J. S. Rainbird, 'The Fire Stations of Imperial Rome', *PBSR*, 54 (1986), 147–69; R. W. Davies, 'Augustus Caesar: A Police System in the Ancient World', in P. J. Stead (ed.) *Pioneers in Policing* (1977), 12–32, esp. 14–16; P. M. Swan (2004), 182; W. Nippel (1995), 97.

[39] *Dig.* 1.15.1–5. Some have argued that police duties were a later development, see especially P. K. Baillie Reynolds (1926), 17 f.; W. Clinton Terry III, and K. V. Hartigan, 'Police Authority and Reform in Augustan Rome and Nineteenth Century England: Localizing and Nationalizing Police work in Traditional and Modern societies', *Law and Human Behavior*, 6:3/4 (1982), 295–311, esp. 301f; W. Nippel (1995), 96–7: 'Their capacity to pursue thieves and runaway slaves should not be overestimated.'

[40] Suet. *Aug.* 25.2: *Libertino milite, praeterquam Romae incendiorum causa et si tumultus in graviore annona metueretur, bis usus est*, 'Only twice were freedmen used as soldiers, except for use as fire-fighters in Rome and if he was in fear of riots when grain was scarce.' The co-ordinating conjunction *et* need not imply two separate emergency forces. It could mean that the vigiles fought fires *and* controlled riots. Curiously, W. Nippel (1995), 96, understands this passage to mean that 'Augustus may have thought of employing the *vigiles* as a sort of riot police if necessary', but then writes: 'but we have no evidence that they were really used in this way'. But surely Suetonius provides such evidence.

[41] *Dig.* 1.15: 'The Prefect of the Vigiles takes cognizance of incendiaries, burglars, thieves, robbers, and harbourers of criminals, unless the culprit is so savage and notorious, that he is turned over to the Prefect of the City.'

The Buck Stops Where? 83

caeduntur, accenduntur alia ipsaque cum maxume flagrantia spolium ex alienis ruinis feruntur.

Whether it [fire] seizes on buildings by arson or accident, these collapses and these blazes are the ruin of cities. For men do not defend their own property, but amid the communal danger hurry like enemies to the loot, and take what belongs to others. In their own homes owners are killed by those stronger than they. Other things are set alight on purpose, and, still blazing, are carried as booty from the ruins of others' houses."[42]

An emergency force capable of maintaining order is obviously what Augustus had in mind.[43] To sum up then: Illyricum was in rebellion; food supply was low owing to destroyed storage, piracy, and rebellion; the public corn dole was being rationed; public business had ceased; fires had broken out, causing destruction and looting; people were probably exposed to extremely high short-term prices; public shows had been cancelled until further notice; and a 5 per cent inheritance tax had been imposed. Dio had evidence that people held Augustus' government accountable:

Ὁ δ' οὖν ὅμιλος, οἷα ὑπό τε τοῦ λιμοῦ καὶ ὑπὸ τοῦ τέλους τοῖς θ' ὑπὸ τοῦ πυρὸς ἀπολωλόσι κεκακωμένος, ἤσχαλλε, καὶ πολλὰ μὲν καὶ φανερῶς νεωτεροποιὰ διελάλουν, πλείω δὲ δὴ βιβλία νύκτωρ ἐξετίθεσαν. Καὶ ταῦτ' ἐλέγετο μὲν ἐκ παρασκευῆς Ποπλίου τινὸς Ῥούφου γίγνεσθαι, ὑπωπτεύετο δὲ ἐς ἄλλους· ὁ μὲν γὰρ Ῥοῦφος οὔτε ἐνθυμηθῆναί τι αὐτῶν οὔτε πρᾶξαι ἐδύνατο, ἕτεροι δὲ τῷ ἐκείνου ὀνόματι καταχρώμενοι καινοτομεῖν ἐπιστεύοντο. Καὶ διὰ τοῦτο ζήτησίς τε αὐτῶν ἐψηφίσθη καὶ μήνυτρα προετέθη· μηνύσεις τε ἐγίγνοντο, καὶ ἡ πόλις καὶ ἐκ τούτων ἐταράττετο.

And so the people, distressed by the results of the famine and of the tax, and by the losses resulting from the fire, were horrified, and were discussing many plans for revolution, even openly, and posted up even more as pamphlets by night. And it was said that all these things had come about from the planning of a certain Publius Rufus, but suspicion was directed against others, for Rufus could neither have concocted nor accomplished any of these things. But others, making use of his name, were understood to be planning revolution. On account of this a search for them was decreed and

---

[42] Sen. *Cont.* 2.1.11–12.
[43] Phenomena that we know well in modern cities perhaps appeared in Rome in the first century BC, necessitating a range of government interventions. Augustus' Principate was an attempt at a solution, though incomplete. The *vigiles* represent an important step in the direction of a centralized emergency services unit.

rewards for informants advertised. Information started to come to light, and because of this, the city was also in a state of commotion."[44]

Ὅμιλος implies a very large group of people: a general dissatisfaction with the government's effectiveness had transformed into a public show of anger and frustration.[45] It is doubtful that the creation of the *vigiles* calmed angry crowds.[46] Hungry, worn-out people who, of a sudden, face the loss of whatever possessions they have left are not prone to cool-headed reason. A tradition of resisting taxation, moreover, should not be lightly dismissed, especially since it was based on the principle of Rome as the ruling element in the empire.[47] Most modern communities evidence anxiety when a new tax is imposed. Exaggerated fears set in even when the proposed rate is low, further fuelling popular resistance. Because the new earmarked tax was set at a flat rate for all classes in the census (aside from the very poor), complaints would have come from all sides. But even contemporaries believed that behind the general protest lay a more sinister motive with political dimensions. Some scholars view the episode as a single unique affair, while others place it within the larger theme of dynastic succession.[48] Identifying the organizers of the protest will indicate if either interpretation is correct.

---

[44] Dio 55.27.1-3.
[45] Cf. P. M. Swan (2004), 183; also T. Wiedemann (1975), 268: 'Perhaps we should not overestimate the extent of opposition to the policies of the Government.'
[46] Cf. P. M. Swan (2004), 183.
[47] C., Nicolet, *The World of the Citizen in Republican Rome* (1980), 184-5. Cf. P. M. Swan (2004), 183, who writes 'It is anything but clear how he [Dio] thought the inheritence tax, which he says exempted the poor, exercised the people.' Swan seems to suggest here that 'ὅμιλος' is to be read as 'the poor'. He is guided by Z. Yavetz, *Plebs and Princeps* (1969), 141. But Yavetz includes in his list *populus*, οἱ πολλοί δῆμος and οἱ ἐν τῇ πόλει. It cannot be maintained that these all refer to the poor. Importantly, however, there is evidence to suggest that the minimum property qualification was set very low. J. F. Gilliam, 'The Minimum Subject to the Vicesima Hereditatium', *AJP*, 73:4 (1952), 397-405, cites papyrus which shows that in the second century AD a property worth 1,900 drachmas (HS 7,600) could be taxed. If this were the case in AD 5, it would suggest that a great part of the population was affected by the tax, including, perhaps, emancipated slaves who had inherited a few thousand sesterces in their master's will.
[48] It is considered a single and unique affair by T. Wiedemann (1975), 264-71, esp. 268; R. Syme (1986), 115-27; K. A. Raaflaub and L. J. Samons, 'Opposition to Augustus' in K. A. Raaflaub and M. Toher, (eds.), *Between Republic and Empire: Interpretations of Augustus and his Principate* (1990), 417-54. The affair is directly related to court politics by: F. Norwood (1963), 153 f; B. Levick (1976), 329 f., (1999), 58 f.; R. A. Birch (1981), 450 f. The affair is not treated by F. B. Marsh (1931); A. E. Pappano (1941), 30-45; R. Detweiler (1970), 289-95; R. Seager (2005).

The Buck Stops Where?

Dio states that a certain Publius Rufus was nominally responsible, and that others were in fact using his name. Publius Rufus is thought to be the same man referred to by Suetonius in his list of men who conspired against Augustus:

Lepidi iuvenis, deinde Varronis Murenae et Fanni Caepionis, mox M. Egnati, exin Plauti Rufi Lucique Pauli progeneri sui . . .

Young Lepidus, then Varro Murena and Fannius Caepio and soon after M. Egnatius, and next Plautius Rufus and Lucius Paulus, husband of his granddaughter.[49]

Suetonius has consciously paired conspirators who he believed worked together. Publius Rufus and Plautius Rufus are surely the same man, and Levick is probably right to name him Publius Plautius Rufus.[50] But the reference to L. Aemilius Paullus has fuelled the most speculation. We have two other references to Aemilius Paullus' disgrace. First from the Scholiast on Juvenal:

Dedit hunc Agrippa sorori: Iuliam neptem Augusti significat, quae nupta Aemilio Paulo cum [h]is [sic] maiestatis crimine perisset, ab avo relegata est. post revocata cum semet vitiis addixisset perpetui exilii damnata est supplicio.

Agrippa [Herod] gave this to his sister: He [Juvenal] means Julia, granddaughter of Augustus, who having been married to Aemilius Paullus, when he had perished under a charge of *maiestas*, was relegated by her grandfather. After being recalled, when she had abandoned herself to her vices, she was condemned to the punishment of perpetual exile.[51]

Next Suetonius, who refers to the cancellation of the future emperor Claudius' betrothal to Aemilius Paullus' daughter:

Priorem, quod parentes eius Augustum offenderant, virginem adhuc repudiavit . . .

He repudiated the former before their marriage, because her parents had offended Augustus . . .[52]

Suetonius' *quod parentes eius Augustum offenderant* would seem to contradict his previous linking of Aemilius Paullus with Plautius Rufus, since we know that Julia was finally relegated in AD 8.[53] But connecting the disgrace of Julia and Aemilius Paullus could be

---

[49] Suet. *Aug.* 19.1.   [50] B. Levick (1999), index.
[51] *Scholia in Iuvenalem*: 158.1–2.   [52] Suet. *Claud.* 26.1.
[53] Under AD 28 Tacitus, *Ann.* 4.71, writes that Julia had been exiled for twenty years: *Illic viginti annis exilium toleravit . . .*

thematic.[54] Needing to explain the failed engagement of Claudius and Aemilia Lepida, Suetonius decided to blame both husband and wife. The Scholiast poses the more difficult problem. He is commenting on Juvenal *Satire* 6.157, in which Juvenal mentions a diamond ring once worn by Queen Berenice:

Hunc dedit olim | barbarus incestae, gestare Agrippa sorori, | observant ubi festa mero pede sabbata reges | et vetus indulget senibus clementia porcis.

This was given long ago | as a present by the barbarian Agrippa to his incestuous sister | where kings observe the Sabbath festival bare foot | and ancient clemency indulges elderly pigs.[55]

Herod Agrippa, the Jewish king, is meant. The Scholiast has either made a terrible mistake and confused Herod Agrippa with Agrippa Postumus, or the manuscript has been garbled in transmission. But the information is not useless. The Scholiast evidently believed that the younger Julia was twice exiled. A minority have accepted the claim, but most reject it as confused, proposing instead that the Scholiast has conflated the relegation of the elder Julia and the younger Julia. But the solution is unconvincing. Reference to the younger Julia's husband and brother indicate the possession of a correct profile, as does the phrase *neptis Augusti*. Norwood has put forward, in my opinion, the best solution: the younger Julia was sent away twice: the first a form of quarantine; the second full-blown relegation.[56] An enforced 'holiday' is a logical assumption. In the wake of Aemilius Paullus' condemnation and the *abdicatio* of Agrippa, it would have been sensible to remove the young woman from the centre of public attention, a policy easily mistaken for tough punishment by historians with an eye to her final disgrace. But even if

---

[54] T. D. Barnes, 'Julia's Child', *Phoenix*, 35:4 (1981), 362–3. Cf. R. Syme (1986), 115 f., for whom Suet. *Claud.* 26.1 is central to proving that Aemilius Paullus was not punished in AD 6. Syme argues that *adulescens* refers to Claudius' seventeenth birthday, which was 1 Aug. AD 8. But *adulescens* cannot be treated so precisely, it is too general.

[55] Juv. *Sat.* 6.157–160.

[56] Twice exiled: F. Norwood (1963), 153 n. 31, though he considers the first 'relegation' to have been an informal arrangement, as with Agrippa Postumus' stay in Surrentum; R. Detweiler (1970), 290 n.12 seems to accept Norwood's view; B. Levick (1976), 331, and (1999), 59, with caution on both occasions. Exiled once: E. Meise, *Untersuchungen zur Geschicte der Julisch-Claudischen Dynastie* (1969), 35–48; R. A. Birch (1981), 454; R. Syme (1986), 123 f.; P. M. Swan (2004), 184 f. Unsure: T. Wiedemann (1975), 268 n. 3; E. Fantham, *Julia Augusti* (2006), 110, 162 n.7.

Aemilius Paullus was exiled *before* his wife, we are left with a still more difficult problem. Dio does not mention L. Aemilius Paullus in connection with the affair.

Dio does not mention a trial in relation to the Rufus affair. Bauman therefore held that the senatorial investigation must have failed.[57] If Bauman is right, then L. Aemilius Paullus' conviction for *maiestas* cannot belong in AD 6. To return to Dio's text:

> But others, making use of his name, were understood to be planning revolution. On account of this a search for them was decreed and rewards for informants advertised. Information started to come to light, and because of this, the city was also in a state of commotion.[58]

That information was submitted to the senate is in fact evidence that the inquiry was not a failure. Much rests on Dio's belief that the submission of information caused 'commotion' in Rome. Bauman supposes that the informants, being slaves, caused 'commotion'. The inquiry thus collapsed under the weight of anxious criticism.[59] But we do not in fact know what percentage of informants, if any, were slaves. It is just as plausible that unrest was caused by the fame of the personality exposed: i.e. L. Aemilius Paullus.

For Bauman, the episode's only legal result was a *senatus consultum*, which allowed for the public investigation of future acts of anonymous defamation, and led eventually to the prosecution of Cassius Severus in AD 8 for *maiestas*.[60] He argues that a decree cited by Suetonius is apposite:

> *Etiam sparsos de se in curia famosos libellos nec expavit et magna cura redarguit ac ne requisitis quidem auctoribus id modo censuit, cognoscendum posthac de iis, qui libellos aut carmina ad infamiam cuiuspiam sub alieno nomine edant.*

---

[57] R. A. Bauman (1974), 28 f.
[58] Dio 55.27.2.
[59] R. A. Bauman (1974), 43 f.; *Dig.* 47.10.5.11: *Et ei, qui indicasset, sivi liber sive servus sit, pro modo substantiae accusatae personae aestimatione iudicis praemium constituitur, servo forsitan et libertate praestanda. Quid enim si publica utilitas ex hoc emergit*, 'And for the person who exposes such offence, whether he be free or slave, there is provided a reward according the wealth of the accused, to be assessed by the judge, and in the case of a slave liberty may follow. For it may be that a public good emerges from the exposure.' There is, however, no evidence that slaves provided the bulk of information, if any, in AD 6.
[60] R. A. Bauman (1974), 50.

And he did not even dread defamatory writings about himself scattered in the Curia, but refuted them with much care, and without searching for the authors he recommended after this that writing or speech which defames anybody and is produced under a false name should be investigated.[61]

I believe Bauman's hypothesis is wrong. Dio does not describe the βιβλία disseminated in AD 6 as being defamatory; he refers only to their containing revolutionary messages. The solution requires examination of two relevant defamation cases: those of Cassius Severus and Titus Labienus.

Tacitus states that Cassius Severus was the first to be charged with *maiestas* for defamatory writings:

Primus Augustus cognitionem de famosis libellis specie legis eius tractavit, commotus Cassii Severi libidine, qua viros feminasque inlustres procacibus scriptis diffamaverat.

Augustus was the first to drag investigations concerning written libel under the law [of *maiestas*]; having been disturbed by the licence of Cassius Severus, who had defamed distinguished men and women in his shameless writings.[62]

---

[61] Suet. *Aug.* 55.
[62] Tac. *Ann.* 1.72. Jerome *Chron.* P176 H: 'Cassius Severus, the outstanding orator, who had mocked the Quintian proverb dies of starvation in the 25th year of his exile, covered with hardly a rag over his genitals.' That places his condemnation in AD 8. The date is nevertheless disputed. Th. Mommsen (1899), 800; R. E. Smith (1951), 169–79, esp. 178; G. W. Clarke, 'Books for the Burning', *Prudentia*, 4: 2 (1972), 67–83, and D. Hennig, 'T. Labienus und der erste Majestätspozeß *de famosis libellis*', *Chiron*, 3 (1973), 245–54, all place Cassius' trial in AD 12 by associating it with Dio 56.27.1 f: καὶ μαθὼν ὅτι βιβλία ἄττα ἐφ' ὕβρει τινῶν συγγράφοιτο, ζήτησιν αὐτῶν ἐποιήσατο, καὶ ἐκεῖνά τε, τὰ μὲν ἐν τῇ πόλει εὑρεθέντα πρὸς τῶν ἀγορανόμων τὰ δὲ ἔξω πρὸς τῶν ἑκασταχόθι ἀρχόντων, κατέφλεξε, καὶ τῶν συνθέντων αὐτὰ ἐκόλασέ τινας. 'And learning that some pamphlets of an insulting nature were being written concerning certain people, he ordered a search be made for them; and those that were found in the city he ordered to be burned by the aediles, and those outside by the chief magistrates in each place, and he punished some of the writers'. None cite Jerome. R. A. Bauman (1974), 29–30, is aware of Jerome, but he too wishes to associate Cassius Severus with Dio 56.27.1. He therefore moves the Dio passage into a lacuna where AD 8 would have been because, he reasons, AD 8 was apparently a tumultuous year, while AD 12 was too peaceful to warrant such an episode. This is a poor and self-fulfilling argument. Logically, Dio's evidence suggests that AD 12 was not peaceful. It is only if we remove Dio that the year seems tranquil, an erroneous method for establishing historical fact. A more recent examination of the evidence has been made by A. D'Hautcourt, 'L'exile de Cassius Severus: hypothèse nouvelle', *Latomus*, 54:2 (1995), 315–18, who argues that the intensification of Cassius' exile to Seriphos mentioned in Tac. *Ann.* 4.21.6 belongs in 12 AD, and that the note in Tacitus under AD 24 actually refers to a re-

The elder Seneca was similarly certain about another Augustan orator, T. Labienus:

In hoc primum excogitata est nova poena; effectum est enim per inimicos ut omnes eius libri comburerentur: res nova et invisitata supplicium de studiis sumi... Eius qui hanc in scripta Labieni sententiam dixerat postea viventis adhuc scripta conbusta sunt: iam non malo exemplo quia suo.

It was for him that there was first devised a new punishment: his enemies saw to it that all his books were burnt. It was a new thing that punishments should be exacted from literature... he who supplied this opinion on Labienus' writings afterwards had his own writings burnt while still alive: no longer an evil penalty, once it became his.[63]

Bauman sidelined the problem of Labienus by tucking him away in a footnote: 'It is probable that no formal charges were preferred against Labienus and that the burning of his books was the only penalty inflicted on him. An extra-forensic remedy such as this was known in the Republic.'[64] Such extra-judicial remedies did occur during the Republic, but reference to a *senatus consultum* indicates a senatorial inquiry and the fact of a penalty implies that a *quaestio* followed.[65] Labienus suffered the penalty of a *lex* and the obvious candidate is the *lex maiestatis*.[66]

---

examination of Cassius' situation, with a verdict to continue to uphold the prior judgments. But this is to damage the natural meaning of Tacitus' words, which explicitly place Cassius' move to Seriphos in AD 24. Dio 56.27.1 refers moreover to multiple authors. The most plausible solution is to place Cassius' condemnation in AD 8, consider the situation in AD 12 to have been wholly unrelated, and place the intensification of Cassius Severus' punishment (from *relegatio* to *deportatio*) to AD 24.

[63] Sen. *Cont.* 10 prae. 5–6. *Eius* is unknown. The editor of the Loeb text suggested Cassius Severus, but see Sen. *Cont.* 10 prae. 8: *Cassi Severi, hominis Labieno invisissimi, belle dicta res ferebatur illo tempore quo libri Labieni ex senatus consulto urebantur: nunc me, inquit, vivum uri oportet qui illos edidici,* 'Cassius Severus, who was the greatest enemy of Labienus', had a beautiful saying that was in circulation at the time when Labienus' books were burnt by decree of the senate: 'Now they should burn me alive; I know those books by heart'. Severus was frankly impressed by Labienus' works, but his comment, as well as being witty, is critical of the decision to burn Labienus' books. Indeed, it points out the futility of such action, since ideas can transcend mere paper. Seneca, on the other hand, is clear that the individual who proposed the penalty was the one who lived to see his works burn. G. W. Clarke (1972), 77, placed Labienus' condemnation in AD 6, but there is no evidence to support this belief.

[64] R. A. Bauman (1974), 31, n. 42.

[65] Sen. *Cont.* 10 prae. 8.

[66] Inferred also by the nature of Labienus' death, Sen. *Cont.* 10 prae. 7: *Non tulit hanc Labienus contumeliam nec superstes esse ingenio suo voluit, sed in monimenta se maiorum suorum ferri iussit atque ita includi, veritus scilicet ne ignis qui nomini suo subiectus erat corpori negaretur: non finivit tantum se ipse sed etiam sepelivit,*

The decision to burn his books would have been discretionary, as was often the case when various forms of *damnatio memoriae* were implemented. But how can both Tacitus and Seneca be correct?

The most important evidence for Labienus comes from Seneca's *Controversiae*. The first is a reminiscence:

Memini aliquando, cum recitaret historiam, magnam partem illum libri convolvisse et dixisse: haec quae transeo post mortem meam legentur. Quanta in illis libertas fuit quam etiam Labienus extimuit!

I remember that once, when he was reciting his history, Labienus rolled up a good part of the book, saying: 'The sections I pass over will be read after my death' How great must have been their *libertas* if even Labienus was frightened of it![67]

Seneca was impressed by Labienus' reluctance, not simply because it was out of character, but because at least one other had already recited a politically sensitive history. Cremutius Cordus praised Cassius, Caesar's assassin, without reprimand from Augustus: Labienus' work must have been especially shocking.[68] The subject of his history is unknown, but reference to a Pompeian spirit, a signpost for ideological opposition, is noteworthy.[69]

Yet a sympathetic Pompeian history does not sufficiently explain his fate. Such things were an accepted activity, and were openly encouraged by Augustus.[70] Labienus must have gone well beyond sympathy and explicitly stated that the wrong side had won the civil war, and shown them as unworthy.[71] That Labienus refused to recite parts of his work publicly does not stand in the way of my hypothesis,

---

'Labienus did not take this insult nor did he wish to outlast his own genius, but he had himself carried into the tomb of his ancestors and walled-up, fearing that the fire which engrossed his books would be denied his body: he not only finished his own life, he buried himself.' Labienus' fear that fire might be denied to his own body, and his desire to bury himself, suggest a charge of *maiestas*, which would have brought with it either death or exile, which both prevented cremation and burial. Indeed, his suicide can be explained as an attempt to protect his testament from interference by the State, see also D. Hennig (1973), 251 f.

[67] Sen. *Cont*. 10 prae. 8.
[68] Tac. *Ann*. 4.34; Dio 57.24.2.
[69] Sen. *Cont*. 10 prae. 5. G. W. Clarke (1972), 77: 'an inveterate supporter of Pompey's cause'.
[70] Tac. *Ann*. 1.10.1 on Augustus: *simulatam Pompeianarum gratiam partium*.
[71] i.e. it was possible to sympathize with Pompey's cause, but openly to lament the victory of Caesar, and later Octavian, was an entirely different matter. Both evidence a 'Pompeian spirit'.

for they could have been seized after information was laid by a friend or slave, or even leaked after circulation among intimates. Either way, Labienus' histories were not merely defamatory but were interpreted as an incitement to sedition. An intention to incite sedition would usually have come under the heading *maiestas*, though the penalty of having one's literary works destroyed might still have been novel.[72] Cassius Severus, on the other hand, was charged with *maiestas* for libel, but not, *contra* Bauman, for anonymous libel.[73] Tacitus blames Cassius Severus' 'writings'; he makes no mention of them being anonymously written. Anecdotes of Cassius Severus show him to be openly vicious, to the point of enjoying his reputation as a slanderer.[74] His ego would not submerge even in exile![75] Cassius Severus marked a far more insidious development because he was charged with *overt* defamation, action that had always been examined through a civil procedure under the *lex Cornelia de iniuriis*. The prosecutors probably argued that some people (*alique*) - a group of people who could

---

[72] Cf. D. Hennig (1973), *passim*, who posits a charge *de famosis libellis*. The case of Cremutius Cordus does not contradict my approach. Tac. *Ann.* 4.34: *Cornelio Cosso Asinio Agrippa consulibus Cremutius Cordus postulatur novo ac tunc primum audito crimine, quod editis annalibus laudatoque M. Bruto C. Cassium Romanorum ultimum dixisset*, 'In the consulships of Cornelius Cossus and Asinius Agrippa, Cremutius Cordus was prosecuted for the new and hitherto unheard of crime of writing a history, praising Brutus and calling C. Cassius the last of the Romans.' The charge against Cordus cannot have been that of simply writing a history (which would have set an impossible precedent to police), but writing a history in which, by praising Brutus and calling Cassius the last of the Romans, he had diminished the majesty of the Roman people and its government, since it could be argued that he had de-legitimized the government. The charge was novel and obviously constructed for the purpose of delation, as is made clear in Seneca's *Consolatio Ad Marciam*; cf. R. H. Martin and A. J. Woodman (1989), 177 f. The commentators take Tacitus to mean that Cordus was the first to be charged with 'writing a history'. Aware that this contradicts Seneca's note concerning Labienus, they argue that Labienus was charged not with writing but with oratory. That is unlikely. Seneca states of Labienus' punishment: 'It was an unheard of novelty that punishment should be exacted from literature.' If he had been charged with offensive oratory, why were his books burned?

[73] R. A. Bauman (1974), 48 f.

[74] We know of at least two of Augustus' friends being attacked. Cassius Severus apparently wrote that Quintus Vitellius, a quaestor under Augustus and the father of the future emperor, was descended from a cobbler whose son, given to making money from confiscated estates, married a common wife (*mulier vulgaris*) Suet. *Vit.* 2; see also Sen. *Cont.* 2.4.11, and the preface of *Cont.* 3; Sen. *Suas.* 6.11; Quint. *Inst.* 10.1.116, 12.10.11 and 6.3.27, where jests are described *asperam*.

[75] Tac. *Ann.* 4.21.

be categorized - were subsumed under the *maiestas* of the Roman people.[76] This interpretation better explains a quote attributed to Tiberius some years later:

Sed et adversus convicia malosque rumores et famosa de se ac suis carmina firmus ac patiens, subinde iactabat in civitate libera linguam mentemque liberas esse debere; et quondam senatu cognitionem de eius modi criminibus ac reis flagitante: 'Non tantum' inquit 'otii habemus, ut implicare nos pluribus negotiis debeamus; si hanc fenestram aperueritis, nihil aliud agi sinetis; omnium inimicitiae hoc praetexto ad vos deferentur.'

But he was firm and patient even against insults, evil rumours and defamatory songs about himself and his own people; he sometimes let out that in a free society speech and thought should be free; and once, when the senate was demanding jurisdiction on crimes and criminals of that sort, he said: We do not have so much free time that we ought to get ourselves involved in extra business; if you open this window, you will leave room for no other business; the private enmities of everyone will be brought before you on this pretext.[77]

Fenestra shows that it is a question of interpreting the law. Clearly a 'loophole' was left which made prosecution possible; it is also obvious that overt libel is meant, especially *omnium inimicitiae*. It is not hard to envisage the evolution. Cassius Severus' prosecution rested on subsuming specific classes (senators, priests, decurions, etc., i.e. those later termed *honestiores*) under the *maiestas* of the State.[78] A window (*fenestra*) for senators to destroy personal enemies thus opened. Tiberius perceived the inherent dangers and in turn did not observe the precedent, with a 'take your personal squabbles elsewhere!'[79] That overt (or indeed anonymous) libel is never treated as *maiestas* in the juristic literature, but continued to be treated under

---

[76] Anonymous libel therefore never attracted a charge of *maiestas*, unless, of course, the victim were a magistrate or the princeps. It could be investigated in a public tribunal, but it made the perpetrator *intestabilis*. The idea that someone could be subjected to a public tribunal and yet suffer a penalty prescribed by a civil procedure is best explained by Paulus' reference to an *actio mixto iure*, PS. 5.4.8. Here, the action comes between the *iudicium publicum* and the *iudicium privatum*.

[77] Suet. *Tib.* 28.

[78] See P. Garnsey (1970), 221 f.

[79] Tac. *Ann.* 1.72 does not contradict this approach: *Mox Tiberius, consultante Pompeio Macro praetore an iudicia maiestatis redderentur, exercendas leges esse respondit. Hunc quoque asperavere carmina incertis auctoribus vulgata in saevitiam superbiamque eius et discordem cum matre animum*, 'Soon after Tiberius, to an inquiry put to the praetor, Pompeius Macer, whether the *maiestas* court should be

the heading *iniuria*,[80] is evidence that Tiberius' position was sustained. Only seditious writings/speeches and the defamation of the princeps or a magistrate remained within the cognizance of the *quaestio maiestatis*.[81] Bauman's argument that events in AD 6 led to the *lex Cornelia de iniuriis* being extended to cover the publication of anonymous defamatory writings, and that, two years later, such writings were judged to have diminished the majesty of the Roman people is probably wrong. Events in AD 6 were unrelated to the question of defamatory writing. They were related instead to the *lex maiestatis* in so far as it was the appropriate law for prosecuting acts of treason.

THE SEDITION OF TIBERIUS' RIVAL
L. AEMILIUS PAULLUS

As with the interpretation of T. Labienus' works, the βιβλία circulated by P. Rufus were held to be seditious (νεωτεροποιός), not defamatory.[82] There was no need to pass a decree extending the scope of the *lex de iniuriis*, for the *lex maiestatis* already covered such behaviour.

---

restored, responded that the law should carry on. Poems of unknown authorship satirising his savagery, arrogance, and his broken relationship with his mother, had also exasperated him.' The statement belongs to AD 15. It relates simply to seditious libel (was the princeps cruel) rather than private contumelies; see also Suet. *Tib.* 58. Pompeius Macer may have been asking whether *senatus consulta* relating to investigations into treason had superseded his courts' judgment; Tiberius said 'no'.

[80] A fragment of Cicero (*De re publica* 4.10.12), which is found in Augustine (*De Civit. Dei* 2.9) shows that defamation was a crime during Cicero's childhood: *nostrae contra duodecim tabulae cum perpaucas res capite sanxissent, in his hanc quoque sanciendam putaverunt, si quis occentavisset sive carmen condidisset quod infamiam faceret flagitiumve alteri*, 'Our twelve tables, on the other hand, though they provided the death penalty for only a few things, did provide it for any person who sang or composed a song which contained a slander or insult to anybody else.' Sulla probably included it in his *lex Cornelia de iniuriis*, at which point the penalty was perhaps downgraded.

[81] Cf. Seneca *De Beneficiis* 3.26.1. Seneca probably refers to the final period of Tiberius' Principate, or at least to the period of Sejanus' rule. For a case of written and spoken libel against the emperor as *maiestas*, see Tac. *Ann.* 14.48, for a recent discussion, see A. Yakobson 'Maiestas, the Imperial Ideology and the Imperial Family: The Evidence of the Senatus Consultum De Cn. Pisone Patre', *Eutopia*, 3: 1–2 (2003), 75–107.

[82] Dio 55.27.1.

94   *The Republic in Danger*

This approach better suits the mood. A highly stressed community will usually blame government when the conditions of life fail to improve. When Rome was gripped by famine in 40 BC, the triumvirs produced an edict establishing a tax on the sale of slaves and inheritance of legacies. People were furious. The edict was torn down amid violent protest. Octavian, while attempting to assuage an angry and bewildered crowd, was pelted with stones.[83] Fierce, even violent, resistance to taxation is not unusual during or in the wake of an economic disaster. But Rome had a history of such resistance even during periods of economic prosperity. Roman citizens had been exempt from most forms of taxation since 167 BC. Revenue was sourced instead from the taxation of provincials and the spoils of war.[84] As with protestors in 40 BC, the authors of the βιβλία probably treated the implementation of the inheritance tax within a discourse of oppression. Augustus had already asked senators to find a sufficient revenue source for the *aerarium militare*. Dio then adds:

ἀμέλει ἄλλων ἄλλα ἐσηγησαμένων ἐκείνων μὲν οὐδὲν ἐδοκίμασε, τὴν δ' εἰκοστὴν τῶν τε κλήρων καὶ τῶν δωρεῶν, ἃς ἂν οἱ τελευτῶντές τισι πλὴν τῶν πάνυ συγγενῶν ἢ καὶ πενήτων καταλείπωσι, κατεστήσατο, ὡς καὶ ἐν τοῖς τοῦ Καίσαρος ὑπομνήμασι τὸ τέλος τοῦτο γεγραμμένον εὑρών· ἐσῆκτο μὲν γὰρ καὶ πρότερόν ποτε, καταλυθὲν δὲ μετὰ ταῦτα αὖθις τότε ἐπανήχθη.

Of course when other men had proposed different schemes, he approved of none, but he established the *vicesima* on inheritances and legacies left by the dying to anyone except very close relatives or the poor, as though he had found the tax written down in Caesar's memoranda. For it had in fact been introduced once before, and having been abolished, was again introduced at this time.[85]

Senatorial submissions steered away from the taxation of citizens as a viable policy, as is evident from Augustus' response. Establishing an archaeology for the tax is a defensive manœuvre; unnecessary if the solution was widely held to be reasonable. That Augustus was obviously responsible for initiating the policy could not be disguised, but his invocation of Caesar (now deified and so beyond criticism) shows

---

[83] App. *BC* 5.67–8.
[84] Cic. *De Off.* 2.76; Plut. *Aemilius Paullus* 38; Val. Max. 4.3.8. The *tributum* was a direct tax on those citizens who could take up arms. It was a 'direct contribution assessed as a proportion of declared wealth', C. Nicolet (1980), 157.
[85] Dio 55.25.5–6.

an unwillingness to take full responsibility. The bolstering of legislation with forty-five-year-old credentials implies criticism. Senators with alternative revenue solutions and opposed to an inheritance tax on principle would be the most likely antagonists. At least one senator is linked to the critical βιβλία published a few months later: L. Aemilus Paullus.

In Dio's narrative rumour alone implicated P. Rufus, and the rumour was considered to be implausible.[86] 'Others' were thought to have been using Rufus' name.[87] If βιβλία were anonymous, then 'others' were evidently spreading the rumours. Nevertheless, as Suetonius makes clear, Rufus was unable to shake public suspicion.[88] He fell either as a double-crossed conspirator or an innocent victim. The only way to fit L. Aemilius Paullus into the picture is to count him as one of the 'others'. This would better explain the 'commotion' which followed the laying of information by informants. Allegations that an important member of the government had orchestrated the popular unrest would have been sensational, embarrassing many senators with close ties to the consul of AD 1.[89] Prior objection to the inheritance tax (whether in senatorial meetings or the *consilium principis*) would lend credence to the testimonies of informants. On this reading, his opponents in the senate argued that, on the basis of information from witnesses and in consideration of his manifest sympathy with ideas present in the βιβλία, Aemilius Paullus should be condemned for intending to incite sedition. The *quaestio maiestatis*,

---

[86] Dio 55.27.1.
[87] Ibid., 27.2.
[88] Suet. *Aug.* 19.
[89] Dio's silence is still a problem. I can only conclude that Dio either passed over the results of the inquiry or more likely followed a tradition which conflated the exile of Paullus with his wife the younger Julia (there is a lacuna in Dio's text for AD 8). The conspiracy of Cn. Cornelius Cinna Magnus (cos. AD 5) is an appropriate example. The younger Seneca placed the affair somewhere between 16 and 13 BC, while Dio placed it in AD 4. Badian is sceptical: 'On Cinna, his [Dio's] date of AD 4 is usually thought to be wrong, though Seneca's main reference is so full of mistakes in names, dates, ages and even the sequence of other conspiracies that it would be hazardous to believe him,' E. Badian (1982), 20–1. Significantly Dio is thought to have used Seneca as a source, M. Adler, 'Die Verschwörung des Cn. Cornelius Cinna bei Seneca und Cassius Dio', ZÖG, 60 (1909), 193–208; F. Millar, *Study of Cassius Dio* (1964), 78–9; M. T. Griffin, *Seneca: A Philosopher in Politics* (1976), 410 ff.; P. M. Swan (2004), 147–8. In both Dio and Seneca, Cinna Magnus plotted against Augustus. As with Cinna Magnus, Aemilius Paullus' story may have suffered in transmission; the details of his trial were obscured.

again in operation, agreed.[90] Most protestors probably wished only for a policy reversal and increased government assistance, but men like Aemilius Paullus had other motives.

Commotion in Rome apparently lasted until the food supply recovered and events to celebrate the memory of the elder Drusus were organized.[91] All public spectacles had been cancelled in August/September: games (provided by the elder Drusus' sons, Germanicus and Claudius) were probably supposed to alleviate general anxiety and restlessness.[92] Games were followed by a dedication of the temple of Castor and Pollux by Tiberius.[93] The dedication can be dated to 27 January AD 7, which, if correct, means that Tiberius returned to Rome from Illyricum to participate in some of the celebrations.[94] Dio knew of a more sinister interpretation:

τά τε γὰρ τῶν πολέμων ἅμα διώκει, καὶ ἐς τὴν πόλιν, ὁπότε παράσχοι, συνεχῶς ἐσεφοίτα, τὸ μέν τι πραγμάτων τινῶν ἕνεκα, τὸ δὲ δὴ πλεῖστον φοβούμενος μὴ ὁ Αὔγουστος ἄλλον τινὰ παρὰ τὴν ἀπουσίαν αὐτοῦ προτιμήσῃ.

And indeed, at the same time, Tiberius was carrying on with the business of war and was continually visiting the city, whenever he had the chance; this was partly on account of his business affairs, but mostly because he was afraid that, on account of his absence, Augustus would show preference to somebody else.[95]

Velleius returned to Rome late in AD 6 to enter the quaestorship, but was soon off to Tiberius in Illyricum as *legatus Augusti*.[96] Quaestors

---

[90] *Scholia in Iuvenalem* 6.158.
[91] Dio 55.27.3–4.
[92] Suet. *Claud.* 2.2; Pliny *NH* 2.96, 8.4.
[93] Dio 55.27.4; Suet. *Tib.* 20; *Fasti Praenestini* = V. Ehrenberg and A. H. M. Jones (1955), 46; Ovid *Fasti* 1.705–8.
[94] Suet. *Claud.* 2.2. Levick, B.; (1976), 327, n. 102; Dio places the dedication at the very end of AD 6, the *Fasti Praenestini* (V. Ehrenberg and A. H. M. Jones (1955), 46), and Ovid *Fasti* 1.705–8 give only the date: 27 Jan. P. M. Swan (2004), 185–6 postulates that Dio has erred by linking thematically two episodes concerned with the elder Drusus, i.e. dedication of the temple by Tiberius and the gladiatorial games put on by Germanicus and Claudius at end of AD 6. Swan thus dates the dedication to 27 Jan. AD 6. It is similarly possible however that Dio has dragged back to the end of AD 6 an event which in fact took place at the very beginning of AD 7, i.e. events were organized to celebrate the life of the elder Drusus over a period of 2–3 months.
[95] Dio 55.27.5.
[96] Vell. 2.111.4; at 2.104.3 Velleius tells us that towards the end of AD 4 he joined Tiberius in Germany as a *praefectus equitum* and that 'for nine continuous years . . . I was a spectator of his superhuman achievements'.

The Buck Stops Where?

designate were formally invested on 5 December, so that Tiberius must still have been in Illyricum when Velleius set out from Rome. Tiberius thus left camp for Rome no later than the first week of January. His policy in the years preceding is instructive. Velleius writes that in December AD 4: *pietas sua Caesarem paene obstructis hieme Alpibus in urbem traxit,* 'piety drew Caesar to the city, though the Alps were almost blocked because of winter'; in December AD 5 Tiberius: *eadem qua priore anno festinatione urbem petens,* 'sought the city with the same haste as the previous year'.[97] Returning to Rome 'with haste' in December AD 5 is understandable. The city was in chaos and the soldiers were threatening to strike. Remaining in camp until late December–January AD 6, regardless of the situation in Rome, was, however, intelligent policy. The stability of north-east Italy was uncertain, with Dalmatians having recently invaded Macedonia a second time.[98] Yet a contemporary opinion, surviving in Dio, shows that Tiberius' position was a topic of dispute:

Μαθὼν οὖν ταῦτα ὁ Αὔγουστος, καὶ ὑποπτεύσας ἐς τὸν Τιβέριον ὡς δυνηθέντα μὲν ἂν διὰ ταχέων αὐτοὺς κρατῆσαι, τρίβοντα δὲ ἐξεπίτηδες ἵν' ὡς ἐπὶ πλεῖστον ἐν τοῖς ὅπλοις ἐπὶ τῇ τοῦ πολέμου προφάσει ᾖ, πέμπει τὸν Γερμανικὸν καίτοι ταμιεύοντα, στρατιώτας οἱ οὐκ εὐγενεῖς μόνον ἀλλὰ καὶ ἐξελευθέρους δούς...

And so Augustus having learned these things, suspecting that Tiberius could have quickly defeated them but was delaying deliberately so that he might be under arms as long as possible on the pretext of war, sends out Germanicus [to Illyricum] although a quaestor, having granted him not only freeborn but also freedmen soldiers...[99]

Tiberius' enemies, who must have put forward this interpretation, were playing games.[100] Far from destabilising Tiberius' position, Germanicus was probably in the same boat as Velleius; both were quaestors attached to Tiberius as *legati Augusti*. To depict Tiberius as the new Salvidienus, desiring to possess the northern legions, was to assault his supporters in the senate and his relationship with Augustus.[101] The accusation ought to be considered in relation to

---

[97] Vell. 2.105.3; 2.107.3.   [98] Dio 55.30.6.   [99] Dio 55.31.1.

[100] B. Levick (1999), 327 f. E. Koestermann, 'Der pannonisch-dalmatinische krieg 6–9n. Chr.', *Hermes*, 81 (1953), 345–78 argues that Dio uses, intermittently, an anti-Tiberian source for this period, but P. M. Swan (2004), 204, points out that Dio's coverage of these years is, on the whole, pro-Tiberian.

[101] Appian *BC* 5.66; Dio 48.33.1; Suet. *Aug.* 66.1.

the circumstances of Tiberius' power. Not even a year had passed since senators had voted him the command, citing a need to protect the commonwealth from a full-scale northern invasion.[102] Augustus agreed, describing Tiberius in a letter as the 'sole defence of the Roman People' (*unicum p. R. praesidium*).[103] Since Illyricum already had a governor, Tiberius' *maius imperium* was extended to cover a larger region.[104] He was put in charge of every legion engaged in the action, which numbered ten of a total for the empire of twenty-eight.[105] Even if this extraordinary command was unanimously supported in the senate, Tiberius' opponents would necessarily have harboured serious misgivings. I propose that the anti-Tiberian rumours, attested for the end of the year, result from these misgivings. People were given to understand that Tiberius planned to seize power in a throwback to the civil wars.

The image of Tiberius the potentate was manipulated to insinuate a strained relationship with both Augustus and Germanicus. When Velleius described Tiberius' return to Rome in December AD 4 as pious, we must have the counter-argument.[106] Tiberius' enemies portrayed him as dishonest and his position weak; his supporters countered by insisting on a close and loyal relationship with Augustus. The accusation that he was planning rebellion appeared in the winter of AD 6/7, to which Dio attached his general explanation for Tiberius' behaviour: 'he was afraid that Augustus might take advantage of his absence to show preference to somebody else'.[107] Dio's statement is born, I believe, from a contemporary account which held that Tiberius faced a serious political rival. But identifying the rival has proved difficult. Levick suggests Agrippa, but that is a stretch.[108] Even with support he was too young, and others were above him in

---

[102] Vell. 2.111.2.
[103] Suet. *Tib*. 21.3.
[104] Tiberius' already possessed *maius imperium* in upper and lower Germany and possibly Gaul, but there is no evidence to suggest that it extended originally to Illyricum.
[105] Vell. 2.113.1; Dio 55.32.1; Suet. *Tib*. 16.1 puts the number at 15, but Velleius ought to be preferred.
[106] A. J. Woodman (1977), 141 suggests that Velleius intends to 'magnify this *pietas* by emphasising the difficulty of the winter journey'. It is certainly reminiscent of Tiberius' rushed journey to see his dying brother (Livy *Per*. 142; Pliny *NH* 7.48) and later his dying father (Vell. 2.123.1; Suet. *Tib*. 21.1).
[107] Dio 55.27.5.
[108] B. Levick (1976), 327 f. and (1999), 58 f.

the pecking order, 'viz'. Germanicus.[109] But Germanicus was also too young and, as his position as a subordinate *legatus* shows, could not yet be described as a threat. We require instead somebody with an impressive pedigree, sufficient experience, and in opposition to Tiberius. The most obvious candidate is again L. Aemilius Paullus.

If Aemilus Paullus had been close to Gaius Caesar, and then sought out his brother-in-law Agrippa, the hypothesis makes sense. Faced with irrelevance and obscurity, oppositional groups often turn to the manipulation of public fear and excitement as a weapon. Thus Aemilius Paullus used general discontent with the new tax and the war to erode public support for the administration. Βιβλία were distributed in combination with talk that Tiberius harboured seditious intent and that Augustus no longer trusted him. This was a trap: if Tiberius stayed in winter camp it was because he desired supreme power; if he came to Rome it was because Augustus favoured another. Tiberius nevertheless returned to Rome to expose the rumours as baseless. This was probably at the instigation of Augustus. Suetonius writes that during the Illyrian rebellion Tiberius was often recalled (*saepius revocaretur*).[110] Augustus probably decided to refute rumour with evidence; the people must see with their own eyes that Tiberius harboured no wicked scheme and that his relationship with Augustus was strong.[111] Dedicating the temple of Castor and Pollux served to reinforce the happy picture. Dio writes that Tiberius inscribed the temple with his and his brother's name. But he wrote his name as Ti. Iulius Augusti *f.* Caesar Claudianus.[112] No other extant inscription or text attests the use of the former *gentilicium* by Tiberius.[113] He was

---

[109] R. A. Birch (1981), 451.
[110] Suet. *Tib.* 16.2.
[111] Rumours suggesting a weakened relationship must be placed within a wider context. Suetonius, *Tib.* 21.2, knew of a tradition which believed that Augustus was unimpressed with Tiberius and secretly ridiculed him: *Scio vulgo persuasum quasi egresso post secretum sermonem Tiberio vox Augusti per cubicularios excepta sit*: '*Miserum populum R., qui sub tam lentis maxillis erit!*, I know that it is commonaly believed that after Tiberius had left the room, following the secret conversation, Augustus' voice was heard by the servants: "What misery for the Roman people, to be crushed by such slow moving jaws!" The influence of a late tradition aside, a belief that Augustus tolerated Tiberius would, logically, have appeared owing to the nature of Tiberius' retirement in 6 BC. Scepticism would have been a natural reaction to Tiberius' adoption.
[112] Dio 55.27.4.
[113] P. M. Swan (2004), 186.

evidently keen, at this moment, to advertise his Claudian ancestry, believing it to be, or hoping to make it, popular with the people - a Claudian event, putting on show even the future emperor Claudius, the family embarrassment. The symbolism, it was hoped, would be unmistakable: Augustus had made his choice; the future of Rome would rest with Livia's descendents, i.e. not Agrippa or, more importantly, Aemilius Paullus.[114] The fall of Aemilius Paullus provides us with a plausible explanation for the *abdicatio* of Agrippa and his transportation to Surrentum.

When dealing with the *abdicatio* of Agrippa, Dio wrote:

Τὸν δὲ δὴ Γερμανικόν, ἀλλ' οὐ τὸν Ἀγρίππαν ἐπὶ τὸν πόλεμον ἐξέπεμψεν, ὅτι δουλοπρεπής τε ἐκεῖνος ἦν καὶ τὰ πλεῖστα ἡλιεύετο, ὅθενπερ καὶ Ποσειδῶνα ἑαυτὸν ἐπωνόμαζε, τῇ τε ὀργῇ προπετεῖ ἐχρῆτο, καὶ τὴν Λιουίαν ὡς μητρυιὰν διέβαλλεν, αὐτῷ τε τῷ Αὐγούστῳ πολλάκις ὑπὲρ τῶν πατρῴων ἐπεκάλει. Καὶ οὐ γὰρ ἐσωφρονίζετο, ἀπεκηρύχθη, καὶ ἥ τε οὐσία αὐτοῦ τῷ στρατιωτικῷ ταμιείῳ ἐδόθη, καὶ αὐτὸς ἐς Πλανασίαν τὴν πρὸς Κύρνῳ νῆσον ἐνεβλήθη.

He sent Germanicus and not Agrippa to the war because the latter was low minded and spent most of his time in fishing, on account of which he used to call himself Poseidon; and he used to give way to violent anger and insulted Livia as 'stepmother', and he often accused Augustus himself regarding his inheritance, and since he was not of moderate mind he was made an *abdicatus* and his property was handed over to the military treasury, and he was himself exiled to Planasia, an island near Corsica.[115]

Dio has telescoped Agrippa's life from AD 5–7 into one episode, but, by reference to Germanicus' commission as a *legatus Augusti*, Agrippa's demise can be tentatively dated. If Germanicus was commissioned between December AD 6 and early AD 7, we can place Agrippa's *abdicatio* towards the end of AD 6, i.e. about the time that Aemilius Paullus was exposed and prosecuted. A close relationship with his much older brother-in-law would explain why Agrippa was removed

---

[114] It is interesting to note that by highlighting *Claudianus* Tiberius could point out a historical connection to the Cornelii, Valerii, Fabii, and even the Aemilii. Julia's children had no such Republican tradition and had to draw on Aeneas and his offspring. Perhaps L. Aemilius Paullus advertised himself as a superior candidate on account of his heritage, or compared himself to one of his famous ancestors, most notably the consul of 182 and 168 BC. For a discussion of this family in late Republican politics, see T. P. Wiseman, 'Rome and the Resplendent Aemilii', in T. P. Wiseman (ed.), *Roman Drama and Roman History*, (1988), 106–20.

[115] Dio 55.32.1 f.

200 km from Rome but not from *patria potestas*.[116] Poor behaviour was declared the reason for *abdicatio*, but behind the pretext lay concern that Agrippa was a liability. He was almost 18, old enough to have strong political opinions, no matter how naïve. He was deemed unsuitable for a high profile public career. He could not be trusted in Rome, or, indeed, anywhere as a free man. It was soon evident to Augustus, however, that Agrippa posed an even more serious threat. He was relegated to the island of Planasia and placed under military guard.

---

[116] Cf. R. A. Birch (1981), 451: 'The first punishment—'abdicatio' and removal to Surrentum—was a curious mixture of extreme severity and surprising leniency... exile in Surrentum was presumably comfortable, probably very comfortable, and as favourable a sentence of this kind as could have been imposed.' Birch has erred by relying on Levick's interpretation of *abdicatio*.

6

Augustus' Final Arrangements

THE *RELEGATIO* OF AGRIPPA

Abdicatio denied Agrippa an income, while confinement in Surrentum prevented interaction with the happenings of Rome. The decision then, after a mere several months, to transport Agrippa to an isolated island off the coast of Corsica and place him under military guard signals a dramatic change in the political climate. It was evidently agreed by Augustus and Tiberius that Agrippa could undermine, or be used to undermine, their plans. We must keep this in mind when considering the evidence.

Velleius writes

Hoc fere tempore Agrippa . . . mira pravitate animi atque ingenii in praecipitia conversus patris atque eiusdem avi sui animum alienavit sibi, moxque crescentibus in dies vitiis dignum furore suo habuit exitum.

About this time Agrippa . . . alienated from himself the affection of his father who was also his grandfather, falling into reckless ways by an amazing depravity of attitude and intellect; and soon, as his vices increased daily, he met the end which his madness deserved.[1]

Plutarch writes:

καὶ ὅτι τῶν μὲν δυεῖν αὐτῷ θυγατριδῶν ἀπολωλότων Ποστουμίου [sic] δ' ὃς ἔτι λοιπός ἐστιν ἐκ διαβολῆς τινος ἐν φυγῇ . . .

'Two of his [Augustus'] grandsons being dead and Postumus, the one surviving, being in exile because of some false accusation . . .'[2]

---

[1] Vell. 2.112.7.   [2] Plut. *De Garrul.* 508.

104   *The Republic in Danger*

Tacitus writes

Nam senem Augustum devinxerat adeo, uti nepotem unicum, Agrippam Postumum, in insulam Planasiam proiecerit, rudem sane bonarum artium et robore corporis stolide ferocem, nullius tamen flagitii conpertum.

For she [Livia] had tied down the aged Augustus to such an extent that he flung on the island of Planasia his only grandson, Agrippa Postumus, who was uncultivated in the arts of virtue and stupidly wild in the strength of his body, but who had nevertheless been convicted of no crime.[3]

Suetonius writes

Agrippam nihilo tractabiliorem, immo in dies amentiorem, in insulam transportavit saepsitque insuper custodia militum. Cavit etiam s.c. ut eodem loci in perpetuum contineretur.

As Agrippa became no more manageable, but rather each day became more uncontrollable, he [Augustus] transported him to an island and, moreover, confined him in military custody. He even took the precaution, by *senatus consultum*, that Agrippa should be confined in that same place for all time.[4]

Aurelius Victor writes

Quamquam alii scribant dolo Liviae exstinctum metuentis, ne, quia privignae filium Agrippam, quem odio novercali in insulam relegaverat, reduci compererat, eo summam rerum adepto poenas daret.

Yet some write that [Augustus] was killed by a deception of Livia, who, since she had gained information that Agrippa (the son of her stepdaughter, whom, as a result of his mother-in-law's hatred, she had relegated to an island)[5] was to be recalled, feared that, when he had obtained control of affairs, she would be punished.[6]

And finally the Scholiast on Juvenal writes

Post revocata cum semet vitiis [Julia] addixisset, perpetuo exilio damnata est supplicio. Huius Agrippa frater propter morum feritatem in Sicilia <insulam> ab Augusto relegatus est, post cuius mortem iussu Tiberii interfectus est. 2) Berenice, soror Ptolom<a>ei; verum neptis Augusti Iulia, cum qua (Agrippa) commisit incestum et propterea ab Augusto relegatus est.

---

[3] Tac. *Ann.* 1.3.
[4] Suet. *Aug.* 65.4.
[5] It is possible to read 'she had relegated to an island'. If so, it would be evidence of a moral argument.
[6] *Epitome de Caesaribus* 1.27.

Augustus' Final Arrangements

After being recalled, when she [Julia] had abandoned herself to her vices, she was condemned to the punishment of perpetual exile. Augustus relegated her brother Agrippa to an island near Sicily for wildness of conduct, after whose death he was put to death by order of Tiberius. 2) Berenice the sister of Ptolemy; but Julia, granddaughter of Augustus, with whom Agrippa committed incest and for that reason was relegated by Augustus.[7]

It is important to note the following: (i) Agrippa was at Surrentum when events causing his relegation occurred; (ii) behavioural problems were somehow linked to Agrippa's relegation; (iii) a tradition held that Livia was somehow to blame; (iv) Tacitus was certain that Agrippa was not convicted of a crime; (v) Plutarch believed that a false accusation played a part; and (vi) a *senatus consultum* was used to legalize Agrippa's incarceration. The evidence is obviously contradictory. The reasons provided for Agrippa's *relegatio* do not satisfactorily explain his treatment. A military guard indicates a political dimension, but our evidence cites only family quarrels. Tacitus was sure that Agrippa was convicted of *no crime*, and he is supported by Suetonius' belief that a *senatus consultum* provided official weight to what was, in fact, the punishment of a son by his father (the senate was probably cognizant on the issue of military custody).[8] The reason given at the time by Augustus must be a pretext, beneath which lay more sensational information. It is simply unbelievable that an insult hurled from Surrentum attracted a *senatus consultum* approving incarceration on an island. We must therefore revisit the existing political climate.

Dio states that in AD 7 the public was distressed by both war and the continuing food shortage. He continues:

καὶ ἐπί γε τῇ σιτοδείᾳ δύο αὖθις ἐκ τῶν ὑπατευκότων ἐπιμελητὰς τοῦ σίτου σὺν ῥαβδούχοις ἀπέδειξε. προσδεόμενος δὲ δὴ χρημάτων ἔς τε τοὺς πολέμους καὶ ἐς τὴν τῶν νυκτοφυλάκων τροφήν, τό τε τέλος τὸ τῆς πεντηκοστῆς ἐπὶ τῇ τῶν ἀνδραπόδων πράσει ἐσήγαγε, καὶ τὸ ἀργύριον τὸ τοῖς στρατηγοῖς τοῖς τὰς ὁπλομαχίας ποιοῦσιν ἐκ τοῦ δημοσίου διδόμενον ἐκέλευσε μηκέτ' ἀναλίσκεσθαι.

---

[7] *Scholia in Iuvenalem* 6.158.
[8] Cf. W. Weber *Princeps* I (1936), 37 f.; J. D. Lewis, 'Primum facinus novi principatus?' in *Auckland Classical Essays presented to E. M. Blaikock* (1970), 165–84; S. Jameson (1975), 309f., who all take the *senatus consultum* plus exile to equal *maiestas* and interdiction.

And in view of the dearth of grain he appointed two ex-consuls as supervisors of the grain supply with lictors. And since he needed money for the wars and for the support of the *vigiles* he introduced a two per cent tax on the sale of slaves and ordered that the silver being given from the *aerarium* to the praetors producing gladiatorial shows no longer be expended.[9]

An inscription dated to August implies widespread anxiety about the food supply:

feriae quod eo die arai Cereri Matri et Opi Augustae ex voto suscepto constituta[e] sunt Cretico et Long. C[os].

Holidays, because on this day altars of Mother Ceres and *Ops Augusta*, in accordance with a vow having been undertaken, were consecrated while Creticus and Longus were consuls.[10]

Dio's notice can be assigned to July and August. A low crop yield is implied by a dedication to the goddess of agriculture, while employing commissioners evidences a rationalization of the market.[11] Moreover, 2 per cent on the sale of slaves no doubt caused resentment and cries of abuse, especially if the burden was passed on to consumers.[12] More importantly, however, Dio's 'distressed by war' could compress in a few words the enduring success of the anti-Tiberian position as it developed throughout the previous year: it was still held that Tiberius harboured evil ambition. If criticism of Augustus' government and the implementation of the new tax do belong to July and August AD 7, it may explain a violent election season.

Dio explains how in AD 8 Augustus' ill health reduced his capacity for full participation in public life:

τότε δὲ τῇ μὲν γερουσίᾳ καὶ ἄνευ ἑαυτοῦ τὰ πολλὰ δικάζειν ἐπέτρεπεν, ἐς δὲ τὸν δῆμον οὐκέτι παρῄει, ἀλλὰ τῷ μὲν προτέρῳ ἔτει πάντας τοὺς ἄρξοντας

---

[9] Dio 55.31.4. The *vigiles* were paid from the *Aerarium Saturni* (Dio 55.26.5), as were the praetors, to put on gladiatorial shows. Increased revenue and spending cuts show that the *Aerarium Saturni* was under considerable stress; mention of *Ops Augusta* on 10 Aug. might indicate that Augustus put in some money of his own.

[10] *Fasti Amiternini* = V. Ehrenberg and A. H. M. Jones (1955), 50.

[11] G. Rickman (1980), 63 f.

[12] Tac. *Ann.* 1.78, in AD 15, is a good example: *Centesimam rerum venalium post bella civilia institutam, deprecante populo edixit Tiberius militare aerarium eo subsidio niti...*, 'When the 1 per cent tax on auctioned goods, which was instituted after the civil wars, caused popular protest, Tiberius stated that the military treasury depended on it...'.

αὐτός, ἐπειδήπερ ἐστασιάζετο, ἀπέδειξε, τούτῳ δὲ καὶ τοῖς ἔπειτα γράμματά τινα ἐκτιθεὶς συνίστη τῷ τε πλήθει καὶ τῷ δήμῳ ὅσους ἐσπούδαζε.

At this time Augustus was allowing the senate to try most cases without him, and he no longer went out before the people, but in the year before he had himself declared all those who were to hold office, because there was disorder, but in this and the following years, having posted up certain bulletins, he would recommend to the plebs and to the people those whom he supported.[13]

Στάσις can mean 'sedition' and 'discord', or even describe a party with a revolutionary platform. Popular anger at the carrying out of the war, the low food supply, and taxation are possible causes. With public spectacles again suspended owing to stress on the treasury, elections provided the one opportunity for most citizens to publicize frustration.[14] Disgust with electoral legislation passed two years earlier, which lessened the impact of the popular vote, may have fuelled the outpouring of violence.

THE *LEX VALERIA CORNELIA*

Five fragments from an inscription found in Etruria in 1947 and 1951, which make up the so-called *Tabula Hebana*, cite electoral legislation passed in AD 5 titled the *lex Valeria et Cornelia*. Augustus is credited with reinstating the popular elections of the Republic in 27 BC. Most elections were in theory open contests, though it should be noted that Augustus continued to hold the consulship until 22 BC. In practice, however, the power of Augustus' personality set apart the elections of the Principate from those of the Republic:

Τοὺς γοῦν ἄρξοντας τοὺς μὲν αὐτὸς ἐκλεγόμενος προεβάλλετο, τοὺς δὲ καὶ ἐπὶ τῷ δήμῳ τῷ τε ὁμίλῳ κατὰ τὸ ἀρχαῖον ποιούμενος ἐπεμελεῖτο ὅπως μήτ' ἀνεπιτήδειοι μήτ' ἐκ παρακελεύσεως ἢ καὶ δεκασμοῦ ἀποδεικνύωνται.

And so as for those who were to hold office, he would select some himself and nominate them; and leaving others to the people and to the plebs,

---

[13] Dio 55.34.2.   [14] Dio 55.31.4.

according to ancient tradition, he would take care that no one should be appointed who was unsuitable nor as a result of faction or bribery.[15]

'Traditional way' refers to the electoral process after the reform of the 'Servian' system in or after 241 BC.[16] The electoral procedure during the Republic is a topic of dispute, and, as such, will not be examined here.[17] It is enough to say that there were 193 centuries, drawn from juniors and seniors in five property classes. One century was chosen by lot from the juniors in the first property class to vote first, known as the *praerogativa*.[18] Since Romans counted units (i.e. centuries), rather than the number of votes overall, candidates were elected in descending order from the first to win 97 units to the last, which apparently required, at the very least, the support of the first and second property class.[19] Importantly, the *praerogativa* was thought to have influence over the voting of those that followed.

The property qualification of the first class in the late Republic is unknown; scholars have suggested figures from HS 100,000 to HS 25,000.[20] It no doubt included a range of socio-economic levels from the extremely wealthy to those of modest prosperity well below the equestrian level. The lot, a neutralizing agent thought to reflect divine will, ensured that the privilege of voting in the *praerogativa* was shared by many.[21] Dionysius of Halicarnassus described

---

[15] Dio 53.21.7, trans. by J. W. Rich (1990), 51.
[16] Livy 1.42.4, 1.43.13; Cic. *De Re Pub.* 2.39–40; Dion. *Ant.* 4.16–21, 7.59.2–8. For discussion, see Th. Mommsen, *Staat.*³ (1887–8), 240–99; E. S. Staveley, 'Cicero and the Comitia Centuriata', *Historia*, 11 (1962), 299–314; L. R. Taylor, *Roman Voting Assemblies* (1966), 85 f.; A. Yakobson, *Elections and Electioneering in Rome*, Historia Einzelschriften Heft, 128 (1999), 54 f.
[17] A good discussion of the various views can be found in A. Yakobson (1999).
[18] For its influence, with some exaggeration, see Cic. *Pro Plancio* 20.49: *An tandem una centuria praerogativa tantum habet auctoritatis ut nemo umquam prior eam tulerit, quin renuntiatus sit aut iis ipsis comitiis consul, aut certe in illum annum*, 'The century which votes first carries of itself such weight that no candidate for the consulship has ever secured its vote without being ultimately declared first consul either at that very election or at any rate for the following year.' Cicero would not make this statement if it were held by many to be obviously false. People must necessarily have believed it to be at least partially true.
[19] Cic. *Phil.* 2.82–3.
[20] A. Yakobson (1999), 44, esp. n. 62, provides an assessment of the various hypotheses.
[21] R. Stewart, *Public Office in Early Rome: Ritual Procedure and Political Practice* (1999), ch 1, and L. R. Taylor (1966), 73 f., show evidence that the lot is taken to be divine. Cf. N. Rosenstein, 'Sorting Out the Lot in Republican Rome', *AJP*, 116:1 (1995), 43–75.

the reformed system as 'more democratic' (than the Servian system), (εἰς τὸ δημοτικώτερον).²²

Dio understands his source/s to mean that the above system was again used after 27 BC and that the system was somehow transformed to accommodate the discretionary power of Augustus. Προεβάλλετο is a disputed term. Most scholars refer to it as *commendatio*, but Swan has shown that Dio uses the term to mean 'nominate' rather than 'commend', for which συνιστάναι is used.²³ Whatever Dio had in mind, it is clear that 'some' canvassed with imperial sponsorship. These are probably the Candidates of Caesar (*candidati Caesaris*), of whom there were usually four.²⁴ Aside from the appearance of *candidati Caesaris*, elections under Augustus before AD 5 were, therefore, conducted in a fashion similar to those of the Republic. The *lex Valeria Cornelia* altered this 'more democratic' system. Ten centuries, voting simultaneously, were employed as a prerogatory group. They were known as the *centuriae C. et L. Caesarum* after Gaius and Lucius and were made up of 600 senators and 3,000 equites, not the *equites equo publico* but older men who were eligible to judge criminal cases.²⁵ The reform was, in effect, a throwback to the timocratic principle of the Servian system. A wealthy class was privileged and their dominance made structural.²⁶

---

²² Dion. *Ant.* 4.21.3. Some have taken this to be a reference to the *lex Valeria Cornelia*: G. Tibiletti *Principe et Magistrati repubblicani* (1953), 60 f.; P. Fraccaro, 'La Procedura del voto nei comizi tributi romani', *Opuscula*, 2 (1957), 235–54; E. S. Staveley, *Greek and Roman Voting and Elections* (1972), 129.

²³ P. M. Swan, 'Προβαλλεσθαι in Dio's Account of Elections under Augustus', *CQ*, 32:2 (1982), 436–40. Προβαλλεσθαι=Dio 44.11.4; 54.17.1; 54.30.2; 55.13.3; 60.3.2; 60.15.1: Συνιστάναι=37.44.3; 55.34.2; 58.20.3.

²⁴ Vell. 2.124.4. Tac. *Ann.* 1.15: ... *moderante Tiberio ne plures quam quattuor candidatos commendaret sine repulsa et ambitu designandos*, '... Tiberius limiting himself to the recommendation of no more than four candidates, to be designated without rejection or competition.' Tiberius must here be following an Augustan precedent, see A. H. M. Jones, 'The Elections under Augustus', *JRS*, 45 (1955), 9–21; D. C. A. Shotter, 'Elections under Tiberius', *CQ*, 16:2 (1966), 321–32; A. J. Holladay, 'The Election of Magistrates in the Early Principate', *Latomus*, 37 (1978), 874–93, esp. 88.

²⁵ M.H. Crawford (ed.), *Roman Statutes I*, BICS Supplement 64 (1996), 507–47, for Tabula Hebana, see specifically 519–21 and 530–2. On the status of the eligible equestrians, see A. H. M. Jones (1955), 15 f. We do not know how the change affected other parts of the *comitia centuriata*. Senators and many equites had voted in the first class, but the first class was not necessarily reduced by ten centuries. Either way the innovation had definite consequences.

²⁶ The emergence of this oligarchy was organic, not grounded in the Augustan period. Many new equestrians in the Augustan age probably owed their station to the

Brunt supposed that the law was introduced to satisfy equestrian pride, but that is implausible.[27] The beneficiaries of the legislation posed no threat to the government, indeed, they had already profited greatly from Augustus' administrative revolution. A band of elderly equestrians demanding the right to vote first at elections would have been quickly, and safely, ignored. It makes more sense to believe that Augustus was attempting to take greater control of the elections. Brunt based his criticism of this approach on the consul lists for the period immediately before AD 5: they show, as far as we can tell, that Augustus would have been pleased with those elected.[28] But this is inadequate. We possess the names of relatively few praetors, aediles, and quaestors for the same period. Under 27 BC Dio writes:

ὅ τε δῆμος ἐς τὰς ἀρχαιρεσίας καὶ τὸ πλῆθος αὖ συνελέγετο· οὐ μέντοι καὶ ἐπράττετό τι ὃ μὴ καὶ ἐκεῖνον ἤρεσκε . . . ἐπεμελεῖτο ὅπως μήτ' ἀνεπιτήδειοι μήτ' ἐκ παρακελεύσεως ἢ καὶ δεκασμοῦ ἀποδεικνύωνται.

The people and plebs were still meeting for elections, but nothing was done which did not please him (Augustus) also . . . he took care that no one should be appointed who was unsuitable or as a result of faction or bribery.[29]

Two points are necessary. First, no example of Augustus removing a candidate from the ballot is recorded before the inception of the *lex Valeria Cornelia*. The only instance recorded in which Augustus personally chose the candidates is, in fact, the elections of AD 7; an episode which survives only in Dio. Dio has probably erred by inferring a substantive policy from an isolated episode. The removal of candidates for bribery or factional violence is, moreover, unrelated to the removal of 'undesirables'. Accusations of bribery could be used as a pretext, but evidence suggests that bribery did, in fact, occur and was cause for concern.[30] We should not consider the removal of candidates on suspicion of criminal activity as evidence for Augustus'

---

ambitions of their father, grandfather, or great-grandfather. C. Nicolet, *L'Ordre équestre à l'époque républicaine* (312–43 av. J.-C.), I (1996); S. Demougin (1988), *passim*; E. Gabba, 'The Roman Professional Army from Marius to Augustus', in *Republican Rome: The Armies and the Allies*, trans. by P. J. Cuff, (1976), 20–69.

[27] P. Brunt, 'The Lex Valeria Cornelia', *JRS*, 51 (1961), 71–83.
[28] Ibid., 74f. He points out that the proportion of established *nobiles* and new *nobiles* who reached the consulship remained the same in the periods 5 BC to AD 5 and AD 6 to AD 15; as did the number of *novi homines* in the suffect consulship.
[29] Dio 53.21.6–7.
[30] Tac. *Ann*. 1.15.

ability to control the *comitia* every year. The second point refers to the comment: 'nothing was done that did not please him also'. Augustus would have surely congratulated all the successful candidates. To rebuke the *comitia* for electing an eligible candidate would have made ridiculous his claim that free elections had been restored. Dio is confused. He accepts the claim that free elections were reintroduced, but interprets Augustus' public approval of those elected as proof that he was secretly pulling the strings.[31] If we accept that Augustus' power over the *comitia* was not certain, then the introduction of the *lex Valeria Cornelia* explains itself. A passage from Velleius describing events in 19 BC is instructive:

Praeclarum excellentis viri factum C. Sentii Saturnini circa ea tempora consulis ne fraudetur memoria... tum in comitiis habendis praecipuum egit consulem: nam et quaesturam petentes, quos indignos iudicavit profiteri vetuit, et, cum id facturos se perseverarent, consularem, si in campum descendissent, vindictam minatus est, et Egnatium florentem favore publico sperantemque ut praeturam aedilitati, ita consulatum praeturae se iuncturum, profiteri vetuit et, cum id non obtinuisset, iuravit, etiam si factus esset consul suffragiis populi, tamen se eum non renuntiaturum.

The admirable deed of an excellent man, C. Sentius Saturninus, who was consul around this time [19 BC], should not be lost to memory... in holding the elections he acted as a distinguished consul: for he would not allow those seeking the quaestorship whom he judged unworthy to put forward their names as candidates, and when they persevered, he threatened that if they

---

[31] An approach subsequently accepted by modern scholars. It is commonly held that Augustus could have controlled the elections, but chose not to: A. H. M. Jones (1955), 11 f. P. Brunt (1961), 78 f.; B. Levick, 'Imperial Control of the Elections Under the Early Principate: Commendatio, Suffragatio, Nominatio', *Historia*, 16 (1967), 207–30, esp. 226–7; A. J. Holladay (1978), 885 f. But even if Augustus was able to control, *de facto*, the list of successful candidates read by the presiding magistrate, it does not follow that he could control the *comitia*. Any eligible candidate could write themselves into, or be written into, the election without prior approval from the presiding magistrate, thus Tiberius' policy described at Tac. *Ann.* 1.81: *Plerumque eos tantum apud se professos disseruit, quorum nomina consulibus edidisset; posse et alios profiteri, si gratiae aut meritis confiderent*, 'Generally he declared that no one had applied to him for nomination, except those whose names he had divulged to the consuls; others were still able to apply, if they had confidence in their influence or merits.' Tacitus was sceptical, but his scepticism is tempered by his own admission of confusion: *De comitiis consularibus, quae tum primum illo principe ac deinceps fuere, vix quicquam firmare ausim: adeo diversa non modo apud auctores, sed in ipsius orationibus reperiuntur*, 'Concerning the consular elections, from the first to the last of this Principate, I can hardly provide any positive statement: so different is the evidence, not only in the authors [of history] but in Tiberius' own speeches.'

came down to the Campus Martius he would exercise his consular power to punish them, and he would not allow Egnatius, who was flourishing in popular favour and was expecting his consulship to immediately follow his praetorship as his praetorship had immediately followed his aedileship, to register his name as a candidate, and when this would not work, he swore an oath that if Egnatius was made consul by the votes of the people he would not publicly declare him elected.[32]

Refusing to receive 'unworthy' candidates had little effect. Candidates could 'write' themselves into, or be written into, the election. But the presiding magistrate could not be made to announce a result. Saturninus was thus forced to use his power as the presiding officer to thwart a popular movement in full swing. Dio's narrative shows why obstruction was deemed necessary:

Ὑπάτευε μὲν δὴ ἐν τῷ ἔτει ἐκείνῳ Γάιος Σέντιος· ἐπεὶ δὲ καὶ τὸν συνάρξοντα αὐτῷ προσαποδειχθῆναι ἔδει (ὁ γὰρ Αὔγουστος οὐδὲ τότε τηρηθεῖσάν οἱ τὴν ἀρχὴν ἐδέξατο), στάσις τε αὖθις ἐν τῇ Ῥώμῃ συνηνέχθη καὶ σφαγαὶ συνέβησαν, ὥστε τοὺς βουλευτὰς φρουρὰν τῷ Σεντίῳ ψηφίσασθαι. ἐπειδή τε μὴ ἠθέλησεν αὐτῇ χρήσασθαι, πρέσβεις πρὸς τὸν Αὔγουστον, μετὰ δύο ῥαβδούχων ἕκαστον, ἔπεμψαν.

Indeed, Gaius Sentius was consul that year. And when it became necessary to have a colleague appointed in addition to him (for Augustus did not accept at that time either the office which had been kept for him), disorder again broke out in Rome and killings occurred, such that the senators voted for a guard for Sentius. When he refused to use it, they sent envoys to Augustus, each with two lictors.[33]

The election of a replacement consul probably occurred early in the year, which would explain why the quaestorian elections were also troublesome. The motive behind Egnatius' rejection was political, but the explanation was legal. He had breached the *lex annalis*.[34] Velleius states that Egnatius' praetorship followed immediately (*continuare*) after his aedileship, and that he was hoping for the consulship to

---

[32] Vell. 2.92.   [33] Dio 54.10.1.
[34] Dio 55.20.1 f. Dio, in what is certainly a reconstructed speech put into the mouth of Augustus in 29 BC, tells us that Augustus made alterations to the *lex annalis*. The quaestorship could be reached at 25 and the praetorship at 30. We are told also that the aedileship or tribunate were to be held in the intervening years (though patricians were exempted), see G. V. Sumner, 'The Lex Annalis under Caesar', *Phoenix*, 25:3 (1971), 246–71. A *biennium* had never been required for plebian offices; a one-year interval sufficed: the minimum age for the tribunate or aedileship was thus 26.

follow his praetorship immediately.[35] Similarly, Dio writes: 'he had been elected praetor illegally'.[36] Egnatius must have held the aedileship in 21 BC and the praetorship in 20 BC.[37] Though he did not participate in the consular elections of 20 BC for the consular year 19 BC, his participation in the extraordinary election of January 19 BC defied the required *biennium* stipulated by the *lex annalis*. This provided just grounds for Saturninus' intervention, which was not an abuse of arbitrary power. Egnatius had simply not satisfied the legal requirements.[38] This tells us nothing about arbitrary interference in the elections.

The quaestorian elections, on the other hand, are more instructive. If the quaestorian elections were held around the same time as the election for a replacement consul, they may have been affected by the violence and murders cited by Dio. Egnatius was a popular figure, and may have supported candidates for the quaestorship. Either way, when Saturninus threatened those who set foot inside the Campus Martius with consular power, he was no doubt acting *pro re publica*. A *senatus consultum* providing an armed escort certainly looks like an emergency. For a government seeking popularity, this option was untenable in the long term. The *lex Valeria Cornelia* was supposed to be the final solution. Faith was placed in equestrians, who were qualified to dispense justice, to vote responsibly. That their role became fixed is significant. Every election by the *comitia centuriata* would be led by the same people from the same cross-section of

---

[35] Vell. 2.91.3, 92.4; Dio 53.24.4-6.

[36] Dio 53.24.4-5.

[37] H. A. Andersen, *Cassius Dio und die Begründung des Principates* (1938), 29, n. 74, argues for an aedileship in 22 and a praetorship in 21. J. W. Rich (1990), 159, following Andersen, concludes that 'Egnatius did not literally seek to join the consulship to the praetorship, but his candidature was in breech of the legal two-year interval.' But that is to read Velleius *contra naturam*; he clearly means *the next year*. Andersen's approach is an attempt to reconcile Dio and Velleius, since Dio, though he places Egnatius' aedileship in 26 BC, seems also to provide a place for Egnatius' aedileship in 22, the year in which, according to Dio, Augustus gave instruction to the aediles about fire-fighting (54.2.4). Dio's dating is clearly a mess on this point, and I believe we are best served by sticking with Velleius.

[38] When members of the imperial family were in breach of the *lex annalis*, they received the senate's dispensation. The election of Gaius to the consulship in 6 BC is anomalous, but even he had to wait while a *senatus consultum* was procured which allowed him to take the consulship five years hence. Egnatius was infringing what had become the privilege of the *domus Caesaris* alone.

society every year. The elimination of the lot as a neutral device is important.

The lot could inspire voters to interpret the vote of the *praerogativa* as the will of destiny. The vote of the *centuriae Caesarum*, on the other hand, could not be interpreted in this way. It must have been viewed as a timocracy tied to the government: the 'democratic' traditions of the Republic set aside to gratify and co-opt a wealthy class. It no longer represented the will of the gods, but the will of the *domus Caesaris* (they were indeed the *centuriae Caesarum*). The legislation may not have been implemented in time for the elections in AD 5, while the elections in AD 6 may have suffered from the emergencies affecting Rome. It is, therefore, conceivable that the elections in AD 7 were the first to experience the full force of the legislation. Στάσις attested for the election season of AD 7 could evidence a popular backlash.

THE ELECTIONS OF AD 7

We do not know what election was affected or at what point in the election process Augustus intervened. I nevertheless propose that Augustus intervened only after the *centuriae Caesarum* had voted. Dio uses the verb ἀπέδειξε to explain the manner of Augustus' intervention. Cary, in the Loeb edition, translates it with 'appointed', while Swan, in his recent commentary, uses 'designated'.[39] The discretionary power implied by the terms 'appoint' or 'designate' has led some to argue that Augustus could circumvent electoral procedure in a time of crisis.[40] But if we translate ἀπέδειξε as 'declared', an alternative solution presents itself.[41]

---

[39] P. M. Swan (2004), 220.
[40] A. H. M Jones (1955), 12; P. A. Brunt (1961), 78; B. Levick (1967), 207 and n. 3; A. J. Holladay (1978), 878. Clause four of the *Lex de Imperio Vespasiani* (*ILS* 244) states that the princeps' *commendati* and *suffragati* were treated *extra ordinem*. Levick (213) argues that the absence of a precedent associated with this clause implies that it was created especially for Vespasian. But that does not account for Tac. *Ann.* 1.15, where Tacitus writes that Tiberius' *commendationes* were to be accepted *sine repulsa*. Levick rejects the historicity of Tacitus' words, but that is a self-fulfilling approach. Nevertheless, F. R. D. Goodyear (1972), 194, seems to agree with Levick.
[41] To be taken as Greek for *renuntio*.

Dio remarks, while commenting on elections in AD 32, that when there was an insufficient number of candidates or electoral strife (φιλονεικία) fewer candidates were chosen.[42] Tacitus knew of a similar policy. During the praetorian elections of AD 60, when *acrior ambitus* broke out, Nero intervened by appointing to legionary commands the supernumerary candidates. The number of remaining candidates, therefore, equalled the number of vacancies.[43] Should a similar policy have been adopted in AD 7, it would have been implemented in one of two ways. Augustus could have eliminated the last few names from a list compiled by the presiding magistrate, or eliminated those coming last after the *centuriae Caesarum* had voted. I believe the second is more likely. If the presiding magistrate devised his list arbitrarily, then simply eliminating those candidates at the bottom would invite an accusation of corruption. Implied improbity might be dispelled if the ranking of candidates was determined by lot, which was often employed as a neutral mechanism to avoid conflict, but since all candidates were necessarily equal at the beginning of an election, the use of a device with the potential to imply divine support, before votes were even taken, is unlikely.[44] It was for this reason that, during the Republic, elections were postponed until such time as an orderly vote could be taken.[45] We are, therefore, left with the second option: eliminating superfluous names after the *centuriae Caesarum* had 'destined' certain candidates.

At the praetorian elections of AD 7 about 16 candidates, 4 being *candidati Caesaris*, would compete for 12 vacancies.[46] On the day of election the *centuriae* would assemble, the names of the candidates would be written up, and after the usual ceremonies the *centuriae*

---

[42] Dio 58.20.4–5.

[43] Tac. *Ann.* 14.28.1.

[44] Dio 58.20.3. Commenting on Tiberius' policy in regard to praetorian, quaestorian, and minor elections, Dio writes: 'he selected as many as he wished and referred them to the senate, some with his recommendation, in which event they were chosen unanimously, but in the case of others conditioning their selection upon the merit of their claims, upon mutual agreement, or upon the lot'. But Dio is ambiguous. We know that some minor posts were filled by lot, but there is no explicit evidence that the lot was used for the quaestorship or praetorship. Moreover, if an election was marred by violence owing to an 'undesirable' candidate, the lot would not ensure his defeat, unless, of course, he was proved to be complicit.

[45] Such as the postponed consular and praetorian elections for 52 BC, marred by gang violence, Asc. 30C.

[46] Dio 56.25.4.

Caesarum would have been asked to vote. A crier would then declare the results of the prerogative vote, with some apparently 'destined' and some not.[47] At this point indignation may have erupted. Those ranked last had faithful support in the lower classes, causing shouts that the *centuriae Caesarum* were out of touch. For citizens painfully aware that the government no longer belonged to them, this would have been too much. Violence ensued.[48]

It is not sufficiently appreciated that the ranking of successful candidates was perceived to be a gauge of *dignitas*.[49] Brunt argues that the *centuriae Caesarum* did not alter the type of person elected, but a defeated candidate would not have been consoled by the fact that the winners were the same *type* as he![50] Where plebs and equites had once dominated the ranking of candidates, that power now resided chiefly within the *centuriae Caesarum*. But indignation levelled at the new equestrian oligarchy, which swamped the senators, would come from each of the orders. The senatorial order was witnessing the creation of a rival elite, other equestrians were made to feel left out and forgotten, while the plebs were further alienated from power by an equestrian oligarchy they did not identify with and who owed them no favours—a primitive Tory mob. Στάσις was a reaction to the early election results inasmuch as they represented the inequitable and untraditional nature of the new electoral legislation. Since people were voting when unrest developed, a few hundred malcontents would have been sufficient to force the presiding magistrate to order the *centuriae* to disband and people to go home. The *consilium principis* would then have been convened, where, according to this interpretation, it was decided that the supernumeraries should

---

[47] For the crier announcing the results of the prerogative vote, see Cic. *Phil.* 2.82–3. The nature of *destinatio* is unclear. *Destinati* cannot have been automatically elected since a candidate could be 'written' into an election at any moment. Perhaps the term was simply a way of distinguishing those selected by the *centuriae Caesarum* - a badge of honour for those selected and a signpost for conservative voters who tend to follow a lead. Perhaps in an election that involved 16 candidates and 12 spaces, there were 12 *destinati* after the prerogative vote, i.e. those chosen to fill the number of spaces. The *comitia* would still vote on all 16 candidates, but the 12 *destinati* would have an advantage.

[48] Anger was not universal, since Augustus was obviously able to gather enough support to pass the laws in the first place. Nevertheless, the law only had to infuriate a few thousand people for a disturbance to become dangerous.

[49] Asc. 92C; the opening chapters of Cic. *De Lege Agraria* 2.

[50] P. A. Brunt (1961), 73 f.

be eliminated from the list. With the list equalling the number of places, the *comitia* would again be called to vote. The process would necessarily have been a rubber stamp, and any disturbance treated as seditious, since the entire Principate was being placed in question. If a pamphlet critical of Augustus and written using Agrippa's name was published at this time, we may have the political dimension inherent in, but not explicitly connected to, Agrippa's *relegatio*.

Suetonius states that Augustus fined a plebeian, Junius Novatus, who was caught circulating a letter attributed to Agrippa Postumus:

Cum ille Agrippae iuvenis nomine asperrimam de se epistulam in vulgus edidisset.

When he had circulated a letter among the people which was very critical of Augustus under the name of the young Agrippa.[51]

The letter must have: (i) appeared to be Agrippa's work; (ii) criticized Augustus; (iii) allowed for Augustus to treat Novatus leniently; and, (iv) included material that warranted Agrippa's *relegatio* and incarceration. Convincing the public that Agrippa authored such a document would not have been difficult. Humiliation often breeds resentment. Reconciling the final two criteria is more difficult, however. A fine seems too lenient if the contents of the letter were seditious. But a letter merely critical of Augustus is not enough to warrant Agrippa's incarceration. Criticism of Augustus and Livia in general, or even an accusation that Augustus used adoption to get at Agrippa's money, might explain *abdicatio* and possibly even *relegatio*, but surely not incarceration. Of the two options, it is more reasonable to suppose that Augustus underplayed his hand against Novatus than overplayed his hand against Agrippa. If the case was discussed in the senate, Augustus may have decided to give his opinion first. Since Augustus was the chief victim, the case could have been heard in the *quaestio maiestatis*, but he may have suggested that Novatus, being guilty of publishing covert libel, ought to be tried *de iniuriis* instead. Augustus deemed Novatus an insignificant threat, and so clemency

---

[51] Suet. *Aug.* 51. B. Levick (1976), 332, also places the Novatus letter between the *abdicatio* and *relegatio* of Agrippa. Curiously, the episode is not discussed by R. A. Bauman (1974), in his chapter on defamation, though he shows on p. 30 that he is aware if it.

was advertised at no great expense to the government.[52] Probably the letter attacked Augustus and put forward a strong anti-government position. For the letter to appear authentic, the author must have known Agrippa, opposed Augustus and, no doubt, Tiberius, and had the support of those who had been involved with Aemilius Paullus but survived the fireworks of AD 6. As the evidence is arranged here, criticism of the war effort, a food shortage, στάσις at the elections, and the circulation of a letter highly critical of Augustus all occurred around the same time. This was not a coincidence but a sustained attack on the government by malcontents constantly seeking to whip up popular fear and resentment. Reeling from the effects of the *lex Valeria Cornelia* and frustrated by the government's inability to improve the basic conditions of life, many citizens were no doubt vulnerable to such propaganda. But what were the authors hoping to accomplish by using Agrippa's name?

Many scholars have assumed that Agrippa was a central figure in an anti-Tiberian 'faction'.[53] The basic theme in almost every approach, no matter how the evidence is assembled, is that Agrippa was relegated and incarcerated for involvement in an anti-Tiberian conspiracy. Levick and Norwood have had the greatest impact on recent scholarship. Levick noted that Surrentum is only about 25 km from Misenum, a naval base that Agrippa's father had created.[54] Levick assumed that fishing occurred on the open water, and, in turn, that Agrippa had crossed the harbour and visited the naval base. The focus of his visit was to stir up revolt and hinder foreign grain from reaching the capital and, in doing so, weaken Augustus' position.[55] Meanwhile, at Rome Agrippa's supporters attempted to 'write' him into the consular election. The attempt was thwarted when

[52] S. Jameson (1975), 301: 'Augustus let him off lightly with a fine, which suggests, perhaps, that the incident was one which proved useful to Augustus in providing a reason for Agrippa's removal'; R. A. Birch, (1981), 450.

[53] A. E. Pappano (1941), 40; F. Norwood (1963), 154 f.; E. Meise (1969), 35 f.; R. Detweiler (1970), 290: 'perhaps Augustus was seeking to prevent any civil dissension which might arise from political plots centering on Agrippa'; J. H. Corbett (1974), 94; B. Levick (1976), 332 f. and (1999), 56 f. Cf. R. Seager (1972), 40: 'It is unlikely anyone could have considered him a serious contender for the Principate'; R. A. Birch (1981), 451: 'It would be rash to infer that Agrippa—still only 17—was a prime mover'.

[54] Outlined in B. Levick (1999), 59 f. and more fully developed in (1976) 333 f.

[55] A view seemingly supported by R. A. Birch (1981), 452, support which somewhat undermines his concern not to be "rash".

Augustus took control of the elections and appointed the magistrates himself. There is nothing to disprove this theory, but neither is there any way to test its veracity. Indeed, there are far too many assumptions: (i) we are not sure the reference to Neptune refers to Agrippa's stay at Surrentum, he could easily have been fishing in the Tiber, or any country estate;[56] (ii) owing to difficulties experienced throughout the empire, such as piracy near Sardinia, we cannot be sure how much of the fleet was at Misenum; and (iii) we do not know the nature of Agrippa's stay at Surrentum, i.e. was he free to move about, or was he subject to *libera custodia*?[57] It is furthermore unlikely that Agrippa's election was a viable goal. Had Agrippa won *in absentia*, the presiding magistrate could simply declare Agrippa ineligible, on account of age, and refuse to declare him as the winner. Aside from public support, which was already evident, no strategic advantage would be gained.

An even more extreme position was taken by Norwood, who accepts the evidence of the Scholiast on Juvenal as authentic.[58] The Scholiast apparently believed that Julia's final exile was caused by an incestuous relationship with Agrippa (*cum qua (Agrippa) commisit incestum*).[59] From this Norwood produced a marvellous tale, in which Agrippa and Julia were both sent to Surrentum because of the cloud hanging over Aemilius Paullus. While in Surrentum, Julia employed Ovid to act as Agrippa's tutor. Ovid taught Agrippa his *Ars Amatoria*; the result was a sexual awakening between brother and sister, which left Julia pregnant. While in Surrentum the two became embroiled in the revolutionary designs of Paullus' faction, and were accidentally caught by Ovid discussing seditious plans. Rumour reached Augustus and Agrippa was banished, followed in AD 8 by Julia and Ovid. Though Norwood's approach is based on evidence,

---

[56] A. E. Pappano (1941), 35, first associated the reference to fishing with Agrippa's stay in Surrentum. It has since become an established fact, E. Fantham (2006), 106: 'Dio reports that Agrippa spent his exile fishing...'. Dio does not say this.

[57] The nature of Agrippa's stay in Surrentum depends upon one's view of *abdicatio*. R. A. Birch (1981), 451, following Levick's interpretation of *abdicatio*, writes: 'Exile in Surrentum was presumably comfortable, probably very comfortable, and as favourable a sentence as could have been imposed.' As this thesis has shown, this interpretation cannot be right. Agrippa may have been physically comfortable, but he was probably supervised closely, see M. Wurm (1972), 54, 60.

[58] F. Norwood, 'The Riddle of Ovid's Relegatio', *CP*, 58:3 (1963), 150–63.

[59] *Scholia in Iuvenalem* 6.158.

his interpretation is unsatisfactory.[60] At the crux of Norwood's thesis is the statement *possibly* in the Scholiast that Agrippa and Julia were lovers. It is true that Julia was eventually found guilty of *adulteria*, and that she gave birth to a child who was later abandoned, but this does not necessarily support the Scholiast.[61] I accepted above the Scholiast's belief that Paullus was indicted for *maiestas*, since Suetonius links Paullus with conspiracy against Augustus. The Scholiast, moreover, does not confuse Paullus with a character from Juvenal, making cross-contamination unlikely. In the case of Julia and Agrippa's sexual relationship, there is clear evidence for cross-contamination.

The Scholiast comments on Juvenal's treatment of the Jewish king Herod Agrippa and his sister Berenice, whose relationship Juvenal describes as incestuous.[62] Juvenal's message has been evidently garbled, either by the Scholiast or a copyist. The Scholiast may, it is true, have known of a tradition which described Agrippa and Julia as incestuous, but that is an argument from silence. Indeed, the absence of incest in any other source, especially Suetonius, is surely the last nail in the proverbial coffin. Norwood's hypothesis should, therefore, be rejected: Agrippa was probably not an 'active' participant in any plot. He was 200 km away from Rome, no doubt in one of Augustus' villas. Furthermore, since *abdicatio* was not accompanied by *emancipatio*, Agrippa was probably surrounded by a host of Augustus' servants and freedmen, and was controlled by a *rector*. The idea, inherent in the approach of some scholars, that his stay at Surrentum was recreational cannot be right. *Abdicatio* evidences Augustus' anger with Agrippa; retention of *patria potestas* shows that he did not trust Agrippa; dismissal to Surrentum indicates that Agrippa was to have no contact with Rome. We should hence assume that Agrippa was socially isolated.[63] In this way, Agrippa was not *relegatus* because of what he did, but because of what people wanted him to do or to be.

Aemilius Paullus' supporters were left isolated, vulnerable, and under heavy scrutiny at the beginning of AD 7. His exile seems to have left a vacuum. His credentials are impressive: noble blood; 'royal'

---

[60] R. A. Bauman (1967), 243, n. 134 seems to misinterpret Norwood when he writes: '(he) may be right to suggest that the Agrippa whom the Scholiast attests as having corrupted her was not her brother, Agrippa Postumus, but Herodes Agrippa'.
[61] Suet. *Aug.* 65.4.
[62] Juv. *Sat.* 6.157–160.
[63] The suggestion made above that Julia might have been 'sent' on a holiday at this time does not contradict this theory. She was probably sent to the other side of Italy.

wife; a daughter in the direct line from Augustus; a successful political career; and support among the people. Those are hard shoes to fill. Agrippa seems to have been the preferred replacement. The libellous letter made Agrippa a mouthpiece for the opposition, whether he liked it or not. He was just 18, unready for such a role, but he was older than his brothers when designated to be consuls and only slightly younger than Gaius as consul in office and commander in the east.[64] Agrippa's personality may have become inextricably linked to unrest. Thus, Augustus did not use *relegatio* and incarceration because Agrippa had committed a crime, hence Tacitus' *nullius flagitii compertum*, but because he now represented a dangerous potentiality.[65]

It has been argued above that Agrippa was *abdicatus* because of manifest sympathy with Tiberius' political opponents; a position perhaps revealed within the walls of the *domus Caesaris*. A son exhibiting such sympathies was a potential embarrassment and he was packed off accordingly. Once Agrippa was the opposition mouthpiece there was no option left but to pack him off for good. That military custody was held to be necessary implies that Surrentum was no longer safe. Perhaps a desire, or a plan even, to retrieve Agrippa had become known to Augustus, causing understandable alarm. This was probably the point at which Livia, whose involvement in the banishment of Agrippa was either known or suspected by later historians, was made to enter the scene. Her decision to support the

---

[64] Augustus is, of course, the elephant in the room. His position at the age of 19 was celebrated.

[65] *Nullius flagitii compertum* stands against theories which hold that Agrippa was tried for *maiestas*. A. E. Papanno (1941), 36: 'It can *hardly be doubted* that the immediate cause for severe punishment visited upon Agrippa was his violent and tactless accusation of Augustus. If so, then Tacitus' "*nullius flagitii compertum*" is not strictly true' (my italics). But a false accusation hardly requires incarceration. F. Norwood (1963), 154, alters Tacitus' meaning to fit a schema: 'Tacitus going so far as to say he had been *discovered* in no crime' (my italics). Tacitus does not say this. R. A. Bauman (1974), 31: 'A senatus consultum... makes it *certain* that the transfer to Planasia was pursuant to a trial' (my italics). To introduce to the senate a question concerning Agrippa does not make a trial; S. Jameson (1975), 302 f. argues that confiscation of property must relate to interdiction not relegation, and takes this to mean that Agrippa's offence was 'loosely embraced under the law of *maiestas*' but that he 'appears not to have stood trial'. First, how can Agrippa's property have been *confiscated* if he was not *sui iuris*? Agrippa owned no property to confiscate. Secondly, how can an offence 'loosely' embrace *maiestas*? It was either *maiestas* or it was not. Thirdly, if a person were interdicted for offences under the heading *maiestas*, then there *must* have been a trial, if only a show. Probably there was no trial.

exile of Agrippa, as well as his incarceration, in a forum such as the family council may well have been explained as sinister interference, something like: 'I have heard it said that many people want him returned from Surrentum.' Blaming Livia for the entire mess certainly fits with a desire to portray Agrippa as a viable alternative to Tiberius. Whatever Livia's involvement, Agrippa was ultimately punished by Augustus via *patria potestas*, not by a public trial. The *senatus consultum* that followed performed at least two functions: (i) it provided that Augustus' death would have no effect upon Agrippa's situation; becoming *sui iuris* would not free Agrippa from military custody; and (ii) the decree may have been procured with a view to the uncertain future. Perhaps it was designed to take from Tiberius the *invidia* of keeping Agrippa in exile on Augustus' expected death - he was soon to be 70. It was certainly held that Agrippa was a threat to the succession policy and that perpetual exile with military custody was the only effective means, short of execution, of preventing his interfering. A great deal of scholarship, however, attempts to connect the younger Julia to the 'revolutionary' supporters of Agrippa. Indeed, she is often portrayed as a dominant figure within an anti-Tiberian movement. This image is born out of a political interpretation of Julia's exile in AD 8.

7

The Exiles of the Younger Julia, D. Junius Silanus, and the poet Ovid

Many link Agrippa's exile with the exile of his sister Julia.[1] The approach is logical. Her husband was the conspirator Aemilius Paullus; her exile occurred less than one year after her brother's; she was exiled to an island; her daughter's betrothal to the future emperor Claudius was cancelled; her house was razed to the ground; and she was refused burial in the Julian mausoleum.[2] These facts have been used to construct an *a posteriori* image of the younger Julia as conspirator, suspected of plotting against Augustus.[3] The image is wrong. Julia was punished for unchaste conduct, not conspiracy, though her behaviour admittedly had political consequences. Aside from the Scholiast on Juvenal, whose details we rejected already, Tacitus supplies the best evidence when treating the return to Rome of D. Junius Silanus:

Ut valida divo Augusto in rem publicam fortuna, ita domi improspera fuit ob impudicitiam filiae ac neptis quas urbe depulit, adulterosque earum morte aut fuga punivit. Nam culpam inter viros ac feminas vulgatam gravi nomine laesarum religionum ac violatae maiestatis appellando clementiam maiorum

---

[1] J. C. Tarver (1902), 257 f.; F. Norwood (1963), 154 f.; E. Meise (1969), 35 f.; R. Detweiler (1970), 290 f.; B. Levick (1976), *passim*, and (1999), 60 f.; R. A. Birch (1981), 455 f.; I. Cogitore, 'Mancipii Unius Audacia (Tac, Annals II, 39, 1): Le Faux Agrippa Postumus Face au Pouvoir de Tibère', *Revue Des Études Latines,* 68 (1991), 123–35; R. A. Bauman (1992), 120 f.; E. Fantham (2006), 111.

[2] Tac. *Ann.* 4.71.4 supplies the date and location of her exile; see Suet. *Claud.* 26.1 for her daughter's betrothal; for the destruction of her house and the decision to refuse her burial in the Julian mausoleum see Suet. *Aug.* 72.3.

[3] As K. A. Raaflaub and L. J. Samons (1990), 430 note: 'Scholars generally agree that the charges of adultery against Julia... were only pretexts designed to conceal political and conspiratorial involvement...'.

124   *The Republic in Danger*

suasque ipse leges egrediebatur... D. Silanus in nepti Augusti adulter, quamquam non ultra foret saevitum quam ut amicitia Caesaris prohiberetur, exilium sibi demonstrari intellexit...

Though a powerful fortune was with the divine Augustus in state affairs, his fortune was less prosperous at home on account of the unchaste conduct of his daughter and granddaughter, whom he expelled from the city and punished their adulterous lovers with death or exile. For calling a common fault between men and women by the serious name of sacrilege and violated *maiestas* he went outside the clemency of our ancestors and his own laws... D. Silanus, the adulterous lover of the granddaughter of Augustus, although he did not suffer anything more severe than the loss of Caesar's friendship, understood it to mean his exile.[4]

He later writes

Per idem tempus Iulia mortem obiit, quam neptem Augustus convictam adulterii damnaverat proieceratque in insulam Trimerum, haud procul Apulis litoribus. Illic viginti annis exilium toleravit Augustae ope sustentata...

About this time Julia died; Augustus had condemned his granddaughter on a charge of adultery and flung her on the island of Trimerus, not far from the shores of Apulia. There she endured twenty years of exile, sustained by the resources of Augusta [i.e. out of Livia's purse].[5]

Suetonius writes

Iulias, filiam et neptem, omnibus probris contaminatas relegavit... ex nepte Iulia post damnationem editum infantem adgnosci alique vetuit.

He relegated the Julias, his daughter and granddaughter, who had been contaminated by every form of infamy... and he did not allow the child born to his granddaughter Julia after her condemnation to be recognized and nourished.[6]

Julia's husband, L. Aemilius Paullus, was condemned in AD 6 under the title of *maiestas*. If Julia was charged with actual adultery, then Aemilius Paullus suffered not *interdictio* but *relegatio*, i.e. their marriage survived his condemnation.[7] But this cannot be right. Seditious

---

[4] Tac. *Ann.* 3.24.
[5] Tac. *Ann.* 4.71.4.
[6] Suet. *Aug.* 65.
[7] The status of L. Aemilius Paullus is a topic of dispute. B. Levick (1976), 331, believes he was executed late in AD 6 or early in AD 7. Her view was accepted by E. Fantham (2006), 110. R. A. Birch (1981), 453 noted the inherent problem of Levick's thesis: how could Julia be charged with adultery if Paullus was dead? He

Exiles of the Younger Julia, D. Junius Silanus, and poet Ovid 125

acts proved to have diminished the *maiestas* of the Roman People would have attracted *interdictio aqua et igni*.[8] Since, as has been shown already, Julia's disgrace was separate from that of her husband, only one plausible solution remains: Julia was not charged with

---

suggested exile, but did not consider whether that meant relegation or interdiction. R. Syme (1986), 115-27, argues that Aemilius Paullus was in fact alive until AD 14. Minutes of the Arval Brethren, (*ILS* 5026) state that on 12 May they chose Drusus Caesar to replace 'L. Paullus'. Syme convincingly argues that Drusus replaced L. Aemilius Paullus (cos. AD1), not an unattested son. Syme, however, places his condemnation in AD 8; that time frame was rejected above.

[8] *Aqua et igni interdictio* was the statutory penalty for *maiestas* in the late Republic, replacing voluntary exile, Cic. *Phil.* 1.9.23. See also Tac. *Ann.* 3.50.4 and *P. S.* 5.29. It meant, among other things, loss of Roman citizenship. For general discussion, see A. H. J. Greenidge (1901), 510f.; J. E. Allison and J. D. Cloud, 'The Lex Julia Maiestatis', *Latomus*, 21 (1962), 711-31. Some have argued that *aqua et igni interdictio* did not mean loss of citizenship, J. L. Strachan-Davidson II (1912), 39 f.; A. H. M. Jones (1972), 109; B. Levick, 'Poena Legis Maiestatis', *Historia*, 28 (1979), 358-79; G. P. Kelly, *A History of Exile in the Roman Republic* (2006), 45 f. Three pieces of evidence are put forward to show this: Cic. *Pro. Caec.* 34.100 states explicitly that citizenship cannot be taken away from him, but is abandoned by the exile only when he takes up the citizenship of another community. But it is dangerous to use Cicero here as a guide to the law. It was in his interest to argue that he remained a citizen while in exile. Cic. *Har. Resp.* 17, shows Cicero replying to Clodius' question *cuius civitatis es*? by suggesting that he belongs 'to a State which could not exist without me' and then states that he could have said 'Rome'. Again, however, the context is problematic; Cicero was trying to save his house by arguing, *inter alia*, that he had remained a Roman citizen in exile, and therefore the legal owner of the house. Incidentally, Clodius was pointing out that it was the intention of his law (by which Cicero was banished) to deem Cicero a non-citizen; otherwise his question is self-defeating. Cicero's specious approach is exemplified by his response to Antony's intention to allow an appeal to those interdicted, *Phil.* 1.23: 'Does this not annul Caesar's laws that bid that those convicted of violence and treason be interdicted from fire and water', i.e. on this occasion Cicero argues that those interdicted were not protected by the various appeal laws (such as the *lex Porcia*) - they had no citizen rights. Q. Pompeius Rufus was interdicted in 51 BC, and we are told that while in exile he took his mother to court for withholding a *fideicommissum*, Val. Max. 4.2.7. This appears to be the best evidence in favour of Stachan-Davidson's interpretation, but it is not clearcut. A *fideicommissum* was not a signpost to citizenship in this period - it was not subject to formalization until the Augustan era (Iust. *Inst.* 2.23.1) and even then it could be used to circumvent the *lex Falcidia* until the time of Vespasian (J. Crook (1967), 125-7). It was a device for providing a legacy to those whose ability to inherit was restricted, e.g. by the *lex Voconia*. As to the fact that Pompeius Rufus was allowed to 'have his day in court', albeit *in absentia*, this was probably due to a belief that his mother had acted outrageously - the verdict in his favour a legal anomaly. It was commonly held that even exiles should live out their lives in relative comfort. R. A. Birch (1981), 453, and T. D. Barnes (1981), 362-3, seem, nevertheless, to believe that Paullus suffered *relegatio* since both insist that Julia committed adultery.

126   *The Republic in Danger*

adultery. In Roman law *interdictio* dissolved marriage; a wife was *sui iuris* or returned to the *potestas* of her father. It is universally held that Julia was *sui iuris*.[9] As such, any sexual relationship developed after that moment would be *stuprum*, not *adulterium*.[10] The crime of *stuprum* was treated under the title *lex Iulia de adulteriis*: *Lex stuprum et adulterium promiscui et καταχρηστικώτερον appellat*. 'The law refers to *adulteria* and *stuprum* indiscriminately and with rather a misuse of terms.'[11] Tacitus thus records the law by which Julia was condemned, not her actual crime. This interpretation better explains the treatment of Julia's lover, D. Junius Silanus.

Theories which take Julia's crime to have been adulterous, or seditious even, fail to explain Augustus' treatment of Junius Silanus.[12] If suspicion of conspiracy dogged the younger Julia, it is untenable to hold that Augustus considered Junius Silanus an innocent bystander. What did he think they discussed while together in bed? Similarly, if Julia had committed adultery, then Junius Silanus should have experienced at least *relegatio*.[13] Paulus writes concerning the *lex Iulia de adulteriis*:

Adulterii convictas mulieres dimidia parte dotis et tertia parte bonorum ac relegatione in insulam placuit coerceri: adulteris vero viris pari in insulam relegatione dimidiam bonorum partem auferri, dummodo in diversas insulas relegentur.

It has been held that women convicted of adultery shall be punished with the loss of half of their dowry and one third of their estates, and by relegation to an island. The adulterer, moreover, shall be deprived of half his property, and

---

[9] *PIR*² I 421.
[10] G. Rizzelli, 'Stuprum e adulterium nella cultura e la lex Iulia de adulteriis', *Bullettino dell'Istituto di Diritto Romano*, 29 (1987), 355–88; E. Fantham, 'Stuprum: Public Attitudes and Penalties for Sexual Offences in Republican Rome', *EMC*, 10 (1991), 267–91.
[11] Papinian *Adulterers Book 1* = *Dig.* 48.5.6.1.
[12] B. Levick (1999), 61, accepts that Augustus was mild toward Junius Silanus. She sees it as a function of the Government's confidence. But if Julia was a political player worthy of exile, then the Government was evidently not confident. E. Fantham (2006), 110, wonders whether Junius Silanus informed against his lover. But that is unlikely if the child was his and there is no evidence that Julia had other lovers.
[13] A. J. Woodman, in R. H. Martin, and A. J. Woodman (1996), 226, notes that Junius Silanus 'in fact paid a lesser penalty than the *lex* demanded'. It is improbable that Junius Silanus would have escaped trial had the charge been adultery proper with a princess of the *domus Caesaris*.

shall also be punished by relegation to an island; provided the parties are exiled to different islands.[14]

Amicitia Caesaris prohiberi would have been a significant reduction of the statutory penalty for violating a marriage, especially one arranged, probably, by Augustus for a princess of the imperial house. That Augustus' own law was contravened and his moral programme repudiated would have made his treatment of Junius Silanus seem even more absurd. Only a charge of *stuprum* provides a satisfactory solution. But if Julia had committed *stuprum*, then we must explain the confiscation of her entire property, the demolition of her house, and Augustus' decision to deny her burial in the family mausoleum; we must explain why Tacitus mentions violated *maiestas* and *laesae religiones*.[15] Ovid's exile now enters the discussion.

Ovid insists that his relegation, in the very same year, was caused by a poem and an error (*carmen et error*).[16] *Carmen* is the *Ars Amatoria*, but Ovid will not disclose the *error*. His reason is obvious. The *Ars Amatoria* was defensible; his *error* was not. This, he tells us, is not because he was guilty of a crime (*scelus*) but because he was partly at fault (*culpa*), i.e. he did not show intent.[17] That he was relegated by neither *senatus consultum* nor *lex,* but was instead ordered to Tomis by Augustus, did not lose citizen status, and that he kept his property supports his claim.[18] The *error* was instead the real force behind his relegation:

---

[14] *PS.* 2.26.14; P. Garnsey (1970), 116. O. F. Robinson, *The Criminal Law of Ancient Rome* (1995), 66, 138, n. 185 takes Paulus to mean that *relegatio* was added to the statute in the 3rd century AD. But see Pliny *Ep.* 6.3.5–6.

[15] The confiscation of Julia's entire estate is implied by Livia's financial assistance. Perhaps, despite Julia being *sui iuris*, the house belonged to Augustus, who thus destroyed a house now polluted. Why, however, was Julia considered for burial in the Julian mausoleum when she should have been buried with the Vipsanii? J. Linderski (1988), 191, argues that Augustus' tomb was open to all of his decendants, not simply those with agnatic connection, basing his conclusion on the work of F. De Visscher, *Le Droit de tombeaux romains* (1963), 93–138. It is moreover important to note that Agrippa was buried in the Julian Mausoleum, Dio 54.28.5: 'Augustus... buried him [Agrippa] in his own [Augustus'] mausoleum, though Agrippa had taken one for himself in the Campus Martius.' It is probably the case, therefore, that Augustus had meant in his will for all of Agrippa's children to be buried in the Julian Mausoleum. In his final will, drawn up in AD 13, Augustus took care to state explicitly that this was no longer the case for the younger Julia, or indeed her mother.

[16] *Trist.* 2.207.
[17] *Trist.* 3.1.52; *Ex Pont.* 1.6.25–6.
[18] *Trist.* 2.130.

128   *The Republic in Danger*

nec quicquam, quod lege vetor committere, feci: | *est tamen his gravior noxa fatenda mihi.* | *neve roges, quae sit, stultam conscripsimus Artem.* | *Innocuas nobis haec vetat esse manus.* | *Ecquid praeterea peccarim? quaerere noli,* | *ut lateat sola culpa sub Arte mea.*

I have committed no act which is forbidden by the law | I must however confess a more significant offence | you must not ask what it is; we have composed a silly 'Art'; | this forbids our hands from being innocent; | have I sinned further? Do not ask this, | so that my fault may hide behind my Art alone.[19]

Ovid wants us to know that his *error* was not an illegal act. Whatever the pleas of the condemned are worth, Ovid would have us believe that his fault was passive in nature:

Cur aliquid vidi? cur noxia lumina feci? | *cur imprudenti cognita culpa mihi?* | *inscius Actaeon vidit sine veste Dianam:* | *praeda fuit canibus non minus ille suis.* | *Scilicet in superis etiam fortuna luenda est,* | *nec veniam laeso numine casus habet.*

Why did I see something? Why did I make my eyes guilty? | Why was a fault convicted in me without my own intention? | Actaeon was unwitting when he saw Diana without clothes: | he was none the less the prey of his own dogs. | Obviously when you are dealing with gods even chance is punishable, | nor does accident receive pardon when a divine power has been harmed.[20]

That which Ovid witnessed is elsewhere described as a crime (*crimen*) and evil actions (*facta mali*).[21] Celebrities allegedly filled the scene. Extolling the virtues of a discreet social life, Ovid warns against socializing with great names: *si quicquam credis amico vive tibi et longe nomina magna fuge,* 'If in anything you believe a friend, live for yourself and flee far away from great names.'[22] If this alludes to circumstances surrounding his *error*, then Ovid was attending a party when he witnessed a crime by accident.[23] The crime affected Augustus directly:

---

[19] *Ex Pont.* 2.9.71–6.
[20] *Trist.* 2.103–108 f.
[21] *Trist.* 3.6.28. Thus a recent attempt to equate Ovid's *error* with having written the *Metamorphoses* cannot be right, S. G. Nugent, 'Tristia 2: Ovid and Augustus', in K. A. Raaflaub and M. Toher (1990), 239–57.
[22] *Trist.* 3.4.1–4. Used by F. Norwood (1963), 156; B. Levick (1999), 60.
[23] *Trist.* 3.6.11–13.

Perdiderint cum me duo crimina, carmen et error, | *alterius facti culpa silenda mihi:* | *nam non sum tanti, renovem ut tua vulnera, Caesar,* | *quem nimio plus est indoluisse semel.* | *altera pars superest, qua turpi carmine factus* | *arguor obsceni doctor adulterii.*

Though two charges, a poem and an error, have ruined me, | of the circumstances of the second fault I will remain silent; | for I am not of such importance that I would renew your wounds, O Caesar, | for whom it was more than too much to have pained once. | The other crime remains, that through a disgraceful poem | I am accused of becoming the teacher of foul adultery.[24]

The relevance of the allegorical *laeso numine* cited above is here exposed. Augustus, described elsewhere by Ovid as a god, is held to have been injured. This calls to mind Tacitus' *laesae religiones*. That Ovid unwittingly saw Julia in a compromising position which, when it was later made known, was held to have embarrassed Augustus, is the most plausible scenario. That Julia was with Junius Silanus at the time is also probable. Thus, sometime after the exile of her husband, Julia was discovered in a relationship with D. Junius Silanus; a 'baby bump' probably gave it away.[25] Hell broke loose when Augustus found out. He treated dynastic alliances with extreme care, and frowned severely upon this particular match. But the baby posed the greatest problem: Julia had really messed things up. The senate was notified and a public inquiry set up, with the *lex Iulia de adulteriis* providing the terms of reference. As Brunt has shown, this *lex* provided for the sale of slaves to the state for the purpose of interrogation.[26] Ovid seems to suggest that slaves were interrogated:

Causa meae cunctis nimium quoque nota ruinae | *indicio non est testificanda meo.* | *quid referam comitumque nefas famulosque nocentes?*

The cause of my ruin, which is only too well known by all | must not be revealed by my own evidence. | Why refer to the wickedness of friends and guilty slaves?[27]

Famuli nocentes is reminiscent of an Augustan edict from the second half of AD 8:

---

[24] *Trist.* 2.207–12.
[25] As pointed out by T. D. Barnes (1981), *passim*.
[26] P. Brunt, 'Evidence Given under Torture in the Principate', *ZSS*, 97 (1980), 256–65.
[27] *Trist.* 4.10.99–101.

130   *The Republic in Danger*

Edictum divi Augusti, quod proposuit Vibio Habito et Lucio Aproniano consulibus, in hunc modum exstat: '*Quaestiones neque semper in omni causa et persona desiderari debere arbitror, et, cum capitalia et atrociora maleficia non aliter explorari et inuestigari possunt quam per servorum quaestiones, efficacissimas eas esse ad requirendam veritatem existimo et habendas censeo.*'

An edict of the deified Augustus, which he issued to the consuls Vibius Habitus and Lucius Apronianus, is extant as follows: 'I do not think that interrogations are required in every case and person, but when capital and more horrible crimes cannot be explored and investigated in any other way than through the interrogations of slaves, I am of the opinion that [such interrogations] are most effective for the purpose of investigating the truth, and I declare that they must be held."[28]

The edict was cited by Paulus in his *De Adulteriis*. 'Capital' has puzzled some scholars, since adultery was not a capital offence.[29] Bauman relates the edict to the case of Cassius Severus.[30] But that does not explain why Paulus saw fit to place it under the title *adulterium*. Moreover, it has been shown already that Cassius Severus was indicted for overt libel; such an edict would have been unnecessary. The key is not capital but the nebulous *atrociora maleficia*. The absence of a device to strengthen the comparative, i.e. *etiam*, implies equality: 'capital crimes or other more horrible crimes', where 'more' does not imply a greater quality than 'capital'.[31] This is logical, for what can be more severe than a capital offence, since capital offences carried the severest penalty? Augustus, then, had in mind offences that he held to be grave but, nevertheless, were not capital. *Stuprum* involving a princess plus an unplanned pregnancy in the *domus Caesaris* is a good candidate. If the law *de adulteriis* limited the

---

[28] Paulus *Adulterers Book 2* = *Dig.* 48.18.8pr.
[29] P. Brunt (1980), 258; Dio 55.5.4 writes that in 8 BC Augustus proposed a bill, which was passed, allowing for slaves to be sold to the *actor publicus* in certain criminal cases. The bill was justified on the grounds that 'it was necessary because the loophole had enabled many to conspire both against Augustus himself and the magistrates'. J. W. Rich (1990), 223, and P. M. Swan (2004), 61, both take this to be a reference to the *lex maiestatis*. They are probably right. The practice was used in the case of Drusus Libo in AD 16, Tac. *Ann.* 2.30.3, and C. Junius Silanus in AD 22, Tac. *Ann.* 3.67.3. The loophole to which Augustus seems to have been referring is the manumission of slaves before they could give evidence *in caput domini* in significant cases; the case of Milo's slaves as recounted by Asconius 34C is a good example.
[30] R. A. Bauman (1974), 43 f.
[31] So P. Garnsey (1970), 214: 'more serious and capital crimes'.

interrogation of slaves to cases of adultery proper, then perhaps the legality of interrogating slaves in a case of *stuprum* was questioned; Augustus replied that this particular offence must be treated *as if* it were capital.[32] The inquiry was obviously not set up to discover whether *stuprum* had occurred; Julia was pregnant. But as Ovid's experience shows, Augustus was determined to clear away the rot. Perhaps, as Levick supposes, Ovid witnessed, or took some part in, the impromptu wedding of Julia and Junius Silanus.[33] Whatever occurred, Julia's condemnation for a sexual offence was not a pretext to disguise seditious behaviour. We must therefore explain Tacitus' violated *maiestas* and *laesae religiones*:

For calling a common fault between men and women by the serious name of sacrilege and violated *maiestas* he went outside (*egredior*) the clemency of our ancestors and his own laws.[34]

Egredior means 'to pass outside of' or to 'diverge from'. Law is, of course, interpretative, but Tacitus means for us to understand that Augustus *transgressed* the rule of law and custom; that his interpretation of the crime was cruel and self-serving.[35] By what right did he do this? Augustus cannot have argued that the *maiestas populi Romani* was diminished by Julia's affair. If he had, Silanus should have been more seriously punished. Similarly, Augustus cannot have argued that the act of *stuprum* in and of itself caused him injury. *Patria potestas* was no doubt used for the elder Julia, but what device was used to punish the younger Julia? My preferred solution is radical,

---

[32] *Cod. Iust.* 9.9.3 states that interrogation was not allowed in a case of incest, but for adultery proper alone. O. F. Robinson (1995), 64, is probably right to conclude that *stuprum* was exempted also.

[33] B. Levick (1999) 54 f., supported, perhaps, by E. Fantham (2006), 111. The act could still be interpreted as *stuprum*. This view is based on a corrupt and fragmentary text Περὶ τοῦ Καισαρείού γένους, written around the time of Nero, which states: Δύο θυγάτερες Ἰουλία ἰλανω (ed. Lamporos supplies Σιλανῷ) γαμηθεῖσα καὶ Ἀγριππῖνα ἡ μετὰ ταῦτα Γερμανικῷ τῷ Δρούσου. '(There were) two daughters, Julia, who was married to Silanus, and Agrippina, who after these events (was married to) Germanicus, son of Drusus.' Admittedly the idea makes sense. A marriage might have been considered logical with a child 'on the way', while Junius Silanus would have been innocent of any charge: it was not an offence to court and marry a woman. *Renuntiatio amicitiae* is therefore an obvious solution for Augustus: 'you have committed no crime, but you have offended me and my house.'

[34] Tac. *Ann.* 3.24.

[35] Thus some are of the opinion that Augustus' *voluntas* was the motivating force for all criminal legislation during the period, B. Biondi, 'La legislazione di *Augusto*', *Scritti Giuridici*, 2 (1965), 61–98, esp. 85 f.

but, I believe, best explains the nature of the younger Julia's condemnation: she was Augustus' daughter by adoption.

The second edition of the *Prosopographia Imperii Romani* had for Julia: IULIA (*Vipsania Iulia sine dubio, sed gentilicium reticetur*). This is, so far as I can tell, accepted universally by modern scholars. But *sine dubio* is a careless phrase. Why was Julia not Vipsania Agrippina? By what right did she claim the *nomen* Julia?[36] If she was *sui iuris*, by what right did Augustus confiscate her property? By what right did Augustus order the death of Julia's child? Surely these questions evoke serious doubt. Each question, left unanswered by her being *sui iuris*, is explained perfectly by *patria potestas*.[37] Moreover, 'violated *maiestas*' and *laesae religiones* are appropriate if Augustus were Julia's father by adoption: Julia should have *revered* Augustus as her *pater*, while Silanus had only the *officium* of *amicitia* to observe. Perhaps *patria maiestas* is here relevant.[38] The term is of no interest to the jurists, but appears only in a few writers of the early Principate.[39] As with *abdicatio*, Augustus may have employed a nebulous device for the purpose of punishing severely moral defects exposed in his children: Julia did not violate the *maiestas populi Romani*, but the *maiestas* of her *pater familias*.

It remains possible, however, that Julia was *sui iuris*. The effect of this interpretation is quite different. If Julia were *sui iuris*, then Augustus evidently held her to be, as a direct descendant, subject to his *potestas*, if not in law, then certainly in fact.[40] As was the case in

---

[36] I note, however, that the daughter of Nero Claudius Drusus and Antonia was named Livia Julia. Thus, the question of Julia's *nomen* is perhaps not as important as questions concerning her treatment by Augustus. Nevertheless, that no ancient source attests an adoption for Julia is no bar. Aside from Livia, when do we ever hear of female adoptions in the early Principate?

[37] Contra L. F., Raditsa, 'Augustus' Legislation concerning Marriage, Procreation, Love Affairs and Adultery', *ANRW* II, 13 (1980), 279–339, esp. 290–5, who argues that the adulterous affairs of the elder Julia were deemed to have injured the *pater patriae*, who was the moral guardian of Rome. Raditsa believes that Augustus had no choice but to appear as a martyr. But if the title *pater patriae* protected Augustus from all forms of injury, then *everybody* would have been vulnerable; this was clearly not the case.

[38] Woodman's comments are given as his own in R. H. Martin and A. J. Woodman, (1996), 227 f.

[39] Livy 4.45.8; Val. Max. 5.1 ext. 2; Quint. *Decl. Min.* 376.3.

[40] For the idea that the *domus Augusta* was treated *as* a civic institution see B. Severy (2003), *passim*, and A. Yakobson (2003). I do not hold that the *domus Augusta* was a civic institution, only that it was being treated as such. This postulated *maiestas* of the *domus Augusta* is not to be confused with the unreal concept produced

my preferred scenario above, Silanus, in contradistinction, had only the *officium* of *amicitia* to observe.[41] Since, however, Julia was *sui iuris*, Augustus was forced to deal with her transgression in a public setting. Though the crime was *stuprum*, Augustus nevertheless secured her relegation and the confiscation of her property: he had transgressed, *egredior*, the penalties imposed by his own law and *mos maiorum*. In addition, he demolished a house now polluted by fornication and refused Julia burial with her father, grandfather, cousins, and siblings. Augustus argued that Julia's unplanned pregnancy violated the majesty of his own house, the *domus Augusta*. Whichever is correct, Julia had problematized a well thought-out and balanced dynasty. The world was introduced to another child with a direct connection to the *pater patriae*. But the affair, as the evidence assembled here shows, was unconnected to the exile of Agrippa or Aemilius Paullus even. It was an entirely independent event and of little interest to the history of Agrippa Postumus, aside from its relevance to the overarching theme of Augustus' dynastic plans and, perhaps, his belief in the *domus Augusta* as a civic institution.

by R. A. Bauman (1967), 243 f. I do not accept his belief that violated majesty was a type of treason developed by Augustus as an alternative to the *crimen maiestatis imminutae* to protect himself and the *domus Caesaris* and treated in an imperial court. It would have been awkward and immodest for Augustus to argue that Julia had violated his majesty as princeps and thus committed sacrilege. That he was the *pater patriae* probably made his situation all the more embarrassing. Cf. J. E. Allison and J. D. Cloud (1962), 721 f., who argue that the case was heard under the *lex Iulia de adulteriis*, but that Augustus used the language of violated majesty and sacrilege to justify *extra-ordinem* penalties. If, however, Julia's crime had violated the *maiestas populi Romani*, Silanus would have suffered *interdictio*, or at least *relegatio*. Silanus suffered only *amicitia Caesaris prohiberi* precisely because the *maiestas populi Romani* was not violated.

[41] In the case of Agrippa, Augustus decided that his *de facto* influence was inadequate and so secured *patria potestas*. The case of the younger Julia shows the inherent problem with Augustus' approach to those members of his family who were not subject to his *potestas*.

8

Novus Principatus: An Imperial Co-operative

The setbacks that began to pile up in AD 5 wore away at the government's confidence, since only lack of confidence explains treating Cassius Severus' public outbursts as *maistas* in AD 8. But Augustus' frailty cannot have helped. He had withdrawn from attendance at the assemblies and senatorial investigations, and entrusted foreign embassies to a board of three ex-consuls.[1] Three years later, in AD 11, his already poor health deteriorated; a boon for those who claimed special knowledge of the future. In addition to cracking down on the activities of seers, Augustus also published his personal horoscope.[2] Publication of an official horoscope is evidence that 'false' copies were in circulation. People were obviously excited by the prospect of Augustus' death and what it would bring. A passage from Dio concerning events concurrent with Augustus' edict may be important. At the praetorian elections of AD 11, all 16 candidates were elected, though there were not 16 spaces to fill:

> ...Καὶ στρατηγοὶ ἑκκαίδεκα ἦρξαν, ἐπειδὴ τοσοῦτοί τε τῆς ἀρχῆς ἀντεποιήσαντο καὶ οὐδένα αὐτῶν λυπῆσαι ὁ Αὔγουστος, οἷα ἐν τοιούτοις ὤν, ἠθέλησεν· οὐ μὴν καὶ τοῖς ἄλλοις τοῖς ἐφεξῆς ἔτεσι ταὐτὸν ἐγένετο, ἀλλ' οἱ δώδεκα ἐπὶ πολὺ κατέστησαν.

Sixteen praetors held office since that number had competed for the positions and Augustus, being in such difficult circumstances, was not willing to offend any of them. The same was not the case however for the years immediately following, but twelve [praetors] were appointed for a long time.[3]

---

[1] Dio 55.33.5 = Xiph. 114.15–30; Dio 55.34.2.
[2] Dio 56.25.5.
[3] Dio 56.25.4.

How was this achieved? Augustus could not tell the centuries how to vote, nor were they compelled to follow his *suffragia* or *commendationes*.[4] He must, therefore, have increased the number of vacancies for that year to 16, thereby allowing the election to continue without interference while ensuring that all were successful.[5] The election was thus perfunctory. Striking is Dio's belief that Augustus had no other option. What was so difficult about Augustus' situation? The praetorian elections might usefully be linked to the decree on horoscopes. A widely held belief, or simply chatter, that Augustus would soon die would explain the pressure being exerted by candidates - they were unsure of support in the post-Augustan era. Beneath Dio's account lies an implicit logic: Augustus was threatened by men who would only take yes for an answer, i.e. Augustus' *auctoritas* was made to serve their selfish ends and not his own.[6] The nature of the threat is not known, but it is surely not a coincidence that both Tiberius and Germanicus were away from Rome; they had missed the violent elections of AD 7 as well.[7] Augustus' solution was meant to arrest anxiety, made acute by the widely held belief that a succession was imminent. He was probably too weak to fight and felt that violence must be avoided at any cost. Still, it was made known that he was not ready to give up the ghost. A modern scientific mind has freed many from the bondage-like determinism of astrological charts, but in AD 11 a great part of the population believed in their predictions. The 'official' horoscope was no doubt unspecific about the time of death, highlighting instead his extraordinary destiny.[8]

The belief that Augustus was near death can also be linked to legislation passed in AD 12 concerning the regulation of exiles. Dio

---

[4] B. Levick (1967), *passim*.

[5] As supposed by A. E. Astin, 'Nominare in Accounts of Elections in the Early Principate', *Latomus*, 28 (1969), 863–74, esp. 872; A. J. Holladay (1978), 881.

[6] Even if the candidates were fighting for legionary commands in the wars, or, indeed, the year simply witnessed unusually tense rivalry, it does not explain why Augustus was unable to 'offend any of them', which implies a weakened position.

[7] Dio 56.25.1–3 states that both were in Germany for most of AD 11, celebrating Augustus' birthday (23 Sept.) north of the Rhine.

[8] So the famous story of a young Octavian and Marcus Vipsanius Agrippa having their horoscope read, the latter promised a great and glorious future, the former presented with a prostrated astrologer. Suetonius tells us that after this incident Augustus made public his horoscope, but this does not mean Dio is wrong. It could be that the horoscope was made public twice. Indeed, how many copies would survive more than fifty years? Suet. *Aug.* 94.12.

provides some details. Those who had suffered *aqua et igni interdictio* could no longer live on the mainland or any island within 50 miles; they could not cross the sea, possess more than one transport and two oared boats, employ more than 20 slaves or freedmen, and own more than HS 500,000.[9] The decree provided for the punishment of exiles who infringed the new rules and, more interestingly, non-exiles who aided infringements. Some exiles, Dio says many, were evidently living outside their allotted districts in a manner that irked the government.[10] A limit of HS 500,000 signals the social standing of those in question; the life of an *exul* seemed more like an extended vacation than a punishment, and by AD 12 was too paradoxical to ignore.[11] The development of these rules may have been in response to the discovery of plans to rescue a few high-profile exiles.

It must be significant that Augustus' death triggered an attempt to rescue Agrippa Postumus from Planasia; it was probably always the plan. In AD 11 the declining health of Augustus provided individuals

---

[9] Dio 56.27.2-3.

[10] R. A. Bauman, (1974), 28-30, and B. Levick (1979), 358-79, both view this legislation as the point at which *aqua et igni interdictio* became *deportatio in insulam*. They are followed by P. M. Swan (2004), 288f; cf. J. L. Strachan-Davidson II (1912), 55f., and A. H. M. Jones (1972), 109-10, both of whom place the development firmly in the Tiberian period. These views require some revision. Dio's language shows that change had occurred already: 'As there were many exiles who were either living outside of the districts *to which they had been banished* or living too luxuriously *in the proper places* . . .'. In the Republic interdiction from fire and water did not specify a place of exile, only that the exile could not set foot on Roman soil. On the effects during the Republic, see in general Th. Mommsen, *Straf.* (1899), 972-9; A. H. J. Greenidge (1901), 512f; G. P. Kelly (2006), 17-65. On the other hand, we have evidence that in the Republic *relegatio* - banishment by magisterial *coercitio* - might carry with it a specific area of exile. Augustus probably merged the effects of *relegatio* with *interdictio* early in his Principate. It should be remembered that Sempronius Gracchus, who was evidently charged with a capital offence in 2 BC, was exiled to the island of Cercina in the Gulf of Gabes, Africa.

[11] The rulings would have allowed for confiscation of property. Confiscation can be found accompanying exile as early as 212 BC, Livy 25.4.9-10. In 26 BC Cornelius Gallus had his entire property confiscated, as did Drusus Libo in AD 16. In 52 BC, T. Annius Milo was exiled for his part in the murder of P. Clodius. We are told that his property was confiscated, Plut. *Cic.* 35; Dio 40.54.2; Cic. *Ad Att.* 5.8.2. Nevertheless, Milo's friends ensured that he was provided with either income and/or capital. More strikingly, C. Verres, exiled in 70 BC for *repetundae*, apparently took with him into exile a boatload of goods gained while governor of Sicily, Lact. *Inst. Div.* 2.4.35-6, Cic. *In. Ver.* 5.44, Pliny *NH* 34.6. But in the case of Cn. Piso's accomplices, Sempronius Bassus and Visellius Karus, their property was sold in AD 20 'by the praetors in charge of the treasury', *SCPP*, 120f. Obviously, the statute provided guidance; details varied from case to case. Suet. *Iul.* 42.3 is problematic, see G. P. Kelly (2006), 25f.

138   *The Republic in Danger*

opposed to Tiberius with cause for concern. While Augustus lived, the supreme power of Tiberius was a potentiality only - albeit the likely one. The plan to rescue Agrippa in AD 14 is evidence that some were desperate enough to bet against the odds. I propose that a similar attempt was made in late AD 11 or early AD 12. Stress should be laid on the clause:

τιμωρηθήσεσθαι καὶ αὐτοὺς ἐκείνους καὶ τοὺς ἄλλους τούς τι παρὰ ταῦτα συμπράξαντάς σφισιν ἐπαπειλήσας.

Having threatened to punish both these [exiles] themselves and others who had in any way assisted them in contravention of these [rules].[12]

It is possible that in response to a single catalytic episode, the government formed a broad sweeping policy to resolve a systemic problem in the treatment of exiles. I believe that this episode was the attempted rescue of Agrippa Postumus and his mother, Julia, by L. Audasius and Asinius Epicadus, irrespective of the fact that their places of exile had not been breached.[13] Suetonius lists the men among those who had conspired against Augustus:

L. Audasi falsarum tabularum rei ac neque aetate neque corpore integri, item Asini Epicadi ex gente Parthina ibridae . . . Audasius atque Epicadus Iuliam filiam et Agrippam nepotem ex insulis, quibus continebantur, rapere ad exercitus . . .

L. Audasius, who had been accused of falsifying documents and was old and feeble, and Asinius Epicadus, a half-breed from the Parthini . . . Audasius and Epicadus [planned] to seize Julia, daughter [of Augustus], and Agrippa, grandson [of Augustus], from their islands, where they were being held, and rush them off to the armies . . .[14]

Levick dates the episode to AD 8, arguing that the younger Julia was instrumental in its planning and attempted execution.[15] This is in part because Levick requires a political dimension to explain the exile of the younger Julia, and also because the younger Julia is not named by Suetonius as a target for the conspirators. Conspiracy, however, was not part of the younger Julia's disgrace, nor is it necessary to

---

[12] Dio. 56.27.3.
[13] S. Jameson (1975), also proposes a connection. It must be noted also that there were evidently many exiles, of whom we know the names of very few.
[14] Suet. *Aug.* 19.
[15] B. Levick (1999), 61.

believe that Suetonius has supplied, or even knew, every fact. The two men may have been arrested before they were able to leave Italy or Rome even. Nor would a subsequent investigation bring to light every detail. Much would have relied on the information of slaves and informants, and by the time the two were sentenced, all that could be said was that it was believed they were attempting to free Agrippa and his mother.[16] There were others who might have been considered; L. Aemilius Paullus and the elder Julia's lover, Sempronius Gracchus, being the most obvious candidates. Indeed, both - with Agrippa - died during the succession of Tiberius. Sempronius died perhaps towards the end of AD 14. He was put to death by *milites* on the island of Cercina, off the coast of Africa. Tacitus does not provide a date, supplying only the general *eodem anno*.[17] Tiberius shifted blame for the execution onto L. Asprenas, proconsul of Africa. The execution was probably performed on hearing that Augustus was dead; as was the case with Agrippa Postumus. The demise of L. Aemilius Paullus is even more suggestive. Syme has shown that L. Aemilius Paullus is the same man who was replaced by Drusus Caesar as an Arval Brother on 12 May AD 14—three months before Augustus finally died.[18] It reads: *in locum L. [...] Paulli*.[19] As Syme points out, membership was not extinguished by exile but by death alone.[20] Though L. Aemilius Paullus possibly died from complications arising from the nature of his exile, the timing is suspicious.

Asinius Epicadus had Illyrian heritage. Some connection to the Asinii is evident and Levick may be right when she suggests that Asinius Pollio took him in war.[21] Of all the attested Audasii, the overwhelming majority come from the same 130 km stretch of highway in Cisalpine Gaul, including Mediolanum, Bergomum, Brixia, and Verona.[22] Though excavations indicate the existence of Augustan veteran colonies in the area, there is also evidence for

---

[16] It is plausible even that the younger Julia was not named because she was not part of this group; a member of the smart set with her own concerns, interested not in politics but socializing at parties, or simply, in a different political group (which included Junius Silanus).
[17] Tac. *Ann.* 1.53.3.
[18] R. Syme (1986) 123f.
[19] *ILS* 5026.
[20] Pliny *NH* 18.6; Pliny *Ep.* 4.8.1; Plut. *Quaest. Rom.* 99.
[21] B. Levick (1976), 337, n. 135.
[22] Mediolanum = *CIL* V² 5749; Bergomum = *CIL* V² 5150; Brixia = *CIL* V² 8879; Verona = *CIL* V² 3503, 3504, 3505.

disaffection.[23] But Audasius' criminal record is the most revealing: he was a forger. The conspirators were not planning to attack the prison on Planasia but to use falsified release documents instead. A parchment, with what appeared to be Augustus' seal, containing instruction for Agrippa's release, written in the princeps' style and type and presented by an appropriate looking individual, is a necessary postulation. Rhegium, moreover, might have been a naval base, which would explain Augustus' decision to send his daughter Julia there when attempting to appease angry crowds in AD 4.[24] It would also explain why the conspirators were not interested in causing a stir. It was believed, or argued in court, that the escapees were to be taken to the armies; no legions are specified. A clue is furnished if we take this conspiracy to have been the prototype for Clemens. In that case they were to be taken to the German legions; either way civil war was to be the result.[25]

In AD 11 Tiberius and Germanicus campaigned in Germany, dispatched for the purpose of re-establishing a northern defence weakened by the Varian disaster.[26] Both men celebrated Augustus' birthday on 23 September while north of the Rhine, and Velleius adds that Tiberius later made winter camp.[27] Dio has both in Rome by January.[28] The conspirators would not have approached the legions while both Tiberius and Germanicus were present - they would have waited until the onset of winter, making their expedition to Planasia and Rhegium even more dangerous. A late date would explain why legislation was not passed until AD 12; the plan was

[23] A story survives in Plutarch (*Comp. Dion. and Brut.* 5) of the magistrates of Mediolanum being thrown into confusion when Augustus happened to stop by and was greeted with statues of Brutus and Cassius. Augustus is said to have laughed, using the episode to advertise the government's tolerance, but the fact that the story exists suggests that not all were convinced by an eloquent smile. A story with a similar theme is cited by Suet. *De Rhet.* 6, who states that within the forum in Mediolanum there was a statue of Brutus, to which a famous orator declared: 'once again Italy was being reduced to the form of a province'. G. C. F. Chilver, *Cisalpine Gaul: Social and Economic History from 49 B.C. to the Death of Trajan* (1941), 9f., argues that the entire region was chosen for colonization by Augustus in order to stamp out disaffection, but such tendencies would not necessarily dissolve in a melting pot of new and old citizens.
[24] J. Linderski (1988), 184, esp. n. 10.
[25] Tac. *Ann.* 1.39.1-2.
[26] Dio 56.25.1-3.
[27] Vell. 2.120.1-2.
[28] Dio 56.26.1.

discovered during the early stages of its operation, or was exposed before the conspirators had even left Rome. An inquiry was held, the names of Audasius and Epicadus were brought to light and both were sentenced at subsequent trials, though precise details never surfaced. As with the Clemens affair, the government was left with small-fry con–artists, rumour, and suggestive testimony.[29] Still it was supposed, or established in court, that at least Agrippa and his mother, Julia, were the targets of an attempted rescue. The government was left to wonder about other exiles. A sweeping review was held, exposing fundamental problems within the system. Those opposed to the coming succession kept up their attack regardless.

Dio records under AD 12 the distribution of vituperative pamphlets aimed at prominent members of the government:

καὶ μαθὼν ὅτι βιβλία ἄττα ἐφ' ὕβρει τινῶν συγγράφοιτο, ζήτησιν αὐτῶν ἐποιήσατο, καὶ ἐκεῖνά τε, τὰ μὲν ἐν τῇ πόλει εὑρεθέντα πρὸς τῶν ἀγορανόμων τὰ δὲ ἔξω πρὸς τῶν ἑκασταχόθι ἀρχόντων, κατέφλεξε, καὶ τῶν συνθέντων αὐτὰ ἐκόλασέ τινας.

And learning that some pamphlets of an insulting nature were being written concerning certain people, he ordered a search be made for them; and those that were found in the city he ordered to be burned by the aediles, and those outside by the chief magistrates in each place, and he punished some of the writers.[30]

The nature of the authorship and the extent of publication are unknown. The arrest of authors indicates overt authorship, but may also follow an extensive investigation condensed into a single paragraph by Dio.[31] 'Those outside' is similarly ambiguous. The range of publication may have been a region of Italy, the whole of Italy, or perhaps even empire-wide. Obscurity, however, does not preclude contextualization. The reaction implies anger (searching for pamphlets, perhaps door-to-door, burning them, punishing authors) and anxiety. Anger presumably because the victims were important people; anxiety because the criticisms were widely held and/or believable. A combination of Augustus' ill health with the prospect of succession is a plausible context. It was certainly the most pressing concern for

---

[29] As with rumour surrounding Clemens' insurrection, Tac. *Ann.* 2.40.3.
[30] Dio 56.27.1.
[31] As was shown above, *contra* R. A. Bauman (1974), 29–30, and A. D'Hautcourt (1995), 315–18, Cassius Severus was not involved.

142 *The Republic in Danger*

Tiberius' bitterest enemies. A *relatio* read on the first sitting day of the senate is evidence for such a connection:

ὁ δὲ δὴ Αὔγουστος ἐκεῖνόν τε ὡς καὶ ἐπὶ γήρως ὢν τῇ βουλῇ καὶ ταύτην τῷ Τιβερίῳ παρακατέθετο. ἀνέγνω δὲ τὸ βιβλίον οὐκ αὐτός (οὐ γὰρ οἷός τε ἦν γεγωνίσκειν) ἀλλ' ὁ Γερμανικός, ὥσπερ εἰώθει.

But Augustus, giving his old age as the reason, entrusted Germanicus to the senate and the senate itself to Tiberius. Augustus himself did not read the letter (since he could not make himself heard) but Germanicus did, as was usual.[32]

Scholars have not considered associating the defamatory pamphlets with Augustus' letter. The timeframe is, however, acceptable. In Dio's treatment of AD 12, the pamphlets are placed after the letter of Augustus to the senate but before the *Ludi Martiales*, which occurred on 10 May. If Dio simply recounts events as they appeared in the senatorial *acta*, or a senatorial historian, the pamphlets were published sometime between January and May. The time between publication and senatorial inquiry may only have been a week; at most it was a month. The pamphlets could certainly have been written as early as January. Augustus' central message would have certainly aroused protest and indignation from those already dissatisfied.

Entrusting Germanicus to the care of the senate is fair enough, but entrusting the senate to Tiberius is outrageous. Hammond translates παρακατατίθεμαι as 'to commend', but he is mistaken.[33] Its literal meaning is 'to place alongside'; its usual sense is to 'entrust', as when a father entrusts his son to the care of a guardian in a will. When Dio means 'commend', he uses συνιστάναι.[34] The treatment of Germanicus' children Nero and Drusus in AD 23 is here instructive. In AD 20 Nero was commended (*commendare*) to the senate on taking the *toga virilis*; his brother Drusus followed suit at the beginning of AD 23.[35] After the death of Germanicus, the boys were placed in the care of their uncle, the younger Drusus. When Drusus died on 14 September AD 23, Tiberius approached the senate thus:

---

[32] Dio 56.26.2.
[33] M. Hammond, *The Augustan Principate in Theory and Practice during the Julio-Claudian Period* (1933), 273, n. 15.
[34] Dio 37.44.3; 58.20.3. Both instances refer to elections, but the idea is the same. Tacitus uses '*commendare*' for both elections and the sponsorship of imperial youths on taking the *toga virilis*.
[35] For Nero, see Tac. *Ann*. 3.29; for Drusus, see Tac. *Ann*. 4.4.

Erepto Druso preces ad vos converto disque et patria coram obtestor: Augusti pronepotes, clarissimis maioribus genitos, suscipite regite, vestram meamque vicem explete. Hi vobis, Nero et Druse, parentum loco.

Drusus has been taken away and so I direct my prayers towards you and I implore you before the gods and the fatherland: take up and direct the grandchildren of Augustus, scions of most illustrious ancestors, and fulfil your duty and mine. Nero and Drusus, these men will take the place of your parents.[36]

Since both Nero and Drusus had already been 'commended' to the senate, this occasion supplied an entirely different theme.[37] The senate, in a moral sense, *adopted* the boys. The terms *suscipio, rego,* and *expleo* are important.[38] They imply the moral authority of a father, and thus the immature and incomplete nature of a child. Treating the same episode Dio uses παρακατατίθεμαι:

Ὁ μὲν οὖν οὕτως διώλετο, ὁ δέ γε Τιβέριος εἰς τὸ συνέδριον ἀφικόμενος ἐκεῖνόν τε ἀπωδύρατο καὶ τὸν Νέρωνα τόν τε Δροῦσον τοὺς τοῦ Γερμανικοῦ παῖδας τῇ γερουσίᾳ παρακατέθετο.

Thus he [Drusus] perished; but Tiberius, having arrived at the senate house, both lamented him publicly and entrusted Nero and Drusus, the sons of Germanicus, to the senate.[39]

Treating Augustus' letter of AD 12, Dio must mean that Tiberius was 'entrusted' with the senate as if he were a guardian exercising moral authority over an orphan.[40] This is a surprising approach by Augustus.[41] The letter presented Augustus' *res publica* as nothing less than monarchic, bringing into question his long-standing claim that the senate was supreme. Since Augustus remained *princeps senatus* until death, he evidently wanted the senators to extend to Tiberius the same level of respect he had himself received. Tiberius was to be treated *as* a *pater*! Curiously, this piece of evidence is absent from notable biographies of Tiberius and, more surprisingly, from the most

---

[36] Tac. *Ann.* 4.8.
[37] Cf. B. Levick (1999), 162: 'Nero and Drusus were brought in and commended to the *patres*.'
[38] A father 'takes up' (*suscipio*) a baby to accept it into the family.
[39] Dio 57.22.4ᵃ = Zon. 11.2.
[40] Since Dio seems to be following the *acta senatus* he has likely used the correct term. Indeed, as with Nero and Drusus in AD 23, Germanicus had already been 'commended' to the senate. Dio ought to be trusted on this.
[41] P. M. Swan (2004), 285, describes it as 'remarkable'.

144   *The Republic in Danger*

important modern works on the 'constitution' of the early Principate.[42]

Scholars look to *senatus consulta* in AD 12 and 13 that provided Tiberius with *imperium* equal to that of Augustus and reinstated his *tribunicia potestas* for another term.[43] But the emphasis is superficial. Augustus was, in fact, organizing his powers over time into a defined totality; on each occasion that Tiberius received a form of power a new aspect of the Principate was established: *statio imperii*.[44] Aside from Augustus' personal charisma, which afforded the princeps a certain type of power, by AD 13 Augustus and Tiberius were equal; the position of *pontifex maximus* alone separated them. Augustus was manufacturing a structure with which to guide succession.[45] What, then, was he hoping to achieve in his address to the senate in AD 12? Keeping in mind the prospect of succession, the answer must lie in the distinction made between Tiberius and Germanicus.

At 26, Germanicus represented the long-term future. Tiberius was in his fifties and might be expected to last another decade or so, but

---

[42] The passage is not considered by: Th. Mommsen *Staat.* (1888), esp. his section on the relationship between princeps and Senate, III 2, 894–902; A. H. J. Greenidge (1901); W. Weber (1936); J. Crook, *Consilium Principis* (1955); Sattler, P. *Augustus un der Senat* (1960); J. Bleicken, *Senatsgericht und Kaisergericht* (1962); F. Miller, *The Emperor in the Roman World* (1977); R. J. A. Talbert (1984), and 'Augustus and the Senate', *Greece and Rome*, 31:1 (1984), 55–63; P. A. Brunt 'The Role of the Senate in Augustus' Government', *CQ*, 34:2 (1984), 423–44; W. K. Lacey, *Augustus and the Principate* (1996); cf. M. Hammond, (1933), 273, n. 15.

[43] Dio 56.28.1; Vell. 2.121.1; Suet. *Tib.* 21.1. Velleius writes that Tiberius received *imperium* equal to that held by Augustus 'in all provinces and armies'. Suetonius adds that the *lex* also allowed for Tiberius to hold a census with Augustus, and perform a *lustrum*. In *RG* 8. Augustus writes: 'In my sixth consulship with Marcus Agrippa as colleague, I carried out a census of the people, and I performed a *lustrum* after a lapse of 42 years.' Agrippa and Augustus were both consuls in 28 BC. He goes on: 'I performed a *lustrum* with consular *imperium*, with Tiberius my son, as colleague (*conlega*), in the consulship of Sex. Pompeius and Sextus Appuleius.' *Conlegus* indicates that Tiberius also had consular *imperium*. Moreover, Tiberius was able to summon and use the praetorians within Rome in the first weeks of September, a right that required *imperium*. That it was within the *pomerium* indicates consular *imperium* (Tac. *Ann.* 1.7.5; Suet. *Tib.* 24). Cf. P. A. Brunt, 'C. Fabricius Tuscus and an Augustan Dilectus', *ZPE*, 13 (1974), 161–85 who dates Tiberius' consular *imperium* to AD 4; also A. H. M. Jones, *Studies in Roman Government and Law* (1960), and D. Hoyos 'The Legal Powers of Augustus: Some Modern Views', *Ancient Society Resources for Teachers*, 8:1 no.1 (1983), 42–6, who date it to 17 Sept. AD 14.

[44] Vell. 2.124.2; *SCPP* 129–30.

[45] The position of *pontifex maximus* was not essential to supreme power, but preferred. Augustus waited until 12 BC (*RG* 10.2); Tiberius waited until 15 March AD 15 (*ILS* 154; V. Ehrenberg and A. H. M. Jones (1955), 47).

Germanicus would potentially enjoy dominance for thirty to forty years, perhaps more. That Drusus was not named shows only that his position did not require definition.[46] The letter of AD 12 shows that interest in Germanicus caught Augustus' and Tiberius' attention; it was made clear who was to succeed. That people might have held positive expectations about Germanicus' consulship is not surprising. A self-imposed exile on Rhodes from 6 BC to AD 2, interdiction from public activities from AD 2 to AD 4, and continual campaigning from AD 4 to AD 12 must have affected Tiberius' relationship with the senate. Between AD 4 and AD 12 Tiberius could only have attended the senate from January to perhaps April. He would then leave Rome for the northern provinces, and would not return again until winter (sometimes late October, generally early December), by which time the senate was already in recess until January. If Tiberius attended the senate from January to April, and the senate met twice a month, then Tiberius attended approximately 64 out of a possible 216 senate meetings. If we take into account his Rhodian exile, then from 6 BC to AD 12 Tiberius attended 64 of a minimum 432 senate meetings (15 per cent); he probably attended even fewer. In Tiberius' absence, senators would have formed alliances, friendships, cliques that did not include Augustus' heir. Indeed, methods for transactiong senatorial business would have been developed that required very little imput from Tiberius, or none at all. Only his closest allies would have kept his interests alive. It is, therefore, very possible that senators became more comfortable around the young consul Germanicus than Augustus' intended successor: this would have been a problem for Augustus, as well as Tiberius. Augustus' letter prevented Germanicus from *unintentionally* fostering a relationship with the senate which could prove awkward for Tiberius, and parts of the senate from *intentionally* fostering such a relationship with Germanicus. Indeed, though we have highlighted a division between those who supported Agrippa and those who supported Augustus' succession plan,

---

[46] G. V. Sumner, 'Germanicus and Drusus Caesar', *Latomus*, 26 (1967), 413–35, takes it to mean that Germanicus was, at this time, preferred over Drusus. I believe he is right. It was probably the case that Drusus' position structurally renewed the relationship of L. Caesar to his brother C. Caesar. Nevertheless, Drusus, on this occasion, was omitted because he was not consul, i.e. there was no reason for confusion on any level. Cf. B. Levick, 'Drusus Caesar and the Adoptions of AD 4', *Latomus*, 25 (1966), 226–44, argues that both were treated as equals; they were to serve as dual *principes*.

political divisions are rarely symmetrical. We should not assume that men loyal to Augustus were happy to transfer support to Tiberius; some would have looked to Germanicus instead, while still others would have hoped for Drusus to succeed Tiberius at the expense of Germanicus. For those opposed to Tiberius, Germanicus and Drusus, the image of the *domus Caesaris* divided would be used to satisfy their own political agenda. Augustus' letter was meant to right a faltering ship, but as the evidence is assembled here, the immediate result was the publishing of dissent.

The government's theatrical reaction evidences the seriousness of the criticism. Something like calling Tiberius a new *dominus*, or a *rex* even, would have been both defamatory and seditious.[47] The senate, along with the *comitia* and *quaestiones*, provided the appearance of continuity with the free past: as symbols they were central to Augustus' new *res publica*. As with Labienus' histories, the regime reacted because the pamphlets threatened to destabilize support for an insecure government sensitive to accusations of tyranny. Concerning senatorial freedom under Augustus, Suetonius writes:

Sententias de maiore negotio non more atque ordine sed prout libuisset perrogabat, ut perinde quisque animum intenderet ac si censendum magis quam adsentiendum esset.

Concerning more important business he asked senators to give their opinions not in the customary order but pretty well as he fancied, so that each man might direct his thoughts towards the business, as if he was using judgement more than acquiescing.[48]

Dio provides an appropriate example when treating a debate that emerged in AD 13 concerning the *vicesima hereditatium*. Augustus sent a βιβλίον to the senate on the issue when an uprising seemed imminent (καὶ ἐδόκει τι νεώτερον ἔσεσθαι); he was evidently too weak to attend in person. Dio continues:

---

[47] As has been shown already, it would be *maiestas* on account of the ruling against Cassius Severus in AD 8 and the fact that he held magisterial *imperium*. But it might also be held that the succession plan was part of the *statio imperii*. Indeed, Tiberius' adoption was accompanied by an official rider. Any attempt to undermine the succession might, therefore, have been interpreted by the government as *contra rem publicam*.
[48] Suet. *Aug.* 35.4; see also Dio 56.41.1.

Novus Principatus: *An Imperial Co-operative*

καὶ ὅπως γε μὴ τοῦ Γερμανικοῦ τοῦ τε Δρούσου γνώμην τινὰ εἰπόντων ὑποτοπήσωσί τε ἐκ τῆς αὐτοῦ ἐντολῆς τοῦτο γεγονέναι καὶ ἀνεξέταστον αὐτὴν ἕλωνται, προσέταξε μηδέτερον αὐτῶν μηδὲν εἰπεῖν.

Also to keep the senators from suspecting that some view of Germanicus or Drusus was said on his instructions and from preferring it uncritically, Augustus instructed them both to say nothing.[49]

Direct taxation was contentious, and for that reason alone Augustus was keen to include senators in discussions and make them share responsibility. Thus, as Suetonius points out, senators were given a say on the big issues. Concerning ordinary business, however, Augustus was happy to affect debate.[50] But Suetonius supplies evidence that his approach had critics:

In senatu verba facienti dictum est: 'Non intellexi', *et ab alio:* 'Contra dicerem tibi, si locum haberem.' *Interdum ob immodicas disceptantium altercationes e curia per iram se proripienti quidam ingesserunt licere oportere senatoribus de re p. loqui.*

Speaking in the senate, it was said to him: 'I do not understand' and by another: 'I would speak against you, if I had the opportunity.' Sometimes, while he was rushing out of the House in anger because of the excessive wrangling of the disputants, some shouted at him that senators ought to be allowed to speak on public affairs.[51]

De re publica does not refer to *maius negotium*, but all matters brought before senators. Offering a summation of Augustus' Principate, in order to advertise an ideal mixed constitution, Dio has Tiberius say:

... οὔτε ἐν ταῖς διαγνώμαις τὴν ἐξουσίαν τῆς διαψηφίσεως κατέλυσεν, ἀλλὰ καὶ τὴν ἀσφάλειαν τῆς παρρησίας προσέθηκεν.

---

[49] Dio 56.28.5.
[50] Tiberius is said to have stated at the funeral of Augustus: οἷς ἐξ ἴσου καὶ αὐτὸς τὴν γνώμην ἐδίδου καὶ μεθ' ὧν συμμεθίστατο (Dio. 56.41.1). J. Crook (1955), 131, erroneously states 'What is important is that Augustus did not waste his time and vocal powers on everyday matters (except merely to give his *sententia*, which is quite different).' As was shown above, Augustus' *sententia* was treated as the deciding opinion, which in fact made his use of it in 'everyday matters' autocratic. Far from wasting his time, he was controlling the administration of the empire.
[51] Suet. *Aug.* 54.

Nor did he abolish their [senators'] power of deciding matters by vote in their deliberations but in addition he gave them the security to speak frankly.[52]

That senators were allowed to vote on issues is hardly worthy of praise. Dio would have us believe that senators voted by the grace of Augustus, who could have abolished the right altogether. Ἀσφάλεια, moreover, does not mean that senators were merely allowed to give their opinion, but that they were allowed to speak frankly without worrying about recriminations, i.e. their careers and lives were safe from harm. As with the right to vote on issues *de re publica*, the implicit suggestion that this was a privilege offered by Augustus shows just how superficial the façade had become. Παρακατατίθεμαι momentarily made visible the true autocratic nature of Augustus' *res publica*, leaving some, perhaps many, shocked and disapproving. Such disapproval, or anger even, may have informed Tiberius' future relationship with the senate. Tiberius' performance in the senate between AD 14 and AD 20 is a topic of dispute precisely because his approach was ambiguous. It has been described in both ancient Rome and modern scholarship as hypocritical, naïve, sinister, or Republican. It was certainly awkward; awkwardness caused by, or perhaps made worse by, his infrequent attendance.[53] A brief examination of Tiberius' relationship with the senate is here instructive.

We are told that as *princeps* Tiberius brought most matters, no matter how insignificant, to the senate, and that when a matter was being discussed he generally remained silent or gave his opinion out of turn.[54] Both Suetonius and Dio state that Tiberius lost debates, and Dio cites an instance in AD 16 when a tribune vetoed a motion that had been passed against Tiberius' advice.[55] Tiberius' style was

---

[52] Dio 56.40.3.
[53] B. Levick (1976), *passim*, held that Tiberius was to some extent misunderstood by a weak and incompetent senate; G. Kampff, 'Three Senate Meetings in the Early Principate', *Phoenix*, 17: 1 (1963), 25–58, goes further: Tiberius wished to restore Republicanism, but was foiled by a self-interested elite. A somewhat weaker conclusion is drawn by R. Seager (1972), 248: 'Tiberius made repeated efforts in the early years of his reign to force the senate to assume its responsibilities, and his sincerity cannot be doubted.' Seager blamed Augustus' heavy-handed approach, which left the senate unable to respond to Tiberius' 'Republicanism'. R. Syme (1986) (see index under Tiberius) agrees with Tacitus: Tiberius was hypocritical. These are, of course, simply a sample of what is a very extensive bibliography.
[54] Dio 57.7.3; Suet. *Tib*. 30.1.
[55] Suet. *Tib*. 31.1; Dio 57.7.5; 57.15.9.

distinctive, and perhaps disturbing.[56] He was not, however, 'Republican'. He was inclined simply to let debate run its course by suppressing his opinion or else speaking out of turn. A senatorial inquiry into an allegation of treason against Granius Marcellus in AD 15 is a good example:

Ad quod exarsit adeo, ut rupta taciturnitate proclamaret se quoque in ea causa laturum sententiam palam et iuratum, 'quo' ceteris eadem necessitas fieret. Manebant etiam tum vestigia morientis libertatis. Igitur Cn. Piso 'quo' inquit 'loco censebis, Caesar? Si primus, habebo quod sequar: si post omnis, vereor ne inprudens dissentiam.'

At this his fury blazed forth so that it ruptured his taciturnity and he proclaimed that in this case he would himself also give his opinion, openly and under oath, that the others might be under the same obligation. There lingered even then remnants of expiring freedom. And so C. Piso said: 'In which place will you vote Caesar? If first, I shall have something to follow, if last, I fear differing from you unawares.'[57]

Se quoque implies that his general policy was silence, but Piso's interjection, itself telling, shows the inherent power of Tiberius' opinion; senatorial freedom of expression relied almost solely on Tiberius remaining silent.[58] The strength of a Piso or an Asinius Gallus alone could defy the unwritten law. Though the policy seems to have been borrowed from Augustus, there was, in fact, a significant difference. Where Tiberius' general policy was to be silent or speak out of turn, Augustus limited such behaviour to important business of the house only.[59] Tiberius' approach was probably a reaction both to

---

[56] Or else it was sinister. Dio 57.7.5 writes that sometimes, after division on an issue, Tiberius would say: 'If I had been giving my views, I should have proposed this or that.' This is intimidation. Why would an opinion be offered *post eventum*, if not to advertise a difference of opinion? It would only place those who had voted contrary to his stated desire on edge. Otherwise it evidences a severe lack of tact and an inability to appreciate the nature of his position: in a word, naivety.

[57] Tac. *Ann.* 1.74.4–5.

[58] For various interpretations of this passage, see F. R. D. Goodyear (1981), 162f. Goodyear, on p. 164, takes *se quoque* to mean that Tiberius remained silent only sometimes, but Tacitus' point is that Tiberius has 'ruptured' a standard practice.

[59] J. Crook (1955), 129, writes 'This must imply that when major issues were afoot he took over the function of the consuls and made the *relatio* himself.' *Perrogo* at Suet. *Aug.* 35.4 certainly suggests that Augustus made the *relatio*, but the logic of the sentence suggests that in it he refrained from giving his opinion. Crook argues that '*Maiora negotia* he certainly proposed [his own measures], and with a formal, dignified and perhaps long set speech.' If Crook means that Augustus' *relatio* on

criticism of Augustus and to his own infrequent exposure to the senate from 6 BC to AD 12.[60] But for many, Tiberius' policy was a façade, albeit with a milder complexion. Suetonius was not fooled:

Quin etiam speciem libertatis quandam induxit conservatis senatui ac magistratibus et maiestate pristina et potestate.

And he even introduced the appearance of liberty by maintaining the ancient majesty and power of the senate and magistrates.[61]

Species is loaded with cynicism, and may reflect contemporary opinion; the *res publica* was a contradiction, no matter how *libertas* was explained. Tiberius' awkwardness, or guile, made the growing magnetism of Germanicus an issue. At the beginning of AD 13, a decision to reconfigure and strengthen one of the primary advisory councils, the *semenstre consilium*, should be interpreted, along with the letter of AD 12, as Augustus' and Tiberius' response to lingering doubt. Dio writes under AD 13:

Καὶ συμβούλους ὑπὸ τοῦ γήρως, ὑφ' οὗπερ οὐδ' ἐς τὸ βουλευτήριον ἔτι πλὴν σπανιώτατα συνεφοίτα, εἴκοσιν ἐτησίους ᾐτήσατο· πρότερον γὰρ καθ' ἕκμηνον πεντεκαίδεκα προσετίθετο. Καὶ προσεψηφίσθη, πάνθ' ὅσα ἂν αὐτῷ μετά τε τοῦ Τιβερίου καὶ μετ' ἐκείνων τῶν τε ἀεὶ ὑπατευόντων καὶ τῶν ἐς τοῦτο ἀποδεδειγμένων, τῶν τε ἐγγόνων αὐτοῦ τῶν ποιητῶν δῆλον ὅτι, τῶν τε ἄλλων ὅσους ἂν ἑκάστοτε προσπαραλάβῃ, βουλευομένῳ δόξῃ, κύρια ὡς καὶ πάσῃ τῇ γερουσίᾳ ἀρέσαντα εἶναι.

Because of his age, on account of which he was no longer attending the senate except very rarely, he asked for twenty annual counsellors. For previously he would take fifteen every six months. It was also voted that all those measures—which were deemed right by him, in his consultation with Tiberius, and with those counsellors, and with the current consuls, and with the

---

these occasions included his opinion, Suetonius' point is made redundant, i.e. Augustus asked for senators to give their opinions out of order in order to ensure that his opinion was not immediately accepted.

[60] Cf. Pompey's parliamentary inadequacy—despite the desire of most senators to accommodate him.

[61] Suet. *Tib.* 30.1; see also Tac. *Ann.* 1.77.3. For the alternative interpretation, see Vell. 2.126.2, who writes that under Tiberius the *maiestas* of the senate was regained: *accessit . . . senatui maiestas*. A. J. Woodman (1977), 240, points out that this device (i.e. the restoration of senatorial freedom) was to be a *topos* throughout the Principate; cf. B. Levick (1999), 92 f., who believes that Velleius reflects Tiberius' actual goal, i.e. it was not cynical marketing.

consuls designate, and with his own offspring (obviously the adopted ones), and with however many others he might include on each occasion—that these measures be valid, as if having been ratified by the whole senate.[62]

The council was provisional. It is not attested after AD 14.[63] Where the original groups, both the *consilium principis* and the *semenstre consilium*, had been probouleutic, the new committee was invested with the authority to pass decrees. Evidently Augustus wished to remain intimately involved with the empire's administration, not happy on the sidelines. But why make the change now? During the period AD 8–12 the two councils (which Tiberius must have participated in whenever in Rome) no doubt ensured that Augustus was kept informed, despite his absence from the senate, and indeed, was able to shape policy.[64] Dio's belief that by early AD 12 Augustus was too weak to be heard, and seemed close to death, should be taken as evidence that his contribution was diminished, though certainly not abandoned. As was stated above, Tiberius spent the years AD 4–12 on campaign - his first full year in Rome was to be AD 13; the new *consilium* allowed a select group, led no doubt by Tiberius, to effect a smooth transition.[65] To sum up, then, in January AD 12 the senate was publicly placed in Tiberius' care; in late AD 12 the senate and people invested him with *imperium* equal to that of Augustus; in October AD 12 he was allowed to triumph and offer a largess to the people (activity Augustus had jealously made his own); his period of *tribunicia potestas* was extended; he was given the right to hold a census with Augustus; and, finally, at the beginning of AD 13, he was provided with a machine with which senatorial debate, on most occasions, could be circumvented.[66] It is not coincidental that Augustus' testament was finalized on 3 April AD 13; Tiberius was now armed for sole leadership.[67]

---

[62] Dio 56.28.2.
[63] J. Crook (1955), 16f.; P. M. Swan (2004), 295; cf. A. Magdelain, *Auctoritas Principis* (1947), 89f.; R. J. A. Talbert (1984), 488.
[64] For Augustus' absence, see Dio 55.33.5–34.3.
[65] J. Crook (1955), 15f.
[66] A *senatus consultum* and *lex* is attested by Vell. 2.120.1 for *imperium*. The *SCPP* 33–4, states that Germanicus' *imperium* in the east was founded on a 'law put before the people' in AD 18. For providing largesse, see Suet. *Tib*. 20. In 11 BC he had similarly fed the people, Dio 55.2.4, but significantly, he did not supply gifts of money. The year is disputed, but AD 12 is the most suitable since Tiberius was away from Rome for all of AD 11. See A. J. Woodman (1977), 212. For the ability of the *consilium* to pass decrees there is no direct proof, but logically the *consilium* would not be given the power to pass decrees if it did not intend to pass them. We should assume that Augustus authored the new arrangements at Tiberius' (or possibly Livia's) request.
[67] Suet. *Aug*. 101.1.

In reformulating the *consilia*, Augustus exhibited a lack of faith, or outright distrust, in sections of the senate to ensure a stable political environment and he must have had good reason. That the re-organization of *consilia* coincided with a renewed opposition to the inheritance tax cannot be coincidental. Immediately after discussing the *semenstre consilium* Dio writes:

ἐπεί τε ἐπὶ τῇ εἰκοστῇ πάντες ὡς εἰπεῖν ἐβαρύνοντο καὶ ἐδόκει τι νεώτερον ἔσεσθαι, ἔπεμψε βιβλίον ἐς τὴν βουλήν, κελεύων ἄλλους τινὰς αὐτὴν πόρους ἐπιζητῆσαι.

Since everybody, so to speak, was disturbed about the *vicesima* and it seemed there was about to be an uprising, he sent to the senate a letter urging it to look for some alternative sources of revenue.[68]

Augustus asked Germanicus and Drusus not to provide an opinion but to report to him on the senate's deliberations:

καὶ ἐλέχθη μὲν πολλά, καί τινα καὶ διὰ βιβλίων τῷ Αὐγούστῳ ἐδηλώθη· καταμαθὼν δὲ ἐξ αὐτῶν πάντα μᾶλλον ἢ ἐκεῖνο ἑτοίμους σφᾶς ὑπομεῖναι ὄντας, ἐπί τε τοὺς ἀγροὺς καὶ ἐπὶ τὰς οἰκίας τὴν συντέλειαν ἤγαγε, καὶ παραχρῆμα μηδέν εἰπών, μήθ' ὅσον μήθ' ὅπως αὐτὸ δώσουσιν, ἔπεμψεν ἄλλους ἄλλῃ τά τε τῶν ἰδιωτῶν καὶ τὰ τῶν πόλεων κτήματα ἀπογραψομένους, ἵν' ὡς καὶ μειζόνως ζημιωθησόμενοι δείσωσι καὶ τὴν εἰκοστὴν τελεῖν ἀνθέλωνται.

Many views were stated; while some were even communicated to Augustus through letters. Having learned from these that senators were ready to submit to all other forms of tax rather than that the one in force, he transferred the levy to lands and buildings and immediately, having said nothing about either how much or in what way they would pay it, sent different people to different places to register the properties of individuals and cities, in order that they should fear suffering even greater losses, and so be content to pay the five percent tax.[69]

Dio understood his source/s to mean that discontent with the inheritance tax was developing into civil unrest. Since it was not in Augustus' interest to exaggerate, or indeed invent, opposition, the reports are probably true. The tax had survived for almost eight years, and this is the first evidence we have for spirited opposition to its implementation since AD 7. Why the sudden outburst? Swan suggests

---

[68] Dio 56.28.6.
[69] Dio 56.28.5–6.

that 'it perhaps took some years for enough heirs to be affected to fuel a crisis.'[70] But the tax cannot have destroyed confidence in the economy; in principle oppressive, the tax was in reality a trifle. We should not suppose that losing HS 5,000 to the government seriously affected someone inheriting HS 100,000. Objections were politically rather than economically inspired, and the only plausible political explanation for the re-emergence of opposition to the tax is the permanent presence of Tiberius in Rome.[71] Protestors were testing the future princeps.

Dio mentions only the attendance of Germanicus and Drusus at the relevant senatorial debate/s. Tiberius' absence from the meeting, at first sight remarkable, makes sense. The presence of his two sons indicates how deeply Tiberius was affected, but his absence suggests caution. He was quarantined from the inevitable unpleasantness that would accompany an open defence of the government's position. It is important to note that while debate ran its course in the senate, policy was being implemented by the reconstructed *semestre consilium*, at which Tiberius was probably present.[72] Communication between Augustus and the senate was conducted via letters, but Augustus must here refer to his *consilium*. It was the *consilium* that reacted to the threat of violence by bringing the matter before the senate. As was shown above, on sensitive issues such as taxation, the government advertised senatorial self-determination. But importantly, when it became obvious that senators 'were ready to submit to any form of tax' other than the inheritance tax, the *consilium* used its new power to decree an audit of land and buildings. We lose the full text of Dio at ἰδιωτῶν καὶ, but his epitomator, Xiphilinus, understood him to mean that the government's strategy was to limit outcomes to two separate

---

[70] P. M. Swan (2004), 296.
[71] C. Nicolet (1980), 184–5, distinguishes the *vicesima* from *tributum* on the ground that the latter was an exceptional measure. As a permanent feature the *vicesima hereditatium* signalled a significant break from Republicanism.
[72] A papyrus dated to AD 13 attests Tiberius' attendance at the meeting of a *consilium*, listening to Alexandrian envoys. Tiberius is named immediately after Augustus in the official minutes. Though this could refer to the board of three ex-consuls formed to listen to foreign envoys, that Alexandria is concerned makes the *semestre consilium* more likely. P. *Oxy.* 2436 = R. K. Sherk, *Rome and the Greek East to the Death of Augustus* (1984), no.111; P. M. Swan (2004), 295: '[this papyrus] may be an audience of Alexandrian envoys before our *consilium*'.

proposals. Xiphilinus writes only that Augustus wanted senators to fear even greater losses under the new tax, and so accept the 5 per cent tax on inheritances as the better option. He then adds 'and this is what actually happened'.[73] Tenants, and not landlords, tend to bear such burdens, but landlords are usually held responsible.[74] The counter-proposal would, therefore, have attracted popular and elite resistance: it was much easier to pay 5 per cent on windfalls.[75]

Despite the protest's popular dimensions, dissent was none the less artificial. The initial protest in AD 6, though sponsored by persons within the imperial house like Aemilius Paullus, was understandable; resistance to taxation is attested in most societies. Resentment no doubt lingered, but passionate violence had given way to subdued indifference. The crescendo of discontent allegedly threatening Rome in AD 13 was surely manufactured. People certainly talked about the unfair nature of the tax and the possibility of large-scale riots - perhaps gangs of men were paid to cause unrest. The troublemakers, however, were not interested in new policy proposals. They wished to place Tiberius in an uncomfortable and unpopular position at a time when he was poised to succeed Augustus - Tiberius was kept away from the fight.

Tiberius was marked out as successor in AD 4, but the details were not secured until AD 13. Augustus' death was the final requirement. It must have been clear to most observers that Augustus was close to the end. A popular tumult regarding the tax was, therefore, a reaction to the penultimate process of succession. Those opposed to Tiberius complained that the inheritance tax was unfit for Roman citizens, implying that they were being treated like subjects. Men on the street

---

[73] Augustus' 'threat' was, in fact, a return to fiscal policy during the triumvirate, see Dio 47.14.2–3 for a tax on houses and country estates.

[74] Landlords would also be exposed to the unpopularity of collecting higher rents. A rental crisis in England in 1549 contributed to Kett's rebellion, in which the rebel manifesto singled out revenue-raising as a chief concern for the commons. Significantly, Kett was a landlord. Indeed, each Tudor rebellion evidenced a symbiotic relationship between landlords and commons; landlords required the physical presence of the commons while the commons required the landlords for political legitimation, A. Fletcher (1968), see index.

[75] D. Kienast (1999), 407, took the alternative seriously. He argues that Augustus *wanted* a tax on land and buildings. That would have been very risky. It is illogical to believe that Augustus would make a precarious situation even worse by suggesting a tax that was sure to upset people. Augustus cannot have believed that such a tax would be less odious. Rather than evidence naivety, the situation shows that Augustus was expert at intimidation.

perhaps used the language of tyranny. The government, with Tiberius hiding behind the lines, reasserted its position. This is not a surprise. War was an expensive endeavour and required ever-increasing levels of public administration. Since Augustus did not want individual citizens to offer voluntary payments, thereby feudalizing the government, taxation was the only alternative. This is an area of tension for all governments, but especially authoritarian governments uninterested in private philanthropy. The government alone paid for public utilities and services, and costs soon blew out once the defence and organization of the entire empire was considered. The opposition was utilizing a philosophical doctrine relevant to city-state Republicanism to counter the pragmatic policy decisions of a government administering an empire. This contest is relevant to the final accession of Tiberius and his famous hesitation.

9

The Hesitation of Tiberius

Augustus died at Nola on 19 August AD 14.[1] Tiberius alone now held *imperium* both inside and outside Italy, as well as tribunician power.[2] *Auctoritas* equal to that of Augustus was alone lacking. Tiberius utilized his position immediately. Tacitus writes:

simul excessisse Augustum et rerum potiri Neronem fama eadem tulit.

The same single report carried news that Augustus was dead and that Nero was in control of things.[3]

and

Sed defuncto Augusto signum praetoriis cohortibus ut imperator dederat; excubiae, arma, cetera aulae ...

But on the death of Augustus he had given the signal to the praetorian cohorts as imperator, he had guards (of watch), weapons of war, and every aspect of a royal court ...[4]

Dio writes:

τοιοῦτος οὖν δή τις ὢν ἔς τε τὰ στρατόπεδα καὶ ἐς τὰ ἔθνη πάντα ὡς αὐτοκράτωρ εὐθὺς ἀπὸ τῆς Νώλης ἐπέστειλε, μὴ λέγων αὐτοκράτωρ εἶναι·

---

[1] Suet. *Aug.* 99.2–100.1; Vell. 2.123; Tac. *Ann.* 1.5; Dio 56.30.5f.
[2] D. Hoyos (1983), 43f., has argued that Tiberius did not have, in Sept. AD 14, consular *imperium* valid inside Italy. According to Hoyos, the law of AD 12 provided Tiberius only with *imperium* equal to that of Augustus in the provinces. But Tiberius' ability to command the praetorians inside the *pomerium* in the first weeks of Sept. surely rested on a legal right, and Tacitus makes specific reference to his giving orders within Rome 'as Imperator', that is, as someone who held *imperium* (Tac. *Ann.* 1.7.5). The obvious type of *imperium* is consular.
[3] Tac. *Ann.* 1.5.
[4] Ibid., 1.7.

158   *The Republic in Danger*

And so indeed he, being a man of this sort, sent a letter immediately, as emperor, from Nola to all the legions and provinces, though not claiming to be emperor...[5]

Suetonius writes:

Principatum, quamvis neque occupare confestim neque agere dubitasset, et statione militum, hoc est vi et specie dominationis assumpta...

Although he did not hesitate to seize immediately and exercise the Principate, and with a guard of soldiers, that is with the power and appearance of domination having been assumed...[6]

In response to the report, an oath of allegiance to Tiberius was immediately sworn:[7]

Sex. Pompeius et Sex. Appuleius consules primi in verba Tiberii Caesaris iuravere, apudque eos Seius Strabo et C. Turranius, ille praetoriarum cohortium praefectus, hic annonae; mox senatus milesque et populus.

The consuls Sex. Pompeius and Sex. Appuleius were the first to swear an oath to Tiberius Caesar and in their presence so did Seius Strabo, prefect of the praetorian cohorts, and C. Turranius, prefect of the corn supply; next the senate, the soldiers and the people (did the same).[8]

And when news of Augustus' death reached Germanicus in Gaul:

seque et proximos et Belgarum civitates in verba eius adigit.

To himself, those around him, and the Belgic cities he [Germanicus] administered the oath of allegiance to Tiberius.[9]

Dio notes further:

---

[5] Dio 57.2.1. It must be remembered that Dio's Greek does not capture the *imperator*/emperor dichotomy in the Latin.
[6] Suet. *Tib.* 24.1.
[7] It is not necessary here to discuss the nature of this oath. It is important simply to point out that Tiberius' position was necessarily perceived as superior and required suitable recognition. A brief discussion, with bibliography, is given by F. R. D. Goodyear (1972), 138f. T. E. J. Wiedemann in *CAH* 10², 203, argues that the oath was a private affair, neither public nor constitutional. That the consuls swore the oath together in the presence of the two most powerful public servants suggests that Wiedemann is wrong. Tacitus' narrative implies public organization, with the consuls in the lead. Moreover, the idea that a political act is unconstitutional is problematic for Roman history. Rome had no defined constitution.
[8] Tac. *Ann.* 1.7.2.
[9] Ibid., 1.34.1.

The Hesitation of Tiberius

τοὺς μὲν γὰρ ἐν τῇ Ἰταλίᾳ ὄντας τοῖς ὅρκοις τοῖς ὑπὸ τοῦ Αὐγούστου καταδειχθεῖσι προκατέλαβεν·

For he [Tiberius] had won over those who were in Italy by means of the oaths that were established by Augustus...[10]

Fama in Tacitus means literally a rumour, i.e. 'it was said that...'. But there must have been an official letter, replete with Tiberius' formal title. This was his right as holder of *imperium* in every province. Tiberius' note was in part an assumption of power.[11] Though the desired effect was witnessed almost immediately, i.e. an empire-wide oath, we should suspect prior orchestration. Augustus had invested heavily in Tiberius and surely planned for the moment. It is reasonable to suppose that key stakeholders - the consuls, the senior prefects, Germanicus and Drusus - knew in advance what was expected of them and acted accordingly. By the time Tiberius reached Rome most of the empire would have pledged allegiance. Effects were evident once he was in Rome: *miles in forum miles in curiam comitabatur*, 'soldiers accompanied him in the forum, soldiers accompanied him in the curia.'[12] By *miles*, Tacitus must mean that a bodyguard of praetorians occupied civic spaces disarmed under the Republic. Contemporaries interpreted this public show of force as the definition of real power, echoed perhaps in Suetonius: 'and with a guard of soldiers, that is with the power and appearance of domination having been assumed...'.[13] Thus, in the weeks following Augustus' death, Tiberius possessed *tribunicia potestas*, consular *imperium* inside and outside Italy, the allegiance of the legions, praetorians, *vigiles,* and urban cohorts, as well as the consuls, the social orders, and the various administrative branches, and armed soldiers accompanied him everywhere: Tiberius was the unquestioned ruler of Rome. Further to his position within the body politic, he was also now the *pater familias* of the *domus Caesaris*. As Wiedemann points out, Tiberius was in control of the most extensive supply of assets in the empire.[14] The number of freedmen paid out of

---

[10] Dio 57.3.2.
[11] Perhaps *fama* is a deliberate distortion by Tacitus, or his source, meant to thrown suspicion on an act that was in fact legal and appropriate.
[12] Tac. *Ann.* 1.7.5.
[13] Suet. *Tib.* 24.
[14] *CAH* 10² 202f.; this point formed the basis of Millar's criticism of D. Timpe *Untersuchungen zur Kontinuität des frühen Prinzipats*, Historia Einzelschriften, Heft

Augustus' fortune while working in the public interest was enormous, while the number of families engaged in a patron–client relationship with the *domus Caesaris*, including foreign monarchs, provided a means for social control 'with which no other household could compete'. Nevertheless, for a period of weeks following Augustus' death, Tiberius seemed hesitant when speaking in the senate about the prospect of being princeps, or as the contemporary Velleius put it, of accepting the Principate (*principatus*).[15] Velleius writes:

Una tamen veluti luctatio civitatis fuit, pugnantis cum Caesare senatus populique Romani, ut stationi paternae succederet, illius, ut potius aequalem civem quam eminentem liceret agere principem. Tandem magis ratione quam honore victus est, cum quidquid tuendum non suscepisset, periturum videret, solique huic contigit paene diutius recusare principatum, quam, ut occuparent eum, alii armis pugnauerant.

There was however one civil dispute, as it were, when the senate and people of Rome fought with Caesar to make him succeed to the position of his father while he (countered) that he would prefer to be allowed to be an equal citizen rather than be singled out in the role of princeps. At last he was conquered more by reason than by the offered honour since he saw that whatever he did not take under his protection would perish. He is the only one to whose lot it has fallen to refuse the principate for a longer time, nearly, than others had fought to secure it.[16]

Ovid, responding to the news some time after the event, writes:

Nam patris Augusti docui mortale fuisse | corpus in aetherias numen abisse domos | esse parem virtute patri qui frena rogatus | saepe recusati ceperit imperii...

For I have taught that the body of father Augustus was mortal, | that his godhead has departed for celestial abodes, | that equal in virtue to his father is

---

5 (1962), in his review article 'The Early Principate', *CR*, 13:3 (1963), 327-9. Millar argues that the key to understanding the Principate lies not in its 'constitution' but the process by which the 'Roman world came to accept so easily and so quickly the existence of a ruling house.' Millar's position essentially leads to analysis which places heavy significance on patron–client relationships as they operated in the Republican period.

[15] On what it was that Tiberius was refusing/hesitating to accept, see: T. Hillard (2010) 163 n. 27, 'Velleius 2.124.2 and the Reluctant Princeps: The Evolution of Roman Perceptions of Leadership', in Cowen, *E. Velleius Paterculus: Making History* (2010) (I would like to thank Tom Hillard for allowing me to see an advanced copy of his paper). Cf. D. Hoyos (1983), 42–6.

[16] Vell. 2.124.2.

he who, having been asked, has taken the reins | of the often refused *imperium*.[17]

Tacitus writes:

Litteras ad exercitus tamquam adepto principatu misit, nusquam cunctabundus nisi cum in senatu loqueretur.

He sent letters to the army as if he had obtained the Principate, and being hesitant nowhere except when speaking in the senate.[18]

Suetonius writes:

Diu tamen recusavit, impudentissimo mimo nunc adhortantis amicos increpans ut ignaros, quanta belua esset imperium, nunc precantem senatum et procumbentem sibi ad genua ambiguis responsis et callida cunctatione suspendens, ut quidam patientiam rumperent atque unus in tumultu proclamaret: 'Aut agat aut desistat!' Alter coram exprobraret ceteros, quod polliciti sint tarde praestare, sed ipsum, quod praestet tarde polliceri.

For a long time however he refused, with a most shameless mime now reproaching friends who encouraged him, saying that they were ignorant how beast-like supreme power was, and now with ambiguous responses and cunning delay leaving in suspense the senate praying and prostrate at his knees, so that some lost patience and one shouted in the turmoil: 'Let him take it or leave it!' Another openly taunted that others were slow to perform what they promised, but that he was slow to promise what he was already delivering."[19]

Dio writes:

ταῦτά τε οὖν οὕτως ἔπρασσε, καὶ τὰ τῆς ἀρχῆς ἔργῳ πάντα διοικῶν ἠρνεῖτο μηδὲν αὐτῆς δεῖσθαι.

And so he did these things in this way and, while actually administering all the business of the empire, he declared he did not want any of it.[20]

Persistent hesitation did yield finally to acceptance.[21] Suetonius possessed evidence that Tiberius eventually agreed to act as the

---

[17] *Ex. Pont.* 4.13.25–8. The sitting consul, Sex. Pompeius, was a source of information to Ovid while the latter was in exile.
[18] Tac. *Ann.* 1.7.5.
[19] Suet. *Tib.* 24.1.
[20] Dio 57.2.3.
[21] Cf. B. Levick (1999), 248, n. 24. Levick has argued that Tiberius never accepted supreme power, and rejects the concept of a *dies imperii* (day of power assumed). Suetonius' passage is relegated to a footnote and treated as 'misleadingly positive'. Ovid is not discussed.

162   *The Republic in Danger*

supreme power, while the contemporaries Ovid and Velleius both employ words that indicate positive action:

Tandem quasi coactus et querens miseram et onerosam iniungi sibi servitutem, recepit imperium; nec tamen aliter, quam ut depositurum se quandoque spem faceret.

Finally, as if forced, and complaining that a miserable and onerous slavery was being forced upon him, he accepted *imperium*; in such a way however that he expressed the hope that he might someday lay it down.[22]

Suetonius had in front of him a source which included part of Tiberius' speech: *Ipsius verba sunt: Dum veniam ad id tempus, quo vobis aequum possit videri dare vos aliquam senectuti meae requiem*, 'His own words are: Until I come to that time, in which it may seem right to you to give some rest to my old age.' The speech was probably recorded by a senatorial historian, such as Servilius Nonianus, or else the daily records of the senate.[23] As I shall show later, the declaration was made sometime between 17 September and the praetorian elections of AD 14.

How can Tiberius have assumed power and engaged in a *recusatio* concurrently? The situation is a topic of dispute because it is a question of psychology. The historical sources provide three main causes for Tiberius' hesitancy: (i) the execution, sometime between 19 August and early September, of Agrippa Postumus; (ii) the popularity of Germanicus; and (iii) the mutiny, in late August early September, of the German and Pannonian legions.[24] Suetonius alone adds a fourth reason: Drusus Libo.[25] Modern scholars on the whole reject the idea that Tiberius was responding to emerging political threats. Abstract nouns are preferred to real phenomena. The first edition of the *Cambridge Ancient History*, for instance, uses *moderatio* to explain Tiberius' reluctance; the recent second edition focuses on

---

[22] Suet. *Tib.* 24.2.
[23] A. Macé, *Essai sur Suétone* (1900), 363–58, puts forward Servilius Nonianus as a candidate; H. Lindsay, *Suetonius: Tiberius* (1995), adds Aufidius Bassus. Even with a positive declaration, however, Tiberius' propensity for obscuration meant that ambiguity remained even four months later in AD 15: Tac. *Ann.* 1.72.2; also Dio 57.8.4–5 and 58.17.3.
[24] On Agrippa Postumus, see the next chapter. For Germanicus, see Tac. *Ann.* 1.7.6; Suet. *Tib.* 25.2; Dio 57.4.1, 6.2–7.2. For the mutiny, see: Suet. *Tib.* 25.1; Dio 57.4.1.
[25] Suet. *Tib.* 25.1.

dissimulatio.[26] The result is the triumph of two opposite views: (i) Tiberius wanted power but was required to engage in a show of what has been termed 'decent papal reluctance'; or (ii) Tiberius was forced to take power but in fact wished to reorganize the State along more Republican lines. Various theories lie between these two interpretations.[27]

The idea that Tiberius, to use a convenient term, was Republican, and that his rhetoric reflected a deep-seated philosophical conviction, should be abandoned. As senators were quick to point out, Tiberius did not hesitate to use the instruments of supreme power, i.e. the legions and praetorians. Actions tend to speak louder than words, and Tiberius showed, beyond doubt, that he was interested in the maintenance of authoritarian power. 'Decent papal reluctance', on the other hand, has some value. Romans, as with most peoples, distrusted political leaders who seemed to covet power, and so a manœuvre was used to overcome native prejudice: emergency powers were refused when first offered and were finally accepted only through a discourse of reluctance.[28] Tiberius was himself familiar with the art. In AD 4 he was voted *tribunicia potestas* 'in spite of his continued objection both in private and in the senate'.[29] The situation in AD 14 was, however, different, in so far as Tiberius was not refusing new powers but showing a reluctance to keep powers that already belonged to him. The occasion was reminiscent of the so-called Augustan settlement of 27 BC. In a long speech to the senate, Octavian proposed to abdicate his unprecedented public position and return to life as a normal citizen. The essence of his speech, as it was known to Dio, is instructive when compared to that attributed to Tiberius in AD 14:

---

[26] *CAH* 10¹ (1934), 611 f. *CAH* 10² 205 f.
[27] See, e.g., F. B. Marsh (1931), 45; *CAH* 10¹ (1934), 611 f.; J. Béranger 'Le refus du pouviur', *MH*, 5 (1948), 178–96; F. R. D. Goodyear (1972), 169 f.; M. M. Sage, 'Tacitus and the Accession of Tiberius', *Ancient Society*, 13/14 (1982/1983), 293–321; A. Wallace-Hadrill, 'Civilis Princeps: Between Citizen and King', *JRS,* 72 (1982), 32–48; R. Syme (1939) 438–439, and (1986), 449; *CAH* 10², 205. Cf. H. H. Scullard (1976), 278 f.; G. Kampff (1963), 25–58; R. Seager (1972), 56: 'to deny Tiberius' sincerity is perverse"; B. Levick (1999), 68f. T. Hillard (2004), seems to accept the view that the act was not ritual without the corollary that Tiberius was sincerely disinterested in power. Nonetheless, Hillard does not believe that he was responding to political threats.
[28] For a general history of the phenomenon, see U. Huttner, *Recusatio Imperii: Ein Politisches Ritual Zwischen Ethik und Taktik* (2004).
[29] Vell. 2.103.3.

ὑμῖν γάρ, ὑμῖν τοῖς ἀρίστοις καὶ φρονιμωτάτοις πάντα τὰ κοινὰ ἀνατίθημι
... αὐτός τε γὰρ καὶ πεπόνημαι καὶ τεταλαιπώρημαι, καὶ οὐκέτ᾽ οὔτε τῇ ψυχῇ
οὔτε τῷ σώματι ἀντέχειν δύναμαι... καὶ διὰ ταῦτα καὶ ἰδιωτεῦσαι μᾶλλον
εὐκλεῶς ἢ μοναρχῆσαι ἐπικινδύνως αἱροῦμαι. Καὶ τὰ κοινὰ κοινῶς ἂν πολὺ
βέλτιον ἅτε καὶ ὑπὸ πολλῶν ἅμα διαγόμενα καὶ μὴ ἐς ἕνα τινὰ ἀνηρτημένα
διοικοῖτο.

For to you, best and most mindful of men, I entrust all the public affairs...
and as for myself, indeed, I have both laboured and suffered, and no longer
can I withstand it, neither in my mind nor in my body... and because of this,
I choose to live in glory as a private citizen, rather than to live in danger as a
monarch. And as for public affairs, they would be far better administered
publicly, since they would be handled by many men acting together, and not
be dependent on a single man.[30]

By 'public affairs' Augustus is said to have meant the armies, laws, and provinces, both traditional provinces and those acquired by Octavian while acting in the interest of the State.[31] Contemporary interpretations of his motive were varied: he honestly wished to restore Republican *praxis*; or he was deceiving the senate and in fact wished to hold on to power. During the debate Octavian's supporters were said to have been: 'shouting out... begging for monarchy and putting forward all the arguments in its favour, until they compelled him... to accept autocratic power.'[32] Octavian's power was subsequently sustained, albeit in part diminished. He was to administer some provinces, while the rest were to remain with the people of Rome, the so-called senatorial provinces.[33] The events of 17 September AD 14 were markedly similar to those of 27 BC.[34] In his *relatio*, one of the consuls put the motion that Tiberius be recognized as leader of

---

[30] Dio 53.8.5–8.
[31] Ibid., 4.4.
[32] Dio 53.11.4. Octavian's friends would hold that he sincerely wished to restore Republican practice, and would then argue that the *res publica* needed him to remain in an extraordinary position. Thus, Octavian is made to appear genuinely sympathetic to Republicanism, while being saved the *invidia* of justifying his own favoured position as supreme ruler: he was forced by passionate argument to remain in a dominant position. It should be noted, however, that some of Octavian's friends may well have desired the restoration of Republican *praxis*.
[33] Ibid., 12.2–8. F. Millar, 'Senatorial Provinces: An Institutionalized Ghost', *Ancient World*, 20 (1989), 1–5; J. W. Rich (1990), 140 f.
[34] This is an often made comparison. R. Syme (1939), 439; J. Béranger, 'Recherches sur l'aspect idéologique du principat', *Schweiz. Beitr. Z. Altertum swissenshaft*, 6 (1953), 152 f.; G. Kampff (1963), 39; T. Hillard (2004), *passim*.

the *res publica*.³⁵ The wording of the motion is lost, but its essence remains in Velleius, Suetonius and Tacitus.³⁶ Tacitus writes:

Dixit forte Tiberius se ut non toti rei publicae parem, ita quaecumque pars sibi mandaretur eius tutelam suscepturum. Tum Asinius Gallus 'Interrogo' inquit, 'Caesar, quam partem rei publicae mandari tibi velis'... respondit nequaquam decorum pudori suo legere aliquid aut evitare ex eo cui in universum excusari mallet.

Tiberius said that he himself was unequal to [the task of governing] the entire *res publica*, but would undertake to look after whichever part might be committed to him. Asinius Gallus then said: 'I inquire, Caesar, which part of the *res publica* do you wish to have committed to you'... and Tiberius responded that it was by no means appropriate to his personal sense of propriety to choose or avoid any part of something from which he would prefer to be excused completely.³⁷

It was probably at the same meeting that Quintus Haterius allegedly said '*Quo usque patieris Caesar non adesse caput rei publicae*', 'how long, Caesar, will you let the *res publica* lack a head'; and Mamercus Scaurus pronounced that '*spem esse ex eo non inritas fore senatus preces quod relationi consulum iure tribuniciae potestatis non intercessisset*', 'There was hope that the senate's prayers might not be in vain, since he had not vetoed the *relatio* of the consuls by the use of his Tribunician power.'³⁸ Dio writes:

Καὶ τὸ μὲν πρῶτον καὶ πᾶσαν αὐτὴν διά τε τὴν ἡλικίαν (ἐξ γὰρ καὶ πεντήκοντα ἔτη ἐγεγόνει) καὶ δι' ἀμβλυωπίαν (πλεῖστον γὰρ τοῦ σκότους βλέπων ἐλάχιστα τῆς ἡμέρας ἑώρα) ἐξίστασθαι ἔλεγεν· ἔπειτα δὲ κοινωνούς τέ τινας καὶ συνάρχοντας, οὔτι γε καὶ πάντων καθάπαξ ὥσπερ ἐν ὀλιγαρχίᾳ, ἀλλ' ἐς τρία μέρη νέμων αὐτήν, ᾔτει, καὶ τὸ μὲν αὐτὸς ἔχειν ἠξίου, τῶν δὲ ἑτέρων ἄλλοις παρεχώρει. ἦν δὲ ταῦτα ἓν μὲν ἥ τε 'Ρώμη καὶ ἡ ἄλλη 'Ιταλία, ἕτερον δὲ τὰ στρατόπεδα, καὶ ἕτερον οἱ λοιποὶ ὑπήκοοι.

And at first he kept saying that he would retire from all of it on account of his age (for he was aged fifty-six) and on account of his near-sightedness (for, though he saw very well in the dark, he saw very poorly in the day); and after that he asked for some associates and colleagues, though, indeed, he did not

---

³⁵ F. R. D. Goodyear (1972), 174 f.
³⁶ I agree with Levick (1999), 78 f., that the *relatio* contained an idea like that expressed in *statio paternae*, as preserved by Vell. 2.124. It did not ask that Tiberius take new powers (*imperia*), but that he accept the Principate (*principatus*).
³⁷ Tac. *Ann.* 1.12.1–2.
³⁸ Ibid., 1.13.

166   *The Republic in Danger*

intend for them [to rule] over everything, as in an oligarchy, but, dividing it into three parts, that he was to keep one part himself, while he would give over the remaining parts to them. And one of these parts consisted of Rome and the rest of Italy, another of the legions, and another of the remaining subject-peoples.[39]

Every element of the Augustan discourse is present: Tiberius is tired; Tiberius would prefer to be a private citizen; the empire cannot be administered effectively by one man; administration ought to be shared by treating the empire as a sum of independent parts. These were not throwaway lines. They possessed real historical meaning within Roman politics.[40] It is important to note, however, that at the senate meetings on 17 September, Tiberius did not so much accept the Principate as cease to refuse it:

Fessusque clamore omnium, expostulatione singulorum flexit paulatim, non ut fateretur suscipi a se imperium, sed ut negare et rogari desineret.

Exhausted by the universal clamour and the insistence of individuals he changed his attitude little by little, not so as to admit that he had taken up supreme power but so as to cease to refuse and to be asked.[41]

Modern audiences can appreciate why this failed to satisfy those hoping for closure; evasion is a skill important to politicians. Thus, accusations of 'feigned hesitancy' persisted: '*trepida civitas incusare*

---

[39] Dio 57.2.4–5.
[40] J. W. Rich (1990), 136, believes Dio has invented Augustus' speech, noting that the structure evidences typical signs of artifice, especially echoes of Thucydides. He notes also that such speeches (i.e. resignation of powers by a supreme magistrate holding an extra-ordinary command) were common in rhetorical schools, citing Quint. *Inst.* 3.8.53. Even so, this was a famous occasion, records of which surely survived well into the Principate. The style and phraseology may not be authentic, but the underlying message should not be doubted. P. M. Swan, 'Cassius Dio on Augustus: A Poverty of Annalistic Sources?', *Phoenix*, 41: 3 (1987), 272–91, shows that Dio's main source was written in the Augustan era or shortly after. Moreover, as U. Huttner (2004) has shown, the discourse of reluctance had a long history in Rome. That Augustus would not have utilized such a discourse at that moment is unlikely. Indeed, the discourse is present in the *Res Gestae* (5–7), and, interestingly, is very much present in Livy's first pentad, such as the famous story of Cincinnatus (Livy 3.21).
[41] Tac. *Ann.* 1.13.5–6. Tacitus does not state explicitly that Tiberius' message changed *on* the 17th, but the date can be inferred from a combination of evidence. Tacitus implies that Tiberius' position changed at the same meeting of the senate at which Augustus was declared a god. The *Fasti Amiternini* and the *Fasti Oppiani* state that a decree was passed making Augustus a god on 17 Sept. (V. Ehrenberg and A. H. M. Jones (1955), 52). Cf. K. Wellesley, 'The Dies Imperii of Tiberius', *JRS*, 57 (1967), 23–30, and M. Sage (1982/83), 310.

The Hesitation of Tiberius

Tiberium quod dum patres et plebem invalida et inermia cunctatione ficta ludificetur...' 'The terrified citizenry accused Tiberius 'while with his fictional hesitation he was ridiculing the senate and plebs, weak and unarmed...'[42] Tiberius was able to alter his message but not able to offer a positive declaration. Though 'decent papal reluctance' partly explains Tiberius' attitude between Augustus' death and 17 September, it does not explain his transition to silence. Silence in the face of a request being, after all, a condition pregnant with more than a polite sense of moderation; the hallmark of reluctance decently offered. It indicates uncertainty. Senators no doubt remembered that Tiberius had once before abandoned his post, on the grounds that he was tired and in need of rest, when faced with an awkward political landscape in 6 BC.[43] Tiberius' silence would have seemed both frustrating as well as unnerving because his *recusatio* was *not* a nod to mere formality: he was actually hesitant in the face of something or someone. A standard concentration on philosophical mindsets within modern scholarship devalues the explicit evidence of Suetonius concerning the cause of Tiberius' approach:

Cunctandi causa erat metus undique imminentium discriminum... Nam et servus Agrippae Clemens nomine non contemnendam manum in ultionem domini compararet et L. Scribonius Libo vir nobilis res novas clam moliebatur et duplex seditio militum in Illyrico et in Germania exorta est.

The cause of his hesitation was fear of the imminent dangers all around him... For a slave of Agrippa's, Clemens by name, had put together a not contemptible force to avenge his dead master; L. Scribonius Libo, a *nobilis*, was secretly planning revolution; and in two places, Illyricum and Germany, sedition broke out among the troops.[44]

The following chapters will show that it is possible to construct a coherent model using Suetonius' interpretation while explaining the

---

[42] Tac. *Ann.* 1.46.1.
[43] Suet. *Tib.*10.
[44] Suet. *Tib.* 25.1. A. Lang (1911), 32, calls it 'improbable' and 'exaggerated': it is rejected by A. Passerini (1948), 224 f.; G. Kampff (1963), 45, criticizes Suetonius for a complete unconcern about chronology; R. Seager (1972), 89, calls it false, but admits that both Clemens and Drusus Libo were possibly active in AD 14; F. R. D. Goodyear (1972), 173, n.1, calls this list a 'muddle', and (1981), 307 'careless misunderstanding'; Levick (1999) 150, 224 f: "Suetonius' idea we need not accept"; M. Sage (1982/83), 299, calls it 'impossible'; H. Lindsay (1995), 110, describes the list as 'implausible'. Cf. U. Silvagni, *L'Impero e le donne dei Cesari,* II (1909), 270; F. B. Marsh (1926), 298, accepts Suetonius' chronology but not his interpretation; R. S. Rogers (1935), 12 f.

gradual nature of Tiberius' position *vis-à-vis* the senate. In particular, that Drusus Libo was an issue for Tiberius in the early weeks of September AD 14. Before dealing with the debate on 17 September, however, we must consider the death of Agrippa Postumus. Though Suetonius refers only to Clemens, Agrippa's death lies at the heart of the story; the event by which Tacitus defined the Tiberian Principate. We must, therefore, return to Agrippa.

10

"Did You Hear About Agrippa?"

Where was Tiberius when Augustus died? According to the extant sources he was either on his way to Illyricum or sitting inside a Nolan villa as Augustus breathed his last. In his research Dio found that most 'respectable' historians preferred the first scenario:

ταῦτα γὰρ οὕτω τοῖς τε πλείοσι καὶ τοῖς ἀξιοπιστοτέροις γέγραπται· εἰσὶ γάρ τινες οἳ καὶ παραγενέσθαι τὸν Τιβέριον τῇ νόσῳ αὐτοῦ καὶ ἐπισκήψεις τινὰς παρ' αὐτοῦ λαβεῖν ἔφασαν.

These things, indeed, are attested by most writers, and by the more trustworthy ones; for there are some who claim that Tiberius was present for his [Augustus'] illness, and that he received some instructions from him.[1]

Tacitus is equivocal:

Utcumque se ea res habuit, vixdum ingressus Illyricum Tiberius properis matris litteris accitur; neque satis conpertum est spirantem adhuc Augustum apud urbem Nolam an exanimem reppererit.

Whatever the truth was, having just entered Illyricum, Tiberius was summoned by an urgent letter from his mother; it is not really known whether near the city of Nola he discovered Augustus as yet still breathing or lifeless.[2]

A belief that Tiberius was absent is associated with a tradition that accused Livia of murdering Augustus because he considered pardoning Agrippa. Plutarch writes:

Φούλβιος (sic) δ' ὁ Καίσαρος ἑταῖρος τοῦ Σεβαστοῦ γέροντος ἤδη γεγονότος ἀκούσας ὀδυρομένου τὴν περὶ τὸν οἶκον ἐρημίαν, καὶ ὅτι τῶν μὲν δυεῖν αὐτῷ θυγατριδῶν ἀπολωλότων Ποστουμίου (sic) δ' ὃς ἔτι λοιπός ἐστιν ἐκ διαβολῆς τινος ἐν φυγῇ ὄντος ἀναγκάζεται τὸν τῆς γυναικὸς υἱὸν ἐπεισάγειν τῇ διαδοχῇ

---

[1] Dio 56.31.1.   [2] Tac. *Ann.* 1.5.3–4.

τῆς ἡγεμονίας, καίπερ οἰκτείρων καὶ βουλευόμενος ἐκ τῆς ὑπερορίας ἀνακαλεῖσθαι τὸν θυγατριδοῦν· ταῦθ᾽ ὁ Φούλβιος ἀκούσας ἐξήνεγκε πρὸς τὴν ἑαυτοῦ γυναῖκα, πρὸς δὲ Λιβίαν ἐκείνη, Λιβία δὲ καθήψατο πικρῶς Καίσαρος, εἰ πάλαι ταῦτ᾽ ἐγνωκὼς οὐ μεταπέμπεται τὸν θυγατριδοῦν, ἀλλ᾽ εἰς ἔχθραν καὶ πόλεμον αὐτὴν τῷ διαδόχῳ τῆς ἀρχῆς καθίστησιν.

Fulvius [sic], the friend of Caesar Augustus, heard the emperor, now an old man, lamenting the desolation of his house: two of his grandsons were dead, and Postumius [sic], the only one surviving, was in exile because of some false accusation, and thus he was forced to import his wife's son into the imperial succession; yet he pitied his grandson and was planning to recall him from abroad. Fulvius [sic] divulged what he had heard to his own wife, and she to Livia; and Livia bitterly rebuked Caesar: if he had formed this design long ago, why did he not send for his grandson, instead of making her an object of enmity and strife to the successor to the empire.[3]

Though lacking detail the elder Pliny includes elements of the story in his list of miseries which affected Augustus:

inde suspicio in Fabium arcanorumque proditionem, hinc uxoris et Tiberi cogitationes, suprema eius cura.

Then his suspicion of Fabius and the betrayal of secrets, and the intrigues of his wife and Tiberius that tormented his last days.[4]

Tacitus writes:

Quippe rumor incesserat paucos ante mensis Augustum, electis consciis et comite uno Fabio Maximo,[5] Planasiam vectum ad visendum Agrippam; multas illic utrimque lacrimas et signa caritatis spemque ex eo fore ut iuvenis penatibus avi redderetur: Quod Maximum uxori Marciae aperuisse, illam Liviae.

For a rumour went around that a few months before, Augustus, with a few chosen friends in the know and one companion, Fabius Maximus, had sailed to Planasia to see Agrippa; with many tears shed, signs of affection and hope that the young man was about to be returned to the household of his grandfather. Maximus told this to his wife Marcia, who in turn told Livia.[6]

---

[3] Plut. *Moralia: De Garrul.* 11.
[4] Pliny *NH* 7.150.
[5] For this ambiguous sentence, see F. R. D. Goodyear (1972), 131.
[6] Tac. *Ann.* 1.5.

"Did You Hear About Agrippa?"

Dio elaborates:

Ὁ δ᾽ οὖν Αὔγουστος νοσήσας μετήλλαξε· καί τινα ὑποψίαν τοῦ θανάτου αὐτοῦ ἡ Λιουία ἔλαβεν, ἐπειδὴ πρὸς τὸν Ἀγρίππαν κρύφα ἐς τὴν νῆσον διέπλευσε καὶ ἐδόκει οἱ καὶ παντάπασι καταλλαγήσεσθαι. Δείσασα γάρ, ὥς φασι, μὴ καὶ ἐπὶ τῇ μοναρχίᾳ αὐτὸν καταγάγῃ, σῦκά τινα ἐπὶ δένδροις ἔτ᾽ ἐπόντα, ἀφ᾽ ὧν ὁ Αὔγουστος αὐτοχειρίᾳ συκάζειν εἰώθει, φαρμάκῳ ἔχρισε, καὶ αὐτή τε ἅμα τὰ ἀνήλιφα ἤσθιε κἀκείνῳ τὰ πεφαρμαγμένα προσέβαλλεν.

And so Augustus fell ill and passed away. And Livia incurred some suspicion over his death, since he had sailed over to the island to see Agrippa in secret, and seemed to be about to be reconciled with him in every way. For in her fear, as they say, lest Augustus might restore Agrippa to sovereignty, she smeared with poison some figs which were still on trees, from which Augustus was accustomed to pick by hand. She herself ate the good ones and offered the poisoned ones to him.[7]

Aurelius Victor writes:

Quamquam alii scribant dolo Liviae exstinctum metuentis, ne, quia privignae filium Agrippam, quem odio novercali in insulam relegaverat, reduci compererat, eo summam rerum adepto poenas daret.

Yet some write that [Augustus] was killed by a deception of Livia, who, since she had gained information that Agrippa (the son of her stepdaughter, whom, as a result of his mother-in-law's hatred, he/she had relegated to an island) was to be recalled, feared that, when he had obtained control of affairs, she would be punished.[8]

The alternative scenario, i.e. Tiberius witnessed Augustus' final moments, appears in Velleius and Suetonius (who ignore the existence of the first altogether), and is acknowledged by Dio and Tacitus, though the latter two undercut its validity by seeming to prefer the first. Velleius writes:

Et ingravescente in dies valetudine, cum sciret, quis volenti omnia post se salva remanere accersendus foret, festinanter revocavit filium; ille ad patrem patriae expectato revolavit maturius. Tum securum se Augustus praedicans circumfususque amplexibus Tiberii sui, commendans illi sua atque ipsius opera nec quidquam iam de fine, si fata poscerent, recusans, subrefectus primo conspectu alloquioque carissimi sibi spiritus, mox, cum omnem curam fata vincerent, in sua resolutus initia Pompeio Apuleioque consulibus septuagesimo et sexto anno animam caelestem caelo reddidit.

---

[7] Dio 56.30.1. [8] *Epitome de Caesaribus*: 1.27.

172   *The Republic in Danger*

As his health daily worsened, he knew for whom he must send if he wished to leave everything after him secure, he sent in haste for his son to return; [Tiberius] hurried back to the father of his country earlier than he was expected. Then Augustus, pronouncing himself secure and enfolded in his dear Tiberius' embraces, commending to him their joint work and no longer refusing to meet his end if the fates should require it, revived a little at the first sight of Tiberius and the greeting of the spirit most dear to him, but soon, since destiny conquers every care, he resolved into his own elements and in the consulship of Pompeius and Apuleius in his seventy-sixth year rendered his heavenly soul to heaven.[9]

Suetonius writes:

Sed in redeundo adgravata valitudine tandem Nolae succubuit revocatumque ex itinere Tiberium diu secreto sermone detinuit, neque post ulli maiori negotio animum accommodavit.

But as he was returning his illness was aggravated and he finally succumbed at Nola, and recalling Tiberius from his journey, he detained him for a long time in private conversation, after which he did not attend to any important business.[10]

The first scenario is comparable to the story of Nero's accession: an unpopular Nero is adopted by the princeps; the adoption is engineered by Nero's scheming mother, Agrippina; Agrippina murders the princeps after a dispossessed heir re-enters the picture; Agrippina orders the house to be surrounded by guards.[11] This last image mirrored Livy's treatment of the accession of Servius Tullius.[12] Some scholars have, therefore, assumed that the interpretation emerged after AD 54, and is not therefore relevant to Tiberius' reign.[13] I believe that this interpretation is wrong and that the

---

[9] Vell. 2.123.1–2.   [10] Suet. *Aug.* 98.5.

[11] The comparison was discovered by M. P. Charlesworth, 'Tiberius and the Death of Augustus', *AJP*, 44:2 (1923), 145–57.

[12] Livy 1.41; M. P. Charlesworth, 'Livia and Tanaquil', *CR*, 41 (1927), 55–7; R. H. Martin, 'Tacitus and the Death of Augustus', *CQ*, 5 (1955), 123–8; F. R. D. Goodyear (1972), 128.

[13] B. R. Motzo, 'I Commentari di Agrippina madre di Nerone', *Studi di Storia e Filologia*, 1 (1927), 38 f.; F. B. Marsh (1931), 50, seems to follow Charlesworth; R. S. Rogers (1935), 3 f.; W. Allen Jun. 'The Death of Agrippa Postumus', *TAPA*, 78 (1947), 131–9; R. H. Martin (1955), *passim*; C. Questa, 'La Morte di Augusto Secondo Cassio Dione', *PP*, 14 (1959), 41–53; J. D. Lewis (1970), 176 f., agrees that the story is not a product of the Tiberian period, but cannot believe it was invented by the younger Agrippina. Lewis simply dates its construction to after Tiberius' death;

tradition was in fact contemporary.[14] The conspiracy of Clemens, the Pseudo-Agrippa, in AD 16 is the evidence.[15]

The conspirators required evidence that Agrippa was the legitimate heir of Augustus, since the *senatus consultum* of AD 7 - by which Agrippa was incarcerated - necessarily proved Augustus' repudiation of his estranged son. Agrippa obviously had supporters, but his exile was still a problem. A rumour that Agrippa and Augustus were, in fact, reconciled shortly before Augustus' death was the solution.[16] Fabius Maximus was an ideal character. Official records attest that he and Augustus had left Rome together in May AD 14; he had subsequently committed suicide because of some dispute with Augustus.[17] Neither Fabius nor Augustus could be called on to verify or dispute the story. There was, moreover, sufficient circumstantial evidence to evince plausibility.[18] Livia was known to have hated Agrippa, and if her involvement in his exile was popularly believed, it would not have been difficult to convince people of her guilt. Livia's poor reaction to news of Augustus' trip to Planasia was therefore crucial to the story, as was her subsequent decision to murder him. The role of Livia allowed the conspirators to argue that Agrippa's full restoration was prevented only by the schemes of a wicked stepmother.[19] The

F. R. D. Goodyear (1972), 126, with some reservations; R. Mellor, *Tacitus* (1993), 44 f.; A. Barrett (2002), 243 f.

[14] My position is not to be mistaken for that adopted by R. A. Bauman (1992), 127f., and 'Tanaquil-Livia and the Death of Augustus', *Historia*, 43 (1994), 177-8, who locates the stories firmly in the Tiberian Principate, but takes them to be historically accurate, i.e. not hostile rumour lacking substance.

[15] R. Detweiler (1970), 291, says that most scholars hold this view (he does not); in all my research I have found only one scholar who explicitly connects Agrippa's execution with the story of Clemens. A. E. Pappano (1941), 41, makes the connection, but we differ considerably in detail. Pappano conflates the conspiracy of Clemens with that of Audasius and Epicadus cited at Suet. *Aug.* 19. Furthermore, Pappano suggests that the story appeared *while* the conspiracy was being planned. That is unlikely. The story would necessarily come after the event.

[16] It is accepted as historical by V. Gardthausen, *RE* 10, 183-5; S. Jameson (1975), 310; B. Levick (1999), 64.

[17] *Acta Fratrum Arvalium* 1, 29 (ed. Henzen).

[18] The death of Princess Diana is a modern example. Some continue to believe that Princess Diana and Dodi Al Fayed were murdered in a palace-sponsored plot. This thinking has found traction in the pages of 'gossip magazines' and 'tabloid' newspapers, which have subsequently affected the thinking of, no doubt, many people.

[19] Tac. *Ann.* 1.72.3 states: *Hunc quoque asperavere carmina incertis auctoribus vulgata in saevitiam superbiamque eius et discordem cum matre animum*, 'Poems of unknown authorship satirising his savagery, arrogance, and his broken relationship with his mother, had also exasperated him.' These 'poems', if Tacitus supplies a

presence of this interpretation in several historical sources shows that some people accepted the story as true—I believe it was invented in AD 16. When Tacitus wrote his *Annals,* rumour had evidently become valid history (as Dio observed), providing historians interested in the symmetry of history with a device through which the reader could predict tyranny.[20] Suetonius, however, was still able to follow the alternative, and no doubt official, history. But we need not accept that particular version as true.

Aside from satisfying a human need for last-goodbyes, Tibe[rius] had little reason to speak with Augustus on 19 Augustus AD 14; [the] occasion of Augustus' death must have been well planned. For [one] and half years Augustus and Tiberius had been organizing the app[ro]priate powers for transition. It is untenable to think that the fam[ily] council (or the *semenstre consilium*) had not discussed, and in fa[ct] agreed on, the appropriate course of action. Augustus' careful planning of his own funeral evidences such a mindset.[21] Tiberius' position was, moreover, beyond question. He was certainly Augustus' heir and chosen successor. Velleius' *commendo* is suspect. It seeks to justify the continuation of the Principate as an intermediate structure: 'there is still work to do; continue on the path we have *both* been following'. It is not uncommon for governments to manufacture history in order to counter the claims of revolutionaries. But, more importantly, the official version sought to exculpate Livia and Tiberius while rubbishing claims that Agrippa was preferred: (i) Augustus did not change his mind. He commended the Principate to Tiberius; and (ii) Livia could not have intervened because Tiberius was already present to receive Augustus' last instructions. This reaction to popular rumour cannot be trusted. That Tiberius' absence was held to be true by the 'best' historians (which probably includes those who lived at the time) suggests that it was. But it was a decision made in Rome that caused

---

coherent chronology, appeared before AD 15 (which begins at *Ann.* 1.55). That Tiberius and his mother were probably on good terms would not have prevented his enemies from constructing a malicious image, perhaps built upon Tiberius' decision not to allow Livia to be officially titled *mater patriae*. The same methodology is used today by all gossip magazines. Cf. F. R. D. Goodyear (1981), 153, who believes the passage is not datable.

[20] Thus the same mechanisms were associated with Nero.
[21] Suet. *Aug.* 101.4; Dio 56.33.1.

"Did You Hear About Agrippa?" 175

Tiberius problems. The sources must be quoted in full, starting with Tacitus:

Primum facinus novi principatus fuit Postumi Agrippae caedes, quem ignarum inermemque quamvis firmatus animo centurio aegre confecit. Nihil de ea re Tiberius apud senatum disseruit: patris iussa simulabat, quibus praescripsisset tribuno custodiae adposito ne cunctaretur Agrippam morte adficere quandoque ipse supremum diem explevisset. Multa sine dubio saevaque Augustus de moribus adulescentis questus, ut exilium eius senatus consulto sanciretur perfecerat: ceterum in nullius umquam suorum necem duravit, neque mortem nepoti pro securitate privigni inlatam credibile erat. Propius vero Tiberium ac Liviam, illum metu, hanc novercalibus odiis, suspecti et invisi iuvenis caedem festinavisse. Nuntianti centurioni, ut mos militiae, factum esse quod imperasset, neque imperasse sese et rationem facti reddendam apud senatum respondit. Quod postquam Sallustius Crispus particeps secretorum (is ad tribunum miserat codicillos) comperit, metuens ne reus subderetur, iuxta periculoso ficta seu vera promeret monuit Liviam ne arcana domus, ne consilia amicorum, ministeria militum vulgarentur, neve Tiberius vim principatus resolveret cuncta ad senatum vocando: eam condicionem esse imperandi, ut non aliter ratio constet quam si uni reddatur.

The first act of the new Principate was the slaying of Agrippa Postumus, who, though surprised and unarmed, was nevertheless executed by a centurion of resolute spirit with some difficulty. Tiberius did not discuss the matter in the senate: he simulated orders from his father, which instructed the tribune in charge of the prison not to delay the death of Agrippa once he himself had met his final day. Without doubt Augustus had many times complained bitterly of the young man's character, and he had procured a *senatus consultum* to sanction his exile: but he never steeled himself to the killing of any of his relatives, and it was incredible that the death of a grandson had been brought about for the security of a stepson. It was closer to the truth that Tiberius and Livia, the one from fear the other from a stepmother's enmity, hurried on the destruction of a youth whom they suspected and hated. When the centurion reported, according to military custom, that he had 'executed the command', Tiberius replied that he had given no order, and that accountability for the act must be supplied to the senate. When afterwards Sallustius Crispus, a partner in imperial secrets (he had sent the letters to the tribune) found this out, fearing that he would be falsely substituted as the defendant, and that the danger would be the same whether he spoke the truth or lied, he warned Livia that the secrets of the imperial house, the counsels of its friends, or any services performed by the soldiers should not be divulged, and that Tiberius should not weaken the power of the Principate by referring

The Republic in Danger

everything to the senate, for 'the condition' he said 'of holding power is that an account cannot be balanced unless it is rendered to one person.'[22]

Suetonius writes:

Excessum Augusti non prius palam fecit, quam Agrippa iuvene interempto. Hunc tribunus militum custos appositus occidit lectis codicillis, quibus ut id faceret iubebatur; quos codicillos dubium fuit, Augustusne moriens reliquisset, quo materiam tumultus post se subduceret; an nomine Augusti Livia et ea conscio Tiberio an ignaro, dictasset. Tiberius renuntianti tribuno, factum esse quod imperasset, neque imperasse se et redditurum eum senatui rationem respondit, invidiam scilicet in praesentia vitans. Nam mox silentio rem obliteravit.

The death of Augustus was not made public before the young Agrippa had been done away with. A military tribune, appointed to guard him, killed him on reading a note, in which he was ordered to do the deed. It was not known whose the letter was, whether the dying Augustus left it, to remove a source of uprising after his death; or whether Livia wrote it in Augustus' name, and in that case, whether Tiberius was cognizant or ignorant. Tiberius replied to the tribune, who reported that he had carried out his order, that he had given no such order and that he (i.e. the tribune) must provide an account to the senate, obviously attempting to avoid odium for the time being. For soon he buried the matter in silence.[23]

While Dio writes:

Τὸν μὲν γὰρ Ἀγρίππαν παραχρῆμα ἀπὸ τῆς Νώλης πέμψας τινὰ ἀπέκτεινε· καὶ ἔλεγε μὲν μὴ ἐκ τῆς ἑαυτοῦ προστάξεως τοῦτο γεγονέναι, ἐπηπείλει τε τῷ δράσαντι, οὐ μὴν καὶ τιμωρίαν τινὰ αὐτοῦ ἐποιήσατο, ἀλλ' εἴα τοὺς ἀνθρώπους λογοποιεῖν, τοὺς μὲν ὅτι ὁ Αὔγουστος αὐτὸν ὑπὸ τὴν τελευτὴν ἀπεχρήσατο, τοὺς δ' ὅτι ὁ ἑκατόνταρχος ὁ τὴν φρουρὰν αὐτοῦ ἔχων καινοτομοῦντά τι ἀπέσφαξεν αὐτογνωμονήσας, ἄλλους ὡς ἡ Λιουία, ἀλλ' οὐκ ἐκεῖνος, ἀποθανεῖν αὐτὸν ἐκέλευσεν.

And, having immediately sent from Nola, he put Agrippa to death; and he continued to say that this had not occurred as a result of his own order(s), and made threats against the perpetrator; yet he did not impose any punishment on him at all, but allowed men to make up stories, some to the effect that Augustus had put him out of the way just prior to his death, and others to the effect that the centurion, who was charged with his protection, had slain him on his own initiative for some revolutionary activity, and still others to the effect that Livia, rather than Tiberius, had given the order for him to perish.[24]

---

[22] Tac. *Ann.* 1.6.   [23] Suet. *Tib.* 22.   [24] Dio 57.3.5.

Tiberius' desire to hold a senatorial inquiry into Agrippa's execution is the key. Tiberius' ignorance of the execution is implied as is his earnest desire for exoneration. Tiberius knew that a public inquiry would clear his name. But its survival in sources with obvious anti-Tiberian elements indicates that it was held to be true, rather than constructed *post factum*. Such a complicated story that allowed for a positive interpretation of Tiberius would surely have been eliminated by his opponents had it not been widely held to be true. Unable to navigate round such an obvious fact, opponents chose instead to present it in the worst possible light. Tiberius was probably informed while alone (the messenger would not blurt the information out while Tiberius was in the presence of other people, no matter their rank), but soon after declared before witnesses that he had received the information and would lay it before the senate. The presence of witnesses ensured its place within the mainstream histories.[25] Tiberius' decision not to bring the matter before the senate was thus interpreted as evidence of deceit, but this is probably wrong. If Tiberius was in any way complicit, then his request for a public inquiry was stupid and reckless. Unlike modern government inquiries, a senatorial inquiry could not be whitewashed. The silence and co-operation of Tiberius' enemies was not assured. The most logical explanation is, therefore, the one provided by Tacitus: someone convinced Tiberius not to have an inquiry.

Sallustius Crispus' involvement appears only in Tacitus. He was about 70 in AD 14 and seems to have been, at that time, Augustus' chief adviser.[26] In an obituary Tacitus remarks that Crispus possessed greater *potentia* than 'many who triumphed or held the consulship'.[27] A tradition, known only to Tacitus, evidently knew of Crispus' involvement.[28] Indeed, Tacitus believed that Crispus was in trouble

---

[25] Evidently, Crispus was not with him at the time. It is clear from Tacitus' narrative that Tiberius was not immediately convinced to remain silent. That this quote was accepted as fact almost immediately by both contemporaries and historians tells against the position of some modern scholars who argue that Agrippa did not die in AD 14 or, at least, was not executed: W. Allen Jun. (1947), *passim*; J. Bellemore (2000), *passim*.

[26] Tac. *Ann*. 3.30; A. Stein, *RE* 18 2097; H. W. Benario, 'The End of Sallustius Crispus', *CJ*, 57: 7 (1962), 321–2.

[27] Tac. *Ann*. 3.30.2.

[28] *Contra* D. C. A Shotter, 'The Problems in Tacitus' Annals I', *Mnem*., 18 (1965), 359–61. Shotter argues that Tiberius attempted to shift blame onto Crispus. But Tiberius could not blame Crispus. That would involve damaging his mother's

'whether he spoke the truth or lied', i.e. the truth was an admission of guilt, while a lie would seriously embarrass the government. Who would be affected by a lie? It cannot have been Tiberius, for the reasons given above. We should instead look to Augustus. If Tiberius were genuinely ignorant of the execution, which I believe he was, then Augustus cannot have been complicit; he would not have withheld such a plan from his successor.[29] It is furthermore irrational to believe

reputation and, more importantly, admitting that he was convinced not to have an inquiry. Tacitus shows in his obituary of Crispus that biographical material was available. Sallustius Crispus had an adopted son, C. Sallustius Crispus Passienus (suff. 27). Suetonius, *Nero* 6.3, writes that Passienus was for a time married to the younger Agrippina. Would the story have entered her memoirs? J. D. Lewis (1970), 181, n. 13, 183, n. 52, believes it did; D. Kehoe (1985), disagrees. The *Scholiast on Juvenal*, 4.81, writes that Passienus was poisoned by Agrippina. R. Syme (1986), 160, n. 33 dates his death to pre AD 47. Whether or not the death was suspicious, it would have allowed Agrippina to treat her ex-husband's father with impunity. Some modern historians would reject this approach, holding that Agrippina's work was pro-Julian (as argued by Charlesworth). This is problematical. Agrippina's situation depended not on Agrippa Postumus but her father, Germanicus. Germanicus would not have sympathized with Agrippa's claim. Agrippina's memoirs would have treated Agrippa as a pretender, an illegitimate force. Nevertheless, it would explain why Tacitus is the only extant historian who treats Crispus' involvement. Dio and Suetonius would mention Crispus if they knew about him. Since we know Dio and Suetonius have read various sources, we must conclude that Tacitus, in using the private memoirs of the younger Agrippina, has landed a scoop, and he wants us to know it. This is especially clear at Tac. *Ann.* 4.53.2, when writing about a different episode: *Id ego, a scriptoribus annalium non traditum, repperi in commentariis Agrippinae filiae quae Neronis principis mater vitam suam et casus suorum posteris memoravit*. 'This, not noticed by writers of history, I found in the memoirs of her daughter Agrippina, mother of Nero, who recorded for posterity her life and that of her house.' This is Tacitus gloating. But Agrippina's evidence put Tacitus into a twist. He at first seems to follow mainstream thinking: 'Augustus is said to have done it, but I think Tiberius and Livia were guilty.' But he then introduces his scoop, and the effect obfuscates the entire passage. He knows Crispus did it, but he still wants Tiberius to be guilty. Cf. H. Furneax (1896), 31, n. 1, wonders whether Sallustius Crispus may have authored his own memoirs, which stayed within his family. If he did, Agrippina would certainly have had access to them. The ramifications of this conclusion extend, however, beyond the memoirs of the younger Agrippina: it weakens the belief that Tacitus seriously affected either Suetonius or Dio. It would suggest that where Suetonius and Dio seem to echo Tacitus, they in fact echo an earlier common source, not Tacitus himself. They have both skipped over Tacitus, probably preferring Servilius Nonianus, Aufidius Bassus, Cluvius Rufus, Fabius Rusticus, and perhaps even the elder Seneca.

[29] Cf. A. Spengel, 'Zur Geschichte des Kaisers Tiberius', *Sitzungsberichte der K. B. Akademie der Wissenschaften zu München* (1903), 5–11; M. P. Charlesworth (1923), 156; E. Hohl (1935), 352–3; F. Norwood (1963), 163; R. Seager (1972), 42; B. Levick (1999), 65 f.; T. E. J. Wiedemann, *CAH*, 10^2, 202; nor can Augustus have ordered the execution as an emergency measure before Tiberius arrived at Nola. Livia,

that Augustus incarcerated Agrippa in AD 7 only to have him executed a few days before he died in AD 14. The contemporary analysis was probably correct: Augustus could not bring himself to execute family. Evidence could nevertheless be produced which made Augustus a suspect; it must have been the written order to execute.

A soldier, no matter what rank, would not execute a member of the imperial family without formal orders; only Augustus' or Tiberius' seal was probably sufficient.[30] If both are innocent, then someone must have ordered the execution on their behalf. Since Tiberius believed an inquiry would exonerate him the seal must have belonged to Augustus: Crispus ordered the execution of Agrippa on Augustus' behalf, using Augustus' seal. It would not have been an original idea, but an interpretation of the effects of the *senatus consultum* of AD 7, by which Agrippa was incarcerated. The order was not sent from Nola, but from Rome. If Crispus had been at Nola when Tiberius arrived, he would have informed Tiberius immediately. Indeed, even if he had left, others, such as Livia, would have known and told Tiberius. It is clear that Tiberius was first told about Agrippa's death by a centurion holding the instructions in his hand. This implies that no one at Nola knew of Agrippa's execution; that Livia was therefore innocent; and that Crispus was somewhere else. Rome is the best bet. As Augustus' chief minister, Crispus probably stayed in Rome to continue day-to-day business while Augustus toured Italy. To perform this function, Crispus would require a copy of Augustus' seal.[31] This approach perfectly explains Crispus' belief that an inquiry would ruin him, and the fact that some were able to attribute the order to Augustus.[32]

who would have been privy to such an order if it was sent from Nola by Augustus, would have told Tiberius immediately on his arrival, i.e. Tiberius would not have been informed by a centurion a week later.

[30] Otherwise it would have been in the government's interest to have an inquiry. Tac. *Ann.* 1.5.3; Suet. *Tib.* 22; Dio 57.3.5 all attest written instruction for Agrippa's execution.

[31] Dio's belief that a letter was sent from Nola to Planasia is not a problem. It comes from a tradition that blamed Tiberius, and therefore held that the instructions *must* have come from Nola.

[32] Indeed, if the execution was grounded in an interpretation of the *senatus consultum* of AD 7 (which seems likely) then Crispus could argue that he acted according to the terms of the decree, in line with Augustus' intentions when he sponsored its passage through the senate. It would be argued that Augustus had *intended* Agrippa to be executed were the rules pertaining to his incarceration to be breached. This idea may have become distorted within a hostile historical tradition, producing in Tacitus a sentence which seems, on the face of it, to be contradictory, Tac. *Ann.* 1.6: *Nihil de ea*

180 *The Republic in Danger*

But, more importantly, it explains why some suspected Livia. Livia probably possessed Augustus' seal between his death and Tiberius' arrival in Nola. If Crispus were to lie at an inquiry, then suspicion might leave Livia vulnerable. Thus Suetonius and Dio knew of an alternative history in which Livia wrote the letter herself. Tiberius would have known that Livia was innocent; if she knew anything, she would have told him immediately on his arrival at Nola. Tiberius and Livia were probably unaware of Crispus' guilt; Tiberius was right to demand an inquiry. If we accept the historicity of Crispus' and Livia's conversation, then Tiberius abandoned his plans for a public inquiry only once he was in Rome. Interestingly, Tacitus had evidence that Tiberius' relationship with Crispus subsequently soured:

interficiendi Postumi Agrippae conscius, aetate provecta speciem magis in amicitia principis quam vim tenuit.

He knew of the death of Agrippa Postumus, but with advancing years he held more the appearance than the reality of the princeps' friendship.[33]

By agreeing not to hold an inquiry, Tiberius denied himself an opportunity for public exoneration; he may never have forgiven Crispus for placing him in such a position. It is important to note, however, that despite Suetonius' statement: *Nam mox silentio rem obliteravit*, 'for soon he buried the matter in silence', Dio's belief that Tiberius continued to deny his involvement suggests that some official statement was made.[34] Since the matter was never discussed in the senate, the statement was probably something like: 'Agrippa Caesar was put to death on account of a disturbance affecting the security of the *res publica*'. The recent actions of Audasius and Epicadus made it at least plausible for the regime to allege conspiracies and disturbances around Agrippa. But governments that produce equivocal statements invite popular speculation. Some blamed Tiberius and interpreted his request for an inquiry as deceitful, basing their analysis on a logical but defective test: *cui bono*? Others were happy to

---

re Tiberius apud senatum disseruit: patris iussa simulabat, quibus praescripsisset tribuno custodiae adposito ne cunctaretur Agrippam morte adficere quandoque ipse supremum diem explevisset, 'Tiberius did not discuss the matter in the senate: he simulated orders from his father, which instructed the tribune in charge of the prison not to delay the death of Agrippa once he himself had met his final day.'

[33] Tac. *Ann.* 3.30.3.
[34] Once people were talking, some official statement was necessary. Cf. J. Bellemore (2000), 99; and I. Cogitore (1991), 133.

blame the centurion, while still others looked to either Augustus or Livia. But revelations about Crispus probably surfaced much later.[35] It is important to note, however, that Tiberius never withdrew friendship from Crispus.[36] Crispus must have convinced Tiberius that his actions were justified; Tiberius agreed and used him again on Clemens.

Justification for execution precludes arbitrary action as a plausible explanation; Crispus cannot have said: 'Well, Tiberius always said Agrippa was an inconvenience.' An order for execution would not have been given without just cause; a belief that people were planning to free Agrippa is the obvious solution, especially since an actual attempt had already been made. Dio's report may contain traces of the original language when he writes 'the centurion who was guarding him had slain him on his own responsibility because of some revolutionary dealings'. The government could not, at the time, publicly blame the centurion; had it been possible, a public inquiry would have been beneficial. There were probably too many witnesses. It was nevertheless in the regime's interest to let rumour circulate. The question of sources is here relevant.

The death of Agrippa Postumus would not have been treated in a historical work while Tiberius still lived. Velleius, by placing the affair firmly in Augustus' reign, shows what was expected of those who cared about Tiberius' opinion.[37] But holding the centurion responsible necessarily frees the government from blame - we need a pro-Tiberian source able to engage with the subject during the Tiberian Principate. I believe we can do no better than Tiberius' own works. Suetonius refers to *commentarii* and *acta* which survived at least to the time of Domitian.[38] Tiberius, moreover, wrote an autobiography, a *commentarius de vita sua*, which, though apparently brief, touched on the execution of Sejanus[39] and possibly Sempronius Gracchus in AD 14:

---

[35] J. D. Lewis (1970), 168; W. Allen Jun. (1947), 133; P. Sinclair, *Tacitus the Sententious Historian: A Sociology of Rhetoric in Annales 1-6* (1995), 5 f., treat the episode as unhistorical.
[36] As demonstrated by H. W. Benario (1962), 321-2.
[37] Cf. A. J. Woodman (1977), 170.
[38] Suet. *Dom.* 20.
[39] Suet. *Tib.* 61.1.

Quidam non Roma eos milites, sed ab L. Asprenate pro consule Africae missos tradidere auctore Tiberio, qui famam caedis posse in Asprenatem verti frustra speraverat.

Some [state] that the soldiers were sent not from Rome but from L. Asprenas, pronconsul of Africa; Tiberius authored this view, who had hoped in vain that the infamy of murder could be transferred to Asprenas.[40]

The work was perhaps designed to exonerate Tiberius from the most shocking aspects of his Principate, of which Agrippa's death was the first and perhaps most famous. It represents, therefore, a historical revision written almost twenty years after the fact.

Dio's passage: 'the centurion who was guarding him had slain him on his own responsibility because of some revolutionary dealings', thus conflates two separate messages: (i) Tiberius was not responsible for Agrippa's execution, and (ii) the execution was justified because Agrippa had revolutionary designs.[41] The first came much later and from Tiberius. The government used the second in AD 14. Justification was necessary. Dio provides anecdotal evidence which may be related to the question of Agrippa:

ἤδη μὲν γὰρ ἤκουσα ὅτι, ἐπειδὴ ἡ Λιουία ἄκοντος τοῦ Αὐγούστου τὴν ἀρχὴν αὐτῷ περιπεποιηκέναι ἐλέγετο, ἔπραττεν, ὅπως μὴ παρ' ἐκείνης (καὶ γὰρ πάνυ αὐτῇ ἤχθετο) ἀλλὰ παρὰ τῆς βουλῆς ἀναγκαστός, ὡς καὶ κατὰ ἀρετὴν σφων προήκων, δόξειεν αὐτὴν εἰληφέναι·

Now, in fact, I have heard that, when it began to be said that Livia had, against Augustus's will, brought about the rule for Tiberius, he contrived so as to appear not to have received it from her (and indeed he was utterly hateful towards her), but under compulsion from the senate, since he was superior to them in excellence.[42]

Two ideas are present. The first comes from Agrippa's supporters, and relates to the message reconstructed above: Livia murdered Augustus, sponsored Agrippa's execution, and thus provided Tiberius with the Principate. The other is quite separate: Tiberius despised his mother, and thus removed himself from the suspicion that surrounded her. An attempt to undermine the public's perception of Tiberius' relationship with his mother is attested for the period.[43]

---

[40] Tac. *Ann.* 1.53.6.
[41] Of course, Dio is probably not responsible for the conflation, which may well have begun with Tiberius.
[42] Dio 57.3.3.   [43] Tac. *Ann.* 1.72.

Dio's source understood that innuendo and dissent, manufactured, in my view, by Agrippa's supporters, affected Tiberius' behaviour following the death of Augustus. In concert with other events, it compelled him to seek out senatorial support - not to make legal the execution of Agrippa but to legitimize further his own position. But there was more than public relations at stake. Dio cites an exchange between Tiberius and an unknown senator at the first senatorial meeting following Tiberius' return from Nola. Tiberius called the meeting via his *tribunicia potestas* to discuss topics relevant to Augustus' funeral:

Τούς τε σωματοφύλακας ἀμφ' αὐτὸν ἤδη ἔχων ἐδεῖτο δὴ τῆς γερουσίας συνάρασθαί οἱ ὥστε μηδὲν βίαιον ἐν τῇ τοῦ σώματος αὐτοῦ ταφῇ παθεῖν· ἐδεδίει γὰρ δῆθεν μή τινες αὐτὸ ἁρπάσαντες ἐν τῇ ἀγορᾷ, ὥσπερ τὸ τοῦ Καίσαρος, καύσωσι. καὶ ἐπειδή γε κομψευσάμενός τις ἐπὶ τούτῳ φρουρὰν αὐτῷ ὡς οὐκ ἔχοντι δοθῆναι ἐσηγήσατο, τόν τε χλευασμὸν αὐτοῦ συνῆκε, καὶ ἔφη καὶ ὅτι "οἱ στρατιῶται οὐκ ἐμοὶ ἀλλὰ δημόσιοί εἰσι."

And while he already had bodyguards around him, he in fact asked the senate to give him assistance, so that he might not suffer any violence at the burial of Augustus' body; for he was afraid, in truth, lest people, having seized Augustus' body in the forum, as they had seized Caesar's, would burn it. And when somebody, making a joke, suggested that a guard be given to him, as though he had none, he understood the man's irony and actually said that 'the guards do not belong to me, but to the State.'[44]

Tiberius would hardly have asked for State troops to replace those already in his service (praetorians), which he believed were also State troops. 'Assistance' cannot refer to the urban cohorts. Tiberius must have been asking senators to join him in person. His response to the comedian was a veiled request: 'I would prefer that this were a public rather than private initiative'. The image is profound: Tiberius followed by a train of 600 senators, flanked by praetorian guardsmen, and accompanied by the equites in full military array. If news of Agrippa's execution was made public the morning after Tiberius reached Rome, the above request, made on the very same day, indicates actual distress.[45] Universal solidarity beyond that evidenced

---

[44] Dio 57.2.2-3.
[45] According to Dio (56.31.3), the senate met the day after the funeral procession (in which Tiberius participated) reached Rome. Rome would have been informed of Augustus' death by the 21st or 22nd. Crispus' letter would reach Ostia within a day. From Ostia it would be taken, by boat, to Planasia in 1-3 days. If the report reached

by an oath was required: he wanted action, not mere words. Tiberius' approach to the senate following the death of Augustus was thus affected by emerging political situations. As I have so far suggested, the personality of Agrippa, hijacked by those who had formerly supported Gaius, had been persistently used to foster a demagogic reaction to Tiberius - now, as Augustus' legacy was being carried out, serious questions were asked about Tiberius' involvement in Agrippa's demise. Kampff may be right to associate the picture of a nervous capital painted by Velleius with news of Agrippa's demise:

Quid tunc homines timuerint, quae senatus trepidatio, quae populi confusio, quis urbis metus, in quam arto salutis exitiique fuerimus confinio, neque mihi tam festinanti exprimere vacat neque cui vacat potest.

Of the fear of men at this time, the trepidation of the senate, the confusion of the people, the fears of the city, of the narrow boundary between safety and destruction on which we found ourselves, I have not the time to describe as I hasten along, and nor could he [describe these things] who had the time.[46]

As Woodman has pointed out, the *recusatio* confirms the historicity of that which Velleius refuses to describe.[47] Velleius has dressed censorship up as a virtue. But even more interesting is *cui vacat potest*. Even an historian with space to give a full account of the situation still cannot do so! But Agrippa's death was not the only problem for Tiberius. While Tiberius tried, awkwardly, to overlook Agrippa's unauthorized execution, news reached Rome of sedition in lower Germany and unrest within the nobility. Scholars agree that Tiberius' behaviour in the senate on 17 September was not affected by events in lower Germany. I believe this is wrong.

Planasia on the 24th or 25th, Agrippa would have been executed immediately. The letter was returned not to Rome but to Tiberius, who was somewhere between Nola and Rome as part of the funeral procession.

[46] Vell. 2.124.1; G. Kampff (1963), 27.
[47] A. J. Woodman (1977), 221. Cf. R. Syme (1939) 437: "[Velleius'] exaggeration is palpable and shameless".

11

Germanicus: Successor to Tiberius or Augustus?

Three legions camped at Emona in Pannonia and four legions camped near Cologne in Lower Germany mutinied on hearing that Augustus was dead and Tiberius was in control of things.[1] Their respective locations vis-à-vis Rome indicate independent situations.[2] All seven legions none the less wanted the same things: an increase in the normal pay rate; better severance conditions; reduction in the length of service; and an immediate release from the standards for those who had served twenty years. Further to this, the legions in Lower Germany demanded immediate payment of the donatives left them by Augustus, while some troops even tried to co-opt Germanicus by declaring him *Imperator* and offering him supreme power. It was with this in mind that Tacitus wrote concerning Tiberius' 'hesitation':

Causa praecipua ex formidine ne Germanicus, in cuius manu tot legiones immensa sociorum auxilia, mirus apud populum favor, habere imperium quam exspectare mallet.

The chief cause of fear was that Germanicus, in whose hands were so many legions, such large auxiliaries of the allies and such wonderful popular goodwill, might prefer to have the Empire, rather than wait for it.[3]

---

[1] Tac. *Ann.* 1.16, 31.
[2] News probably reached Pannonia by about 25–7 August, if modern predictions are correct that a courier carrying an emergency note could travel as much as 150 km per day. See W. M. Ramsay, 'The Speed of the Roman Imperial Post', *JRS*, 15 (1925) 60–74; N. J. E. Austin and N. B. Rankov, *Exploratio: Military and Political Intelligence in the Roman World from the Second Punic War to the Battle of Adrianople* (1995), 124f. Cf. K. Wellesley (1967), 25 n. 9, who suggests a top speed of 125 miles per day.
[3] Tac. *Ann.* 1.7.6.

Connecting the mutinies—particularly mutiny in Lower Germany—with Tiberius' behaviour in the senate is an ancient interpretation rejected by modern scholars.[4] There are two reasons for this: one is chronological; the other is psychological. Wellesley and Levick posit that news of the mutiny, especially mutiny in Lower Germany, cannot have reached Rome before the first senatorial meeting, which must have occurred between 30 August and 4 September.[5] But Wellesley's placing of Tiberius' acceptance of supreme power in early September is not supported by evidence, while Levick's belief that Tiberius' decision cannot have been affected by the mutinies, since his 'hesitation' ceased before they had settled down, ignores the possibility that unforeseen issues emerged hastening a final solution, despite the ongoing nature of the mutiny.[6] In terms of psychology, it has been suggested that had Tiberius feared mutiny he would not have hesitated at all, but would have wrapped himself in power immediately.[7] But this, too, is weak. Debate in the senate centred on Tiberius recognizing powers that already belonged to him, not his accepting them. Tiberius had, moreover, shown a propensity to retreat when threatened: to Rhodes when threatened with political irrelevance; and from Rhodes when threatened with his life. Equivocation was central to the exercise. Chronological and psychological objections can, therefore, be put aside. It can be shown instead that the mutinies did affect the political situation in Rome, and thus Tiberius' performance in the senate on 17 September AD 14.

---

[4] The link is accepted by: F. B. Marsh (1931), 57f. It is rejected by G. Kampff (1963); K. Wellesley (1967); B. Levick (1999), 68–81; M. Sage (1982/83); *CAH*, 10², 206.

[5] K. Wellesley (1967), *passim*; B. Levick (1999), 68–81. Dating the first senatorial meeting depends on our dating the arrival of Augustus' body in Rome. Suet. *Aug.* 100.2 states that the procession travelled only at night, during the day Augustus' body was kept indoors at 'each town'. Levick has counted 13 towns between Nola and Rome in which she believes the body rested. Though Suetonius' '*cuiusque*' implies every town, he may have meant 'each town they stopped at'. The distance between Nola and Rome is roughly 200 km, so that Levick estimates the cortege travelled 15.4 km a night. If we assume that by 'night' Suetonius means that the procession marched from say 6 p.m. to 5 a.m, then Levick would have it that the procession moved at about 1.4 km/h, this is perhaps too slow. The cortege which carried Tiberius' body in AD 37 seems to have taken 10 days to cover almost the same distance, which would give us a speed of about 1.8 km/h. Either way, if the procession began between 21st and 22nd, it would have reached Rome anywhere between 1 and 4 Sept.

[6] B. Levick (1999), 75.

[7] Ibid., 71.

A belief that the situation in Lower Germany was reported in Rome only after 17 September is central to Levick's argument that it had no effect on the succession debate.[8] She cites Tacitus as evidence, but he implies the opposite:

At Romae nondum cognito qui fuisset exitus in Illyrico, et legionum Germanicarum motu audito, trepida civitas incusare Tiberium quod, dum patres et plebem, invalida et inermia, cunctatione ficta ludificetur, dissideat interim miles neque duorum adulescentium nondum adulta auctoritate comprimi queat. Ire ipsum et opponere maiestatem imperatoriam debuisse cessuris ubi principem longa experientia eundemque severitatis et munificentiae summum vidissent.

At Rome meanwhile, while the outcome in Illyricum was not yet known, and having heard about the mutiny of the German legions, the fearful citizen-body reproached Tiberius that while he was mocking the senate and people, elements lacking strength and arms, with assumed hesitation, in the meantime the troops were in mutiny and could not be put down by the immature *auctoritas* of two young men. He should have gone himself and confronted with the imperial majesty those who would have submitted once they saw a princeps with long experience and supreme in his ability to dispense severity and reward.[9]

Having left Rome on 17 or 18 September, Drusus reached the Pannonian legions, stationed at Emona, on 26 September, and the situation was already settled by the 27th.[10] On the morning of the 27th

---

[8] Ibid., 73f.; also M. M. Sage (1982/83), 305, but strangely, Sage holds that news nevertheless arrived in Rome before 17 Sept., 305 n. 70.

[9] Tac. *Ann.* 1.45. Tacitus purports to provide public opinion, i.e. what people were saying at dinner parties and on the street. In so doing, his narrative is necessarily a construction. But this does not mean the message is artificial. Tacitus places the episode within a chronological structure. This would imply that he is working from an analytical source. It is plausible that a source such as Servilius Nonianus or Aufidius Bassus provided a clear and analytical account of various criticisms of Tiberius made during these few weeks; a more extensive exposition was condensed by Tacitus for the purpose of dramatic effect: a showdown between the people and the princeps.

[10] Tac. *Ann.* 1.14 states that the senate voted (on 17 Sept., see V. Ehrenberg and A. H. M. Jones (1955), 52) that Germanicus should be given proconsular *imperium* and that a commission be sent to Lower Germany to confer it in person and to offer condolences for Augustus' death. Tacitus adds that the same things were not voted for Drusus: *ea causa quod designatus consul Drusus praesensque erat*. Since Drusus was consul designate, he did not require a proconsular command. He did not require official condolence by proxy because he was present in the senate, '*praesens*', see H. H. Schmitt, 'Der pannonische Aufstand d. J. 14 und der Regierungsantritt des

Drusus promised to send a letter to Tiberius concerning the legions' requests. It probably informed Tiberius and the senate that the situation was, for now, under control.[11] If dispatched on 28 September, Drusus' letter, revealing the upshot of events in Illyricum, should have reached Rome no later than 3 or 4 October. The above attack on Tiberius therefore occurred between 17 September and 4 October. Tacitus places the episode after the delegation to Germanicus, which had left for Cologne on the 18th, had reached their destination and inspired further violence.[12] But the phrase *et legionum Germanicarum motu audito* cannot refer to the nature of their arrival. Fifteen days is insufficient for the delegation to reach Cologne and for news of their arrival to reach Rome.[13] The phrase must instead mean something like: 'and having heard (already) about the mutiny of the German legions...'. A clue is provided by the tense of the final sentence: 'He *should have* gone...'. The clause 'while the outcome in Illyricum was not yet known' implies moreover that something was known about the outcome in Lower Germany, or at least the direction in which events were expected to run. Tacitus' notice thus suggests the existence of an initial report by Germanicus on the situation in Germany, which probably arrived in Rome before 17 September; political manœuvring on 17 September was the result.[14]

Approximately 22,000 Roman soldiers were stationed in Lower Germany when mutiny broke out; that represents a formidable threat.[15] Germanicus was somewhere in Gaul when informed.[16] On

---

Tiberius,' *Historia*, 7 (1958), 378–83; R. Seager (1972), 60, and B. Levick (1999), 72. Cf. M. Sage (1982/83).

[11] Tac. *Ann.* 1.25.3.
[12] Tac. *Ann.* 1.39f.
[13] Since the delegation comprised a large group, necessarily with protection, 150 km per day is out of the question. Even if the group traveled between 7 a.m. and 6 p.m. at a healthy 5 km/h it would have taken 20 days to reach Cologne. They probably reached Cologne between 8 and 18 Oct. An emergency courier back to Rome would have taken a further 7–10 days.
[14] G. V. Sumner review of E. Koestermann 'Cornelius Tacitus: Annalen, Band 1: Buch 1–3', *Phoenix*, 20. 1 (1966), 76–85, believes that the decision to send a senatorial delegation to Germanicus on the 17th is proof that Rome was ignorant of the situation in Lower Germany. That is illogical. The news which reached Rome told of both the rebellion and its pacification by Germanicus. Tiberius would have considered the situation settled. Sending a senatorial delegation to Lower Germany is, therefore, an attempt to shore-up an already improved situation.
[15] Tac. *Ann.* 1.31.1; H. M. D. Parker (1958), 118f.
[16] Tac. *Ann.* 1.34.1f.

arrival at the camp, Germanicus was apparently confronted by many soldiers, who persisted, in spite of Germanicus' *imperium*, in their insubordination.[17] Germanicus spoke immediately but his rhetoric failed to placate. Indeed, it incited further indignation:

Ut seditionem attigit, ubi modestia militaris, ubi veteris disciplinae decus... rogitans, nudant universi corpora, cicatrices ex vulneribus, verberum notas exprobrant.

But when he touched on the sedition and asked: where was the military composure? Where the discipline of ancient renown?... They all tore off their clothes and reproachfully exhibited the scars of battle and the imprints of the lash.[18]

By questioning the soldiers' virtue he underestimated the prevailing psychology; these soldiers were not concerned with duty or loyalty, but justice. Nevertheless, during this exchange some proclaimed Germanicus 'emperor' and offered to support him against Tiberius.[19] Wiedemann states: 'we may be sceptical about how serious this offer was', while Levick has: 'the attempt to proclaim Germanicus was not seriously meant...'.[20] But it cannot have been a joke, or a half-hearted/lukewarm proposal. The men who shouted *imperator* and offered Germanicus supreme power were gambling with their lives; intended sedition and willingness for civil war is always serious business. Germanicus' response, a threat to commit suicide to evidence loyalty, shows that he took the offer very seriously.[21] Having retreated to his tent for consultation with advisers, Germanicus decided on a settlement:

Igitur... placitum ut epistulae nomine principis scriberentur: missionem dari vicena stipendia meritis, exauctorari qui sena dena fecissent ac retineri sub vexillo ceterorum inmunes nisi propulsandi hostis, legata quae petiverant exsolvi duplicarique.

Therefore... it was agreed that a letter should be written in the name of the princeps: those who had served 20 years were to be given discharge; those who had completed 16 years were to be released from duty and retained under the standard with immunity from everything else except holding off an enemy; the legacies which they had asked for were to be paid and doubled.[22]

---

[17] Tac. *Ann.* 1.34.
[18] Tac. *Ann.* 1.34–5.
[19] Tac. *Ann.* 1.35.3; Dio 57.5.1–2; Suet. *Tib.* 25.2; Vell. 2.125.
[20] *CAH* 10² 208; similarly B. Levick (1999), 247, n. 6.
[21] Tac. *Ann.* 1.35.3f.   [22] Tac. *Ann.* 1.36.

The letter was probably read out between 2 and 4 September. Germanicus cannot have wanted the legions to believe that Tiberius was responding to their demands; that possibility was beyond their technology. The letter must instead have been presented as arriving with those Tiberius had sent from Nola. Tiberius had meant to improve the conditions of employment even before the mutinies![23] This evidences naivety and desperation; the soldiers, not surprisingly, were unimpressed.[24] If Tiberius had written the letter, why did Germanicus not refer to it immediately on arrival? The terms were nevertheless accepted and the legions were ordered to depart for their respective winter camps, but Legions V and XXI refused until Augustus' legacy was paid to them: *ex viatico amicorum ipsiusque Caesaris pecunia*.[25] Germanicus then left for Upper Germany, where, perhaps for the second time in a matter of weeks, the oath of allegiance was administered to Legions II, XIII, XIV, and XVI.[26] The report from Germany, alluded to by Tacitus, was probably sent by Germanicus shortly after the troops in Lower Germany had left for their winter camp, i.e. once the situation was considered settled. If sent between 4 and 6 September, it would have reached Rome before the 17th. Hence, prior to 17 September, Tiberius and the senate were probably aware of the fact of mutiny, the legions' demands, and Germanicus' response. They were also aware that four legions had offered to support Germanicus against Tiberius.[27] Some in the crowd were reportedly hostile to Germanicus, but the image which formed in the minds of those in Rome lacked nuance.[28] Velleius, in Rome when Germanicus' report arrived, understood that the soldiers:

---

[23] Perhaps he meant to shame the legions by his reconstructed chronology.
[24] Tac. *Ann.* 1.37; cf. Dio 57.5.5–6.
[25] Tac. *Ann.* 1.37.1.
[26] Tac. *Ann.* 1.37.3.
[27] It would have been dangerous for Germanicus to not include in his report the offer of supreme command by sections of the legions. It was far better to be open and honest with Tiberius, lest he should invite suspicion when the story finally broke. Indeed, aside from Germanicus' letters to Tiberius and the senate, one would expect that various companions would include the episode in their letters home: in the same way Q. Cicero had sent letters to his brother M. Cicero from Caesar's camp in Gaul. Though Q. Cicero's letters took some time to reach Rome, officers in AD 14 might have sent them with the couriers carrying Germanicus' letters.
[28] *CAH* 10² 208: 'We may be sceptical...'; R. Seager (1972), 64: 'Only a small, minority among the mutineers attempted to push Germanicus into rebellion...'. There is no evidence to support Seager's 'small minority'. On the contrary, we possess only evidence that suggests a large number of soldiers nominated Germanicus for

novum ducem, novum statum, novam quaerebant rem publicam, 'wanted a new leader, a new order of things, and a new *res publica*'.[29] The situation was analysed in Rome to a high degree of sophistication.[30] The belief that legionaries wanted a *dux*, rather than a *princeps*, is telling. It implies a militarization of power. But the idea of 'constitutional' reform is best evidenced by the distinction made between *status* and *res publica*: a 'state of things' and the 'State'. This is not Republican language. *Dux* signals instead the presence of a military dictator, in opposition to the civilian Principate then being enacted in Italy. Velleius, with his contemporaries, believed that the legions were aiming to dismantle the balanced structure built by Augustus—the *optimus status* in Augustus' own words—and replace it with militant demagogy: a *novus status* and hence *nova res publica*.[31] For Velleius, this was best evidenced by their approach to the legitimate organs of power: *quin etiam ausi sunt minari daturos se senatui daturos principi leges,* 'they even dared to threaten to give laws to the senate and princeps.'[32] Most senators and equestrians would share Velleius' opinion, whether they supported Tiberius or not.

---

supreme power, Vell. 2.125.2 (*non qui sequerentur*)'. Velleius, admittedly, treats both the situation in Lower Germany and that in Pannonia together, but *dux* (*qui contra rem publicam duceret*) again reminds us of Germanicus. M. M. Sage (1982/83), 315, holds that Velleius' comments are ambiguous because they lack detail. But Velleius was writing while Tiberius still lived. Rumours about Germanicus would not be described in detail; unable to ignore the issue completely he did the next best thing.

[29] Vell. 2.125.1.

[30] It is dismissed as unhistorical by A. Spengel (1903), Heft 1, 18; M. M. Sage (1982/83), 315, though Sage's position is not entirely clear. That people in Rome were discussing the situation of Germanicus is accepted by E. Koestermann, 'Die Feldzuge des Germanicus 14-16 n.Chr', *Historia*, 6 (1957), 429-79; D. C. A. Shotter 'Tacitus, Tiberius and Germanicus', *Historia,* 17 (1968), 194-214; R. Seager (1972), 64; B. Levick (1999), 247, n. 6, seems to accept it as historical, but with reservations.

[31] The soldiers, with cynical realism, would not tolerate a universally accepted facade. They knew the reality of power. They knew with whom they must deal. Moreover, *SCPP,* 160f. shows that the soldiers were *treated* as belonging to the princeps, and were encouraged, or reminded, to view the *domus Caesaris* as their patron house: *qui sub auspicis et imperio principis nostri milites essent, quam fidem pietatemq(ue) domui Aug(ustae) p[raesta]rent, eam sperare perpetuo praestaturos, cum scirent salutem imperi nostri in eius dom[u]<s> custodia posita<m> esse{t}.* 'That all soldiers under the auspices and command of our princeps would forever display the fidelity and devotion that they were displaying to the house of Augustus, since they knew the safety of our empire had been placed in the custody of that house.' For *Optimus Status,* see Suet. *Aug.* 28.2.

[32] Vell. 2.125.

It must be accepted that Tiberius cannot have known how many supported Germanicus before 17 September. As with modern parliamentary leaders, the true extent of support is often unknown until the day of a leadership ballot. Tiberius, of course, was not facing a leadership ballot, but the situation in Cologne, known to the public, made Germanicus' situation topical.[33] As Tacitus notes, Germanicus' performance in Lower Germany was attacked.[34] It was argued that Tiberius should have dealt with the matter instead. Despite the critical language, the theme is pro-Tiberian. Its essence no doubt appeared soon after Germanicus' report reached Rome; Tiberius benefited the most whether the scene was orchestrated or not. Tiberius, of course, had nothing to fear from Germanicus. The latter needed only to wait. But attempts had been made as recently as AD 12 to destabilize Tiberius' position by advertising Germanicus as a viable alternative. The troublemakers were not necessarily Germanicus' friends.[35] From AD 4 to AD 14 Tiberius' enemies consistently attempted to drive a wedge between Tiberius and Augustus: from AD 4 to AD 7 Tiberius was accused of fostering the northern legions in order to seize power; after AD 6 it was said that Augustus preferred Germanicus.[36] Tiberius' awkwardness in AD 14 shows that persistent insinuation was effective. The moment lent itself to the Augustan discourse of shared responsibility. Suetonius' decision to link the question of Germanicus' position within the *res publica* with Tiberius' 'reluctance' is telling:

Quem maxime casum timens, partes sibi quas senatui liberet, tuendas in re. p. depoposcit, quando universae sufficere solus nemo posset nisi cum altero vel etiam cum pluribus.

---

[33] This is made clear by Augustus' letter to the senate in AD 12 and the constant references to Germanicus in this episode. Some modern scholars have attempted to make such references inventions of Caligula's reign, but that ignores the logicality of the situation. Being called *Imperator* by soldiers evidences a wider discussion about the nature of Germanicus' position *vis-a-vis* the *domus Caesaris*. To ignore the potential for such a dynamic within a society of nobles is naive.

[34] Though Tac. *Ann.* 1.45 refers to a period later than 17 Sept., criticism of Germanicus would necessarily have occurred when news of the situation first broke.

[35] *Contra* E. Ciaceri (1944), 271f., and I. Cogitore (1991), 128f., who seem to argue that Agrippina was leading a circle of Julians in opposition to Tiberius, despite the fact that Germanicus was 'next in line'.

[36] What was insinuation between AD 4 and 20 was presented as fact by the pro-Germanicus tradition, established after Tiberius' death and encouraged by Gaius, i.e. they did not make these stories up, but re-cast them within a new discourse.

Germanicus: Successor to Tiberius or Augustus? 193

This, his greatest fear, caused Tiberius to require the senate to assign him a part in the *res publica*, to be looked after by him, since no one could bear everything unless with [the help of] another or even more.[37]

Suetonius takes *alter* to be a veiled reference to Germanicus; I believe he is right. The senate might register under *pluribus*, but if the task were to be limited to one other, then Germanicus was the only plausible candidate.[38] In response, Tiberius' supporters stacked the debate, praising Tiberius as the most fit to govern while insinuating that others were not qualified. Our sources record very little dissent. The most vehement comment attested is 'Let him take it or leave it', and it is inconceivable that anyone would have said: 'Perhaps you should share power with Germanicus', or 'Germanicus could lead us, if you would prefer to retire from politics'.[39] The pro-Tiberian message swept away all before it, silencing critics while leaving heavyweights like Asinius Gallus floundering. Tiberius had thrown down a challenge, aware that no one would dare accept.

Once the possibility of having to share supreme power was eliminated, Tiberius was able to stop refusing it. Secure, Tiberius put the motion that *imperium proconsulare* should be conferred on Germanicus, advertising his trust and support but stopping short of granting *tribunicia potestas*.[40] Anyone hoping to use Germanicus to trip up Tiberius was thus confronted, wedged, and overcome. This marked the point at which Tiberius ceased actively to refuse supreme power. He felt, however, that he could not yet explicitly recognize his position and positively accept its moral consequences. With the 'Germanicus question' settled on the 17th, we need another factor to explain Tiberius' ongoing behaviour in the senate. 'Decent Papal reluctance' is weak. It does not account for the subtle change in message on the 17th, nor adequately explain the long delay. Levick's belief that Tiberius never formally accepted the Principate is contradicted by actual evidence; while Woodman's position, that Tiberius did not in

---

[37] Suet. *Tib.* 25.2.
[38] As was the case in AD 12, Drusus' position does not seem to have become a topic of discussion.
[39] Suet. *Tib.* 24.
[40] Since Augustus conferred *tribunicia potestas* on Vipsanius Agrippa (Dio 54.12.4; 54.28.1) and Tiberius (Dio 55.9.4–5; Vell. 2.103f.) only once they were well into their thirties and forties, it would have been easy for Tiberius simply to cite the Augustan precedent: Germanicus and Drusus were still too young.

fact want supreme power, fails to account for the fact that Tiberius had immediately possessed and utilized the instruments of violent coercion, i.e. the praetorians and the armies.[41] I propose that M. Scribonius Drusus Libo provides the solution.

[41] A. J. Woodman, *Tacitus Reviewed* (1998).

12

Alternative Government

AN AWKWARD ALLIANCE

Was M. Scribonius Drusus Libo a problem for Tiberius in September AD 14? Suetonius thinks he was. Tacitus and Dio are ambiguous. Suetonius writes:

L. Scribonius Libo [sic] vir nobilis res novas clam moliebatur... Libonem, ne quid in novitate acerbius fieret, secundo demum anno in senatu coarguit, medio temporis spatio tantum cavere contentus; nam et inter pontifices sacrificanti simul pro secespita plumbeum cultrum subiciendum curavit et secretum petenti non nisi adhibito Druso filio dedit dextramque obambulantis veluti incumbens, quoad perageretur sermo, continuit.

L. Scribonius Libo, a nobleman, was secretly planning revolution... Not wanting to make things too difficult at the beginning [of his reign], Tiberius waited two years before attacking Libo in the senate; in the meantime, however, he was content to be on his guard; for, when sacrificing together among the pontiffs, he took care to substitute the sacrificial knife for a lead one, and when he [Libo] sought a private audience he [Tiberius] gave it only if his son Drusus was present and leaning, as it were, on his right arm as he walked, held it until the conversation had finished.[1]

Tacitus writes:

Firmius Catus senator, ex intima Libonis amicitia, iuvenem inprovidum et facilem inanibus ad Chaldaeorum promissa, magorum sacra, somniorum etiam interpretes impulit, dum proavum Pompeium, amitam Scriboniam, quae quondam Augusti coniunx fuerat, consobrinos Caesares, plenam imaginibus domum ostentat... Ut satis testium et qui servi eadem noscerent

---

[1] Suet. *Tib.* 25.3. Suetonius has evidently made a mistake by conflating the consul of AD 16, L. Scribonius Libo, and his brother M. Scribonius Drusus Libo.

repperit, aditum ad principem postulat, demonstrato crimine et reo per Flaccum Vescularium equitem Romanum, cui propior cum Tiberio usus erat. Caesar indicium haud aspernatus congressus abnuit: posse enim eodem Flacco internuntio sermones commeare. Atque interim Libonem ornat praetura, convictibus adhibet...

Firmius Catus, a senator and close friend of Libo's, urged the short-sighted and stupid young man to resort to the promises of astrologers, the rites of magicians, and also dream interpreters, and to boast about his great-grandfather Pompeius, his paternal aunt Scribonia, former wife of Augustus, his imperial cousins, his house crowded with ancestral images... When he found enough witnesses and slaves who had the same information, he asked for access to the princeps, having indicated the charge and the defendant through Vescularius Flaccus, a Roman knight who was more intimate with Tiberius. Caesar, not rejecting the information, declined an interview: 'it was possible for the information to be passed on via the same intermediary Flaccus.' Meanwhile he distinguished Libo with a praetorship and invited him to dinner parties.[2]

Dio writes:

τοῦτό τε οὖν οὐχ ὁμολογούμενον ἔπραξε, καὶ Λούκιον Σκριβώνιον Λίβωνα, νεανίσκον εὐπατρίδην δόξαντά τι νεωτερίζειν, τέως μὲν ἔρρωτο, οὐκ ἔκρινε, νοσήσαντα δὲ ἐπιθάνατον ἔν τε σκιμποδίῳ καταστέγῳ, ὁποίῳ αἱ τῶν βουλευτῶν γυναῖκες χρῶνται, ἐς τὴν γερουσίαν ἐσεκόμισε...

And so he did this, acting inconsistently; likewise for Lucius Scribonius Libo, a young noble who appeared to be undertaking some revolutionary activity; as long as he was healthy, he did not bring him to trial; but when he was ill to the point of death, he had him brought into the senate in a covered litter, of the kind that the wives of senators use...[3]

Suetonius separates by two years the initial suspicion of Drusus Libo from his eventual demise, while Tacitus and Dio describe a timelapse. Most scholars reject Suetonius' account, preferring Tacitus instead. But Tacitus' account does not necessarily invalidate Suetonius: dating Drusus Libo's praetorship is the key. Three options are available to us: a praetorship in 15; a praetorship in 16; a praetorship in 17. Alternatively, Drusus Libo may have been a *candidatus*

---

[2] Tac. *Ann.* 2.27.2.
[3] Dio 57.15.4; Dio, too, has erred by naming the consul of 16 rather than his brother. An early source has obviously confused the two brothers, though Tacitus shows that correct information was nevertheless at hand.

Caesaris for an election that had not yet taken place.[4] I prefer a praetorship in 15, and hence election to the praetorship in AD 14.

That Drusus Libo was praetor, or praetor-designate, when prosecuted in AD 16 is unlikely. Prosecution of a magistrate, or magistrate designate, is unusual, and usually commented on by the sources. Moreover, as Weinrib has shown, a prosecution would only go ahead once the magistrate had abdicated from office.[5] In AD 21 two men brought a charge of *maiestas* against the praetor Magius Caecilianus.[6] Tacitus, who, it should be added, does mention Magius' praetorship, writes only that Tiberius charged the *delatores* with *calumnia*.[7] Dio, who is similarly brief, adds that on hearing the charge, Magius 'left the senate and having taken off his robe of office returned, demanding as a private citizen to have the complaint lodged at once'—i.e. Magius abdicated from office.[8] Dio records many other instances of the phenomenon.[9] That the sources, and especially Dio, do not mention Drusus Libo's abdication or his being arraigned while praetor, or praetor-designate, is evidence, *ex silentio* as it is, that the first two options are unlikely. On the other hand, a *candidatus Caesaris* for a future election requires a relatively late date for the praetorian elections, and distorts the natural sense of our sources, especially Tacitus (it should be noted that a natural reading of the text also suffers from making Drusus Libo a praetor-designate).[10] Weinrib supports his view that Drusus Libo was a *candidatus Caesaris* by suggesting that the praetorian elections in AD 16 occurred after Libo's trial. The argument is based on the fact that elections in AD 14

---

[4] For praetor in AD 16 or 17 see *PIR*[1] S 214; R. Syme (1958), 1.399, and (1986), 256; E. Koestermann (1963), 300; G. V. Sumner (1966), 81; E. J. Weinrib, 'The Prosecution of Roman Magistrates', *Phoenix*, 22:1 (1968), 32–56, with some variation; F. R. D. Goodyear (1981), 270–1, esp. 271, n. 3; S. Rutledge (2001), 371, n. 5. For praetor in AD 15, see R. Seager (1972), 90; B. Levick (1999), 270, n. 114; M. M. Sage (1982/83), 299, n. 34.

[5] G. V. Sumner (1966), 81; E. J. Weinrib (1968), *passim*. It should be noted, however, that a designate was not immune from prosecution, E. J. Weinrib (1968), 51 f.

[6] Tac. *Ann.* 3.37.1; Dio 57.21.1.

[7] Tac. *Ann.* 3.37.1.

[8] Dio 57.21.1.

[9] Dio shows consistent interest in the prosecution, or attempted prosecution, of magistrates, for instance: Dio 37.34.2; 39.7.3; 39.18.1; 40.55.1; 46.49.1; 55.10.15; 56.24.7; 57.21.1; 58.8.3; 59.23.8. Tacitus also mentions the subject on occasion: Tac. *Ann.* 12.4; *Ann.* 13.44; *Ann.* 14.48.2; *Ann.* 4.22.1; *Hist.* 3.35 f.; Vell. 2.124.4.

[10] E. J. Weinrib (1968), 33 n. 7.

occurred in late September/early October. But the elections of AD 14 should not be used to date elections in AD 16.[11] When Augustus died, his *commendationes* were already published, suggesting that the elections were to be held in late August or early September.[12] Augustus' death and funeral caused public business to cease, a situation that would have affected the timing of the praetorian election as well. That the elections were overdue is perhaps also suggested by the fact that Tiberius turned his attention to their re-organisation immediately on accepting the principate.[13] Moreover, Tacitus (who mentions dinner parties), Suetonius (who mentions religious ceremonies and informal meetings), and Dio (who suggests that Tiberius bided his time) all imply that more than a few weeks separate the initial entrapment by Catus and Drusus Libo's final destruction.[14] Indeed, Tacitus' 'origin, stages, and end of this affair' (*eius negotii initium, ordinem, finem curatius disseram*...) seems to describe a lengthy process, the natural sense of which is seriously damaged by a chronology which places the whole episode inside a month or two.[15] We are therefore left with a praetorship in AD 15 and, hence, election to the praetorship in AD 14.

Designation as a *candidatus Caesaris* in AD 14 accords with Velleius' description of his own election to the praetorship in that year: *proxime a nobilissimis ac sacerdotalibus viris destinari praetoribus contigit*, 'were together destined for the praetorship immediately after those from the noblest houses and those who had held priesthoods'.[16] Both *nobilissimus* and *sacerdotalis* cover Drusus

---

[11] Weinrib further argues that Tac. *Ann.* 2.36, in which Asinius Gallus proposed a decree to the effect that 'elections should determine the magistrates for the next five years...' refers to the praetorian elections of AD 16. Though Tacitus goes on to mention aspects of the proposal that would affect the praetorship, it is conceivable that the intention was to determine for five years all magistracies. Moreover, as F. R. D. Goodyear (1981), 270, points out, the episode is loosely dated by Tacitus. It is connected thematically (*et certamen Gallo adversus Caesarem exortum est*) to *Ann.* 2.35.1: *Res eo anno prolatas haud referrem*... Tacitus may have felt that the dispute was not suitably placed between the close of action in Germany and the prosecution of Drusus Libo; he chose instead to register in succession disputes that had taken place in the senate from *Ann.* 2.33.1 to *Ann.* 2.38; a totality without a precise chronological structure.
[12] This is the view of C. J. Simpson, 'Tacitus and the Praetorian Elections of A.D. 14', *La Parola Del Passato*, 36 (1981), 295–311, esp. 299.
[13] Vell. 2.124.3–4.
[14] Tac. *Ann.* 2.28.2; Suet. *Tib.* 25.3; Dio 57.15.4.
[15] Tac. *Ann.* 2.27.1 f.
[16] Vell. 2.124.4.

Libo.[17] Velleius adds that he and his brother were 'the last to be commended by Augustus and the first to be commended by Tiberius'.[18] Tiberius, who limited himself to four recommendations, would not have repudiated or added to Augustus' *commendationes* while they remained valid.[19] Since Augustus would not have preferred a pair of Velleii to an important young aristocrat of impeccable family, Drusus Libo, like Velleius and his brother, was probably commended by Augustus and Tiberius.[20] He was possibly praetor *suo anno*. It has been argued, nonetheless, that a praetorship in 15 causes problems for our understanding of the affair.

Scholars seem to agree generally that if Suetonius is to be believed, and the praetorship is to be placed in AD 15, then one *must* hold that the plot which was discovered in September AD 16 was *formed* in AD 14.[21] But opposition often seems consistent, even though its manifestations appear intermittently. That which is termed a 'plot' is very often nothing more than a collection of separate decisions (often reactive) artificially linked owing to a common theme. I believe the best solution is to treat Drusus Libo's activities in AD 14 and AD 16 separately. On that reading, a tradition endeavouring to understand the final damnation of Drusus Libo, or, better, those trying to

---

[17] Cf. W. K. Lacey, 'Nominatio and the elections under Tiberius', *Historia*, 12 (1963) 167–76, esp. 170, and C. J. Simpson (1981), 303, who take '*a*' to mean 'by' rather than 'after'. See R. Frei-Stolba, *Untersuchungen zu den Wahlen in der römischen Kaiserzeit* (1967), 143–4; and A. J. Woodman (1977), 227, for argument in favour of 'after'.

[18] Vell. 2.124. 4.

[19] Tac. *Ann*. 1.15.

[20] That Tacitus mentions only Tiberius' *commendatio* vis-à-vis Drusus Libo is not a problem. He is interested in the fact that Tiberius agreed to commend a political rival. Indeed, introducing Augustus' *commendatio* would cause problems for his approach, which is to present Tiberius as two-faced.

[21] F. R. D. Goodyear (1981), 270; cf. R. S. Rogers (1935), 14: 'Libo's plot had been in progress since the commencement of Tiberius' rule'; R. Seager (1972), 90; B. Levick (1999), 150; cf. the suggestion of U. Silvagni (rev. 1909), 270, that Drusus Libo was behind the mutinies in Illyricum, a theory seemingly based on an incorrect reading of Suetonius *Tib*. 25. Goodyear also believes that 'the earlier we put his praetorship, the more puzzling becomes our sources' emphasis on Libo's youth'. But the sources only use general terms which have no specific meaning: Tacitus uses *iuvenis*, Seneca uses *adulescens*, and Dio uses νεανίσκο. Goodyear posits an accelerated *cursus*, i.e. Drusus Libo was treated as if he were an imperial youth. But this surely would interest at least one of our sources. As was shown above, dispensation required the approval of the senate in response to a personal request from the princeps, an extraordinary privilege extended only to members of the *domus Caesaris*. A dispensation for Drusus Libo, passed over in silence by the sources, is simply improbable.

destroy him in AD 16, telescoped two separate incidents; a synthesis convenient and provocative. Suetonius' *clam* is thus a device to explain the long delay; it reflects an interpretation not historical fact. When put this way, objections to a praetorship in AD 15 dissolve. What, then, occurred in September AD 14 to deserve Suetonius' treatment, and in particular, his use of language appropriate to revolution (*res novas clam moliebatur*)?

Astrology is a key topic for the prosecution in AD 16. Drusus Libo's accusers may have argued, or proved, that he had first consulted astrologers in AD 14. If this is correct, then Suetonius' *clam* may, in fact, relate to the senate's findings. It was in the prosecution's interest to establish one coherent plan, rather than a mixed bag of offences. The story of Firmius Catus seems, however, authentic. Catus is said to have collected witnesses and slaves and taken their information to Vescularius Flaccus, Tiberius' close friend.[22] News that witnesses (who were not slaves) were being collected would spread quickly, especially within the senatorial class; notoriety that would prove useful to the prosecution in September AD 16, something like: 'Two years ago Firmius Catus had evidence that Drusus Libo was plotting revolution; he was saved only by the clemency of our princeps...' Catus could not construct a serious charge from ambitious spirit; *maiestas* was possible only once the necromantic parchment surfaced in AD 16. But the essence of Catus' accusation is not entirely obscure.

Drusus Libo is said to have meditated on his Pompeian ancestry and his imperial cousins, (*consobrini Caesares*).[23] Both are relevant to the political atmosphere of September AD 14. At *Ann.* 1.10 Tacitus purports to record criticisms of Augustus which surfaced in the weeks following his death. Though the structure is probably Tacitean, we need not reject the contents. Defamation concerned Augustus in his final years; criticism, of what was essentially authoritarianism, should not surprise us. Tacitus writes that people accused Augustus, *inter alia*, of having feigned a Pompeian spirit. If this reflects a contemporary idea, then Pompeism (an anachronistic but useful label), which had come to mean the principle of Republican government, was evidently topical in the weeks following Augustus' death: 'our leaders talk of a free Republic... etc.'[24] Tiberius' use of the Augustan

---

[22] Tac. *Ann.* 2.28.1.   [23] Tac. *Ann.* 2.27.2.
[24] Suet. *Tib.* 57.2, writes that Tiberius, at the beginning of his reign, made reference to Pompeiani in the senate: *Nec multo post in senatu Pompeio cuidam equiti R.*

discourse of shared responsibility on 17 September is here apposite. As was the case in 27 BC, the rhetoric was necessary because the topic was relevant. The Principate was enacted as an emergency structure and this was not forgotten. As Velleius admits, people *did not know* what to expect of the post-Augustan era.[25] Tiberius was in a position of supreme power, but some probably wondered: 'Do we really need him?' It is conceivable that during these few weeks Drusus Libo was somehow made to represent a Pompeian position, a hypothesis supported by Tacitus' belief that he had spoken out about something: *cunctaque eius dicta factaque, cum prohibere posset, scire malebat . . .,* 'He [Tiberius] could have checked his *every word and action*, but wished instead to know them'.[26] Reference to *consobrini Caesares* is significant: Gaius, Lucius, Agrippa, Julia, and Agrippina (and thus Germanicus by marriage) are the most likely candidates, being second-cousins by blood.

Men who had formerly supported Gaius, Aemilius Paullus, and finally Agrippa embraced the politics of reform to destabilize a government moving firmly into Tiberius' grasp. Perhaps they took up, or were already associated with, the Republican ideology earlier ascribed to the elder Drusus and later taken up by his grandson Caligula, but their aim was nevertheless to defeat Tiberius.[27] As

---

quiddam perneganti, dum vincula minatur, affirmavit fore ut ex Pompeio Pompeianus fieret, acerba cavillatione simul hominis nomen incessens veteremque partium fortunam, 'Not long afterwards, when a Roman knight named Pompeius opposed some business in the senate, he threatened him with chains and declared that from a Pompeius he would make him a Pompeian, a cruel pun on the man's name and the fortune of the old party.'

[25] Vell. 2.124; At *Ann.*1.10 Tacitus writes that 'not a few began to talk of *libertas*'. Cf. R. Syme (1939) 437.

[26] Tac. *Ann.* 2.28.2. Tacitus means that Drusus Libo's words and actions could have been checked by Tiberius in AD 14, who decided, instead, to gather more information. It should also be noted that his grandfather L. Scribonius Libo (cos. 34), wrote a history probably from the Pompeian perspective (App. BC 3.11). Even if the history was obscure (though it need not have been), it would have been known to those inside the Scribonian house. For a general discussion of this work see L. Canfora, 'Appiano ed il « Liber Annalis » di Libone', *Studi Classici Orientali,* 12 (1963), 207–11. For the view that Libo's work was not obscure see K. Welch, 'Alternative Memoirs: Tales from the 'Other Side' 'of the Civil War', in C. Smith and A. Powell (eds.) *The Lost Memoirs of Augustus* (2009), 195–223.

[27] Suet. *Claud.* 1.4: 'Drusus was, they say, no less eager for personal glory than devoted to Republicanism . . . He also openly announced that, as soon as he came to power, he would restore the old form of government'; *Tib.* 50.1: 'He [Tiberius] first showed his hatred of his kindred in the case of his brother Drusus, producing a letter of his, in which Drusus discussed with him the question of compelling Augustus to restore the Republic.'

recently as AD 12 libellous pamphlets had described Tiberius, probably, as a future ruler and suggested that Augustus had established *de facto* monarchy. Violent protests had been engineered to oppose the *vicesima hereditatium* on a principle grounded in city-state Republicanism: 'We are not vanquished foreigners; we are Roman citizens!' This approach had been advocated by Aemilius Paullus and artificially associated with Agrippa. Agrippa's continued existence, in exile, had allowed his supporters to hope; his execution was a serious blow to them. I believe that these men now turned their attention to Drusus Libo, the prospect of which weighed on Tiberius' mind as he approached the senate on 17 September AD 14.

My hypothesis depends upon dating (in relative terms) the praetorian elections of AD 14. Having discussed the debate on 17 September, Tacitus writes:

Candidatos praeturae duodecim nominavit, numerum ab Augusto traditum; et hortante senatu ut augeret, iure iurando obstrinixit se non excessurum. Tum primum e campo comitia ad patres translata sunt...

He nominated 12 candidates for the praetorship, the number handed down by Augustus; and when the senate pressed him to increase [that number], he bound himself by an oath that he would not exceed [it]. Then for the first time the elections were moved from the Campus to the senate...[28]

Does *tum* mean 'at that time' or 'next'? Velleius' treatment of the same occasion is important:

Post redditum caelo patrem et corpus eius humanis honoribus, numen divinis honoratum, primum principalium eius operum fuit ordinatio comitiorum... Quo tempore mihi fratrique meo, candidatis Caesaris, proxime a nobilissimis ac sacerdotalibus viris destinari praetoribus contigit, consecutis quidem, ut neque post nos quemquam divus Augustus neque ante nos Caear commendaret Tiberius.

After heaven had received his father, and human honours had been paid to his body as divine honours were paid to his *numen*, his first imperial task was the organization of the *comitia*...At which time my brother and I, as Caesar's candidates, were together destined for the praetorship immediately after those from the noblest houses and those who had held priesthoods and indeed, we were the last to be commended by Augustus and the first to be commended by Tiberius Caesar.[29]

---

[28] Tac. *Ann.* 1.14.6–15.1.   [29] Vell. 2.124.3–4.

Alternative Government 203

The first sentence refers both to Augustus' funeral and his deification on 17 September. It was only afterwards (*post*) that Tiberius went about changing the electoral procedure. Scholars nevertheless hold that these occurred, along with Tiberius' proclamation (as it is described at *Ann.* 1.14.6), on the one day: 17 September.[30] Velleius' *post* and Tacitus' *tum* thus refer to procedural progression: matter (a), was discussed, then (b), and (c), etc. But Velleius should not be read this way. He is clear that the rationalization of electoral procedure was Tiberius' first task *as princeps*, i.e. Tiberius had by then formally accepted supreme power: this did not happen on 17 September. Rationalization of electoral procedure therefore occurred sometime after the 17th.

As Velleius suggests, Tiberius may have formally accepted the Principate on the same day that he sponsored a rationalization of the electoral procedure. Senators were then asked to vote on the candidates for that year. Velleius, his brother, and Drusus Libo were all successful.[31] Their election required only ratification by the *centuriae Caesarum* and the people.[32] The situation described by Tacitus at *Ann.* 1.14.6 and Velleius at 2.124.3-4 therefore occurred after 17 September but before the final election. Tacitus' description of this event is a topic of *great* dispute. Leaving aside the contested term *nominatio* (a book in itself), I nevertheless accept the view put forward by Jones that men did not ask for more candidates, but more praetorships.[33] A tactic that had proved successful in AD 11 was now

---

[30] W. K. Lacey (1963), 167–76, esp. 171; F. De Visscher, 'Tacite et les réformes électorales d'Auguste et de Tibère', *Studi in Onore di V. Arangio-Ruiz*, II (1953), 428; B. Levick (1967), 218 f; C. J. Simpson (1981), 299; cf. M. M. Sage (1982/83), 308 f.

[31] This perfectly explains *ILS* 944: ... *viacure* ... [*q.tr.p.*] *l. pr. leg.*[*pro pr. Imp. C*] *aesaris Augusti* [*i*]*ter. per commendation. Ti. Caesaris ab senatu cos. dest. patrono.* Here, a man has been commended by Tiberius and destined by the senate. Since the senate had *de facto* superseded the *centuriae Caesarum*, candidates were right to think of themselves as *destinati* once the senate had voted them in.

[32] Inscriptional evidence shows that the people continued to assemble to vote in the *Comitia Centuriata*. They would have been voting, however, on a fixed number of candidates provided by the senate. The real election was, therefore, in the senate. The *Comitia* was now a rubber stamp.

[33] A. H. M. Jones (1955), 19; I do not agree with Jones that Tacitus has misunderstood his source, or that he had made a mistake, but simply that he has used clumsy language. See also *Ann.* 2.36: *princeps duodecim candidatos in annos singulos nominaret*. It is quite obvious that Tacitus is not interested in providing a technical interpretation of these events, but that does not mean he failed to understand them. On the contested term *nominatio,* see Th. Mommsen, *Staat.* II³ (1887/88), 917 f.; H. Siber, 'Die Wahlreform des Tiberius', *Festschrift Paul Koschaker*, I (1939), 171 f.;

employed against the 'new guy' - Tiberius, unlike Augustus, stood firm: 'Augustus intended 12 praetorships, and that's how many you'll get!'[34] Perhaps the empowerment of the senate as a prerogative body was offered as compensation: 'You cannot have more praetorships. But how about determining the election results?' The reforms would have enjoyed the support of many within the senatorial order, especially those lacking popular standing.[35] It was probably on this day that Tiberius published his recommendations, among them being Drusus Libo.

We do not know how many days, or weeks, separate the meeting on the 17th from Tiberius' proclamation concerning praetorships. 'Days' are nevertheless more appropriate than 'weeks'. Augustus published his *commendationes* for the praetorian elections in August; his death would have caused the elections to be postponed. Elections would remain in abeyance for Augustus' funeral and then for his deification on the 17th. The senate's failure to secure a positive declaration from Tiberius on the latter occasion would not, however,

---

M. Hammond, *The Antonine Monarchy* (1959), 266; W. K. Lacey (1963), 167–76; D. C. A. Shotter (1966), 321–23; B. Levick (1967), 207–30; and A. E. Astin (1969), 863–74.

[34] Cf. J. A. Crook, 'The Election of Magistrates in the Early Principate', *CR*, 20: 1 (1970), 65–8, esp. 67.

[35] Vell. 2.124.3 f., writes that the rationalization of the electoral process was managed in concert with written instructions left behind by Augustus. Most take this to mean that Augustus authored the measures outlined by Tacitus at *Ann.* 1.15.1. Though Velleius is explicit, there is good reason to question his information. As Velleius' own election shows, the elections were in full swing when Augustus died. It is, therefore, hard to believe that Augustus intended to change the election process but had not done so before 19 August. Why would he sit on such a proposal only for Tiberius to use it immediately and claim that it was Augustus' desire that it be implemented? On the other hand, it could be a public relations device. In AD 6 Augustus linked the implementation of the *vicesima hereditatium* to papers left behind by the now divine Julius (Dio 55.25.5–6). No one would dare ask to see the papers. Indeed, it is worth noting that Augustus had recently been made a State-sponsored God. It was, therefore, in Tiberius' interest to associate a potentially unpopular proposal with the now-divine Augustus. How could anybody refuse a proposal created by a man that everybody had recently agreed deserved deification? Velleius would certainly accept Tiberius' proposed archaeology without question. Cf. A. J. Woodman (1977), 227, argues that instruction for the change was found in the three or four books left behind by Augustus, Suet. *Aug.*101.4; Dio 56.34.3. But Woodman's suggestion fails to explain Augustus' decision not to institute the change before he had published his *commendationes*, which probably occurred shortly before the day of election. As C. J. Simpson (1981) points out, Augustus' active schedule at this time, and Tiberius' decision to leave for Illyricum, suggest that death came as a surprise.

justify their continued suspension. Indeed, when Tacitus writes that Tiberius 'ceased to refuse and to be asked', he implies that the senate moved on with other business, leaving Tiberius' situation unanswered. According to this interpretation, Tiberius turned his attention to the now overdue praetorian elections soon after the debate on the 17th. Catus thus began to supply information against Drusus Libo shortly before 17 September, i.e. Tiberius went into the meeting unsure of Drusus Libo's support.[36] We need not speculate on a 'real' plot to commit violent acts against the State.

As was noted previously, Tiberius had relatively little experience in the senate from 6 BC to AD 13, a period of almost twenty years! He was, no doubt, well represented by friends and allies, but his absence would still have caused problems. Cliques, relationships, alliances, and factions would have formed by necessity in his absence: they are the hallmark of any deliberative body. Indeed, they are the mechanisms by which a great deal of work gets done. When Tiberius finally returned to Rome to lead the senate in AD 13, he may have found himself on the outside looking in. No doubt he could rely on a great number of senators, but there would have been many with whom he had no connection or familiarity: they may have found his presence an annoyance at best, and at worse a threat to the established order of things. Certainly, he would not have known which, and his skill in the senate betrays his lack of confidence. That an important aristocrat like Drusus Libo, who advertised Claudian, Scribonian, Julian, and Pompeian connections, might consider an alliance with Gaius' old friends would have concerned Tiberius greatly—that is, it would have made him hesitate. It is thus naïve to think that only a 'real' plot could or would have worried Tiberius. A coalition of Drusus Libo's

---

[36] *Contra* R. Seager (1972), 90, who argues, despite Tacitus, that Drusus Libo was designated praetor before Catus laid his information. He places Catus' attack in October-December. B. Levick (1999), 150, holds that Tiberius was first aware of a problem with Drusus Libo 'immediately after Tiberius' accession to the Principate'. I am unsure what Levick means by this, since she has elsewhere argued that Tiberius never formally accepted the Principate. Levick agrees with Seager that Tiberius was, in Tacitus' narrative, clearly princeps when Catus laid his information. Tacitus does use the term 'princeps', but that proves nothing. Tacitus reflects the reality of power, an approach made obvious with his treatment of Tiberius' accession; he does not concern himself with strict legal definitions. Moreover, Tacitus followed a tradition which telescoped the events of AD 14 and AD 16; Drusus Libo was for Tacitus *not* relevant to the question of Tiberius' hesitation. He was uninterested therefore in clarification.

supporters with those who had formerly supported Gaius, Aemilius Paullus and Agrippa posed danger to Tiberius, Germanicus, and Drusus, and would be seen as provocative. If the coalition were to solidify, then Tiberius' position would destabilize. His control of the instruments of power would remain, but his legitimacy as princeps would be questionable. The future position of Germanicus and Drusus would be even less clear. Catus thus offered to supply information and prepared the way for future entrapment. But the information was tenuous at best and at worst unsubstantiated. In any case, there was no evidence of a capital crime. Tiberius could not destroy an important member of the aristocracy (who was not stuck on an island) without good evidence of serious wrongdoing, but nor did he wish to. Negotiation was the better approach.

Here is my proposed chronology: (i) in the final week of August, Tiberius is told about the execution of Agrippa; (ii) in early September, Agrippa's execution is talked about in Rome, but not discussed in the senate; rumour circulates that Agrippa was murdered by Livia and Tiberius; (iii) Tiberius, meanwhile, is informed about the situation in Pannonia, and then, shortly before 17 September, the situation in Lower Germany; (iv) at this time Tiberius is also made aware of an emerging coalition between the aristocrat Drusus Libo and Agrippa's known supporters; (v) on 17 September Tiberius deals successfully with the situation in Germany and its consequences in Rome, as well as the issue of Germanicus, but the situation concerning Drusus Libo remains unresolved; (vi) concerned by the prospect of a new coalition, Tiberius holds off accepting anything until the situation is made clearer; (vii) rather than provoke his enemies into action, Tiberius makes a deal with Drusus Libo, who agrees to accept Tiberius' *commendatio* and by so doing, shows his support for the government;[37] (viii) Tiberius formally agrees in the senate to continue holding supreme power; he accepts the moral responsibility of empire, *statio paterna: dum veniam ad id tempus, quo vobis aequum possit videri dare vos aliquam senectuti meae requiem*, 'Until I come to

---

[37] As Martin Stone points out to me, Drusus Libo could have made a political statement by refusing to seek the praetorship, or else refusing to accept Tiberius' support, running instead as an independent candidate. Both would signal a 'vote of no confidence' in the government, and Tiberius in particular, i.e. Drusus Libo and Tiberius had come to a mutual agreement. Drusus Libo was, therefore, doing Tiberius a favour; he may subsequently have believed that Tiberius was beholden to him.

that time, in which it may seem right to you to give some rest to my old age'.[38] He was almost 56.

I have here shown that a coherent picture can be produced to support Suetonius' contention without rejecting other evidence or being, of itself, implausible. The situation in AD 15 is not clear, though Tacitus hints at economic turmoil, and we know that popular anger with the level of taxation was again an issue.[39] As praetor and *pontifex*, Drusus Libo socialized occasionally with Tiberius, as was appropriate for an important noble and a relative, and performed religious ceremonies. Suetonius and Tacitus hold that Tiberius remained suspicious of him for two years before feeling ready to move. The assertion cannot be tested. But since the government certainly sponsored his prosecution in AD 16, it is plausible. Suspicion, however, does not require the presence of a 'real' plot, the evidence for which emerged only in AD 16. Its appearance signalled Tiberius' failure to convince important members of the aristocracy to support Augustus' succession policy and, with it, his government.

A FALSE DAWN

The decision to leave obscure Agrippa's execution left Tiberius vulnerable to suspicion. Plausible deniability was sacrificed and soon replaced by innuendo: 'Augustus ordered it'; 'I heard it was Livia'; 'No, I have it on good authority that Tiberius is to blame'; 'It was probably Livia and Tiberius'. Gossip is a natural habit but political opponents often make use of and encourage its dissemination. We have, for Agrippa's supporters, two separate and mutually exclusive messages: (i) 'Agrippa was murdered by Tiberius'; and, (ii) 'Agrippa has been saved by the gods and is alive and well.' There are two possibilities: Agrippa's supporters broke into separate factions after his death; or (i) occurred before (ii). The second postulate is the most plausible.

Tacitus implies that the government first became aware of a pseudo-Agrippa only in AD 16. Having described Clemens' plan to rescue Agrippa from Planasia, Tacitus continues:

---

[38] Suet. *Tib.* 24.2.   [39] Tac. *Ann.* 1.78.

Ausa eius inpedivit tarditas onerariae navis: atque interim patrata caede ad maiora et magis praecipitia conversus furatur cineres vectusque Cosam Etruriae promunturium ignotis locis sese abdit, donec crinem barbamque promitteret: nam aetate et forma haud dissimili in dominum erat. Tum per idoneos et secreti eius socios crebrescit vivere Agrippam, occultis primum sermonibus, ut vetita solent, mox vago rumore apud inperitissimi cuiusque promptas auris aut rursum apud turbidos eoque nova cupientis. Atque ipse adire municipia obscuro diei, neque propalam aspici neque diutius isdem locis, sed quia veritas visu et mora, falsa festinatione et incertis valescunt, relinquebat famam aut praeveniebat. Vulgabatur interim per Italiam servatum munere deum Agrippam, credebatur Romae; iamque Ostiam invectum multitudo ingens, iam in urbe clandestini coetus celebrabant, cum Tiberium anceps cura distrahere, vine militum servum suum coerceret an inanem credulitatem tempore ipso vanescere sineret.

'The tardiness of the cargo-boat hindered his bold venture; in the meantime the execution [of Agrippa] was accomplished and so he turned to a more significant and hazardous scheme: he stole the ashes of the deceased, sailed to Cosa, a promontory of Etruria, and hid himself in unknown places until he had grown his hair and beard: for in age and appearance he was not unlike his master. Then, through suitable persons and friends who shared his secret, it was rumoured that Agrippa was alive, first in private conversations, as is usual with forbidden knowledge, and soon in vague rumour which found its way to the open ears of the most ignorant or, on the other hand, those who were trouble makers and consequently fomenters of revolution. He himself entered towns at dusk or dawn, and he was neither to be seen in open places or spending a long time in the same place, but since truth grows in strength by appearance and time and falsehood by haste and uncertainty, he left rumour behind him or preceded it. It was meanwhile rumoured throughout Italy that Agrippa had been saved by heaven, at Rome it was believed; already huge crowds greeted him at Ostia, already secret meetings were being held in the city, while the attention of Tiberius was distracted with conflicting concerns: should he put down his slave by military means or allow idle credulity to vanish over time.[40]

Dio places the whole affair in AD 16:

Κἂν τῷ αὐτῷ ἔτει Κλήμης τις, δοῦλός τε τοῦ Ἀγρίππου γεγονὼς καί πῃ καὶ προσεοικὼς αὐτῷ, ἐπλάσατο αὐτὸς ἐκεῖνος εἶναι . . .

---

[40] Tac. *Ann.* 2.39–40.1.

And in the same year a certain Clemens, who had been a slave of Agrippa, and who resembled him to some extent, pretended to be Agrippa himself ...[41]

Tacitus understood his source to mean that news of Agrippa's survival surfaced only after Clemens had taken refuge in some secret location near Cosa.[42] Clemens surfaced looking, apparently, different. Dio writes only that in AD 16 Agrippa's survival was publicized. Only Suetonius situates news of Agrippa's survival in AD 14. He is mistaken. Commenting on the reasons for Tiberius' hesitation he writes:

Nam et servus Agrippae Clemens nomine non contemnendam manum in ultionem domini compareret . . .

For a slave of Agrippa, Clemens by name, had collected a not contemptible force to avenge his master . . .[43]

In ultionem domini refers not to the attempted rescue of Agrippa but to Clemens' own insurrection. Suetonius furthermore implies that in September AD 14 Tiberius was aware of this development. In contrast to his interpretation of Drusus Libo, which can be supported by the versions of Tacitus and Dio, Suetonius' interpretation of the Clemens affair is impossible. Clemens did not have sufficient time to travel from Planasia to Cosa, hide for long enough to grow his beard and hair, and then gather enough men in Gaul and Italy to cause Tiberius concern by late September AD 14. Suetonius' interpretation was probably his own. It was logical to make Clemens' activities an extension of Agrippa's execution, but in doing so Suetonius

---

[41] Dio 57.16.3.

[42] Tacitus' information, contra J. Bellemore (2000), 93–114, came from more than one source. Clemens' identity and the story of his flight, with Agrippa's ashes, to a promontory at Cosa would not come from his supporters, or even sympathizers; it undermines their position. Most probably the information was official and disseminated *post eventum*. Bellemore, uncomfortable with this conclusion, dismisses the government's evidence and argues that Clemens *was* Agrippa. Bellemore holds that we cannot accept as genuine any information which comes from the inquisition of an authoritarian regime, or indeed any regime. This level of cynicism is not necessary. A public declaration was certainly published which unmasked the pseudo-Agrippa, but Bellemore has not considered the importance of Crispus. It was shown above that Tacitus' treatment of the execution of Agrippa Postumus was largely affected by his reading the memoirs of the younger Agrippina, which preserved a secret history of Sallustius Crispus. That Tacitus alone mentions Crispus in connection with Clemens suggests that he has again referred to his 'scoop' for supplementary information, i.e. details of the affair were known to members of Crispus' family.

[43] Suet. *Tib.* 25.1.

constructed an impossible chronology. A chronology must, therefore, be based upon Tacitus' longer, and more consistent, narrative.

Speculating on the speed of hair growth is a futile exercise. It is better to ask: from the moment that the 'first secret conversations' were held, how long would it take for the government to find out? Two sentences are important: (i) 'Then, through suitable persons and friends who shared his secret, it was rumoured that Agrippa was alive, first in private conversations, as is usual with forbidden knowledge, and soon (*mox*) in vague rumour'; and (ii) 'It was meanwhile rumoured throughout Italy that Agrippa had been saved by heaven, at Rome it was believed; already huge crowds greeted him at Ostia.' *Mox* in the first passage, though not meaning 'soon', necessarily suggests that a long delay between the first secret conversations (*occulti primus sermones*) and the spread of rumour (*vagus rumor*) is unlikely.[44] If Clemens was captured in the final few months of AD 16, then *occulti primum sermones* belong, probably, to the first half of that year.[45] This chronology supports the second postulation given above: in AD 14 it was said that Agrippa had been executed by order of Tiberius; later, in AD 16, it was held that Agrippa had, in fact, survived and intended to overthrow Tiberius. The second message obviates the first, which necessarily became counter-productive. On this reading, the decision to manufacture a pseudo-Agrippa, the recruitment of a few thousand fighters and the emergence of conspiratorial 'cells' within Rome all belong to AD 16.[46] Agrippa's supporters obviously believed that their position was untenable.

Traces of rebel propaganda survive in Tacitus. *Agrippa munere deum servatus* is for the ears of a true believer, but secret 'cells' in Rome would discuss more than propaganda. Tacitus describes the

---

[44] H. J. Rose, 'Mox', *CQ* 21:21 (1927), 657–61, shows that *mox* did not mean 'soon' in either Classical or Silver Latin, but rather, its meaning changed according to the context. It could mean 'next', 'then', or 'soon' but rarely with the sense of 'immediately after' or 'after a very short space of time'. His findings, with some corrections, are supported by G. Norwood, 'Mox', *CJ*, 37: 7 (1941), 421–3. Norwood cites instances in which *mox* is used to pass over several years. It is nevertheless clear that in each context, *mox* is used to describe an event which took place sooner rather than later. Nevertheless, Rose suggests that, aside from a few rare instances which can be explained contextually, *mox* is not used to describe a lengthy time-lapse.

[45] Tacitus and Dio, whose works are annalistic, place the capture of Clemens at the end of AD 16; Suetonius, whose treatment is thematic, places it before the death of Drusus Libo.

[46] Cf. I. Cogitore (1991), 134.

attendees: 'many (*multi*) from the imperial house, equestrians and senators were said to have supported [Clemens] with money and assisted with their advice'.[47] *Multi equites et senatores* would, at these meetings, discuss details of the plot: how will so-and-so be put-away? Who will the praetorians fight for? What about the urban cohorts? Who will take responsibility for the grain supply? These men, whose names remain unknown to us, stand at the centre of this reconstruction. They had supported Gaius, then Aemilius Paullus, and finally Agrippa. Reconciliation with Tiberius was impossible; he had been too often made to feel threatened and humiliated. Distrust was mutual and deep. While Augustus lived they rallied behind prominent members of the imperial family. Aemilius Paullus, consul in AD 1, could plausibly supersede Tiberius. His destruction in AD 6 is testimony to his potential. The use of Agrippa Postumus, young, uncultured, and inexperienced, was, on the other hand, an act of pure desperation. He provided only nomenclature, but the *nomena* were popular and powerful. The government responded accordingly.

The attempt in AD 11 to free Agrippa from incarceration evidences a political reality, i.e. those who opposed Tiberius could not ignore the public's enthusiasm for members of Augustus' family. In AD 14, with Agrippa dead, they allied themselves with an important aristocrat who placed a premium on his connection to the *domus Caesaris* by highlighting his own brand name. Drusus Libo, for his part, accepted Tiberius' olive branch and succeeded to the praetorship (his brother was moreover designated consul in AD 15), but the seed was sown. Seneca, alive when Drusus Libo was arraigned, believed that he had desired the top job. A praetorship, or later a consulate, might temporarily satisfy the ambitious, but their power and influence was limited so long as Rome was dominated by a princeps. AD 16, so far as we know, brought no office or distinction, or military command; an unoccupied Drusus Libo was left alone to reflect on his situation. Others were also, at this moment, reflecting on their situation. *Multi equites et senatores* had come to view as untenable their participation in the current political milieu. The elder Julia, for whom crowds gathered to demand her restoration in AD 4, had starved to death within a year of Tiberius' accession, while her alleged

---

[47] Tac. *Ann.* 2.40.3.

lover, Sempronius Gracchus, was executed; popular sympathy for another victim of Tiberius' scheming might, with the right agent, mutate into violent support. In AD 16, at secret meetings in Rome, *equites et senatores* agreed that Agrippa was still the best agent for change, thus *Agrippa munere deum servatus*. A historical fiction soon emerged: Augustus and Agrippa had, in fact, reconciled, but the murder of Augustus prevented Agrippa's full restitution. Tiberius, desperate for unrivalled domination, ordered Agrippa's immediate execution, but, by the grace of the Gods, Agrippa escaped! The destruction of a suspected ally in the very same year is surely not coincidental.

Men refused to defend Drusus Libo, not because he was a fool but because of his known connection to Agrippa's supporters. Notorious relationships stick to politicians for life. Support could easily be mistaken for sympathy, as would any proposal that appeared lenient; the reaction to Julius Caesar's proposal on 5 December 63 BC that Catiline's associates not be put to death is apposite. Unlike Lentulus Sura and his associates, Drusus Libo was not put in gaol, but the effect was similar. A large group of praetorians would not guard a defendant because he dabbled in necromancy, nor would the government employ such resources to enhance the income of four *delatores*. Had Drusus Libo been considered not dangerous, it would have been in the regime's interest to encourage voluntary exile. Indeed, voluntary exile would prove the case for the prosecution and ensure their full compensation. Instead, troops were used to separate Drusus Libo from suspected confederates. There was, of course, no smoking gun. That is clear from the trial. A parchment listing important figures required interpretation; its use was not manifest, though its existence was. The necromancer Junius, who had discussed the matter with Fulcinius Trio, supplied evidence of a vague but sinister question, something like: 'What does my future hold should anything unfortunate happen to the men on this list?' It was enough to warrant a senatorial investigation and allow for the dismantling of a provocative coalition.

We can only speculate on Drusus Libo's part in the conspiracy. He was an important individual, and so his participation ought to have been significant. But his decision to consult a necromancer demands our caution. It indicates an uncertain psychology rather than confident commitment to a cause, and it is therefore possible that he was still, even with the Pseudo-Agrippa bearing down on Rome, weighing his options. Regardless, Levick is surely right to suppose that the conspirators would have removed Clemens once Tiberius and his entourage were dead.[48] Levick further argues that Drusus Libo was to be nominated princeps and presented, by the people, to the senate.[49] This is unlikely. Drusus and Tiberius were present in Rome and would, therefore, have been put to death, along with their closest allies, but Germanicus, in Germany with thousands of troops, would pose a serious threat to the conspirators. His position was physically and morally superior to anybody who might occupy, or liberate, Rome as princeps. To neutralize Germanicus, the conspirators would require a device by which his position would appear untenable, unpopular, and illegitimate. The best way to counter Germanicus' popularity while avoiding an unpopular war was the abolition of the Principate, which would effectively wedge Germanicus.[50] Aggression by Germanicus would be advertised as a repudiation of his father's purported Republicanism, damaging seriously his popularity in Rome. It would also require the siege of Rome, now housing a free and emboldened senate and people. The *invidia* of tyranny could be avoided only by acknowledging the new *res publica* as legitimate, and, in so doing, mortally wound any claim to supreme power. Germanicus, of course, may have reacted differently, but I believe, that the conspirators in Rome would have had little option but to try and wedge him: a war would have been costly and difficult to win. Having deposed the tyrant and dismantled his government, the conspirators would, therefore, have organized immediately fresh elections in accordance with ancestral custom, i.e. the new electoral arrangements were to be abolished and the people would again determine the outcome of elections. It was with good reason that Tiberius presented his electoral reform as having been designed by the now deified Augustus.[51] The *equites* who made up the *centuriae Caesarum* had no reason to support Tiberius' electoral innovations, which were barely two years old, and may have been satisfied with anything other than the status quo. Nor should we assume that plebeians took to political impotence with satisfaction or indifference. As was noted above, aside from the right to vote according to ancestral custom, distress had remained topical, being communicated to the government via anti-tax protests. We know almost nothing about the

---

[48] B. Levick (1999), 149 f.   [49] Ibid.
[50] Cf. E. Ciaceri (1944), 271.   [51] Vell. 2.124.3.

sate of Rome's economy during these years, save Tacitus' note that people asked Tiberius to abolish the 1 per cent sales tax, and Tiberius' reply that the state could not function without it.[52] Even without more information, it is safe to assume that things were not going well for a large group of people. On this reading, the Tiberian experiment was seen by many as a failure and they were now open to alternatives. That talk of *libertas* and Republican *praxis* resurfaced on the death of Tiberius, and more impressively after the death of Gaius Caesar, is evidence that my conclusion is not impossible, nor even improbable.[53] It certainly explains the presence or Concord. Augustus' use of a discourse which implied the extraordinary, and temporary, nature of the supreme power, and Tiberius' rambling about the eventual laying to rest of a heavy burden allowed people to question the legitimacy of the so called *optimus status*. The paradoxical nature of the Principate sustained interest in a truly free *res publica*.

The ancient belief that Drusus Libo desired the 'top job' is, therefore, a rejection of his Republican image. The prosecution presented evidence of supreme ambition: 'Would he ever have enough money to cover the *Via Appia* from Rome to Brundisium with gold?'[54] The image was accepted by contemporaries: 'He possessed higher ambitions than anyone could have been expected to entertain in that epoch, or a man like himself in any epoch at all.'[55] There were to be no Republican martyrs in the changed conditions of Tiberius' succession. Drusus Libo, nonetheless, was no mere tool.[56] When Catiline entered the senate on 8 November 63 BC, not one of his associates would sit near him. Still, Catiline was no puppet.[57] Clemens' conspiracy nonetheless continued despite Drusus Libo's very public demise. Once a fighting force of thousands assembled, the conspiracy would remain active so long as Clemens was alive or a serious defeat

---

[52] Tac. *Ann* 1.78.2.
[53] Suetonius (*Claud*. 10) has it that on the death of Gaius the consuls, with the support of the senate and the Urban Cohorts, occupied the Forum and Capitol, being determined to protect *libertas*. Suetonius goes on to suggest (*Claud*. 11) that the senate had recorded its desire to 'change the form of government'. The records were apparently destroyed by Claudius as part of a general amnesty following his rise to supreme power. It should be noted, moreover, that Gaius Caesar either abolished or at least reduced the 1 per cent sales tax (Dio 59.9.6; Suet. *Gaius* 16.3).
[54] Tac. *Ann*. 2.30.
[55] Sen. *Ep. Mor.* 70.10.
[56] Cf. L. Freytag (1870), 115.
[57] Cic. *In. Cat.* 1.16.

was suffered. The *multi equites et senatores* were committed to new political order, not the inauguration of one particular aristocrat. Drusus Libo was one of many senators secretly behind Clemens. He was, however, closest to the ruling clique and therefore a major loss.

No manifest evidence existed to prove Drusus Libo's involvement in the Pseudo-Agrippa conspiracy, but the political climate—affected by widespread speculation that Agrippa was marching towards Rome—demanded caution. As with many Romans at that time, Drusus Libo was evidently affected by fatalistic creeds; a strong temptation to know the future proved his undoing. Those most threatened by revolution pounced, while those with the most to gain were in no position to help. Tiberius, and to a greater extent Germanicus and Drusus, profited, but it is important to note Tiberius' own behaviour. His satisfaction should not be doubted, but he wore on his public face signs of distress. Tiberius ostentatiously preferred reconciliation and clemency, while the senate demanded justice in the face of threats to the government. The result belied the nature of the Principate: the princeps should not impose his will on a free senate charged with the protection of the *res publica*, thus: *responsum est ut senatum rogaret*.[58] This is a complex approach to power. On the death of Augustus, Tiberius surrounded himself with the instruments of violent coercion. Praetorians accompanied him everywhere. But the maintenance of authoritarian power requires more than the tools for destruction; it involves public relations. Tiberius advertised *moderatio* and sorrow at the death of a rival whilst the senate was left to accept full responsibility. The irony concealed real tyranny, as the chief victims were made to wear the tyrant's face.

FUTURE DIRECTIONS

In the process of showing that Tiberius' position was threatened by the persistence of a 'real' opposition, a model for understanding Tiberius' Principate has come to light which stands in contrast to those hitherto produced. Scholars who construct a Republican

---

[58] Tac. *Ann.* 2.31.1.

paradigm to interpret Tiberius and the unfolding of his Principate are shown to be seriously mistaken, as are those who insist that moral abstractions like *dissimulatio* or *moderatio* were the key principles by which Tiberius operated. I have shown that Tiberius responded to an actual fear, not simply discourse: anything less than supreme power would have meant his assassination. By grounding the Tiberian Principate firmly in Augustus' Principate, *contra* Tacitus, the above approach is able to explain why this came about. But the benefits of the model advanced here extend well beyond AD 16.

Concerning the affair of Drusus Libo, Levick held that: 'the genuine and remarkable concord between Germanicus and Drusus will have been cemented by the episode.'[59] We cannot be sure this was ever the case, but Tacitus possessed evidence that by AD 17 hostility between their respective friends and supporters had emerged:

Divisa namque et discors aula erat tacitis in Drusum aut Germanicum studiis ... Sed fratres egregie concordes et proximorum certaminibus inconcussi.

For there was division and discord in the court with silent preferences to either Drusus or Germanicus... but the brothers were singularly united and unshaken by the struggles of those around them.[60]

My approach explains this development. Since, as Tacitus writes, there was no public inquiry following the death of Clemens, the *multi equites et senatores* were left to reconsider their position. As I have shown, most could not be reconciled with Tiberius. They required therefore a new figurehead—someone, as we have seen, closely connected to the imperial family. I would suggest that they got behind Germanicus, or, more precisely, Germanicus and Agrippina. This would explain the emergence of hostility between the supporters of Drusus and Germanicus, but it also explains the later treatment of Germanicus' sons following his death. Nero and Drusus were, following the death of their uncle Drusus, accused of conspiracy; both eventually died amid suspicion.[61] The history of Germanicus and his supporters after AD 16 therefore deserves further analysis.

Finally, my approach allows for a new appreciation of the sources. By not grounding Tiberius' Principate in Augustus' Principate, Tacitus fails to comprehend Tiberius' approach to power; we find

---

[59] B. Levick (1999), 152.
[60] Tac. *Ann.* 2.43.5.
[61] Tac. *Ann.* 6.23; Suet. *Tib.* 54; Dio 58.25.4.

ourselves reading Suetonius and Dio with relief! What did Aufidius Bassus, Servilius Nonianus, Cluvius Rufus, or Fabius Rusticus have to offer? A re-examination of Tacitus' sources is required. Tacitus had before him more sources than is usually admitted. Indeed, Syme's belief that Tacitus relied heavily on the *acta senatus* seems to me unlikely. A different approach must also be brought to the memoirs of the younger Agrippina. Tacitus' treatment of the death of Agrippa Postumus and the conspiracy of Clemens suggests that Agrippina's work was not well known and, therefore, had little impact in the first century AD. The absence of Sallustius Crispus in either Suetonius or Dio is suggestive, and weakens the belief that Tacitus seriously affected either historian. A better understanding of the historical works of the first century AD is essential.

APPENDIX 1

A Prosopography of M. Scribonius Drusus Libo

What follows is an attempt to capture the essence of what Drusus Libo had in mind as he considered his place in Roman society:

Firmius Catus senator, ex intima Libonis amicitia, iuvenem inprovidum et facilem inanibus ad Chaldaeorum promissa, magorum sacra, somniorum etiam interpretes impulit, dum proavum Pompeium, amitam Scriboniam, quae quondam Augusti coniunx fuerat, consobrinos Caesares, plenam imaginibus domum ostentat, hortaturque ad luxum et aes alienum, socius libidinum et necessitatum, quo pluribus indiciis inligaret.

Firmius Catus, a senator and close friend of Libo's, urged the short-sighted young man, given to empty things, to resort to the promises of astrologers, the rites of magicians, and also dream interpreters, reminding him of his great-grandfather Pompeius, his paternal aunt Scribonia, former wife of Augustus, his imperial cousins, his house crowded with ancestral images, and urging him to extravagance and debt: Firmius associated himself in these debaucheries and embarrassments, in order to entangle Libo in more evidence.[1]

Marcus Scribonius Libo Drusus would seem an appropriate name for a young man who was born (M.?) Livius Drusus and was later adopted by a Scribonius. He was, in fact, a Scribonius adopted by a Livius. The *Fasti Amiternini* records his name as 'M. Libo', Velleius Paterculus has 'Drusus Libo', Seneca 'Drusus Libo', and Tacitus uses the phrase *e familia Scriboniorum Libo Drusus*.[2] Dio and Suetonius mistake Drusus Libo for his brother, Lucius Scribonius Libo, consul *ordinarius* in AD 16.[3] Hitherto the standard preference is to apply the Tacitean formula, thus Syme, Shotter, and Weinrib.[4] Sumner shows that the preference is wrong.[5] Tacitus alone uses

---

[1] Tac. *Ann.* 2.27.2.
[2] V. Ehrenberg and A. H. M. Jones (1955), 52; Vell. 2.130.3; *Ep. Mor.* 70.10.1; Tac. *Ann.* 2.27.1.
[3] Dio 57.15.4; Suet. *Tib.* 25; see the list of consuls for AD 16 in V. Ehrenberg and A. H. M. Jones (1955), 40.
[4] R. Syme (1986), table 14; D. C. A. Shotter (1972), *passim*; E. J. Weinrib (1968), 247–78.
[5] G. V. Sumner, 'The Truth About Velleius Paterculus: Prolegomena', *HSCP*, 74 (1970), 275, n. 113, who shows other instances where Tacitus has inverted a person's name.

220 Appendix 1: A Prosopography

'Libo Drusus', and as Tacitus himself tells us, one of the posthumous penalties was to deprive Scribonian descendants from ever adopting Drusus as a cognomen: *ne quis Scribonius cognomentum Drusi adsumeret*.[6] The preferred formula was M. Scribonius Drusus Libo. This slight emendation makes it somewhat easier to envisage an adoption. That he was born a Scribonius is certain. Seneca and Tacitus mention *amita Scribonia*, 'Scribonia, an aunt on the father's side', and Tacitus also mentions *proavus Pompeius*, 'Pompey, a great-grandfather'. Scribonia can thus be found on his father's side, and Pompeius was the grandfather of his mother, Pompeia Magna. Drusus Libo was, therefore, a Scribonius adopted by a Livius, but in a manner that allowed for unconventional nomenclature, i.e. he should have been M. Livius Drusus Libo Scribonianus, but was able instead to use M. Scribonius Drusus Libo. Weinrib has argued that Drusus Libo annexed the *cognomen* Drusus after the death of M. Livius Drusus Libo (cos. 15).[7] His hypothesis has not been challenged.

Drusus Libo's brother was L. Scribonius L.f. Libo (cos. AD 16), and hence their father was a L. Scribonius Libo. The father's brother was M. Livius L.f. Drusus Libo (cos. 15).[8] Lucii *filius* signifies that their (i.e. the consul of 15 BC and his brother) father was thus also a L. Scribonius L.f. Libo. He is the consul for 34 BC.[9] There are two points to consider. An eldest son was provided with the *praenomen* Lucius, and that one generation before our man, the second son of a Scribonius Libo had joined the ranks of the Livii Drusi. Weinrib's study of M. Livius L.f. Drusus Libo shows that he was not adopted through either of the formal modes known to us- *adrogatio* or *datio in adoptionem*- for we would not expect L.f., when his *praenomen* is clearly Marcus.[10] Instead, M. Livius Drusus Libo joined the Livii Drusi through the process of testamentary 'adoption'.[11] His testator was M. Livius Drusus

---

[6] Tac. *Ann*. 2.32.2.

[7] E. J. Weinrib (1968), 263–4: 'The proposal of Cn. Lentulus after the fall of M. Scribonius Libo Drusus, *'ne quis Scribonius cognomentum Drusi adsumeret,'* implies that the offender had incorporated the item Drusus into his nomenclature through his own volition rather than that he possessed it from birth on the decision of the father.'

[8] V. Ehrenberg and A. H. M. Jones (1955), 37.

[9] Ibid., 34.

[10] E. J. Weinrib (1968), 252–3.

[11] In this scenario, a man would perform the appropriate rites before a praetor, and then be able to take on the estate of the deceased, his name, the masks of his ancestors, and his *sacra familiaria*. Yet, most important of all, it did not require pontifical approval, because the heir would not be under the *patria potestas* of the *testator*, instead his familial position did not change. Due to this, such an adoption was only defined within the civil law, not the sacral or public laws, and, hence, it was more or less a private agreement between two families. J. Linderski, 'Q. Scipio Imperator', in J. Linderski (ed.), *Imperium Sine Fine: T. Robert S. Broughton and the Roman Republic* Historia Einzelschriften Heft, 105 (1996), 152–3. For alternative theories, see R. Syme

Appendix 1: A Prosopography

Claudianus, a Claudius Pulcher who was adopted by the tribune of 91 BC, M. Livius Drusus. Although M. Livius Drusus Libo did not come under the *patria potestas* of his new father, he did have claims to his titles and estates, which he shared with his new sister, Livia Drusilla. Weinrib goes on to suggest that this eminent position was not underestimated by his young nephew M. Scribonius Drusus Libo, who was so impressed by his uncle's fame that he chose to take on his *praenomen* and *cognomen* out of pure regard.[12] As evidence for this practice, Weinrib cites the example of L. Seius Strabo, who gave his son the *cognomen* Tubero in honour of a family friend.[13] Yet he goes on to acknowledge that: 'this idea is now out of favour'.[14] Other examples cited do not exclude the possibility that a will had been drawn up, and in the case of M. Aurelius Cotta Maximus Messalinus, the evidence actually implies a testament was being followed:

Qui vir animo etiam quam gente nobilior dignissimusque, qui et patrem Corvinum habuisset et cognomen suum Cottae fratri relinqueret...

This man [M. Valerius Messala Messalinus], was more noble in spirit even than in family, who was very worthy to have had Corvinus as a father, and who left behind his own *cognomen* to his brother Cotta.[15]

Weinrib has ignored the active verb *relinquo*: the brother *left behind* his *cognomen*. The *cognomen* was not annexed. This is much like his reading of Tacitus' passage concerning the posthumous penalty suggested by Cn. Lentulus: *ne quis Scribonius cognomentum Drusi adsumeret*.[16] Weinrib takes *adsumere* to mean 'to take', and insists that the verb signifies a one-sided transaction: Cn. Lentulus suggests that no Scribonius shall 'take' the *cognomen* Drusus.[17] But *adsumere* is here used in the widest possible sense, in which 'to take' can mean taking for oneself or to take when offered by another. Weinrib is closest to the mark when he writes in a footnote 'Mommsen's instinctive suggestion of a testamentary adoption by Drusus Libo may be correct (Eph. Ep. I (1872) 146). In this case the nomenclature would be exactly parallel to that of Brutus Albinus.'[18] Annexation of nomenclature did, of course, occur. The *lex Cornelia de falsis*, or an amendment, dealt with the issue in relation to forming wills, as is evidenced by *Dig.*

'Clues to Testamentary adoption', in A. R. Birley (ed.), *Roman Papers IV* (1988), 159–74; and D. R. Shackleton Bailey, *Two Studies in Nomenclature* (1976), 81–91.

[12] E. J. Weinrib (1968), 263–4.
[13] Ibid., 263.
[14] Ibid., 263, n. 65.
[15] Vell. 2.112.2. For the case of P. Suillius Rufus, see Tac. *Ann.* 11.36.5 and 12.25.1. For P. Clodius Thrasea Paetus, see *PIR*² C 103.
[16] Tac. *Ann.* 2.32.2.
[17] E. J. Weinrib (1968), 264.
[18] Ibid., n. 69, 263.

Appendix 1: A Prosopography

48.10.13: *Falsi nominis vel cognominis adseveratio poena falsi coercetur*, 'To lay claim to a false *nomen* or *cognomen* is punished by the penalty for fraud.' But the evidence suggests the perpetrators were usually freedmen or foreigners passing themselves off as citizens.[19] Moreover, it appears that M. Scribonius Drusus Libo was never prosecuted for such a breach, which is perhaps evidence that no breach was ever made. This supports the view that he was adopted in the will of his uncle M. Livius Drusus Libo, on the condition that he *take* his name.

Evidently, Drusus Libo chose to drop the *gentilicium* Livius, preferring instead Scribonius. Shackleton-Bailey cites the case of T. Pomponius Atticus, who was heir to the estate of his uncle, Q. Caecilius, by testamentary adoption. Perhaps soon after Atticus had come into his new power as *heres*, Cicero headed a letter with *Q. Caecilio Q.f. Pomponiano Attico*.[20] The letter shows that a *heres* could revert to his natal nomenclature despite the *condicio nominis ferendi*, since he continued to be called T. Pomponius Atticus.[21] Thus, M. Scribonius Drusus Libo publicized a *cognomen* rich in social and political capital, but, for reasons that are not clear, dropped the equally impressive 'Livius'. Cicero's anecdote, moreover, draws our attention to another reason for viewing Drusus Libo as an adopted son rather than a starry-eyed nephew. No doubt the congratulations given by Cicero referred to the fortune that Atticus had acquired, important when considering the role of testamentary adoptions. Once an heir had performed the appropriate rites before a praetor, he would be able to take on the estate of the deceased, his name, the masks of his ancestors, and his *sacra familiaria*.[22] As a general rule, this whole process favoured heirless nobles who wished for the continuation of the family name without legal fuss. The reason had sufficed for M. Livius Drusus, and, in turn, his adopted son, M. Livius Drusus Claudianus. He had only one daughter, Livia Drusilla, and so adopted

---

[19] Suet. *Claud.* 25.3; Dio 60.17.7.
[20] D. R. Shackleton-Bailey (1976), 85; Cic. *Ad Att.* 3.20. There are other occurrences. When P. Cornelius P.f. Scipio Nasica became Q. Caecilius Metellus Pius Scipio via his testamentary adoption to Q. Caecilius Metellus Pius, Cicero, *De Domo Sua*, 123, could still call him P. Scipio. Linderski (1996), 153–4, has also pointed out that Metellus Pius Scipio's daughter continued to be called Cornelia. In 39 Tiberius Claudius Nero became M. Gallius after a testamentary adoption, but Suetonius, *Tib.* 6.3, tells us that a short while after Tiberius dropped the name. E. J. Weinrib (1967), 257f., has shown that reverting to his natal nomenclature did not detrimentally affect Tiberius' claim to the inheritance.
[21] Suetonius styles him 'Caecilius Atticus', *Tib.* 7. Cicero continues to refer to him as Pomponius in their correspondence. D. R. Shackleton-Bailey (1976), 85; *Onomasticon to Cicero's Letters* (1995), 26–7 Oxford; P. Tansey, *Pulsi maiorum loco? A reconsideration of the Patriciate 218–49 B.C.* Unpublished PhD (1997), 148.
[22] J. Linderski (1996), 152. Cf. R. Syme (1982), 167.

M. Livius Drusus Libo. Now, as far as we know, M. Livius Drusus Libo also had one daughter, Livia Scriboniana and, more importantly, no sons.

Low fertility within the aristocracy concerned the Augustan government; a social phenomenon that had plagued Rome for decades: 'A well-known feature of the social history of Rome is the infertility of the governing class, its failure to rear enough children to maintain its numbers', as Crook put it.[23] *Condicio nominis ferendi* is an artificial reaction to this state of affairs.[24] The object of this device was to ensure a testator's name was carried on after death, and a growing tide of opinion suggests that *condicio nominis ferendi* and testamentary adoption were one and the same.[25] It is here that Weinrib's thesis requires correction. Though he, in fact, advocates this position for M. Livius Drusus Libo, he seems to have downplayed its significance in the case of M. Scribonius Drusus Libo; a brief Livian prosopography reveals why such a process was necessary. The consul of 112 BC was M. Livius Drusus. He had three children: Livia, M. Livius Drusus (tr.pl. 91), and Mam. Aemilius Lepidus Livianus (cos. 77).[26] Livia married both Q. Servilius Caepio (pr. 91), and M. Porcius Cato, neither marriage produced children with the

---

[23] J. A. Crook (1967), 111. A low fertility rate and the consequences this imposed on the perpetuation of the nomenclature of the *pater* can be implied from Ulpian *Dig.* 1.7.15.2-3: *in adrogationibus cognitio vertitur, num forte minor sexaginta annis sit qui adrogat, quia magis liberorum creationi studere debeat: nisi forte morbus aut valetudo in causa sit aut alia iusta causa adrogatio, veluti si coniunctam sibi personam velit adoptare*, 'In cases of *adrgatio* the scrutiny of the court is directed to the question whether perhaps the adrogator is less than sixty years old, because then he should rather be attending to begetting his own children—unless it should so happen that sickness or health is an issue in the case or there is some other just ground for *adrogatio*, such as his being related to the person he wishes to adopt.' The *lex Iulia de maritandis ordinibus* and *lex Papia Poppaea* were seen as important attempts to arrest the problem of fertility through legislation. See introduction to these texts in, *Roman Statutes*, II (1996), 801.

[24] So Sen. *Cont.* 2.1.17.1: *Fabriciorum imagines Metellis patuerunt; Aemiliorum et Scipionum familias adoptio miscuit; etiam abolita saeculis nomina per successores novos fulgent. Sic illa patriciorum nobilitas <a> fundamentis urbis [habet] usque in haec tempora constitit: adoptio fortunae remedium est*, 'The portraits of the Fabricii found room for the Metelli; adoption merged the families of the Aemilii and Scipiones; even names that age has destroyed shine through new heirs. That is how the nobility of the patricians has survived to this day from the founding of the city. Adoption is the remedy for luck.'

[25] C. F. Konrad, 'Notes on Roman Also-Rans', in *Imperium Sine Fine: T. Robert S. Broughton and the Roman Republic*, J. Linderski (ed.), Historia Einzelschriften Heft, 105 (1996), 126, has shown that during the early Principate evidence that the concept of 'testamentary adoption' is nothing more than *condicio nominis ferendi* becomes 'conclusive and abundant'. Also J. Linderski (1996), 152-13; P. Tansey (1997), Appendix I, 143-50; the latter gives a full list of those scholars who adopt this approach at 143 n. 6.

[26] R. Syme (1986) table II; F. Münzer, *Aristocratic Parties and Families*, trans. by T. Ridley (1920, trans. 1999), 268.

cognomen Drusus.[27] M. Livius Drusus (tr.pl. 91) had no children, while Mam. Aemilius Lepidus Livianus, who was clearly adopted by an Aemilius Lepidus, did not take the cognomen Drusus with him.[28] It was thus left to the tribune of 91 to adopt, and he chose a Claudius Pulcher, who became M. Livius Drusus Claudianus. M. Livius Drusus Claudianus had one daughter, who took both *gentilicium* and *cognomen*, but it was not guaranteed that her future children would bear either. This was the situation when M. Livius Drusus Claudianus instituted a Scribonius Libo as *heres*, who became M. Livius Drusus Libo (cos. 15). Thus, immediately after 42 BC Livia and her new stepbrother were the only bearers of this very distinguished *cognomen*.[29]

About this time Livia married Tiberius Claudius Nero (pr. 42); they soon had two children: the future princeps, Tiberius Claudius Nero; and Decimus Claudius Nero (the elder Drusus).[30] Though the name 'Drusus' was not given to either child, some time during his youth Decimus became Nero Claudius Drusus; the plight of 'Drusus' was temporarily reprieved.[31] Nero Claudius Drusus had three children: Germanicus, the future princeps Claudius, and Livia Julia. Germanicus was born Nero Claudius Drusus Germanicus, whilst Claudius was Tiberius Claudius Drusus.[32] In 13 BC Tiberius named his only son Drusus, perhaps fulfilling a mother's request. Tiberius Claudius Drusus' birth in 10 BC therefore brought the number of bearers up to six. But *fortuna* is fickle. While Claudius was still a baby his father, Nero Claudius Drusus, died. It was probably about this time that another Scribonius Libo joined the ranks, though at which point he secured the bequest is beyond us. Either way, having surveyed the recent history of the Livii Drusi, it is not hard to understand why a device like 'testamentary' adoption appealed, especially because 'it merely signifies the instalment of an heir under condition that he take the testator's name'.[33] Since an heir received the deceased's estates, his name, the masks of his ancestors, and his *sacra familiaria*, it is not hard to understand why the situation benefited the Scribonii as well. Thus M. Livius Drusus Claudianus adopted M. Livius

---

[27] F. Munzer (1920, trans. 1999), 270.
[28] Ibid., 268.
[29] M. Livius Drusus Claudianus died in 42 at the battle of Philippi.
[30] Later to become Nero Claudius Drusus (Suet. *Claud.* 1.1).
[31] It must be noted that the change in nomenclature was not solely based on the precarious future of Drusus as a cognomen. We cannot dismiss the political ramifications that followed accusations against Octavian that he was Decimus' father, for to change the child's name to Nero could show an attempt to highlight the boy's natural paternity. For a review of all the arguments, see C. J. Simpson, 'The Change in 'Praenomen' of Drusus Germanicus', *Phoenix*, 42.2 (1988), 173–15.
[32] Suet. *Claud.* 2.
[33] C. F. Konrad (1996), 124.

Drusus Libo, who, in turn, adopted M. Scribonius Drusus Libo, the form of both having been defined through *condicio nominis ferendi*. M. Scribonius Drusus Libo had inherited the masks of not only his natal ancestors but also of the ancestors of the Livii Drusi.[34] With the Scribonii and Pompeii already on display, his collection was certainly impressive, both socially and politically: Weinrib's hypothesis does *not* produce this image.

Having thus established a place for M. Scribonius Drusus Libo, we should now consider his connections. The nomenclature of M. Scribonius Drusus Libo indicates a desire to display his connection both to the Livii Drusi and the Scribonii Libones. As the adopted son of M. Livius Drusus Claudianus, M. Livius Drusus Libo was a brother of sorts to Livia Drusilla and an uncle to Tiberius Claudius Nero, the future princeps. M. Scribonius Drusus Libo could, therefore, claim to be a cousin to the emperor. Indeed, though the passage drips with irony, Tacitus states that Libo frequently dined with Tiberius, and Suetonius cites instances where the two spent time together, even walking arm-in-arm.[35] Both episodes are used to imply Tiberius' fear, but they also indicate that intimate connections were not unusual. No less impressive were Drusus Libo's Scribonian ties. His grandfather was L. Scribonius Libo (cos. 34), a man found in some of the most significant acts of late Republican history.[36]

---

[34] After his appearance in the *fasti*, M. Livius Drusus Libo (cos. 15) does not appear again. Syme has speculated that he may have died a few years after his consulship in 15, perhaps a victim of the plague which probably left three consuls dead in 12 BC, (1986), 153–4 n. 85, though he admits that his approach is speculative.

[35] Tac. *Ann.* 2.28; Suet. *Tib.* 25.

[36] A brief and simplistic biography can be found in W. S. Anderson, *Pompey, his Friends, and the Literature of the First Century* BC. (1961), 41–4. The earliest evidence is possibly *c.* 62 in the form of coins: one a solo effort, the other a joint venture with L. Aemilius M.f. Paullus (cos. 50) to advertise *Concordia*, a show of support for Cicero and his associates. M. H. Crawford, *Roman Republican Coinage*, II (1974), plate 51, 416/1a 417/1a, dates it to 62. D. Weigel, 'The joint issue of L. Libo and Paullus Lepidus', *Society for Ancient Numismatics* (1974), 3–4. Weigel associates L. Aemilius Paullus (cos. 50) with his son Paullus Aemilius Lepidus (*suff.* 34). He dates the coin to 56–5, not 62. Crawford believes *Bonus Eventus* refers to success against the Catilinarians. The other coin celebrates the *Puteal Scribonianum* and thanks *Bonus Eventus*. Festus reveals the Puteal to be the Atrium of Scipio, which had been struck by lightning and destroyed. The task of rebuilding and administering the structure had been given to one of Libo's ancestors, and the note in Festus explains *Bonus Eventus*, thanked for the successful completion of the entire business; Festus 494.34–38 L.; Hor. *Epist.* I.19.1–11. Dating the coin with Lepidus has proved highly contentious, not least because it is central to understanding Libo's age. Part of the problem is pinpointing the identity of Libo's partner, which the legend states was a 'Paulus Lepidus'. Some argue for the *suffectus* of 34 (Groag *PIR*² A 373; Weigel (1974), 3–4), others for his father (Crawford (1974), I.441–2; P. Willems (1883–5), I.486, 495). Since it is not central to the purposes of this chapter, the arguments will not be examined. Suffice to say that no date hitherto suggested has found universal favour.

In 56 BC L. Scribonius Libo appears as a lobbyist for Cn. Pompeius to be given the commission for reinstating Ptolemy VII as king of Egypt.[37] Libo's abilities were endorsed when Pompeius chose Libo's daughter for his son, Sextus Pompeius.[38] Though he again goes missing, the threat of war suited Libo's abilities, and in February of 49 he and L. Cornelius Lentulus Crus (cos. 49) organized troops in Capua. By March Libo had met with Pompeius' senior advisers in Brundisium and, apart from strategy and policy, it seems evident Libo was involved in bribing soldiers.[39] Early in 49, before fighting broke out, Caesar tells us that he sent C. Caninius Rebilus to Libo for the purposes of organizing an interview between himself and Pompey.[40] He adds that Caninius was Libo's *familiaris* and *necessarius* (a very close relationship of some kind). As with many others, Libo obviously had close friends on the other side. The anecdote also signals Libo's high standing, and Caesar adds to the impression when he states elsewhere: *quibuscum communicare de maximis rebus Pompeius consueverat*, 'one with whom Pompey was accustomed to consult about the most important matters'.[41] Defeat in the civil war, and the death of Pompey, did not end the career of Libo. By 46 Libo had befriended Cicero and at some stage during this period had his second son adopted by M. Livius Drusus Claudianus. But these were additional *amici*.[42] His rock remained the *Pompeii*, in the shape of his son-in-law, Sextus Pompeius.

---

[37] Cic. *Ad fam.* 1.1.3; some take this as evidence of a tribunate, so P. Willems (1883-5) I.422, 495-6.

[38] App. *BC* 5.52.; Dio 48.16.3; where Libo is described as Sextus' father-in-law. R. Syme (1986), 255, believed that the marriage occurred: 'perhaps not before the beginning of the Civil War'. It is impossible with current evidence to determine, with real conviction, a date for the marriage. The years 56-49 and 43-2 have both found favour with different scholars: F. Munzer *RE*.II.3.8884; R. Syme (1939), 228, n. 2, who reconsiders his approach in (1986), 255; E. S. Gruen, *The Last Generation of the Roman Republic* (1974), 108; E. J. Weinrib (1967), 249.

[39] The troops in Capua had been raised by T. Ampius Balbus, Cic. *Ad Att.* 8.11B. The advisers at Brundisium included L. Lucceius, Theophanes, Q. Caecilius Metellus Pius Scipio, and Faustus Cornelius Sulla, to which Cicero complains to Atticus: 'do you suppose there are any criminal lengths to which Scipio, Faustus and Libo will not go?' adding: 'their creditors are said to be meeting', *Ad Att.* 9.11.4.

[40] Caes. *BC* 1.26.

[41] *BC* 3.18; Throughout *De bello civili* Caesar portrays Libo as one of Pompey's chief negotiators. When Libo and M. Calpurnius Bibulus (cos. 59) found themselves in trouble while commanding two fleets, they held a parley with two of Caesar's legates, M. Acilius and Statius Murcus, asking that they be allowed to speak to Caesar to arrange peace. Significant is the absence of Pompey's approval, as the decision to negotiate was obviously within Libo's responsibilities, as was the ability to command a truce (3.16. See also 3.15, 3.17, 3.23, 3.90).

[42] *Ad fam.* 7.4; *Ad Att.* 12.18; 12.19.

Appendix 1: A Prosopography

In July of 45 Libo was Sextus' voice at a meeting with Cicero and Brutus.[43] In December of 44 Libo attended a secret meeting at Cicero's house as Sextus' representative.[44] Along with the other attendees, Libo advised Brutus 'not to wait to be authorized by the senate in preserving the safety of the Roman people.'[45] Though Libo was involved with the planning of hostilities that followed the death of Caesar, during the ensuing struggle his diplomacy was again required. At sometime in 40 Libo was part of an embassy to bring M. Antonius over to the side of Sextus.[46] Accompanying Libo on the journey was a C. Sentius Saturninus (cos. 19), who we know was related to Libo.[47] Octavian's response was to offer an alliance with Libo himself by marrying Libo's sister Scribonia, an important event in the history of the family.[48] The treaty of Misenum, though in hindsight a failure, was at the time an attempt at real and long-lasting peace.[49] Libo did well. His sister was married to Octavian, his granddaughter was betrothed to Marcellus - Octavian's nephew and the stepson of Antony - and it was agreed that he would be *consul ordinarius* in 34.[50] Welch argues that Octavian was attempting to destabilize the opposition by co-opting Sextus' most able adviser.[51] But Sextus cannot have felt betrayed, since it was his daughter—and Libo's granddaughter— who was betrothed to Marcellus.[52] Libo was instead mediating the truce

---

[43] *Ad Att.* 16.4.
[44] *Ad Fam.* 11.7: *Cum adhibuisset domi meae Lupus me et Libonem et Servium, consobrinum tuum.*
[45] Ibid. If we cast our minds back to the meeting with Cicero and Brutus in July of 45, questions with exciting implications emerge: how frequent were these meetings? how often did Libo see Brutus? Definite answers are beyond us, but the implications are obvious. If Libo was Sextus' link to Brutus from 45 to the end of 44, was he involved in the plan to assassinate Julius Caesar. His place among those at Cicero's house in December of 44 implies some form of collusion, with Sextus and his forces. That Libo was not arraigned under the *lex Pedia* and was never called an assassin is not a problem—since Sextus was.
[46] App. *BC* 5.52. The group comprised Antonius' mother, Libo, and C. Sentius Saturninus, who was a cousin to Libo on the mother's side, *ILS* 8892; R. Syme, 'The Stemma of the Sentii Saturnini', *Historia*, 13 (1964), 160. About their objective Appian wrote: 'who, being attracted to Antony's capacity for great deeds, sought to bring him into friendly relations with Pompeius and to form an alliance between them against Octavian.'
[47] *AE* 1892 no. 73: *SENTIA LIBONIS...MATER SCRIBONIAE CAESARIS.* Scribonia Caesaris was Libo's sister.
[48] App. *BC* 5.53; Dio 48.16.3; Suet. *Aug.* 62.2.
[49] Though, as Kathryn Welch has pointed out to me, Libo would have preferred to make a settlement with Antony.
[50] App. *BC* 5.73.
[51] K. Welch, 'Sextus Pompeius and the Res Publica in 42–39', in A. Powell and K. Welch (eds.), *Sextus Pompeius* (2002) 31–64.
[52] Concerning this episode, R. Syme (1939), 219, wrote: 'But there was a more important pact than the despairing and impermanent alliance with Pompeius, a more

between Octavian and the Pompeii. The marriage between Octavian and Scribonia lasted long enough to produce a child. Late in 39, as the treaty was falling apart, Octavian sent notice of divorce and married Livia. This may have caused problems.

There is no information on Libo between 38 and 35.[53] He was probably with Sextus in Sicily.[54] Sextus died in 35, but Libo was still able to hold the consulship as planned. If Scribonia's divorce had soured Libo's relationship with Octavian, then the fact that Libo held the consulship, even after the death of Sextus, might mark an attempt by Octavian to mend broken fences and a decision by Libo to accept a renewed offer of friendship. Evidently Octavian needed Libo—Libo, on the other hand, had gone to Antony before he went finally to Octavian! Despite his new alliance with Octavian, Libo's connection with the Pompeii remained unaffected. His eldest son married Pompeia Magna, daughter of Pompeia and L. Cinna (pr. 44).[55] These are the parents of our M. Scribonius Drusus Libo.[56] The importance of this marriage should not be underestimated when considering the role of Drusus Libo in history. It was his mother's ancestry that Drusus Libo is thought to have advertised, and it provided him with a possible slogan for an adventure into politics. On the other hand, the mere fact that the Scribonian House chose to solidify further its connections to the Pompeii is significant in itself. Libo had formed important ties with prominent aristocratic families that his grandson would be induced to remember by the treacherous Catus 45 years later.

Nevertheless, it is the direct descendants of Scribonia who should above all be noted when dealing with the connections of M. Scribonius Drusus Libo. Producing a prosopography for Scribonia is one of the most hazardous and vexatious endeavours known to Roman prosopography. Trouble begins with her two marriages prior to Octavian. Suetonius writes:

glorious marriage than the reluctant nuptials with the morose sister of Pompeius' father-in-law.' How obvious is hindsight. During the feast held by Sextus and Octavian, it is reasonable to believe sanguine faces filled the room, none more so than Libo's.

[53] For the divorce, see Dio 48.34.3; Suet. *Aug.* 62.2.
[54] App *BC* 5.139.
[55] The identity of Pompeia's husband is disputed. It is commonly thought to have been the *suffectus* of 32, so R. Syme (1986), 30, 46–7, 257. I have been persuaded by Patrick Tansey that it must be the praetor of 44. He bases his argument on Seneca, *De. Clem.* 1.9, who states that the father of Cn. Cornelius Cinna Magnus died during the civil wars: the *suffectus* of 32 must, therefore, be excluded.
[56] It was this Pompeia, Sextus' sister, who had given Tiberius presents while fleeing from Octavian in Sicily, presents reportedly exhibited at Baiae as late as the beginning of the second century AD, Suet. *Tib.* 6.3. There was, therefore, possibly a close friendship between Drusus Libo's grandmother and Livia, who were, of course, both refugees.

Appendix 1: A Prosopography

Mox Scriboniam in matrimonium accepit nuptam ante duobus consularibus, ex altero etiam matrem.

Soon he [Octavian] took Scribonia in marriage, [she] had been married before to two ex-consuls, and was a mother by one of them.[57]

One of the husbands is divined from a Propertian elegy, in which the spirit of Cornelia comforts her still living husband.[58] In it Cornelia names Scribonia as her mother and implies that her brother was the consul of 16, P. Cornelius P.f. Scipio. Thus, one of Scribonia's husbands was a P. Cornelius Scipio. The first problem: there is no P. Cornelius Scipio known as consul for the appropriate years. Attempts to bestow the honour on a *suffectus* of 38 proved inadequate, as were those which summoned forth the *suffectus* of 35, appearing in the *Fasti magistrorum vici* as P. Cornelius, but whom the *Fasti Tauromenitani* revealed as P. Cornelius Dolabella.[59] Nevertheless, the quest continues.[60] The second problem comes in the form of an inscription discovered in 1639. It attests a Cornelius Marcellinus as Scribonia's son, thus Cn. Cornelius Lentulus Marcellinus (cos. 56) has been deduced as her husband.[61] Yet Suetonius is sure that Scribonia had children by only one husband. The above is not central to our efforts, but it shows that producing a prosopography for this family is a perilous task and, hence, truly understanding the connections of M. Scribonius Drusus Libo is as difficult as it is important. The other marriage was, of course, to Octavian in 40, and it lasted long enough to produce a third child, Julia.[62] Julia and Cornelia proved the best political and social assets for the Scribonii.

---

[57] Suet. *Aug.* 62.
[58] Prop. *Eleg.* 4.11.
[59] On the *suffectus* of 38, see L. Biondi, 'Intorno un frammento marmoreo di fasti consulari', in *Atti della Pontificia Accademia Romana di Archeologia*, VI (1835), 273–380; *CIL* 1² p. 65; Groag, *PIR*² C 1306, 1395, 1437; *RE.* IIA.1.891 Scribonia no. 32. For the *Fasti magistrorum vici*, see *AE* (1937), no. 62. For the *suffectus* of 35, see R. Syme (1986), 28, 246 f. and 486; T. R. S. Broughton, *MRR* II.406, 555. For *Fasti Tauromenitani* see *AE* (1988), no. 626 a-b, (1991), no. 894. For a history of the *suffectus* of 35 in modern scholarship, see P. Tansey, 'The Perils of Prosopography: The Case of the Cornelii Dolabellae', in *ZPE,* 130 (2000), 265–71.
[60] Patrick Tansey suggested in discussion that the desired Scipio may be one of those who received *consularia ornamenta* from Caesar or Augustus, and that Suetonius was ignorant of the difference.
[61] *CIL* 6.26033: *Libertorum et familiae Scriboniae Caesar(is) et Corneli Marcell(ini) f(ilii) eius [in fr(onte)] (edes) XXXII [in ag]r(o) P(edes) XX*. This may be the same Cornelius Lentulus Marcellinus epigraphically attested as a praetor in 29, *CIL* 11.7412. For a full examination of these characters, see R. Syme (1986), 250 f., 287.
[62] Vell. 2.100.5; Suet. *Aug.* 62.2; Tac. *Ann.* 2.27; Dio 48.16.3, 34.3; App. *BC* 5.53; Zonaras 11.14; *Epitome de Caesaribus* 1.23; *CIL.* 6.7467.

Appendix 1: A Prosopography

Through Julia's marriage to M. Agrippa, M. Scribonius Drusus Libo gained five important cousins: Gaius and Lucius Caesar, the younger Julia, Agrippina, and Agrippa Postumus. Cornelia married Paullus Aemilius L.f. Lepidus (*suff.* 34) and produced M. Aemilius P.f. Lepidus (cos. AD 6 and *capax imperii*) and L. Aemilius P.f. Paullus (cos. AD 1). It has been conjectured that the elder son had more than one wife. The first is thought to be a Vipsania Marcella, whilst the second remains *ignota*.[63] This *ignota* produced M. Aemilius M.f. Lepidus and Aemilia Lepida, both betrothed to Germanicus' children Julia Drusilla and Drusus Caesar, respectively. L. Aemilius Paullus (cos. AD 1), who somehow beat his older brother to the consulship, married his cousin Julia the younger: both were Scribonia's grandchildren. They produced Aemilia Lepida, whose engagement to Tiberius Claudius Drusus Germanicus (Claudius) was terminated when her mother was relegated in AD 8.[64] Aemilia Lepida was instead engaged to marry M. Junius Silanus (cos. AD 19). The evidence, scarce as it is, suggests strongly that Scribonia had remained close to her children and grandchildren as well as the descendants of her brother and, thus, it is reasonable to believe that among such illustrious company, M. Scribonius Drusus Libo was no stranger.[65]

There are two more persons to consider: the unattested but necessary Livia Scriboniana; and P. Sulpicius Quirinius (cos. 12). Livia Scriboniana was the daughter of M. Livius Drusus Libo.[66] She was both a cousin and by adoption a sister to Libo, and her husband was the consul for AD 8, M. Furius Camillus (cos. AD 8). They produced M. Furius Camillus, L. Arruntius Camillus Scribonianus (cos. AD 32), and Livia Medullina.[67] Unfortunately, nothing can be made from her nomenclature, for it is no more than a product of Weinrib's imagination, but her link to the Scribonii Libones is borne out easily enough from her son's *cognomen*, Scribonianus. P. Sulpicius Quirinius is more interesting. Tacitus states that he was a *propinquus* to Drusus Libo, which is commonly taken to mean 'kinsman'. He was a close friend to Tiberius, and capable of taking Drusus Libo's request to the emperor without long delays. The nature of their relationship is not attested. P. Quirinius was married to a Claudia, and then to Aemilia Lepida, so that the link must come from his own family.[68] Nevertheless, he should not be

---

[63] R. Syme (1986), 125 f.
[64] Suet. *Claud.* 26.
[65] Prop. *Eleg.* 4.11 for her intimate relations with Cornelia; Dio, 55.10.14 for her choice to accompany her daughter Julia into exile; Sen. *Ep. Mor.* 70.10 for her presence at Drusus Libo's side during the trial.
[66] Admittedly a postulation, but Weinrib's evidence is strong, as is his reasoning, E. J. Weinrib (1968), 265.
[67] See E. J. Weinrib (1968), 274, *stemma* I.
[68] Syme (1986), table VII.

Appendix 1: A Prosopography

considered a party to Drusus Libo's activities. Indeed, his friendship with Tiberius was most likely the reason he was approached. In his darkest hour, when most of his relatives and friends had deserted him, Drusus Libo pinned his hopes of survival on a staunch Tiberian, something like: 'Please Publius, he trusts you . . .'.[69] The above thus treats Drusus Libo's natal and testamentary connections. We are left to consider the identity of his wife's family.

An inscription found in the middle of the twentieth century attests the existence of Q. Caecilius Drusus Libo. I have shown already that he was the son of Drusus Libo. He was evidently adopted by a Q. Caecilius.[70] The Scribonii Libones and the Caecilii were somehow connected in the late Republic. *CIL* VI 7.37380 attests:

Q CAECILIUS CAECILIAE CRASSI L. HILARUS MEDIC CAECILIA DUARUM SCRIBONIARUM L. ELEUTHERIS EX PARTEM [sic] DIMIDIAE [sic] SIBI E SUI [sic]

Q. Caecilius Hilarus, *libertus* of Caecilia [wife of] Crassus, physician; Caecilia Eleutheris, *liberta* of two Scribonian women, part [of his tomb] for themselves and for their own [i.e. family].

Caecilia Crassi is the daughter of Q. Caecilius Metellus Creticus (cos. 69). Her husband was M. Crassus, eldest son of the triumvir M. Licinius Crassus (cos. 70). Syme has shown that Caecilia Metella was the great-aunt of Q. Caecilius Metellus Creticus Silanus (cos. AD 7) on account of his adoption by a Metellus.[71] But Caecilia Eleutheris is more interesting. She is evidence of a Caecilian and Scribonian connection. Her name should have been Scribonia Eleutheris.[72] There are two solutions: (i) her formal manumission was officially sponsored by a Caecilius, but it was thought appropriate to honour her original owners (perhaps they had informally manumitted the woman by *manumissio inter amicos* and her formal manumission was, therefore, seen as simply a rubber stamp); (ii) Caecilius Hilarus and the soon to be Caecilia Eleutheris wished to marry.[73] Caecilius Hilarus convinced his former master to buy his enslaved girlfriend from the *duae Scriboniae* in order to make her a freedwoman. The *duae Scriboniae* agreed and were, in turn, sincerely thanked by the now Caecilia Eleutheris, who repaid their kindness by

---

[69] For his role in the trial of Libo, see Tac. *Ann.* 2.30; for his staunch support of Tiberius, and Tiberius' trust, see Tac. *Ann.* 3.48.

[70] Cf. J. Scheid (1975), 349–75, who makes him the natural son of a Scribonia and a Caecilius.

[71] R. Syme (1986), *stemma* XVIII.

[72] H. Dessau *ILS* III (1916), *addenda* 9433: *Quomodo liberta earum Caecilia appellari potuerit incertum*; see also H. Gummerus (1932), 47, n. 163; and H. Bloch (1982), 141–50.

[73] For a general discussion of the various forms of manumission, see S. Treggiari (1969), 20–36. Unfortunately, Treggiari does not consider Caecilia Eleutheris.

continuing to acknowledge a connection with her former owners. Either way, we have a connection dating back to the late Republic. The situation of Q. Caecilius Drusus Libo is therefore suggestive: he was adopted into a family probably long associated with the Scribonii Libones. The most likely possibility is that this Q. Caecilius was Drusus Libo's father-in-law.

Immediately following the death of Drusus Libo, Drusus Libo's wife probably moved into the house of a relative while her affairs were put in order. Since Drusus Libo's son was young when his father died, he will have stayed with his mother. We would thus expect the child to have been adopted by a member of his mother's family. This is, of course, speculation, but it is at least a reasonable hypothesis based on circumstantial evidence. M. Scribonius Drusus Libo was married to a Junia (or Caecilia), whose father was probably Q. Caecilius Metellus Creticus Silanus. Since Creticus Silanus was in Syria until AD 17, he evidently did not adopt the child until he had returned to Rome, i.e. a year had passed between Drusus Libo's death and his son's adoption. If this assumption is correct, then Drusus Libo was connected through marriage to an important ally of Germanicus.[74]

This investigation shows Drusus Libo in his social and political station. He stood at the centre of the aristocracy and was connected to its most important and powerful branches. A praetorship in AD 15 suggests a date of birth in or around 15 BC, the year his adoptive father reached the consulship. A date of birth c.15 BC makes Drusus Libo five years younger than Gaius Caesar, two years younger than Lucius Caesar, the same age as Germanicus, one year older than Drusus, and three years older than Agrippa Postumus. Drusus Libo would have spent his youth with these boys: with Gaius, Lucius, and Agrippa he shared the important Scribonia; with Germanicus and Drusus he shared a connection with Livia. He would ultimately view these men as peers, a presumptuous attitude that proved impossible to sustain.

---

[74] Tacitus writes, Tac. *Ann.* 2.43.2: *Sed Tiberius demoverat Syria Creticum Silanum, per adfinitatem conexum Germanico, quia Silani filia Neroni vetustissimo liberorum eius pacta erat, praefeceratque Cn. Pisonem*... 'But Tiberius had removed Creticus Silanus from Syria (he was a marriage connection of Germanicus, whose eldest son, Nero, was betrothed to his daughter), and had appointed Cn. Piso...'.

APPENDIX 2

Family Trees

M. Scribonius Drusus Libo and the Claudian Dynasty

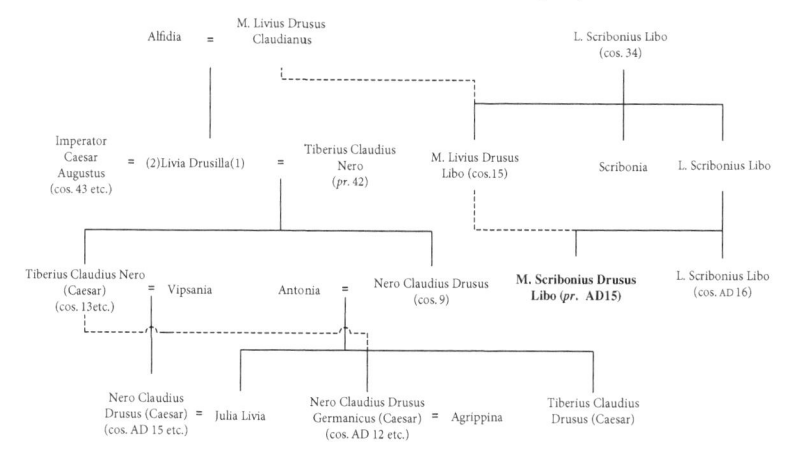

```
                    M. Livius Drusus                                    L. Scribonius Libo
    Alfidia    =    Claudianus                                          (cos. 34)
       |                  |--------------------------------------------------|
       |                  |                                                  |
       |                  |                         |-------------|----------|----------|
Imperator             Tiberius Claudius        M. Livius Drusus    Scribonia   L. Scribonius Libo
Caesar    = (2)Livia Drusilla(1) = Nero         Libo (cos. 15)
Augustus                  (pr. 42)
(cos. 43 etc.)
       |                       |
Tiberius Claudius Nero                Nero Claudius Drusus    M. Scribonius Drusus   L. Scribonius Libo
(Caesar)       = Vipsania   Antonia =   (cos. 9)              Libo (pr. AD 15)        (cos. AD 16)
(cos. 13 etc.)
       |                         |
Nero Claudius                 Nero Claudius Drusus                Tiberius Claudius
Drusus (Caesar) = Julia Livia  Germanicus (Caesar) = Agrippina    Drusus (Caesar)
(cos. AD 15 etc.)              (cos. AD 12 etc.)
```

The Descendants of L. Scribonius Libo and Pompeius Magnus

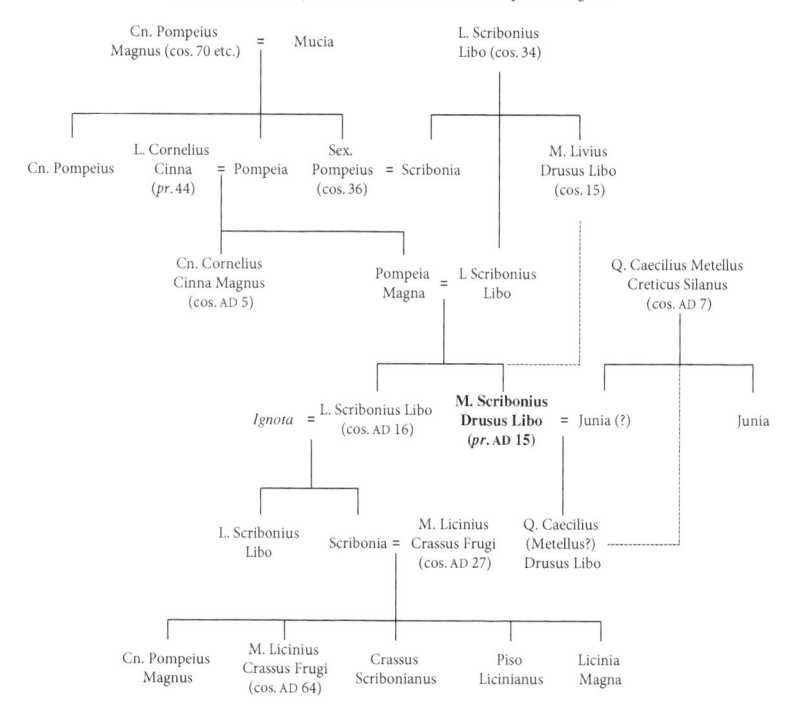

```
Cn. Pompeius                                          L. Scribonius
Magnus (cos. 70 etc.)  =  Mucia                       Libo (cos. 34)
              |                                              |
    |---------|---------|----------|                 |-------|---------|
Cn. Pompeius  L. Cornelius      Sex.                                M. Livius
              Cinna      = Pompeia  Pompeius = Scribonia            Drusus Libo
              (pr. 44)              (cos. 36)                       (cos. 15)
                    |                   |
              Cn. Cornelius        Pompeia    L Scribonius       Q. Caecilius Metellus
              Cinna Magnus         Magna   =  Libo               Creticus Silanus
              (cos. AD 5)                                         (cos. AD 7)
                                        |                              |
                    |-------------------|------------------|
              Ignota = L. Scribonius Libo   M. Scribonius           Junia
                       (cos. AD 16)         Drusus Libo  = Junia (?)
                           |                (pr. AD 15)
              |------------|                    |
        L. Scribonius   Scribonia = M. Licinius      Q. Caecilius
        Libo                        Crassus Frugi    (Metellus?)
                                    (cos. AD 27)     Drusus Libo
                           |
    |--------|-------------|-----------|---------|
Cn. Pompeius  M. Licinius    Crassus     Piso      Licinia
Magnus        Crassus Frugi  Scribonianus Licinianus Magna
              (cos. AD 64)
```

Appendix 2: Family Trees

Scribonia's Descendants

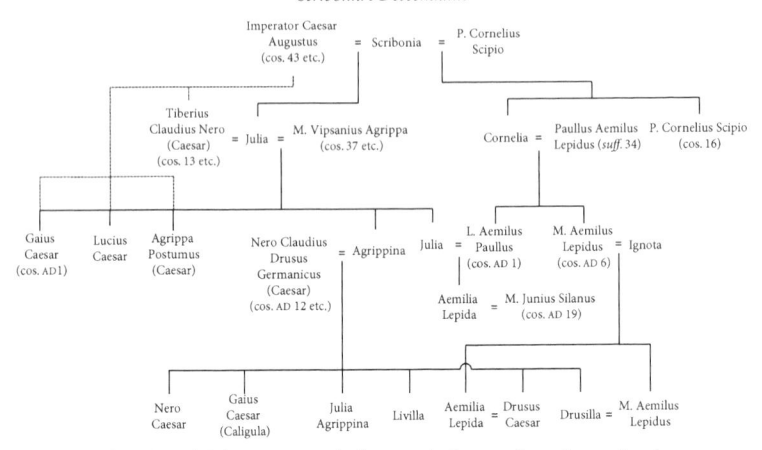

```
                    Imperator Caesar
                        Augustus        = Scribonia =   P. Cornelius
                       (cos. 43 etc.)                      Scipio
```

- Tiberius Claudius Nero (Caesar) (cos. 13 etc.) = Julia = M. Vipsanius Agrippa (cos. 37 etc.)
- Cornelia = Paullus Aemilius Lepidus (*suff.* 34); P. Cornelius Scipio (cos. 16)

Children of Julia & Agrippa: Gaius Caesar (cos. AD 1), Lucius Caesar, Agrippa Postumus (Caesar), Julia, Agrippina (= Nero Claudius Drusus Germanicus (Caesar) (cos. AD 12 etc.))

Children of Cornelia & Paullus: L. Aemilius Paullus (cos. AD 1) = Julia; M. Aemilius Lepidus (cos. AD 6) = Ignota

- Aemilia Lepida = M. Junius Silanus (cos. AD 19)

Children of Agrippina & Germanicus: Nero Caesar, Gaius Caesar (Caligula), Julia Agrippina, Livilla, Drusilla

Aemilia Lepida = Drusus Caesar; Drusilla = M. Aemilius Lepidus

Suet. *Aug.* 62.2: '*nuptam antea duobus consularibus, ex altero etiam materm*'.
There is evidence nonetheless of another child,
appearing in an inscription as 'Cornelius Marcellinus', *CIL* 26033.

APPENDIX 3
Timeline

6 BC–AD 13

6 BC   Tiberius receives *tribunicia potestas*; Gaius Caesar designated consul by *Comitia Centuriata*; Tiberius retires to Rhodes; Gaius made a *pontifex*.

5 BC   Gaius Caesar takes *toga virilis* and is made *princeps iuventutis*, a *sevir turmae*, and is allowed to give his opinion in the senate.

2 BC   Lucius Caesar takes the *toga virilis* and is made a *princeps iuventutis*, a *sevir turmae*, and is allowed to give his opinion in the senate, having been designated consul; the elder Julia is banished; Tiberius and the elder Julia divorce.

1 BC   Gaius Caesar begins tour of the eastern empire.

AD 1   Gaius Caesar and L. Aemilius Paullus are consuls.

AD 2   Lucius Caesar dies in Spain; M. Lollius dies in Syria; Tiberius returns to Rome; Gaius Caesar seriously wounded in Syria.

AD 4   Gaius Caesar dies in January; members of Gaius Caesar's entourage executed in Rome; Tiberius and Agrippa Postumus adopted by Augustus on 26 June; the elder Julia moved to Rhegium; Tiberius receives *tribunicia potestas* and *imperium* for war in Germany.

AD 5   *Lex Valeria Cornelia* passed; Agrippa Postumus takes *toga virilis*; Rome flooded for eight days; food shortage in Rome; legions and praetorian cohorts threaten to strike.

AD 6   January - revolt begins in Illyricum; February to April - *tumultus* declaration is made and an emergency decree authorizing Tiberius' control of the war in Illyricum is passed, troops are levied in Rome, an inheritance tax is instituted; April to May - levied troops reach Illyricum; June to September–a severe grain shortage occurs in Italy, war begins in Illyricum; August to early September–an emergency decree is passed on account of severe grain shortage; September - fires in Rome lead to the formation of the *vigiles*; October to December - mass protests occur and seditious pamphlets emerge, rumour circulates that Tiberius is planning to seize power, Aemilius Paullus is indicted for *maiestas*; late November to December—Agrippa is made *abdicatus* and sent to Surrentum, the younger Julia is sent away from the city, gladiatorial games are presented by Germanicus and Claudius; early December—Germanicus is made a quaestor.

AD 7   Tiberius dedicates temple of Castor and Pollux; Germanicus is quaestor in Illyrian war; food shortage in Rome; sales tax introduced; unrest at elections; Agrippa relegated and incarcerated on island of Planasia by *senatus consultum*.

AD 8   The younger Julia, D. Junius Silanus, and Ovid exiled; Cassius Severus exiled; Augustus' health deteriorates, preventing him from attending elections and most senate meetings.

AD 9   Varian disaster in Germany.

AD 10   Tiberius dedicates temple of Concord on 16 January.

AD 11   Augustus publishes his horoscope; problems with praetorian elections; Asinius Epicadus and Lucius Audasius attempt to free Agrippa Postumus, the elder Julia, and possibly others from their places of exile.

AD 12   Germanicus consul; Germanicus placed in the senate's care and the senate placed in Tiberius' care; pamphlets critical of the government are published; Tiberius receives *imperium* equal to that of Augustus in every province and over every legion.

AD 13   Tiberius receives *tribunicia potestas* for another term; Augustus finalizes his will; *semenstre consilium* reconstructed, able to pass decrees; popular anger concerning *vicesima hereditatium* threatens to erupt.

AD 14–AD 16

May	L. Aemilius Paullus dies.
May–June	Augustus and Tiberius complete census and perform a *lustrum*.
19 August	Augustus dies; Tiberius informed of Augustus' death.
20 August	Tiberius reaches Nola; Tiberius sends letters to the consuls and provinces.
21–22 August	News of Augustus' death reaches Rome; oath of allegiance to Tiberius sworn in Rome; Crispus

Appendix 3: Timeline

	sends to Planasia the order to execute Agrippa Postumus; funeral procession leaves Nola.
24–25 August	Agrippa Postumus executed; Sempronius Gracchus executed (?)
25–27 Aug.	News of Augustus' death reaches troops in Pannonia.
27–28 August	Tiberius informed by centurion that Agrippa Postumus is dead.
28–30 Aug.	News of Augustus' death reaches troops in Lower Germany.
1–4 September	Funeral procession reaches Rome; first senate meeting of the month to discuss funeral arrangements; news circulates in Rome that Agrippa Postumus has been put to death.
4–5 September	News of mutiny in Pannonia reaches Rome; Germanicus sends a report of the unrest in Lower Germany to Rome.
5–16 September	Augustus' funeral; Germanicus' report to Tiberius and the senate reaches Rome; Tiberius is made aware of Drusus Libo's position by Vescularius Flaccus.
17 September	Augustus deified; Germanicus receives *imperium proconsulare*; the senate votes to send to Germanicus a senatorial delegation; Tiberius 'ceases to refuse and to be asked' to accept the supreme power.
18 September	Drusus Caesar leaves for Pannonia.
18–26 September	Tiberius offers to recommend Drusus Libo for the praetorship, as Augustus had done; Drusus Libo accepts Tiberius' offer; Drusus Caesar arrives at camp in Pannonia.
27 September	Drusus Caesar sends report to Rome.
27 October to September	Tiberius formally accepts supreme power; his first act is to sponsor a rationalization of the electoral procedure; at a senatorial meeting senators are asked to vote on the candidates for that year, the winners become 'destined'.

Appendix 3: Timeline

4–6 October	Drusus Caesar's report reaches Rome.
October–December	The elder Julia dies.
AD 15	Drusus Caesar consul; Drusus Libo praetor.
AD 16	L. Scribonius Libo consul; news emerges in Italy and Rome that Agrippa Postumus is alive; Clemens gathers support in northern Italy and southern Gaul; Tiberius asks Germanicus to return to Rome; Germanicus resists.
11 September	Drusus Libo is charged with *maiestas*.
12 September	Drusus Libo commits suicide.
13 September	Senate publishes its opinion on the case of Drusus Libo and public thanks are offered to Jupiter, Mars, and Concord.
October–December	Clemens captured; the conspiracy dissolves.

Bibliography

Abbreviations used in the bibliography and the main text of the book are consistent with those used in L'Année Philologique.

Abbreviation of Journals

AE	L'Année épigraphique: revue des publications épigraphiques relatives a l'antiquité romaine (Paris).
ANRW	Aufstieg und Niedergang der römischen Welt (Berlin).
CIL	Corpus Inscriptionum Latinarum (Berlin).
CJ	The Classical Journal (Ashland).
CR	Classical Review (Oxford).
EMC	Échos du Monde Classique—Classical views (Calgary).
MEFR	Mélanges de l'École française de Rome. Antiquité (Rome)
Mnem	Mnemosyne (Leiden).
MH	Museum Helveticum (Basel).
MRR	T. R. S. Broughton, The Magistrates of the Roman Republic, Vols. 1–2, (New York 1951–2) (Supplement, 1960); Vol. 3, (Atlanta, 1986).
PP	La Parola del Passato (Naples).
PIR^1, PIR^2	Prosopographia Imperii Romani, 1st edn. (Berlin, 1897–8); 2nd edn. (Berlin, 1933).
CAH^1, CAH^2	The Cambridge Ancient History, 1st edn. (Cambridge, 1923–39); 2nd edn. (Cambridge, 1961).
ILS	H. Dessau, Inscriptiones Latinae Selectae (Berlin, 1892–1916).
Inscr. Ital	Inscriptiones Italiae (1931).
HSCP	Harvard Studies in Classical Philology (Cambridge).
JRS	The Journal of Roman Studies (London).
CQ	Classical Quarterly (Oxford).
ZSS	Zeitschrift der Savigny-Stiftung fur Rechtsgeschichte, Romanistische Abteilung (Vienna: Böhlau).
RE	Realencyclopädie der classischen Altertumswissenschaft (Stuttgart, 1893–1972).
REL	Revue des études latines (Paris).
TAPA	Transactions of the American Philological Association, (Baltimore).
PBSR	Papers of the British School at Rome (London).
PCPhS	Proceedings of the Cambridge Philological Society (Cambridge).

ZPE   Zeitschrift für Papyrologie und Epigraphik (Bonn).
AJP   American Journal of Philology (Baltimore).
ZÖG   Zeitschrift für die Österreichischen Gymnasien (Vienna).

Ancient Works

The editions of the main texts used are

Dio = E. Cary, *Dio's Roman History*, Loeb Classical Library, 9 vols. (Harvard University Press, (1914–27).
Justinian, Digest = Th. Mommsen and P., Krueger *The Digest of Justinian*, with an English trans. ed. by A. Watson, vols. (University of Pennsylvania Press, 4 vols. 1985).
Ovid = S. G. P., Owen, *Ovidi Nasonis: Tristium Libri Quinque; Ibis; Ex Ponto Libri Quattuor; Halieutica; Fragmenta* (Oxford Classical Texts, 1912).
Quintilian = M. Winterbottom, *M. Fabi Quintiliani: Institutionis Oratoriae* (Oxford Classical Texts, 1970).
Seneca = M., Winterbottom, *Seneca the Elder: Declamations*, Loeb Classical Library, 2 vols. (Harvard University Press, 1974).
Senatus Consultum Pisone Patre = C., Damon, and D. S., Potter, The 'Senatus Consltum de Cn. Pisone Patre', *AJP*, 120:1 (Spring, 1999).
Suetonius = J. C., Rolfe, *Suetonius, Lives of the Caesars*, Loeb Classical Library, 2 vols, (Harvard University Press, 1914).
Tacitus = C. D., Fisher, *Tacitus Annales* (Oxford Classical Texts, 1906).
Velleius = F. W., Shipley, *Velleius Paterculus and Res Gestae Divi Augusti*, Loeb Classical Library (Harvard University Press, 1924).

Modern Works

Adler, M., 'Die Verschwörung des Cn. Cornelius Cinna bei Seneca und Cassius Dio', *ZÖG*, 60 (1909) 193–208.
T. W., Africa, 'Urban Violence in Imperial Rome', *Journal of Interdisciplinary History*, 2:1 (1971), 3–21.
Aldrete, G. S., *Floods of the Tiber in Ancient Rome* (Baltimore, 2007).
Allen, Jun., W., 'The Death of Agrippa Postumus', *TAPA*, 78 (1947), 131–9.
Allison, J. E., and Cloud, J. D., 'The Lex Julia Maiestatis', *Latomus*, 21 (1962), 711–31.
Alexander, W. H., 'The Culpa of Ovid', *CJ*, 53:7 (1958), 319–25.
Andersen, H. A., *Cassius Dio und die Begründung des Principates* (Berlin, 1938).
Anderson, W. S., *Pompey, his Friends and the Literature of the First Century B.C.*, (Berkeley, 1963).
Arkenberg J. S., 'Licinii Murenae, Terentii Varrones and Varrones Murenae', *Historia*, 42 (1993), 471–91.

Bibliography 241

Astin, A. E., 'Nominare in Accounts of Elections in the Early Principate', *Latomus,* 28 (1969), 863–74.
Atkinson, K. M. T., 'Constitutional and Legal Aspects of the Trials of Marcus Primus and Varro Murena', *Historia,* 9 (1960), 440–73.
Austin, N. J. E., and Rankov, N. B., *Exploratio: Military and Political Intelligence in the Roman World from the Second Punic War to the Battle of Adrianople* (London, 1995).
Badian, E., *Studies in Greek and Roman History* (Oxford, 1964).
—— "Crisis Theories" and the Beginning of the Principate', *Romanitas—Christianitas,* Festschrift J. Straub (1982), 18–41.
Baillie Reynolds, P. K., *The Vigiles of Imperial Rome* (London, 1926).
Barnes, T. D., 'Julia's Child', *Phoenix,* 35:4 (1981), 362–3.
Barrett, A., *Agrippina: Sex, Power and Politics in the Early Empire* (New Haven, 1996).
—— *Livia: First Lady of Imperial Rome* (New Haven, 2002).
Bauman, R. A., 'Tiberius and Murena', *Historia,* 15 (1966), 420–31.
—— *The Crimen Maiestatis in the Roman Republic and Augustan Principate* (Johannesburg, 1967).
—— *Impietas in Principem* (Munich, 1974).
—— *Lawyers and Politics in the Early Roman Empire* (Munich, 1989).
—— *Women and Politics in Ancient Rome* (London, 1992).
—— 'Tanaquil-Livia and the Death of Augustus', *Historia,* 43 (1994), 177–8.
Bellemore, J., 'The Death of Agrippa Postumus and Escape of Clemens', *Eranos,* 98 (2000) 93–114.
Benario, H. W., 'The End of Sallustius Crispus', *CJ,* 57:7 (1962), 321–2.
Béranger, J., 'Le refus du pouvoir', *MH,* 5 (1948), 178–96.
—— 'L'Hérédité du Principat note sur la Transmission du pouvoir Impérial aux Deux Premiers Siècles', *REL,* 17 (1939), 117 ff. = *Principatus* (Geneva, 1972), 137–52.
Biondi, L., 'Intorno un Frammento Marmoreo di Fasti Consulari', in *Atti della Pontificia Accademia Romana di Archeologia,* 6 (1835), 273–380.
Biondi, B. 'La legislazione di Augusto', *Scritti Giuridici,* 2 (1965), 61–98.
Birch, R. A., 'The Correspondence of Augustus: Some Notes on Suetonius, Tiberius 21.4–7', *CQ,* 31:1 (1981), 155–61.
—— 'The Settlement of 26 June A.D. 4 and its Aftermath', *CQ,* 31:2 (1981), 443–56.
Bleicken, J., *Senatsgericht und Kaisergericht –eine Studie zur Entwicklung des Prozeßrechtes im frühen Prinzipat* (Göttingen, 1962).
Bloch, H., 'The Funerary Inscription of the Physician of Caecilia Crassi in the Fogg Art Museum', *HSCP,* 86 (1982), 141–50.
Bodel, J., 'Punishing Piso', *AJP,* 120 (1999), 43–57.
Boucher, J-P., *Gaius Cornelius Gallus* (Paris, 1966).
Brasiello, U., *La Repressione Penale in Diritto Romano* (Naples, 1937).

Bremer, F. P., *Iuris Prudentiae Antehadrianae Quae Supersunt*, Vol.2 (Teubner, 1896–1901).
Brennan, P. M., 'A Rome Away from Rome: Veteran Colonists and Post-Augustan Roman Colonization', in J. P. Descoeoudres (ed.), *Greek Colonists and Native Populations* Sydney, (1990), 491–502.
Brunt, P. 'The Lex Valeria Cornelia', *JRS*, 51 (1961), 71–83.
——'C. Fabricius Tuscus and an Augustan Dilectus', *ZPE*, 13 (1974), 161–85.
——'Evidence Given Under Torture in the Principate', *ZSS*, 97 (1980), 256–65.
——'Princeps and Equites', *JRS*, 73 (1983), 42–75.
——'The Role of the Senate in the Augustus Regime', *CQ*, 34:2 (1984), 423–44.
Buckland, W. W., *Textbook of Roman Law*³, ed. by P. Stein (Cambridge, 1963).
Canfora, L. 'Appiano ed il « Liber Annalis » di Libone', *Studi Classici Orientali*, 12 (1963), 207–11.
Charlesworth, M. P., 'Tiberius and the Death of Augustus', *AJP*, 44 (1923), 145–57.
——'Livia and Tanaquil', *CR*, 41 (1927), 55–7.
Chilton, C. W., 'The Roman Law of Treason under the Early Principate', *JRS*, 45 (1955), 73–81.
Chilver, G. C. F., *Cisalpine Gaul: Social and Economic History from 49 B.C. to the Death of Trajan* (Oxford, 1941).
Ciaceri, E., 'L' Imperatore Tiberio e I Processi di lesa maesta', *Processi Politici e Relazioni Internazionali* (Roma, 1918).
——*Tiberio Successore di Augusto*² (Roma, 1944).
Clarke, G. W., 'The *destinatio* Centuries in AD 14', *Historia*, 13 (1964), 383–4.
——'Books for the Burning', *Prudentia*, 4:2 (1972), 67–83.
Clinton Terry III, W. and Hartigan, K. V., 'Police Authority and Reform in Augustan Rome and Nineteenth Century England: Localizing and Nationalizing Police Work in Traditional and Modern Societies', *Law and Human Behavior*, 6:3/4 (1982), 295–311.
Cogitore, I., 'Mancipii Unius Audacia (Tac, Annals, II, 39, 1): Le Faux Agrippa Postumus Face au Pouvoir de Tibère', *Revue Des Études Latines*, 68 (1991), 123–35.
Cooley, A. E., *Res Gestae Divi Augusti: Text, Translation, and Commentary* (Cambridge, (2009).
Corbett, J. H., 'The Succession Policy of Augustus', *Latomus*, 33 (1974), 87–97.
Cramer, F. H., *Astrology in Roman Law and Politics* (Chicago, 1954).
Crawford, M. H. (ed.), *Roman Republican Coinage*, 2 vols. (Cambridge, 1974).

―― *Roman Statutes*, 2 vols., BICS Supplement, 64 (1996).
Crook, J. A., 'Oktavian und das Testament Cäsars by Walter Schmitthenner', *CR*, 4:2 (1954), 152–4.
―― *Consilium Principis* (Cambridge, 1955).
―― *Law and Life of Rome* (Cornell, 1967).
―― 'The Election of Magistrates in the Early Principate', *CR*, 20:1 (1970), 65–8.
―― 'Was There a Doctrine of Manifest Guilt in the Roman Criminal Law', *PCPS*, 33 (1987), 38–52.
―― *Legal Advocacy in the Roman World* (New York, 1995).
Daly, L. J. 'The Gallus Affair', *Latomus*, 164 (1979), 289–311.
―― 'The Report of Varro Murena's Death (Dio 54.3.5)', *Klio*, 65 (1983), 245–61.
Davies, R. W., 'Augustus Caesar: A Police System in the Ancient World', in P. J. Stead (ed.), *Pioneers in Policing* (Maidenhead, 1977), 12–32.
Demougin, S., *L'ordre équestre sous les Julio-Claudiens* (Rome, 1988).
Dessau, H., *Geschichte der römischen Kaiserzeit*, Vol. 1 (Berlin, 1924–30).
Detweiler, R. 'Historical Perspectives on the Death of Agrippa Postumus', *CJ*, 65 (1970) 289–95.
De Visscher, F., 'Tacite et les réformes éléctorales d'Auguste et de Tibère, *Studi in Onore di V. Arangio-Ruiz* II (Naples, 1953), 428.
D'Hautcourt, A., 'L'exile de Cassius Severus: hypothèse nouvelle', *Latomus*, 54:2 (1995), 315–18.
Drummond, A., *Law, Politics and Power: Sallust and the Execution of the Catilinarian Conspirators*, Historia Einzelschriften Heft, 93 (Stretgaat, 1995).
Düll, R., 'Iudicium domesticum, Abdicatio, und Apokeryxis', *ZSS*, 63 (1943), 54–116.
Duruy, V., *Histoire des Romains* (Paris, 1879–85).
Echols, E., 'The Roman City Police: Origin and Development', *CJ*, 53: 8 (1958), 377–85.
Eck, W., Caballos, A., and Fernández, F. *Das senatus consultum de Cn. Pisone Patre* (Munich, 1996).
Ehrenberg, V., and Jones, A. H. M., *Documents Illustrating the Reigns of Augustus and Tiberius*[2], (Oxford, 1955 rev. 1976).
Fantham, E., 'Stuprum: Public Attitudes and Penalties for Sexual Offences in Republican Rome', *EMC*, 10 (1991), 267–91.
―― *Julia Augusti* (New York, 2006).
Fletcher, A. *Tudor Rebellions* (London, 1968).
Flower, H., *Ancestor Masks and Aristocratic Power in Roman Culture* (Oxford, 1996).
Fraccaro, P., 'La Procedura del voto nei comizi tributi romani', *Opuscula*, 2 (1957), 235–54.

Frank, T., 'The Bacchanalian Cult of 186 B.C.', *CQ*, 21 (1927), 128–132.
—— 'Naevius and Free Speech', *AJP*, 48 (1927), 105–10.
Fraenkel, E., 'Review of Beckmann, Zauberei und Recht in Roms Frühzeit', *Gnomon* 1 (1925), 185–200.
Frei-Stolba, R., *Untersuchungen zu den Wahlen in der römischen Kaiserzeit* (Zurich, 1967).
Freytag, L., *Tiberius und Tacitus* (Berlin, 1870).
Furneaux, H., *The Annals of Tacitus Vol. I: Books I–VI*² (Oxford, 1896).
Gabba, E., 'The Roman Professional Army from Marius to Augustus', in *Republican Rome: The Armies and the Allies*, trans. by P. J. Cuff (1976), 20–69.
Garnsey, P., *Social Status and Legal Privilege in the Roman Empire* (Oxford, 1970).
—— *Famine and Food Supply in the Graeco-Roman World: Responses to Risk and Crisis* (Cambridge, 1988).
Gilliam, J. F., 'The Minimum Subject to the Vicesima Hereditatium', *AJP*, 73: 4 (1952), 397–405.
Goodyear, F. R. D., *The Annals of Tacitus Vol. I (Annals I.1–54)* (Cambridge, 1972).
—— *The Annals of Tacitus Vol. II (Annals I.55–81 and Annals 2)* (Cambridge, 1981).
Gradel, I., *Emperor Worship and Roman Religion* (Oxford, 2002).
Greenidge, A. H. J., 'The Conception of Treason in Roman Law', *Juridical Review*, 7 (1895), 228–40.
—— *The Legal Procedure of Cicero's Time* (Oxford, 1901).
—— *Roman Public Life* (London, 1901).
Griffin, M. T., *Seneca: A Philosopher in Politics* (Oxford, 1976).
—— 'The Senate's Story', *JRS*, 87 (1997), 249–63.
Gruen, E. S., *The Last Generation of the Roman Republic* (Berkeley, 1974).
—— *Studies in Greek Culture and Roman Policy* (Berkeley, 1990).
Gummerus, H., *Der Arztestand im romishen Reiche* I, Societus Scientiarum Fennica, Commentationes Humanarum Litterarum III, 6 (1932).
Hammond, M., *The Augustan Principate in Theory and Practice during the Julio-Claudian Period* (New York, 1933).
—— *The Antonine Monarchy* (Rome, 1959).
Hanslik, R., 'Horaz un Varro Murena', *Rheinisches Museum für Philologie*, 96 (1953), 282–7.
Hennig, D., 'T. Labienus und der erste Majestätspozeß *de famosis libellis*', *Chiron*, 3 (1973), 245–54.
—— *L. Aelius Seianus* (Munich, 1975).
Hillard, T. (2010) 'Velleius 2.124.2 and the Reluctant Princeps: The Evolution of Roman Perceptions of Leadership', in Cowen, E. *Velleius Paterculus: Making History* (2010), 163 n. 27.
Hohl, E., 'Primum facinus novi Principatus', *Hermes*, 70 (1935), 350–5.

Holladay, A. J., 'The Election of Magistrates in the Early Principate', *Latomus*, 37 (1978), 874-93.
Hoyos, D., 'The Legal Powers of Augustus: Some Modern Views', *Ancient Society Resources for Teachers*, 8: 1 (1983), 42-6.
Huttner, U., *Recusatio Imperii: Ein Politisches Ritual zwischen Ethik und Taktik* (Hildesheim, 2004).
Huvelin, P., 'La notion de l'iniuria dans le très ancien droit romain', *Mélanges Appleton*, Annales Univ. Lyon, new ser. ii, 3 (1903), 371-499.
Jameson, S., 'Augustus and Agrippa Postumus', *Historia*, 24 (1975), 287-314.
Jones, A. H. M., 'The Elections under Augustus', *JRS*, 45 (1955), 9-21.
——*Studies in Roman Government and Law* (Oxford, 1960).
——*The Criminal Courts of the Roman Republic and Principate* (Oxford, 1972).
Kampf, G., 'Three Senate Meetings in the Early Principate', *Phoenix*, 17: 1 (1963), 25-58.
Kehoe, D., 'Tacitus and Sallustius Crispus', *CJ*, 80 (1985), 247-54.
Kelly, G. P., *A History of Exile in the Roman Republic* (Cambridge, 2006).
Kennedy, G., 'The Rhetoric of Advocacy in Greece and Rome', *AJP*, 89 (1968), 419-36.
Kienast, D., *Augustus: Prinzeps und Monarch* (Darmstadt, 1999).
Kierdorf, W., 'Die Einleitung des Piso-Prozesses', *Hermes*, 97 (1969), 246-51.
Koestermann, E., 'Der pannonisch-dalmatinische krieg 6-9n. Chr.', *Hermes*, 81 (1953), 345-78.
——'Die Feldzüge des Germanicus 14-16 n. Chr', *Historia*, 6 (1957), 429-79.
——Annalen, I: Buch i-iii(Heidelberg, 1963).
Konrad, C. F., 'Notes on Roman Also-rans', in J. Linderski, (ed.), *Imperium Sine Fine: T. Robert S. Broughton and the Roman Republic*, Historia Einzelschriften Heft, 105 (Stuttqust, 1996).
Kunkel, W. *Über die Entstehung des Senatsgericht* (1969) = *Kleine Schriften* (Weimar, 1974), 267-323.
Lacey, W. K., 'Nominatio and the Elections Under Tiberius', *Historia*, 12 (1963), 167-76.
——*Augustus and the Principate* (ARCA, Lieeds, 1996).
Lang, A., *Beitrage zur Geschichte des Kaisers Tiberius*, diss. (Jena, 1911).
Lange, C. H., *Res Publica Constituta: Actium, Apollo and the Accomplishment of the Triumviral Assignment* (Leiden, 2009).
Leon, E. F., 'Notes on the Background and Character of Libo Drusus', *Classical Journal*, 53: 2 (1957), 77-80.
Levick, B., 'Drusus Caesar and the Adoptions of AD 4', *Latomus*, 25 (1966), 226-44.
——'Imperial Control of the Elections Under the Early Principate: Commendatio, Suffragatio, Nominatio', *Historia*, 16 (1967), 207-30.
——'Abdication and Agrippa Postumus', *Historia*, 21 (1972), 674-97.

——'Tiberius' Retirement to Rhodes in 6 B.C.', *Latomus,* 31 (1972), 779–813.
——'The Fall of Julia the Younger', *Latomus,* 35 (1976), 301–39.
——'Poena Legis Maiestatis', *Historia,* 28 (1979), 358–79.
——'The Senatus Consultum from Larinum', *JRS,* 73 (1983), 97–115.
——*Tiberius the Politician* (London, 1976, rev. 1999).
Levy, E., *Gesammelte Schriften,* Vol 2 (Cologne, 1963).
Lewis, J. D., 'Primum facinus novi principatus?', in *Auckland Classical Essays Presented to E.M. Blaikock* (Auckland, 1970), 165–84.
Linderski, J., 'Julia in Regium', *Zeitschrift fur Papyrologie und Epigraphik,* 72 (1988), 181–200.
——(ed.), *Imperium Sine Fine: T. Robert S. Broughton and the Roman Republic,* Historia Einzelschriften Heft, 105 (Stuttgant, 1996).
——'Q. Scipio Imperator', in J. Linderski (ed.), *Imperium Sine Fine: T. Robert S. Broughton and the Roman Republic,* Historia Einzelschriften Heft, 105 (1996), 145–85.
Lindsay, H., *Suetonius: Tiberius* (London, 1995).
Lindsay, R. J. M., 'Defamation and the Law under Sulla', *CP,* 44: 4 (1949), 240–3.
Lintott, A., *Violence in Republican Rome* (Oxford, 1968).
——*The Constitution of the Roman Republic* (Oxford, 1999).
Macé, A., *Essai sur Suétone* (Paris, 1900).
Macmullen, R., *Enemies of the Roman Order: Treason, Unrest and Alienation in the Empire* (Cambridge, Mass, 1966).
Magdelain, A., *Auctoritas Principis* (Paris, 1947).
Mann, J. C., *Legionary Recruitment and Veteran Settlement During the Principate* (London, 1983).
Marchant, J., 'In Search of Lost Time', *Nature,* 444 (30 November 2006), 534–8.
Marsh, F. B., 'Tacitus and the Aristocratic Tradition', *CP,* 21: 4 (1926), 289–310.
——*Reign of Tiberius* (Oxford, 1931).
Martin, R. H., 'Tacitus and the Death of Augustus', *CQ,* 5 (1955), 123–8.
——and Woodman, A. J., *Tacitus: Annals Book IV* (Cambridge, 1989).
——*The Annals of Tacitus: Book Three* (Cambridge, 1996).
Maschke, R., *Die Persönlichkeitsrechte des röm. Iniuriensystems* (Breslau, 1903).
May, J. M., 'The Rhetoric of Advocacy and Patron–Client Identification: Variation on a Theme', *AJP,* 102: 3 (1981), 308–15.
McFayden, D., 'The Rise of the Princeps' Jurisdiction Within the City of Rome', *Washington University Studies,* Humanities Series, 10: 2 (1923), 181–3.
Meise, E., *Untersuchungen zur Geschicte der Julisch-Claudischen Dynastie* (Munich, 1969).

Mellor, R., *Tacitus* (London, 1993).
Merivale, C., *History of the Romans under the Empire* (London, 1875-6, rev. 1881-3).
Millar, F., 'The Early Principate', *CR*, 13: 3 (1963), 327-9.
—— *A Study of Cassius Dio* (Oxford, 1964).
—— *The Emperor in the Roman World* (London, 1977).
—— 'Senatorial Provinces: An Institutionalized Ghost', *Ancient World*, 20 (1989) 1-5.
Milne, J. G., *A History of Egypt Under Roman Rule*^{3}, (London, 1924).
Mitchell, T. N., 'Cicero and the Senatus Consultum Ultimum', *Historia*, 20 (1971), 47-61.
Mogonet, J., 'La Conjuration de Clemens', *L'Antiquité Classique*, 23 (1954), 321-30.
Momigliano, A., 'Review of Freedom of Speech in the Roman Republic by Laura Robinson', *JRS*, 32 (1942), 120-4.
—— 'Review of The Cambridge Ancient History, Vol. X, The Augustan Empire 44 B.C.-A.D. 70', *JRS*, 34 (1944), 109-16.
Mommsen, Th., *Römisches Staatsrecht*^{3}, 3 vols. (Berlin, 1871-88).
—— *Römisches Strafrecht* (Leipzig, 1899).
Motzo, B. R., 'I Commetari di Agrippina madre di Nerone', *Studi di Storia e Filologia*, 1 (1927), 28-38.
Münzer, F., *Aristocratic Parties and Families*, trans. by T. Ridley (Baltimore, 1999).
Neuhauser, W., *Patronus und Orator*, commentationes Aenipontanae, XIV (1958).
Nicolet, C., *L'Ordre Équestre à l'époque républicaine* (312-43 av. J. C.), I, (Paris, 1966).
—— *The World of the Citizen in Republican Rome*, trans. by P.S. Falla (London, 1980).
Nippel, W. *Public Order in Ancient Rome* (Cambridge, 1995).
Nipperdey, K., *Annales*^{9}, ed. by G. Andresen (Berlin, 1892).
Norwood, F., 'The Riddle of Ovid's Relegatio', *CP*, 58: 3 (1963), 150-63.
Norwood, G., 'Mox', *CJ*, 36: 7 (1941), 421-3.
Ogden, D., *Greek and Roman Necromancy* (Princeton, 2001).
Pagan, V. E., *Conspiracy Narratives in Roman History* (Austin, 2004).
Paladini, M. L., 'La Morte di Agrippa Postumo e la Congiurra di Clemente', *Acme* 1 (1954), 313-29.
Pappano, A. E., 'Agrippa Postumus', *CP*, 36 (1941), 30-45.
Parker, H. M. D., *The Roman Legions* (Cambridge, 1928, rev.,1971).
—— *The Roman Legions*, 2nd edn (Cambridge, 1958).
Passerini, A., 'Per la Storia dell'Imperatore Tiberio', in *Studi giuridici in memoria di P. Ciapessoni* (Pavia, 1948).

Plaumann, G., 'Das sogenannte senatus consultum ultimum', *Klio,* 13 (1913), 322–86.
Powell, D. E., 'Controlling Dissent in the Soviet Union' in *Political Opposition in One-party States,* ed. by L. Schapiro (London, 1972), 201–16.
Purcell, N., 'Livia and the Womanhood of Rome', *PCPhS,* 32 (1986), 78–105.
Questa, C., 'La Morte di Augusto Secondo Cassio Dione', *PP,* 14 (1959), 41–53.
Raaflaub, K. A., and Samons, L. J., 'Opposition to Augustus' in K. A. Raaflaub and M. Toher (eds.), *Between Republic and Empire: Interpretations of Augustus and his Principate* (Berkeley, 1990), 417–54.
Raaflaub, K. A., and Toher, M., *Between Republic and Empire: Interpretations of Auguotuo and his Prinaipate* (Berkeley, 1990).
Raditsa, L. F., 'Augustus' Legislation Concerning Marriage, Procreation, Love Affairs and Adultery', *ANRW,* II, 13 (1980), 278–339.
Rainbird, J. S., 'The Fire Stations of Imperial Rome', *PBSR,* 54 (1986), 147–69.
Ramsay, W. M., 'The Speed of the Roman Imperial Post', *JRS,* 15 (1925), 60–74.
Rehak, P., *Imperium and Cosmos: Augustus and the Northern Campus Martius* (Madison, Wis., 2009).
Rein, W., *Das Criminalrecht der Romer von Romulus bis auf Justinianus* (Leipzig, 1844).
Rich, J. W., *Cassius Dio: The Augustan Succession* (Warminster, 1990).
——and Williams, J. H. C. 'Leges et Iura P.R. Restituit: A New Aureus of Octavian and the Settlement of 28–27 BC', *The Numismatic Chronicle,* 159 (1999), 169–213.
Richardson, J. S., 'The Senate, the Courts, and the SC de Cn. Pisone patre', *CQ,* 47: 2 (1997), 510–18.
Rickman, G., *The Corn Supply of Ancient Rome* (Oxford, 1980).
Rizzelli, G., 'Stuprum e adulterium nella cultura e la lex Iulia de adulteriis', *Bullettino dell'Istituto di Diritto Romano,* 29 (1987), 355–88.
Robinson, L., *Freedom of Speech in the Roman Republic* (Baltimore, 1940).
Robinson, O. F., *The Criminal Law of Ancient Rome* (Baltimore, 1995).
Rogers, R. S., 'The Date of the Banishment of the Astrologers', *CP,* 26 (1931), 203–4.
——'The Conspiracy of Agrippina', *TAPA,* 62 (1931), 141–68.
——*Criminal Trials and Criminal Legislation under Tiberius* (Middletown, 1935).
——'Treason in the Early Empire', *JRS,* 49 (1959), 90–4.
Romer, F. E., 'Gaius Caesar's Military Diplomacy in the East', *TAPA,* 109 (1979), 199–214.
Rose, H. J., 'Mox', *CQ,* 21: 21 (1927), 657–61.

Rosenstein, N., 'Sorting Out the Lot in Republican Rome', *AJP,* 116: 1 (1995), 43–75.
Rowe, G., *Princes and Political Culture: The New Tiberian Senatorial Decrees* (Ann Arbor, 2002).
Rutledge, S., *Imperial Inquisitions: Prosecutors and Informants from Tiberius to Domitian* (London, 2001).
Sage, M. M., 'Tacitus and the Accession of Tiberius', *Ancient Society,* 13/14 (1982/1983), 293–321.
Sattler, P., *Augustus und der Senat: Untersuchungen zur römischen Innenpolitik zwischen 30 und 17 v. Christus* (Göttingen, 1960).
Scheid, J., 'Scribonia Caesaris et les Julio-Claudiens. Problèmes de vocabulaire de parente', *MEFR,* 87 (1975), 349–75.
Schmitt, H. H., 'Der pannonische Aufstand d. J. 14 und der Regierungsantritt des Tiberius', *Historia,* 7 (1958), 378–83.
Schove, D. J., and Fletcher, A., *Chronology of Eclipses and Comets* AD *1–1000* (Suffolk, 1984).
Scullard, H. H., *From the Gracchi to Nero: A History of Rome from 133* BC *to* AD *68* (London, 1957).
Seager, R., *Tiberius* (London, 1972, rev. 2005).
—— 'Review of Bauman R. A. Impietas in Principem', *JRS,* 66 (1976), 230–1.
Severy, B., *Augustus and the Family at the Birth of the Roman Empire* (New York, 2003).
Shackleton-Bailey, D. R., *Two Studies in Nomenclature,* American Philological Association (American Classical Studies, 3 1976).
—— *Onomasticon to Cicero's Letters* (Stuttgart, 1995).
Sherk, R. K., *Rome and the Greek East to the Death of Augustus* (Cambridge, 1984).
Shotter, D. C. A., 'The Problems in Tacitus' Annals I', *Mnem.,* 18 (1965), 359–61.
—— 'Elections under Tiberius', *CQ,* 16: 2 (1966), 321–32.
—— 'Tacitus, Tiberius and Germanicus', *Historia,* 17 (1968), 194–214.
—— 'The Trial of M. Scribonius Libo Drusus', *Historia,* 21 (1972), 88–98.
—— 'The Trial of C. Junius Silanus', *CP,* 67: 2 (1972), 126–31.
—— 'Cn. Cornelius Cinna Magnus and the Adoption of Tiberius', *Latomus,* 33 (1974), 306–13.
Siber, H., 'Die Wahlreform des Tiberius', *Festschrift Paul Koschaker,* I (Weimar, 1939).
Silvagni, U., *L'Impero e le donne dei Cesari*² (Bocra, 1909).
Simpson, C. J., 'Tacitus and the Praetorian Elections of A.D. 14', *La Parola Del Passato,* 36 (1981), 295–311.
—— 'The Change in "Praenomen" of Drusus Germanicus', *Phoenix,* 42: 2 (1988), 173–5.

Sinclair, P., *Tacitus the Sententious Historian: A Sociology of Rhetoric in Annales 1–6* (Pennsylvania, 1995).
Smith, C., and Powell, A., (eds.) *The Lost Memoirs of Augustus* (Swansea, 2008).
Smith, R. E., 'The Law of Libel at Rome', *CQ*, 1:3/4 (1951), 169–79.
Spengel, A., 'Zur Geschichte des Kaisers Tiberius', *Sitzungsberichte der K. B. Akademie der Wissenschaften zu München* (Munich, 1903).
Staveley, E. S., 'Cicero and the Comitia Centuriata', *Historia*, 11 (1962), 299–314.
—— *Greek and Roman Voting and Elections* (London, 1972).
Stewart, R., *Public Office in Early Rome: Ritual Procedure and Political Practice* (Ann Arbor, 1999).
Stockton, D., 'Primus and Murena', *Historia*, 14 (1965), 18–40.
Strachan-Davidson, J. L., *Problems of the Roman Criminal Law*, I (Oxford, 1912).
Sumner, G. V., review of Koestermann, E., 'Cornelius Tacitus: Annalen, Band 1: Buch 1–3', *Phoenix*, 20: 1 (1966), 76–85.
—— 'Germanicus and Drusus Caesar', *Latomus*, 26 (1967), 413–35.
—— 'The Truth about Velleius Paterculus: Prolegomena', *HSCP*, 74 (1970), 257–97.
—— 'The Lex Annalis under Caesar', *Phoenix*, 25: 3 (1971), 246–71.
Swan, M., 'The Consular Fasti of 23 BC, and the Conspiracy of Varro Murena', *HSCP*, 71 (1967), 235–47.
Swan, P. M., '$\Pi\rho o\beta\acute{a}\lambda\lambda\epsilon\sigma\theta a\iota$ in Dio's Account of Elections under Augustus', *CQ*, 32: 2 (1982), 436–40.
—— 'Cassius Dio on Augustus: A Poverty of Annalistic Sources?', *Phoenix*, 41: 3 (1987), 272–91.
—— *The Augustan Succession: An Historical Commentary on Cassius Dio's Roman History, Books 55–56 (9 BC to AD 14)* (Oxford, 2004).
Syme, R., *The Roman Revolution* (Oxford, 1939).
—— *Tacitus*, 2 vols. (Oxford, 1958).
—— 'The Stemma of the Sentii Saturnini', *Historia*, 13 (1964), 156–66.
—— 'Clues to Testamentary Adoption', *Epigraphia e ordine senatorio*, II (Rome, 1982), IV, 197–310.
—— *The Augustan Aristocracy* (Oxford, 1986).
Takacs, S. A., 'Politics and Religion in the Bacchanalian Affair of 186 BCE', *HSCP*, 100 (2000), 301–10.
Talbert, R. J. A., 'Augustus and the Senate', *Greece and Rome*, 31: 1 (1984), 55–63.
—— *The Senate of Imperial Rome* (Princeton, 1984).
Tansey, P., Pulsi maiorum loco? *A Reconsideration of the Patriciate 218–49 BC*, unpublished PhD., University of Sydney, (thesis, 1997).

—— 'The Perils of Prosopography: The Case of the Cornelii Dolabellae', *ZPE*, 130 (2000), 265-71.
Tarver, J. C., *Tiberius the Tyrant* (London, 1902).
Taylor, L. R., *Roman Voting Assemblies* (Ann Arbor, 1966).
Tibiletti, G., *Principe et Magistrati repubblicani* (Rome, 1953).
Timpe, D., *Untersuchungen zur Kontinuität des frühen Prinzipats*, Historia Einzelschriften Heft, 5 (Timpe, 1962).
Toynbee, A., *Hannibal's Legacy: The Hannibalic War's Effects on Roman Life*, Vol. 2 (Oxford, 1965).
Treggiari, S., *Freedmen During the Late Roman Republic* (Oxford, 1969).
Vidman, L., *Fasti Ostienses*[2] (Prague, 1982).
Volkmann, H., *Zur Rechtsprechung im Principat des Augustus: historische Beiträge* (Munich, 1935).
Von Domaszewski, A., *Geschichte der römischen Kaiser* I, (Leipzig, 1909).
Volterra, E., 'Processi penali contro i defunti in diritto romano', *Revue internationale des Droits de l'Antiquite*, 2 (1949), 488-90.
Walker, B., *The Annals of Tacitus* (Manchester, 1952).
Wallace-Hadrill, A., 'Civilis Princeps: Between Citizen and King', *JRS*, 72 (1982), 32-48.
Walsh, P. G., *Livy: His Historical Aims and Methods* (Cambridge, 1967).
Walsh, P. G., 'Making a Drama out of a Crisis: Livy on the Bacchanalia', *Greece and Rome*, 43 (1996), 188-203.
Weber, W., *Princeps: Studien zur Geschichte des Augustus* I (Stuttgart, 1936).
Weigel, D., 'The Joint Issue of L. Libo and Paullus Lepidus', *Society for Ancient Numismatics* (1974), 3-4.
Weinrib, E. J., 'The Family Connections of M. Livius Drusus Libo', *HSCP*, 72 (1967), 247-78.
—— 'The Prosecution of Roman Magistrates', *Phoenix*, 22: 1 (1968), 32-56.
Welch, K., 'Sextus Pompeius and the Res Publica in 42-39 BC', In A. Powell and K. Welch (eds.), *Sextus Pompeius* (London, 2002), 31-64.
Wellesley, K., 'The Dies Imperii of Tiberius', *JRS*, 57 (1967), 23-30.
Wessner, P., *Scholia in Iuvenalem Vetustoria* (Leipzig, 1931).
Wiedemann, T., 'The Political Background to Ovid's Tristia 2', *CQ*, 25: 2 (1975), 264-71.
Willems, P., *Le Sénat de la République romaine* I (Louvain, 1883-15).
Wiseman, T. P., 'The Census in the First Century BC', *JRS*, 59 (1969), 59-75.
—— 'Rome and the Resplendent Aemilii', In T. P. Wiseman (ed.), *Roman Drama and Roman History* (London, 1988), 106-20.
Woodman, A. J., *Velleius Paterculus: The Tiberian Narrative* (Cambridge, 1977).
—— *Velleius Paterculus: The Caesarian and Augustan Narrative* (Cambridge, 1983).
—— 'A Death in the First Act', *Papers of the Leeds International Latin Seminar*, 8 (1995), 257-73.

—— *Tacitus Reviewed* (Oxford, 1998).

Wurm, M. *Apokeryxis, Abdicatio und Exheredatio* (Munich, 1972).

Yakobson, A., 'The Princess of Inscriptions', *Scripta Classica Israelica*, 17 (1998), 206–24.

—— *Elections and Electioneering in Rome: A Study in the Political System of the Late Republic*, Historia Einzelschriften Heft, 128 (Stuetgaet, 1999).

—— 'Maiestas, the Imperial Ideology and the Imperial Family: The Evidence of the Senatus Consultum De Cn. Pisone Patre', *Eutopia*, 3:1–2 (2003), 75–107.

Yavetz, Z. *Plebs and Princeps* (Oxford, 1969).

General Index

Abdicatio
  Fictional device 69 no.30, 71
  not *emancipatio* 69–71
  of Agrippa 67–73, 100–1
  related to *exheredatio* 71–2
Advocacy 29
Aemilia Lepida
  Trial of 21–2
Aemilius Lepidus, M. (cos. AD 6)
  Supports Cn. Piso 30 no.12
  connection to the Scribonii Libones 230, 234
Aemilius Paullus, L. (cos.1)
  Arval Brother 125 no.7, 139
  supports Julia the elder's restoration 48
  supporters 120–1, 211
  sedition 85–7, 95–6
  rival to Tiberius 99, 211
  daughter's engagement called off 85–6
  interdicted from fire and water 124–5
  death 125 no.7, 139
  connection to the Scribonii Libones 230, 234
Agrippa Postumus
  poor behaviour 50–2, 105
  failure of psychological analysis 50
  attracts attention of Gaius' friends 51–2, 60, 201, 211
  adoption by Augustus 47–53, 133 no.41
  denied special privileges 61–2
  suffers *abdicatio* 67–73, 100–1
  disinherited 72–3
  sent to Surrentum 68–9, 120
  exile on Planasia 68–9, 103–7
  not mentioned in Augustus' testament 73 no.41
  letter attacking Augustus 117–18
  not a conspirator 118–22
  relationship with sister 119–20
  guilty of no crime 121 no.65
  attempted rescue 137–41
  reconciliation with Augustus 173
  death 175–81, 207
  escape rumoured 209–10, 212
  family connections 234
Agrippina the younger (memoirs), 177–8 no.28, 217, 234
Apronius, L. (*suff*. AD 8) 8
Archelaus of Cappadocia 59–60
Asinius Epicadus 138–41
Asinius Gallus, C. (cos. AD 8) 8
Astrology and Magic
  Augustan edict 11, 135
  role in Drusus Libo affair 25–6, 200, 212
  decrees of AD 16 and 17 19–22
  widespread interest 25
Audasius, L. 138–41
Augustus Caesar
  Marries Scribonia 227
  settlement of 27 BC 164
  reaction to Gaius' popularity 63–4
  tutors Agrippa Postumus 72–3
  declares emergency in AD 6 80–1
  defamation 88, 91, 200
  failing health 106–7, 135–6, 151
  power over *comitia* 110–11, 114–15
  reforms *cursus honorum* 65–6, 112 no.34
  withdrawal of friendship 12 no.30, 12–13, 126, 127
  target of disaffection 94, 106, 117–18
  treatment of Julia the younger 123, 127
  on interrogation of slaves 130, esp. no.29
  majesty of *domus Caesaris* 133
  tolerates support for Pompeius Magnus 90
  horoscope 135
  death 157
  reconciliation with Agrippa Postumus 173
  death of Agrippa Postumus 178–9

General Index

Aurelius Cotta Maximus Messalinus, M. (cos. AD 20); family connections 234
  Proposal against Drusus Libo 7, 38–9
  friendship with Augustus and Tiberius 39
  takes cognomen from brother 221

Caecilius Drusus Libo, Q. 41–3
Caecilia Eleutheris 42 no.65, 231
Caecilius Hilarus, Q. 42 no.65, 231
Caecilius Metellus Creticus Silanus, Q. (cos. AD 7)
  Adoption of Drusus Libo's son 42, 232
  close to Germanicus 42–3
  connection to the Scribonii Libones 42 no.65, 231, 233
Calpurnius Piso, Cn. (cos.7) 15–17, 30–1
Cassius Severus, 88–9
Catilinarian Conspiracy
  Abandonment of Catiline 35 no.29
  incarceration of suspects 36–7
  state of emergency 12
Claudius Caesar
  Augustus' treatment of, 50–1
  engagement called off 85–6
  family connections 33
Clemens (Ps. Agrippa)
  conspiracy of, 33, 45, 209–14
  many supporters 34–5, 37, 211
  historiography 34 no.24, 209 no.42
  emergence of story 210
  aims of conspirators 213
Concordia 44
Condicio nominis ferendi 42, 220 no.11, 222–3
Corn Supply, see *Food Supply*
Cornelius Gallus, Cn. 12–13
Cornelius Lentulus, Cn. (cos.14)
  Proposal against Drusus Libo 7, 40–3, 221
  close relationship with Tiberius 40
Cremutius Cordus, 91 no.72

Damnatio Memoriae
  Historical precedents 39–40
  used for Drusus Libo 39–42
Defamation 88–93
Drusus Caesar the elder (cos.9)
  Games in honour of, 96
  republican beliefs 201, esp. no.27
  change of nomenclature 224
  family connections 233
Drusus Caesar the younger (cos. AD 15)
  Conduct during trial of Piso 16
  Arval Brother 139
  relationship with Germanicus 145 no.46
  mission to Pannonian legions 187–8
  family connections 233

Egnatius Rufus 112–13
Elections
  Augustan elections before AD 5 109
  elections during Republic 107–9
  influence of *praerogativa* 108
  lex Valeria Cornelia 109–10
  role of equestrians 110
  imperial *cursus* 64–6, 113 no.38, 199 no.21
  role of the lot 114
  elections of AD 7 114–17
  ranking of candidates 116
  praetorian elections of AD 11 135–6
  candidatus Caesaris 198–9
  praetorian elections of AD 14 202–5
  under Tiberius 203–4, esp. no.35

Falanius and Rubrius, affairs of, 15 no.43
Fannius Caepio 13–14
Fires, see *Vigiles*
Firmius Catus 6
Floods, see *Tibur*
Fonteius Agrippa 7
Food Supply 75–7, 81, 83, 94, 105–6, 118, 211, 235
Fulcinius Trio, F. (*suff.* AD 31)
  Prosecution of Drusus Libo 6
  friendship with Sejanus 32 no.17

Gaius Caesar (cos. AD 1) 49, 52, 145 no.46, 201, 232
  friends 53, 60
  elected consul 62–5
  takes *toga virilis* 61–2
  able to express opinions in senate 62 no.4
  eastern command 54–5
  power over Tiberius 57–8

General Index

desire to remain in the east 58-9
members of entourage executed 58
poor relationship with Tiberius 57-8, 64
family connections 234
Germanicus Caesar (cos. AD 12)
adopted by Tiberius 47
marries Agrippina 47, esp. no.5
legatus in Illyrian war 97
portrayed as a rival to Tiberius 97, 145, 192, esp. no 33
entrusted to the care of the senate 142
offered supreme power by mutinous legions 185, 189, 190 no.28
sends report of mutiny to Rome 188, 190 no.27
deals with mutiny 190
imperium proconsulare for war in Germany 193
problem for conspirators 213
attracts interest of Tiberius' enemies 142, 216
children entrusted to the care of the senate 142-3
family connections 233, 234

Julia the elder
Moved to Rhegium 47-8
attempted rescue 137-41
death 211
family connections 234
Julia the younger
Legal status 132-3
sent away from Rome 86
relationship with Junius Silanus 131
stuprum 126
house razed 123, 127 no.15
denied burial 123, 127 no.15
exiled to Trimeus 123
child exposed 132
not a conspirator 133, 139 no.16
daughter's engagement called off 85-6
family connections 234
Julius Caesar, C. (cos.59) 39, 94, 204 no.35, 212, 226
Junius Novatus 117
Junius Silanus, C. (cos. AD 10) 29 no.4
Junius Silanus, D. 126

Labienus, T. 89-90
Legions
Demand better conditions 77, 185
behaviour after Augustus' death 185
offer Germanicus supreme power 189
mutineers' aims 191
belong to *domus Caesaris* 191 no.31
Libera Custodia 36 no.32
Livia Caesaris (Julia Augusta)
possible support for Drusus Libo 32
supporting disgraced family members 32 no.18
treated as the *mater patriae* 32 no.18
exile of Agrippa Postumus 121-2
death of Augustus 173
death of Agrippa Postumus 180
connection to Drusus Libo 225
Livii Drusi 223-4
Livineius Regulus 31 no.12
Livius Drusus, M. (*tr.*91), 221
Livius Drusus Claudianus, M. 220-1, 222
Livius Drusus Libo, M. (cos.15) 220, 225 no.34
Lollius, M. (cos.21) 55-7
Lucius Caesar 49, 52, 61-2, 63, 65, 109, 145 no.46, 201, 232

Maecenas 13
Maiestas
defamation 87-93
Cornelius Gallus 13 no.31
Caepio and Murena 14
Drusus Libo 18-27
legal procedure 11
penalties under statute 21 no.65, 22 no.71, 125 no.8
aqua et igni interdictio 125 no.8, 136-7
post-mortem prosecution 37-8, esp. no.40
relationship with *domus Caesaris* 21-2, 132 no.40
interrogation of slaves 130 no.29
patria maiestas 132
Marcius, P. 8, 24-5

Numen Augusti 15 no.43

Ovidius Naso, 127-31

Papius Mutilus, M. 8
Phrataces, Parthian King 54-5
Pituanius, L. 8, 24-5
Plautius (?) Rufus, P. 85, 93

General Index

Pompeius Magnus, Cn. (cos.70)
 Connection to Scribonii Libones 6, 42, 220, 233
 relationship with L. Scribonius Libo (cos.34) 226
 represents Republicanism 90 esp. no.71, 200 no.24, 201 esp. no.26, 205
Pompeius, Sex. (cos.35) 227–8, 233
Pomponius Atticus, T. 222
Pomponius Flaccus, L. (cos. AD 17) 8

Sallustius Crispus, C. 177–81
Scholiast on Juvenal 85–6
Scribonia Caesaris
 Supports Drusus Libo 7, 31
 marriages and offspring 228–9, 233, 234
Scribonius Drusus Libo, M.
 Birth 232
 testamentary adoption 219–20, 225
 described as young and stupid 8, 27, 199 no.21
 parents 228
 socializes with Tiberius 207
 advertises Claudian connection 211, 225
 connection to Aemilii 230
 wife's family 231–2
 interest in occult 23–5, 212–13
 brought before senate 9–11
 charged with *maiestas* 18, 24–7
 without an advocate 29, 31–3
 supported by women of consular rank 31–2
 in custody 35–7, 212
 damnatio memoriae 38–40
 child 231–2
 praetorship 197–8
 behaviour in AD 14 199–201
 possible association with Gaius' friends 201–2, 205–6, 211
 possible aims 211, 213–14
 alliance with Tiberius 206, 211
 family connections 233
Scribonius Libo, L. (cos.34)
 Memoirs 201 no.27
 early career 225 no.36
 importance to Pompeius Magnus 226
 importance to Sextus Pompeius 227
 truce with Octavian 227–8
 approached Antony 228
 connection to the Sentii Saturnini 227
 descendants 233
Scribonius Libo, L. (cos. AD 16)
 Accompanies brother into senate 32–33
 mistaken for Drusus Libo 219
 family connections 233
Scribonius Storax, M. 41–2
Semenstre Consilium (advisory council), 150–2
Sempronius Gracchus, 139, 182, 212
Senate
 Emergency meeting of, 10–17
 provides *praeiudicium* 12–17
 under Augustus 14, 143, 146–8, 152
 under Tiberius 11, 16, 145, 148–50, 183–4, 215
 Senatus Consultum Ultimum 10
 transfer of elections 204
Sentius Saturninus, C. (cos.19) 111–13
Silius Caecina Largus, C. (cos. AD 13) 10
Sulpicius Quirinius, P. (cos.12)
 Secretly supports Tiberius 55–7
 Gaius' rector 56
 appointed governor of Syria 59
 connection to Drusus Libo 230–1
 delivers message for Drusus Libo 7

Tacitus 177 no.28, 187 no.9, 216, 217
Taxation
 Implementation 78, 106
 resistance to, 84, 94–5, 106, 152–5, 214
 many affected 84 no.47, 153
 importance to Government 84, 214
Terentius Varro Murena, L. 13–14
Tiberius Caesar (Princeps)
 Prosecutes Varro Murena 13–14
 view of *cursus honorum* 64–6
 retires to Rhodes 62–4, 186
 threatened by Gaius' friends 55–6
 returns to Rome as a private citizen 57–8
 adopted by Augustus 47, 53
 accused of planning a coup 97–8, 106
 extraordinary powers 98, 144, esp. no 43, 157
 relationship with Augustus questioned 99, 192
 support of candidates at elections 109 no.24, 115 no.44

subject of abusive literature 141-2, 146, 202
entrusted with senate 142-4
in senate 145, 183, 205-6, 215
supreme power 151, 157, 159
hesitant to assume leadership 160-2, 167, 186, 205
Augustus as a model 166
death of Augustus 159, 174
death of Agrippa Postumus 177, 207
memoirs 181-2
criticised for not dealing with mutinous legions 187-8
first aware of mutiny 190-1
elections 111 no.31, 115 no.44, 203-4, esp. no.35
wanted Cn. Piso defended 30-1, esp. no.12
invokes *Senatus Consultum Ultimum* 10-11
on defamation 92
Republicanism 11, 163, 215-16
family connections 233, 234
Tibur 75-6
Travel, speed of, 57 no.50; 185 no.2; 186 no.5; 188 no.13

Vescularius Flaccus 6
Velleius Paterculus
With Gaius Caesar in the east 54
service during Illyrian wars 79, 96-7, esp. no 96
opinion of mutinous legions 190-1
description of September AD 14 184
treatment of Agrippa's death 181
elected praetor 202-3
Vibius Serenus, C. 7
Vigiles 81-3
Visellius Varro, L. 10
Vitellius, Q. 91 no.74

Index of Sources

Amm. Marc.
   17.4.5: 12 no.28
App.
   BC. 1.60: 39 no.54
   BC. 3.11: 201 no.26
   BC. 5.52: 226 no.38, 227 no.46
   BC. 5.53: 227 no.48, 229 no.62
   BC. 5.66: 97 no.101
   *BC.*5.67–68: 94 no.83
   BC. 5.73: 227 no.50
   BC. 5.139: 228 no.54
Asc.
   30C: 115 no.45
   34C: 130 no.29
   59C: 11 no.27
   73–74C: 80
   92C: 116 no.49
Aurelius Victor
   Epitome de Caesaribus 1.23: 229 no.62
   Epitome de Caesaribus 1.27: 104, 171

Caes.
   BC. 1.26: 226 no.40
   BC. 3.15: 226 no.41
   BC. 3.16: 226 no.41
   BC. 3.17: 226 no.41
   BC. 3.18: 226 no.41
   BC. 3.23: 226 no.41
   BC. 3.90: 226 no.41
Cass.
   Chron. 604: 75
Cic.
   Ad Att. 3.20: 222 no.20
   Ad Att. 5.8.2: 137 no.11
   Ad Att. 8.11b: 226 no.39
   Ad Att. 9.11.4: 226 no.39
   Ad Att. 12.18: 226 no.42
   Ad Att. 12.19: 226 no.42
   Ad Att. 16.4: 227 no.43
   Ad fam. 1.1.3: 226 no.37
   Ad fam. 7.4: 226 no.42
   Ad fam. 11.7: 227 no.44
   De Domo Sua 123: 222 no.20
   De Re Pub. 2.39–40: 108 no.16
   De Re Pub. 4.10.12: 93 no.80
   De Off. 2.76: 94 no.84
   Har. Resp. 17: 125 no.8
   In Cat. 1.16: 35 no.29, 214 no.57
   In Cat. 3.14: 36 no.33
   In Cat. 4.15: 36 no.35
   In Piso. 21.50: 30 no.4
   In Ver. 5.44: 137 no.11
   Phil. 1.9.23: 125 no.8
   Phil. 1.23: 125 no.8
   Phil. 1.32: 41 no.62
   Phil. 2.82–83: 108 no.19, 116 no.47
   Pro Caec. 34.100: 125 no.8
   Pro Plancio 20.49: 108 no.18

Dio
   37.34.2: 197 no.9
   37.44.3: 109 no.23, 142 no.34
   39.7.3: 197 no.9
   39.18.1: 197 no.9
   40.54.2: 137 no.11
   40.55.1: 197 no.9
   44.11.4: 109 no.23
   46.49.1: 197 no.9
   47.14.2–3: 154 no.73
   48.16.3: 226 no.37, 227 no.48, 229 no.62
   48.33.1: 97 no.101
   48.34.3: 228 no.53
   51.19.3: 41 no.62
   52.20.1: 65 no.20
   52.42.6: 80 no.29
   53.4.4: 164 no.31
   53.8.5–8: 164
   53.11.4: 164 no.32
   53.12.2–8: 164 no.33
   53.13.1: 2
   53.16.3: 2
   53.13.5: 59 no.60
   53.21.6: 110
   53.21.7: 107–8, 110
   53.23.5: 12 no.28
   53.23.7: 13
   53.24.4–6: 113 nos. 35 and 36
   53.28.3–4: 65 no.19
   53.32.1: 69 no.27

Index of Sources

53.32.2: 69
53.32.4: 40 no.57
54.1.1–2: 75 no.3
54.2.4: 113 no.37
54.3.3: 14 no.40
54.4.1: 2
54.9.5–7: 54 no.40
54.10.1: 112
54.10.4: 65 no.19
54.12.4: 2, 193 no.40
54.17.1: 109 no.23
54.28.1: 193 no.40
54.28.5: 127 no.15
54.30.2: 109 no.23
55.2.4: 151 no.66
55.5.4: 130 no.29
55.6.1: 2
55.8.6–7: 82 no.37
55.9.2: 53 no.36, 63, 65 no.19
55.9.4: 62, 63 no.13, 193 no.40
55.9.5–8: 62 no.6, 64 no.16
55.9.9–10: 61
55.10a.8: 59 no.56
55.10.9: 52 no.35
55.10.13: 14 no.43
55.10.14: 230 no.65
55.10.15: 197 no.9
55.13.1a: 47 no.2, 48 no.6
55.13.3: 109 no.23
55.20.1: 112 no.34
55.22.3: 75
55.22.4: 61
55.23.1: 77 no.12
55.24.4: 49 no.14
55.24.9: 77–8
55.25.1: 78
55.25.3: 78 no.17
55.25.5: 78 no.18, 94, 204 no.35
55.25.6: 204 no.35.
55.26.1: 76 no.10, 80 no.26
55.26.2: 81 no.33
55.26.3: 81 no.34
55.26.4–5: 81 no.35, 82 no.38, 106 no.9
55.27.1–3: 83–4, 87, 93 no.82, 95 no.86
55.27.3–4: 14 no.43, 51 no.26, 96 no.91, 96 no.93, 99 no.112
55.27.5: 96, 98 no.107
55.30.6: 97 no.98
55.31.1–2: 79 no.22, 97

55.31.4: 81 no.33, 105–106, 107 no.14
55.32.1–2: 50 no.19, 52 no.29, 72 no.38, 98 no.105, 100
55.33.5: 135 no.1, 151 no.64
55.34.2: 106–7, 109 no.23, 135 no.1, 151 no.64
56.34.3: 204 no.35
56.24.7: 197 no.9
56.25.1–3: 136 no.7, 140 no.26
56.25.4: 65 no.19, 115 no.46, 135
56.25.5: 19, 135 no.2
56.26.1: 140 no.28
56.26.2: 142
56.27.1: 89 no.62, 141
56.27.2–3: 137 no.9, 138
56.28.1: 65 no.19, 77 no.11, 144 no.43
56.28.2: 150–1
56.28.4: 152
56.28.5: 147, 152
56.28.6: 152
56.30.1: 171
56.30.5: 157 no.1
56.31.1: 169
56.31.3: 183 no.45
56.33.1: 174 no.21
56.40.3: 147–8
56.41.1: 146 no.48, 147 no.50
57.2.1: 157–8
57.2.3: 161, 183
57.2.4–5: 165–6
57.3.2: 159
57.3.3: 182
57.3.5: 176, 179 no.30
57.4.1: 162 no.24
57.5.5–6: 190 no.24
57.6.2: 11, 162 no.24
57.7.3: 148 no.54
57.7.5: 148 no.55, 149 no.56
57.8.4–5: 162 no.23
57.15: 5
57.15.4: 25 no.82, 196, 198 no.14, 219 no.3
57.15.8: 19 no.57, 20
57.15.9: 11, 25 no.81, 148 no.55
57.16.3: 1, 33, 34, 208–9
57.16.4: 37 no.37
57.21.1: 197 nos.6, 8, and 9
57.22.4a: 143
57.24.1: 2
57.24.2: 90 no.68

Dio (cont.)
   57.24.8: 40 no.59
   58.8.3: 197 no.9
   58.20.3: 109 no.23, 115 no.44, 142 no.34
   58.20.4–5: 115 no.42
   58.25.2: 32 no.17
   58.25.4: 216 no.61
   59.9.6: 214 no.53
   59.23.8: 197 no.9
   60.3.2: 109 no.23
   60.15.1: 109 no.23
   60.17.7: 222 no.19
   62.16.5: 75 no.4
   76.11.1: 19 no.56
   79.7.4: 26
Dion. Hal.
   Ant. 4.16–21: 108 no.16
   Ant. 4.21.3: 109 no.22
   Ant. 7.59.2–8: 108 no.16

Festus
   De Verb. Sig. 494.34–38L: 225 no.36
Florus
   2.31: 77 no.11

Gaius
   Inst. 2.13: 73 no.41
Gell.
   15.7.3: 57 no.54

Heliod.
   6.12–15: 26
Hor.
   Epist. 1.19.1–11: 225 no.36

Jerome
   Chron. 164H: 12 no.28
   Chron. 170H: 76 no.6
   Chron. 176H: 88 no.62
Joseph.
   AJ 15.105: 54 no.40
   AJ 16.25: 59 no.59
   AJ 17.132: 59 no.58
   AJ 17.355: 59.60
Just.
   Cod. 8.46.6: 69
   Cod. 9.9.3: 131 no.32
   Cod. 9.8.6pr: 37 no.40
   Dig. 1.7.15.2–3: 223 no.23
   Dig. 1.15.1: 81 no.35
   Dig. 1.15.1–5: 82 no.39

Dig. 40.9.12.1: 22 no.69
Dig. 47.10.5.11: 87 no.59
Dig. 48.4.3: 30 no.4
Dig. 48.4.11: 37 no.40
Dig. 48.5.6.1: 126 no.11
Dig. 48.8.3.5: 22 no.71
Dig. 48.10.13: 222
Dig. 48.16.15.3: 38 no.40
Dig. 48.18.8pr: 130
Dig. 48.19.28.13: 21 no.65
Dig. 48.21.3: 37 no.39
Inst. 2.23.1: 125 no.8
Juv.
   Sat. 6.157–160: 86, 120 no.62

Lact.
   Inst. Div. 2.4.35–36: 137 no.11
Livy
   1.41: 172 no.12
   1.42.2: 108 no.16
   1.43.13: 108 no.16
   3.21: 166 no.40
   4.45.8: 132 no.39
   6.20.14: 41 no.62
   24.45.8: 36 no.32
   25.4.9–10: 137 no.11
   39.19: 36 no.32
   Per. 67: 36 no.32
   Per 142: 98 no.106
Lucan
   Phars. 6.588–830: 26

Macr.
   1.11.21: 13 no.33, 14 no.38

Orosius
   6.21.18: 77 no.11
   6.21.23: 79 no.19
Ovid
   Am. 3.9.63: 12 no.28
   Ex Pont. 1.6.25–6: 127 no.17
   Ex Pont. 1.9.25–30: 39 no.47
   Ex Pont. 2.8: 39 no.47
   Ex Pont. 2.9.71–76: 128 no.19
   Ex Pont. 4.13.25–28: 160–161
   Fasti 1.705–708: 96 no.93
   Trist. 2.103: 128 no.20
   Trist. 2.130: 127 no.18
   Trist. 2.207: 127 no.16
   Trist. 2.207–212: 129
   Trist. 2.446: 12 no.28
   Trist. 3.1.52: 127 no.17

Index of Sources 261

Trist. 3.4.1–4: 128 no.22
Trist. 3.6.11–13: 128 no.23
Trist. 3.6.28: 128 no.21
Trist. 4.10.99–101: 129
Trist. 5.9: 39 no.47

Paulus
  P.S. 2.26.14: 126–7
  P.S. 5.4.8: 92 no.76
  P.S. 5.21.3: 21
  P.S. 5.23.1: 22 no.71
  P.S. 5.29.1: 21 no.65, 125 no.8
Pliny
  NH 2.96: 96 no.92
  NH 8.4: 96 no.92
  NH 7.48: 98 no.106
  NH 7. 147–150: 68, 76 no.7, 79 no.22, 170
  NH 9.118: 55
  NH 18.6: 139 no.20
  NH 34.6: 137 no.11
Pliny
  Ep. 1.17.3: 39 no.55
  Ep. 4.8.1: 139 no.20
  Ep. 4.15.6: 79 no.24
  Ep. 6.3.5–6: 127 no14
  Ep. 6.29: 29 no.1
  Ep. 7.16: 42 no.65
Plut.
  Aem. Paull. 38: 94 no.84
  Caes. 5–6: 39 no.51
  Cic. 19: 36 no.33
  Cic. 35: 137 no.11
  Cic. 49: 41 no.62
  Comp. Dion. and Brut. 5: 140 no.23
  De Garrul. 508: 103, 169–70
  Mar. 12: 36 no. 32
  Quaest. Rom. 99: 139 no.20
  Sulla 10: 39 no.54
Prop.
  Eleg. 4.11: 229 no.58, 230 no.65

Quint.
  Decl. Min. 376.3: 132 no.40
  Inst. 3.6.96: 71 no.37
  Inst. 3.6.98: 71
  Inst. 3.7.20: 41 no.62
  Inst. 3.8.53: 166 no.40
  Inst. 7.4.11: 71
  Inst. 7.4.27: 73 no.41

Sall.
  Bell. Cat. 42: 81 no.36
  Bell. Cat. 47: 36 no.33
  Bell. Cat. 53: 36 no.34
Scholia in Iuv.
  4.81: 178 no.28
  6.158.1–2: 48 no.8, 85, 96 no.90, 104–5, 119 no.59
Sen.
  Cont. 2.1.9: 70
  Cont. 2.1.11–12: 82–3
  Cont. 1.1.13: 71
  Cont. 2.1.15: 70 no.33
  Cont. 2.1.17.1: 223 no.24
  Cont. 2.1.28: 70, 73 no.41
  Cont. 7.6.22: 30 no.4
  Cont. 10. *prae.* 5–6: 89, 90 no.69
  Cont. 10. *prae.* 7: 89 no.63
  Cont. 10. *prae.* 8: 14 no.43, 89 no.63, 90
Sen.
  Cons. ad Marc. 22
  De Ben. 3.26.1: 93 no.81
  De Brev. Vit. 4.5: 13 no.33
  De Clem. 1.9: 228 no.55
  De Ira 2.5.5: 30 no.4
  Ep. Mor. 70.10: 5, 25, 26, 29, 31, 214 no.55, 230 no.65
Servius
  ad Eclog. 10.1: 12 no.28
  ad Georg. 4.1: 12 no.28
Strabo
  14.5.4: 14 no.39
Suet.
  Aug. 19: 48 no.8, 85, 95 no.88, 138, 173 no.15
  Aug. 25.2: 79 no.22
  Aug. 28.2: 191 no.31
  Aug. 30: 81 no.35
  Aug. 35.4: 146, 149 no.59
  Aug. 41.2: 81 no.34
  Aug. 42: 80 no.28
  Aug. 51.1: 117
  Aug. 54: 147
  Aug. 55: 87–8
  Aug. 56.4: 13 no.34
  Aug. 62.2: 227 no.48, 228 no.53, 229
  Aug. 64.1: 47 no.5
  Aug. 64.3: 72 no.39
  Aug. 65: 47 no.1, 50 no.19, 52 no.35, 124

Suet. (cont.)
  Aug. 65.2: 14.43
  Aug. 65.3: 48 no.6
  Aug. 65.4: 15 no.43, 68, 104, 120 no.61
  Aug. 66.1: 97 no.101
  Aug. 66.2: 12 no.28
  Aug. 66.3: 13 no.35, 69 no.27
  Aug. 67.2: 58
  Aug. 72.3: 123 no.2
  Aug. 94.12: 136 no.8
  Aug. 98.5: 172
  Aug. 99.2–100.1: 157 no.1
  Aug. 100.2: 186 no.5
  Aug. 101: 73 no.41, 152 no.67
  Aug. 101.4: 174 no.21, 204 no.35
  Gaius 1.1: 65 no.19
  Gaius 16.3: 214 no.53
  Claud. 1.1: 224 no.30
  Claud. 1.4: 201 no.27
  Claud. 2: 224 no.32
  Claud. 2.2: 96 no.92
  Claud. 4.1–2: 51, 53 no.37
  Claud. 5: 51 no.27
  Claud. 10: 214 no.53
  Claud. 11: 214 no.53
  Claud. 25.3: 222 no.19
  Claud. 26.1: 85, 123 no.2, 230 no.64
  De Gramm. 5: 12 no.28
  De Gramm. 16: 12 no.30
  De Rhet. 6: 140 no.23
  Dom. 20: 181 no.38
  Iul. 42.3: 137 no.11
  Nero 6.3: 178 no.28
  Nero 38.1: 75 no.4
  Tib. 1: 41 no.62
  Tib. 6.3: 222 no.20, 228 no.56
  Tib. 7: 222 no.21
  Tib. 8.1: 14 no.37
  Tib. 9.1: 54 no.40
  Tib. 10.1: 62 no.6, 69 no.27, 167 no.43
  Tib. 11.1: 62 no.6
  Tib. 11.5: 49 no.12
  Tib. 12.2: 54
  Tib. 13.1–2: 55, 56, 57, 59 no.61
  Tib. 15.1: 57 no.53
  Tib. 15.3: 47 no.4
  Tib. 16.1: 47 no.2, 98 no.105
  Tib. 16.2: 99 no.110
  Tib. 20: 96 no.93, 151 no.66
  Tib. 21.1: 98 no.106, 144 no.43
  Tib. 21.2: 99 no.111

Tib. 21.3: 98 no.103
Tib. 22: 176, 179 no.30
Tib. 24.1: 144 no.43, 158, 159, 161, 193 no.39
Tib. 24.2: 162, 207 no.38
Tib. 25.1: 1, 5, 6, 25 no.82, 33, 34, 162 nos.24 and 25, 167, 199 no.21, 209, 219 no.3, 225 no.35
Tib. 25.2: 162 no.24, 189 no.19, 192–3
Tib. 25.3: 195, 198 no.14
Tib. 28: 92
Tib. 30.1: 11, 148 no.54, 150
Tib. 31.1: 11, 148 no.55
Tib. 36: 20
Tib. 49.1: 21 no.67
Tib. 50.1: 201 no.27
Tib. 54: 216 no.61
Tib. 57.2: 200 no.24
Tib. 61.1: 181 no.39

Tac.
  Ann. 1.3: 50 no.19, 63, 66, 104
  Ann. 1.4: 50 no.20
  Ann. 1.5: 157 no.1, 157 no.3, 170
  Ann. 1.5.3–4: 169, 179 no.30
  Ann. 1.6: 49 no.15, 175–6, 179 no.32
  Ann. 1.7.2: 158
  Ann. 1.7.5: 144 no.43, 157, 157 no.2, 159, 161
  Ann. 1.7.6: 185
  Ann. 1.10.1: 90 no.70, 201 no.25
  Ann. 1.12.1–2: 165
  Ann. 1.13: 165 no.38
  Ann. 1.13.5–6: 166
  Ann. 1.14: 187 no.10
  Ann. 1.14.6: 202, 203
  Ann. 1.15.1: 109 no.24, 110 no.30, 114 no.40, 199 no.19, 202, 204 no.35
  Ann. 1.16: 185 no.1
  Ann. 1.24: 40 no.61
  Ann. 1.25.3: 188 no.11
  Ann. 1.27: 40 no.60
  Ann. 1.31: 185 no.1
  Ann. 1.31.1: 188 no.15
  Ann. 1.34.1: 158, 188 no.16, 189
  Ann. 1.34–35: 189
  Ann. 1.35.3: 189 nos.19 and 21
  Ann. 1.36: 189 no.22
  Ann. 1.37: 190 no.24

Index of Sources

Ann. 1.37.1: 190 no.25
Ann. 1.37.3: 190 no.26
Ann. 1.39.1–2: 140 no.25, 188 no.12
Ann. 1.45: 187, 192 no.34
Ann. 1.46.1: 167 no.42
Ann. 1.53.1: 62 no.6
Ann. 1.53.3: 139 no.17
Ann. 1.53.6: 182
Ann. 1.55: 174 no.19
Ann. 1.72: 88, 92 no.79, 182 no.43
Ann. 1.72.2: 162 no.23
Ann. 1.72.3: 173 no.19
Ann. 1.75.4–5: 149
Ann. 1.77.3: 150 no.61
Ann. 1.78: 106 no.12, 207 no.39
Ann. 1.78.2: 214 no.52
Ann. 1.81.2: 111 no.31
Ann. 2.27.1: 25 no.82, 27, 198 no.15, 219 no.2
Ann. 2.27.2: 6, 196, 200 no.23, 219
Ann. 2.28.1: 200 no.22
Ann. 2.28.2: 198 no.14, 201 no.26, 225 no.35
Ann. 2.28.3: 6, 9, 17, 32 no.17
Ann. 2.29.1: 31
Ann. 2.29.2: 33 no.20
Ann. 2.29: 7, 29
Ann. 2.30: 7, 22 no.74, 23 no.75, 214 no.54, 231 no.69
Ann. 2.30.3: 130 no.29
Ann. 2.31.1: 35, 215 no.58
Ann. 2.31.3: 37 no.39
Ann. 2.32.1: 7, 8, 19 no.57, 20, 24 no.79, 38 no.41, 39 no.50, 44 no.70
Ann. 2.32.2: 220 no.6, 221 no.16
Ann. 2.33.1: 198 no.11
Ann. 2.35.1: 198 no.11
Ann. 2.36: 198 no.11, 203 no.33
Ann. 2.38: 198 no.11
Ann. 2.39.1: 1, 34, 35, 208
Ann. 2.40.1: 33, 37 no.37, 44 no.71, 208
Ann. 2.40.3: 35, 141 no.29, 211 no.47
Ann. 2.42: 60
Ann. 2.43.2: 43 no.66, 232 no.74
Ann. 2.43.5: 216
Ann. 3.8.2: 16 no.46, 31 no.13
Ann. 3.10.3: 16 no.48
Ann. 3.12: 30 no.12
Ann. 3.12.7: 15 no.44
Ann. 3.14.4–6: 16, 31 no.13, 37 no.38

Ann. 3.22: 21 no.67
Ann. 3.23.1: 5
Ann. 3.24.2–3: 123–4, 131
Ann. 3.29: 64–5, 142 no.35
Ann. 3.30: 177 no.26
Ann. 3.30.2: 177 no.27
Ann. 3.30.3: 180 no.33
Ann. 3.37.1: 197 nos.6 and 7
Ann. 3.48: 56, 57 no.51, 231 no.69
Ann. 3.50.4: 125 no.8
Ann. 3.66.1: 29 no.4
Ann. 3.67.2: 29 no.4
Ann. 3.67.3: 130 no.29
Ann. 3.76: 39 no.55
Ann. 4.4: 142 no.35
Ann. 4.7.2: 11
Ann. 4.8: 143
Ann. 4.17: 10
Ann. 4.19: 10
Ann. 4.21.6: 88 no.62
Ann. 4.22.1: 197 no.9
Ann. 4.29.1: 40 no.59
Ann. 4.29.4: 22 no.74
Ann. 4.30: 38 no.40
Ann. 4.34: 40 no.58, 90 no.68
Ann. 4.53.2: 178 no.28
Ann. 4.71.4: 32 no.18, 85 no.53, 123 no.2, 124
Ann. 6.5: 39 no.49
Ann. 6.23: 216 no.61
Ann. 6.51: 62 no.6
Ann. 11.36.5: 221 no.15
Ann. 12.4: 197 no.9
Ann. 12.25.1: 221 no.15
Ann. 13.44: 197 no.9
Ann. 14.28.1: 115 no.43
Ann. 14.48: 93 no.81, 197 no.9
Ann. 15.36: 76 no.6
Ann. 15.39.3: 75 no.4
Hist. 3.35: 197 no.9
Dial. 7: 29 no.1

Ulpian
  Mos. et Rom. 15.2.1: 19 no.58, 20

Val. Max.
  3.8.5: 39 no.54
  4.2.7: 125 no.8
  4.3.8: 94 no.84
  5.1 ext.2: 132 no.39
Vell.
  1.11: 36 no.32

Vell. (cont.)
- 2.69.5: 40 no.56
- 2.91.2: 13 no.33
- 2.91.3: 113 no.35
- 2.92: 111–12
- 2.93.2: 69 no.27
- 2.99.1–2: 62 no.6, 64 no.16
- 2.100.5: 229 no.62
- 2.101.2: 54 no.41
- 2.102.1: 54
- 2.102.3: 52 no.35, 58–9
- 2.103: 47 no.2, 193 no.40
- 2.103.3: 163 no.29
- 2.104.1: 47 no.1, 49 no.13
- 2.104.3: 96 no.96
- 2.105.3: 97 no.97
- 2.107.3: 97 no.97
- 2.110.6: 79 no.19
- 2.111.1–2: 79, 80 no.27, 98 no.102
- 2.111.3: 79 no.23
- 2.111.4: 96 no.96
- 2.112: 50 no.18, 79 no.25
- 2.112.2: 221 no.15
- 2.112.7: 103
- 2.113.1: 98 no.105
- 2.116.2: 77 no.11
- 2.120.1–2: 140 no.27, 151 no.66
- 2.121.1: 144 no.43
- 2.123.1: 98 no.106, 172 no.9
- 2.124.1: 184, 201 no.25
- 2.124.2: 144 no.44, 160
- 2.124.3: 198 no.13, 202, 203, 204 no.35, 213 no.51
- 2.124.4: 109 no.24, 165 no.36, 197 no.9, 198 no.16, 199 no.18, 202, 203
- 2.125: 189 no.19, 191 no.32
- 2.125.1: 191 no.29
- 2.125.2: 191 no.28
- 2.126: 11
- 2.126.2: 150 no.61
- 2.129: 25 no.82
- 2.130.3: 5, 25 no.82, 219 no.2

Inscriptions

AE
- (1892) 73: 227 no.47
- (1937) 62: 229 no.59
- (1964) 82: 41
- (1988) 626 a-b: 229 no.59
- (1991) 894: 229 no.59

V. Ehrenberg and A.H.M. Jones (1955)
- p34: 220 no.8
- p37: 220 no.9
- p40: 219 no.3
- p46: 96 no.93
- p47: 144 no.45
- p50: 106
- p52: 5, 166 no.41, 187 no.10, 219 no.2
- p63: 77 no.11
- p168: 79 no.22

CIL
- I^2 p244: 5, 24, 25
- I^2 p65: 229 no.59
- V^2 3503: 139 no.22
- V^2 3504: 139 no.22
- V^2 3505: 139 no.22
- V^2 5150: 139 no.22
- V^2 5749: 139 no.22
- V^2 8879: 139 no.22
- 6.7467: 229 no.62
- 6.26033: 229 no.61
- 7.37380: 231
- 11.7412: 229 no.61

ILS
- 140: 52 no.35
- 154: 144 no.45
- 244: 114 no.40
- 944: 203 no.31
- 5026: 124 no.7, 139 no.19
- 8892: 227 no.46
- 8995: 12 no.28
- 9433: 42 no.65

Res Gestae
- 5–7: 166 no.40
- 8: 144 no.43
- 10.2: 144 no.45
- 14.1: 61 no.2, 64 no.15, 65 no.19
- 17: 78 no.17
- 34.1: 14 no.41

SCPP
- 4–11: 15
- 20–22: 30 no.12
- 33–34: 151 no.66
- 37–38: 30 no.5
- 45–46: 30 no.9

50–52: 30 no.6
54–55: 30 no.8
71: 16 no.49
93–100: 43 no.69
115–120: 32 no.18
120–123: 16–17, 24 no.80, 137 no.11
129–130: 144 no.44
160: 191 no.31
Sherk
　Documents no. 102, Edict V: 17 no.51
　Documents no. 111: 153 no.72